Who Needs Migrant Workers?

Who Needs Migrant Workers?

Labour Shortages, Immigration, and Public Policy

Edited by
Martin Ruhs and Bridget Anderson

OXFORD
UNIVERSITY PRESS

OXFORD
UNIVERSITY PRESS

Great Clarendon Street, Oxford OX2 6DP
United Kingdom

Oxford University Press is a department of the University of Oxford.
It furthers the University's objective of excellence in research, scholarship,
and education by publishing worldwide. Oxford is a registered trade mark of
Oxford University Press in the UK and in certain other countries

British Library Cataloguing in Publication Data
Data available

Library of Congress Cataloging in Publication Data
Data available

ISBN 978-0-19-958059-0
ISBN 978-0-19-965361-4 (Pbk)

Printed and bound by
CPI Group (UK) Ltd, Croydon, CR0 4YY

Acknowledgements

This book builds on research originally commissioned by the UK's Migration Advisory Committee (MAC), an independent body of academic economists advising the UK government on labour immigration policy. We are grateful to the MAC for its financial support and for its comments on early drafts of some of the chapters. All of the draft chapters were presented and discussed at a workshop in Oxford in May 2009, supported by the ESRC Centre on Migration, Policy and Society (COMPAS) at Oxford University. We are grateful to all workshop participants for their helpful comments and discussions.

We would also like to thank Alexander Eastlake, who helped with formatting and proofreading of the manuscript, as well as Jenny Newman and Vanessa Hughes, who both assisted with the organization of the workshop.

Martin Ruhs and Bridget Anderson
Oxford, October 2009

Contents

Contents

Figures

Tables

List of Contributors

Vanna Aldin is Head of Economics in the Secretariat to the Migration Advisory Committee, an independent public body which advises the government on labour market and immigration issues. A member of the Government Economic Service, her previous research areas include international cooperation, improving estimation of real GDP and productivity, and measurement of government output.

Bridget Anderson is a Senior Research Fellow at the Centre on Migration, Policy and Society, at the University of Oxford. Her research interests include low-waged labour migration, 'trafficking' and citizenship. Publications include *Doing the Dirty Work? The Global Politics of Domestic Labour* published by Zed Books, 2000.

Stephen Bach is Professor of Employment Relations in the Department of Management, King's College London. His research interests include: international migration of health professionals; new ways of working in the public services; human resources management (HRM) in the health sector; public–private partnerships and the future of public service trade unions. His books include: *Employment Relations and the Health Service* (Routledge, 2004) and he is editor of *Managing Human Resources* (Blackwell, 2005).

Jonathan V. Beaverstock is Professor of Economic Geography at the University of Nottingham. He has published widely on highly skilled international labour migration, world cities, international financial centres, and, more recently, business travel. His latest book *International Business Travel in the Global Economy* is co-edited with Ben Derruder, James Faulconbridge, and Frank Witlox and published by Ashgate, 2010.

Alessio Cangiano is a demographer at the Centre on Migration, Policy and Society (COMPAS) at Oxford University. His research focuses on migration and the economic integration of migrants in the UK and Europe. Since 2006, Alessio has been part of the UK research team of an international research project on migrant care workers in ageing societies. His work has focused in particular on the factors underlying the demand for migrant labour and migrant employment patterns in long-term care for older people.

Paul Chan is Lecturer in Project Management in the School of Mechanical, Aerospace and Civil Engineering (MACE) at the University of Manchester. His main research interest lies in human resource management in construction, with particular focus on skills, training and development. He is on the committee of the Association of Researchers in Construction Management (ARCOM) and a member of the UK Construction Skills Network.

Linda Clarke is Professor of European Industrial Relations at the Westminster Business School, University of Westminster, researching training, skills, wage and labour relations in Europe, particularly in the construction sector. She is on the board of the European Institute for Construction Labour Research and her publications include: *A Blueprint for Change: Construction Skills Training in Britain* (Policy Press, 1998) and *Building Capitalism* (Routledge, 1992).

Andrew Dainty is Professor of Construction Sociology at Loughborough University's Department of Civil and Building Engineering. His research focuses on human social action within construction and other project-based sectors and particularly the social rules and processes that affect people working as members of project teams. He is co-author/editor of six books, including *People and Culture in Construction* (Taylor & Francis, 2007) and *Corporate Social Responsibility in the Construction Industry* (Taylor & Francis, 2008).

Robert Elliott is a Professor of Economics and Director of the Health Economics Research Unit at the University of Aberdeen. He has been a member of the ESRC Training Board and President of the Scottish Economic Society. He was appointed to the Low Pay Commission in April 2007. His books include *Advances in Health Economics* (with A. Scott and A. Maynard, eds.; John Wiley, 2002) and *Decentralised Pay Setting: A Study of Collective Bargaining Reform in the Civil Service in Australia, Sweden and the UK* (with K. Bender; Ashgate, 2004).

Andrew Geddes is Professor and Head of the Department of Politics at the University of Sheffield. He has published extensively on comparative European and EU migration policy and politics. Recent publications include *Immigration and European Integration: Beyond Fortress Europe* (Manchester University Press, 2nd edition, 2008). He has been commissioned to work for the Gangmasters Licensing Authority on various aspects of migrant labour and work.

Contributors

Howard Gospel is Professor of Management and Senior Research Fellow at King's College London. He is also an Associate Fellow of the Saïd Business School, University of Oxford, and of the Centre for Economic Performance, London School of Economics, and a Fellow at SKOPE at the University of Oxford. His research interests are employer labour policy, corporate governance and labour management, employee voice systems, and skill formation and training.

Dan James is a Senior Research Officer within the Secretariat to the Migration Advisory Committee, an independent committee which advises the government on labour market and immigration issues. A member of Government Social Research, his previous research areas include violent crime and local and regional government.

Andrew Jones is Reader in Human Geography at Birkbeck College, University of London. Primarily an economic geographer, his research focus is on globalization, transnational firms, and the knowledge economy. His policy work includes research into the globalization of work and international skilled labour mobility. He is author of over 22 journal articles and book chapters, as well as three books, including *Management Consultancy and Banking in an Era of Globalisation* (Palgrave Macmillan, 2003).

Rosemary Lucas is Professor of Employment Relations at Manchester Metropolitan University. Past research has focused on employment relations within the hospitality sector and the exploitative nature of the employment relationship using data from Workplace Employment Relations Surveys and other empirical studies. Previous publications include *Employment Relations in the Hospitality and Tourism Industries* (Routledge, 2004).

Steve Mansfield is a Senior Lecturer at Manchester Metropolitan University. His main research focus is on the use of migrant labour in the hospitality sector and the implications of the Points Based System. This interest came about after working in the industry for a number of years, with responsibility for recruiting and managing workers from different areas of the world.

Philip Martin is Professor of Agricultural and Resource Economics at the University of California-Davis. He has worked on labour and immigration issues for three decades, served on several federal commissions, and testified before Congress numerous times. He works for UN agencies around the world, examining labour migration issues in Eastern Europe and Turkey, North Africa, Latin America, and Asia.

Ken Mayhew is Professor of Education and Economic Performance at Oxford University, Fellow and Tutor in Economics at Pembroke College, Oxford, and

Director of SKOPE, an ESRC-designated research centre on skills, knowledge, and organizational performance. He is a labour economist and a former Economic Director of the UK National Economic Development Office.

Linda McDowell is Professor of Human Geography at the University of Oxford. Her main research interest is the interconnections between economic restructuring, new forms of work, and the transformation of gender relations in contemporary Britain. She has published widely in this area including *Capital Culture* (Blackwell, 1997), *Redundant Masculinities?* (Blackwell, 2003), and *Hard Labour* (UCL Press, 2005). Her most recent book, *Working Bodies* (Wiley-Blackwell, 2009), is about interactive service sector employment and workplace identities.

Jo Moriarty is a Research Fellow in the Social Care Workforce Research Unit at King's College London. She has a long-standing interest in the intersection of paid and unpaid caregiving and this is reflected in her publications. She is a member of the editorial board of the journal *Research, Policy and Planning* and edits the Innovative Practice section of the journal *Dementia: The International Journal of Social Research and Practice*.

Ben Rogaly is Senior Lecturer in Human Geography at the University of Sussex and a member of the Sussex Centre for Migration Research. His latest book (with Becky Taylor), *Moving Histories of Class and Community: Identity, Place and Belonging in Contemporary England*, was published by Palgrave in 2009.

Martin Ruhs is Senior Economist at the Centre on Migration, Policy and Society at Oxford University. Recent publications include 'Economic Research and Labour Immigration Policy' (*Oxford Review of Economic Policy*, 2008) and 'Semi-compliance and Illegality in Migrant Labour Markets' (with Bridget Anderson, *Population, Space and Place*, 2010). He is a member of the Migration Advisory Committee (MAC) which advises the UK government on labour immigration.

Sam Scott has been researching migrant communities and labour markets for over a decade. He has worked for the Gangmasters Licensing Authority and was recently commissioned by the Joseph Rowntree Foundation to look at 'forced labour'. Over the past five years he has published in *International Migration Review* (migrant assimilation), *Geoforum* (community morphology of migration), *JEMS* (social morphology of migration), and *Population, Space and Place* (migrant transnationalism).

Jonathan Wadsworth is Professor of Economics at Royal Holloway College, University of London and a member of the Migration Advisory Committee. His main area of interest is applied labour economics, focusing on issues of immigration, inequality, unemployment compensation schemes, job search, labour mobility, job tenure, wages, unions, health, economic inactivity, and labour markets in Eastern Europe. Jonathan is the co-editor of *The State of Working Britain* volumes, which highlight and comment on significant developments in the labour market.

1

Introduction

Martin Ruhs and Bridget Anderson

1.1 Who Needs Migrant Workers?

The regulation of labour immigration is one of the most important and controversial public policy issues in high-income countries. Many states in Europe and North America have experienced rapid increases in labour immigration over the past 20 years. The current global economic downturn has added further momentum to what in many countries were already highly charged debates about the impacts of rising numbers of migrants on the economic prospects of citizens and on the host economy and society more generally. A survey by the *Financial Times* in March 2009 showed that over three-quarters of adults in Italy and the UK, and about two-thirds in Spain, Germany, and the US, supported the idea of sending migrants who cannot find a job home.[1]

Many high-income countries have changed their rhetoric about immigration, and some have tightened their labour immigration policies in response to the economic downturn. The same UK government that significantly expanded labour immigration in the early 2000s because of its 'enormous economic benefits'[2] claimed in 2008 that 'it's been too easy to get into this country in the past and it's going to get harder'.[3] In early 2009, the UK raised the minimum education and earnings requirements necessary to gain admission under Tier 1 (for highly skilled migrant workers) of the new points-based system, mainly in response to rising unemployment

---

[1] *Financial Times*, 15 Mar. 2009.
[2] Liam Byrne, Immigration Minister, at Home Affairs Select Committee hearing on 27 Nov. 2007.
[3] 'Migrant Numbers "Must be Reduced"', *BBC News*, 18 Oct. 2008.

of British graduates. Spain reduced the annual quota of work permits issued under its *programa de contigentes* from over 15,000 in 2008 to less than 1,000 in 2009, while at the same time eliminating the jobseeker's permit that previously allowed some economic migrants to enter Spain without a prior job offer. Ireland recently reduced the number of jobs eligible for 'green cards' (work permits for skilled migrants) and increased the minimum period employers are required to advertise their job vacancies before applying for a work permit from four to eight weeks. However, for all the political rhetoric accompanying these policy developments, their impact on the numbers of migrant workers admitted has, arguably, been relatively small.

A central question in debates about labour immigration policy is how to link the admission of migrant workers to the 'needs' of the domestic labour market and the national economy more generally. What these needs are, how they vary across sectors and occupations, and how they change during periods of economic growth and crisis are highly contested. There is significant controversy about the role that migrants can, or should, play in meeting 'skills needs' and in reducing 'labour and skills shortages' in particular sectors and occupations. Employers often claim, especially but not only during times of economic growth, that there is a 'need' for migrants to help fill labour and skills shortages and/or to do the jobs that, they allege, 'locals' (a highly contested term) will not or cannot do. Sceptics, including some trades unions, argue that in many cases these claims simply reflect employers' preference for recruiting cheap and exploitable migrant workers over improving wages and employment conditions. Moreover, as unemployment rises, some argue, the economy's need for migrant workers declines. For example, according to Frank Field, Labour MP and Co-chair of the Balanced Migration Group in the UK, 'the immigration policy suitable for a boom is totally unsuitable for a recession'.[4] Parts of the media agree ('It is time we slashed jobs for immigrants'[5]). However, others point out the highly segmented labour market and differentiated economy, suggesting that, even during times of economic downturn, new migrant workers are needed and in some occupations may be critical to economic recovery (Finch et al. 2009).

The policy argument that immigration is required because of 'skills needs' in the domestic economy can reflect one or both of two distinct but related concerns. The first is the provision of a high level of 'human capital' in order to promote long-term economic growth and competitiveness. This line of argument is typically based on endogenous growth models that emphasize

[4] BBC Online News, <http://news.bbc.co.uk/1/hi/7677419.stm>, 18 Oct. 2008.
[5] *Daily Star*, 29 Apr. 2009.

the importance of human capital, knowledge, and research and development for economic growth (see e.g. Romer 1986; Lucas 1988). Human capital models therefore suggest that the immigration of highly skilled workers is to be encouraged even without a job offer. A number of countries have labour immigration policies for admitting highly skilled migrant workers that are in part based on a human capital model, for example, Canada and Australia. Tier 1 of the UK's point-based system is an example of a labour immigration policy that is fully based on a human capital model. Such 'supply-driven' admission policies can become more difficult to politically sustain during an economic downturn.

The analysis in this book largely focuses on a second concern that can underlie the argument that there is a 'need' for migrants' skills. This relates to the aim of using migrant workers to reduce perceived *specific* staff shortages which are typically expressed as labour and/or skills shortages—a highly problematic distinction as discussed in this book. This type of 'shortage' argument is highly contested during both economic growth and even more so during an economic downturn. Because of the contentious nature and high policy salience of the issue, a number of countries, including Australia, Canada, and Spain, have established special government units and/or independent advisory bodies that are tasked to help link the admission of new migrant workers to research and analysis of shortages in the domestic labour market. The UK has recently established the Migration Advisory Committee (MAC), a small independent body of economists tasked to advise the government on where in the UK economy there are skilled labour shortages that can be 'sensibly' addressed by immigration from outside the European Economic Area (EEA). 'Skilled', 'shortage', and 'sensible' are all defined and operationalized by the MAC. A recent proposal for immigration reform in the US, supported by the two major trades unions, includes the establishment of an independent Foreign Workers Adjustment Commission to 'measure labor shortages and recommend the numbers and characteristics of employment-based temporary and permanent immigrants to fill those shortages' (Marshall 2009). All these policy initiatives, and any effort to link labour immigration to domestic labour shortages more generally, need to address the same key question: how do we define, measure, and assess various policy responses to staff shortages?

1.2 Researching Shortages in the Labour Market

There is no universally accepted definition of a labour or skills shortage and no one obvious 'optimal' policy response. The definition of shortage typically underlying employers' calls for migrants to help fill vacancies is that the demand for labour exceeds supply at the *prevailing* wages and employment conditions. Importantly, estimates of employers' 'labour and skills shortages' are typically based on surveys that ask employers about current vacancies that are difficult to fill. In other words, they refer to employers' difficulties with finding the 'right' workers to fill vacancies at *current* wages and employment conditions.

In contrast, a basic economic approach emphasizes the role of the price mechanism in bringing markets that are characterized by excess demand or excess supply into equilibrium. In a simple textbook model of a competitive labour market, where demand and supply of labour are critically determined by the price of labour, most shortages are temporary and eventually eliminated by rising wages that increase supply and reduce demand. In practice, labour markets do not always work as the simple textbook model suggests. Prices can be 'sticky', and whether and how quickly prices clear labour markets critically depend on the reasons for labour shortages, which can include sudden increases in demand and/or inflexible supply. Nevertheless, the fundamental point of the economic approach remains that the existence and size of shortages critically depend on the price of labour. Industries or occupations that suffer from temporary labour shortages can therefore be expected to be characterized by rising relative real wages, employment, and declining and/or relatively low unemployment rates and vacancy rates. Economic assessments of labour shortages have thus typically involved indicators that include changes in relative real wages and employment in specific occupations. For example, Veneri (1999) used three indicators to assess labour shortages in 68 occupations in the US in the 1990s. To be considered in shortage of labour, an occupation had to display: employment growth that was at least 50 per cent higher than the average for all occupations; growth in median weekly earnings that was at least 30 per cent greater than the average for all occupations; and an occupational unemployment rate that was at least 30 per cent lower than the average for all occupations. Using these indicators, Veneri identified shortages in only seven out of the 68 occupations under consideration. Information technology workers, construction workers, and registered nurses—all occupations where US employers were claiming significant shortages—were not found to be in shortage by this economic assessment based on national data.

Although fundamental and necessary, most economists—and the analytical approach taken in this book—agree that analyses based on economic models and indicators are not sufficient to comprehensively assess the existence, nature, and magnitude of shortages in the labour market (e.g. Veneri 1999; MAC 2008). Examinations of national labour market data and employer skills surveys need to be complemented by more in-depth analysis and understanding of the 'micro-foundations' of staff shortages. This includes the micro-level factors affecting employer demand and labour supply and their interaction in particular local labour markets and within particular social contexts, for example, what is considered suitable work for women and men or the social status of certain types of jobs. Such analysis involves a critical assessment of employers' views and claims of labour and/ or skills 'needs' in the context of the institutional and regulatory frameworks affecting specific occupations and/or industries and the economy as a whole. It needs to explore the range of alternative options that employers may have when responding to perceived staff shortages, and the various different ways in which these options are constrained in specific sectors and occupations. The need for a multi-disciplinary micro-level approach to complement the conventional economic analyses of indicators based on large-scale labour market data motivates and frames the methodological approach to the analysis in this book.

1.3 Aims and Chapters of this Book

The research and analysis in this book aim to contribute to public and policy debates about labour shortages and immigration policy in high-income countries. The book discusses the demand for migrant labour both conceptually and empirically in the context of the UK. The conceptual discussion in Chapter 2 (by Bridget Anderson and Martin Ruhs) provides a comprehensive conceptual framework for discussing the relationship between labour shortages, immigration, and public policy in a structured and analytically rigorous way. It integrates theories and existing literature on four key issues in the analysis of staff shortages, immigration, and public policy: (i) the characteristics, dimensions, and determinants of employer demand for labour (*What are employers looking for?*); (ii) characteristics of and segmentations in labour supply (*Who wants to do what?*); (iii) employers' recruitment practices and use of migrant labour (*How and whom do employers recruit?*); and (iv) immigration and alternative responses to perceived staff shortages (*A need for migrant labour?*). Labour demand, supply, recruitment practices, and the alternatives to immigration can and often do change over time and, in particular, between periods of economic growth and crisis. The conceptual analysis of the four fundamental issues above thus includes discussion of the potential effects of the changing economic environment.

Three key issues emerge from the conceptual discussion that are critical to assessments of labour and skills shortages and employer demand for migrant workers and to debates about optimal policy responses. First, labour demand and supply are mutually conditioning rather than generated independently of one another. 'What employers want' can be critically influenced by what employers think they can get from the various pools of available labour, while at the same time, labour supply often adapts to the requirements of demand. This is related to the second issue, that the term 'skills' is both conceptually and empirically ambiguous. It can be used to refer to a wide range of credentialized qualifications, 'soft' skills (e.g. communication or team-working), and personal characteristics (e.g. 'hard-working', 'friendly', 'caring' etc.), which can include a willingness to accept certain wages and employment conditions. Any discussion of skills needs, skills shortages, and skills-based immigration policies thus needs to critically scrutinize what exactly is meant by 'skills' in different contexts. Third, the persistent and in many sectors increasing employer demand for migrant workers can, to a significant degree, be explained by 'system effects' that 'produce' certain types of domestic labour shortages. System effects arise from the institutional and regulatory frameworks of the labour market and from wider public policies (e.g. welfare and social policies, and including immigration policies), many of which are not ostensibly to do with the labour market—hence the book's emphasis on the link between immigration and *public* policy within a dynamic social context. Both system effects and social context are often outside the control of individual employers and workers and in many ways may be heavily (but not exclusively) influenced by the state. Together with the interdependence between labour demand and supply, the analysis of system effects points to the difficulty of constructing and implementing labour immigration policy in isolation from labour market policy and wider economic and social policies and institutions—a key point also made in the commentary on Chapter 2 (by Ken Mayhew).

Based on this conceptual framework, the empirical analysis in the book explores the nature and determinants of staff shortages, and the role of migrant workers, in specific sectors of the UK economy. To set the scene for the in-depth analysis of specific sectors, Chapter 3 (by Vanna Aldin, Dan James, and Jonathan Wadsworth) uses Labour Force Survey data for 2008 and 2002 to describe and explore the determinants of the changing shares of migrant workers in different sectors and occupations of the UK economy.

The statistical analysis in this chapter suggests that the differential intensi-fication of the use of migrant workers across sectors is not simply a matter of certain sectors being able to hire more migrants while at the same time offering low pay, since the sectors that made least use of the growing pool of migrant labour are also low paid. Neither occupational structure, nor part-time working nor self-employment appears to help explain why certain industries have *not* made use of the growing pool of migrant labour. The findings presented in this chapter are tentative, but they do not support simple hypotheses about why some industries use more migrant workers, or why some have increased their use of migrants more rapidly, than others. The chapter concludes that, to better understand the different and chang-ing roles of migrant workers in different sectors and occupations, it is necessary to employ qualitative and in-depth empirical analysis of issues that cannot be captured in a purely quantitative approach.

This in-depth research is provided in the subsequent six chapters which carry out analysis of the development of labour demand, supply, and immigration in six key sectors of the UK economy: health (Chapter 4 by Stephen Bach with a commentary by Robert Elliott); social care (Chapter 5 by Jo Moriarty with a commentary by Alessio Cangiano); hospitality (Chap-ter 6 by Rosemary Lucas and Steve Mansfield with a commentary by Linda McDowell); food production (Chapter 7 by Andrew Geddes and Sam Scott with a commentary by Ben Rogaly); construction (Chapter 8 by Paul Chan, Linda Clarke, and Andrew Dainty, with a commentary by Howard Gospel); and financial services (Chapter 9 by Andrew Jones with a commentary by Jonathan Beaverstock). The main chapters have been complemented by commentaries in order to indicate the wide range of different issues and approaches to these very 'live' debates.

The sectors discussed in this book have been chosen because of their diverse uses of migrant workers and their importance in debates about immigration policy in the UK and most other high-income countries. They include low- and high-wage industries that make relatively heavy or low use of migrants compared to the economy-wide average. Tables 1.1 and 1.2 use the available data from the UK's Labour Force Survey to give a broad picture of the share of migrants in the total workforce in the industries and occupations most relevant to the sectors and jobs discussed in this book (some chapters discuss more than one industry or occupation shown in Table 1.1, and others discuss only sub-industries/sub-occupations for which reliable statistical data about the share of migrants are not available).

Some of these sectors and occupations have been major employers of both high- and low-skilled migrant labour in the UK. Social care, agriculture

Table 1.1 Share (%) of migrants in total workforce in UK industries discussed in this book, 2002 and 2008

Industry	All migrants		
	2002	2008	Change
All industries in UK economy	*8.2*	*13.3*	*+5.1*
Agriculture, hunting, etc. (01)	3.9	6.5	+2.6
Food, beverage manufacturing (15)	8.1	21.4	+13.3
Construction (45)	4.5	7.9	+3.4
Hotels, restaurants (55)	15.7	23.0	+7.3
Financial intermediaries (65)	9.7	13.7	+4.0
Insurance, pensions (66)	7.3	9.1	+1.8
Health, social work (85)	10.1	14.1	+4.0

Notes: The industries in this table are measured at the two-digit level, with 1992 SIC codes in parentheses. Migrants are defined as foreign-born workers. The 'change' column refers to change in percentage points.

Source: Labour Force Survey (2002 and 2008), as reported in Aldin et al., Chapter 3, this volume.

Table 1.2 Share (%) of migrants in total workforce in selected occupations discussed in this book, 2002 and 2008

Occupation	All migrants		
	2002	2008	Change
All occupations in UK economy	*8.2*	*13.3*	*+5.1*
Health professionals (221)	25.1	27.8	+2.7
Business and statistical profs. (242)	12.8	13.7	+0.9
Health associate profs. (321)	14.2	18.2	+4.0
Construction trades (531)	3.8	8.5	+4.7
Building trades (532)	4.6	8.8	+4.2
Food preparation trades (543)	17.1	25.5	+8.4
Healthcare and related (611)	7.9	15.1	+7.2
Process operatives (811)	8.5	25.0	+16.5
Elementary agricultural (911)	2.4	10.7	+8.3
Elementary construction (912)	4.5	11.5	+7.0
Elementary personal services (922)	9.7	16.9	+7.2
Elementary cleaning (923)	8.8	18.4	+9.6

Notes: The occupations in this table are measured at the three-digit level, with 2002 SOC codes in parentheses. Migrants are defined as foreign-born workers. The 'change' column refers to change in percentage points.

Source: Labour Force Survey (2002 and 2008), as reported in Aldin et al., Chapter 3, this volume.

and food processing, and the hospitality sector in particular have recently been at the heart of heated debates about the 'need' for migrant labour and questions about what constitutes 'skill'. Construction experienced rapidly increasing shares of migrants during 2002 and 2008, but construction employment was badly hit by the economic crisis. The health sector is important because it has been a long-standing employer of migrant labour, especially of doctors and nurses. The financial services sector is also included as an example of the human capital approach and because of the impacts of the financial crises on employment.

The in-depth sectoral analyses in Chapters 4 to 9 are based on the conceptual framework and key questions developed in Chapter 2. They explore the determinants of the changing shares of migrants in the workforce over time, consider the likely effects of the current economic downturn on staff shortages and the employment of migrants, and discuss policy implications.

Chapter 4 (by Stephen Bach) examines the distinctive features of migration and labour shortages in the health sector, concentrating on medical and nursing staff. The sector has a long history of employing migrant health professionals, a reflection of the historical under-investment in its workforce and the scope to encourage doctors and nurses to come to the UK to complete their training, and work in the NHS. A key distinguishing feature is that central government control over the financing and staffing policy of the NHS means both labour demand and supply are heavily influenced by government policy—an obvious example of how and why shortages and immigration policy must be analysed within the context of wider economic and social policies. Labour supply in the health sector is regulated by government via training commissions and international recruitment has been an important mechanism to boost labour supply. The chapter by Bach and the chapter commentary (by Robert Elliott) argue that domestic labour shortages in the sector can, to a significant degree, be related to poor workforce planning which, until recently, had been characterized by a persistent shortage of training places. Because the direct costs of training medical practitioners are high and are borne by the state, Elliott argues that health policy-makers might have preferred migration to the more expensive option of increasing the number of training places. The commentary also suggests an important distinction between the labour markets for doctors and nurses: in contrast to the labour market for doctors, which is heavily affected by government workforce planning and policies, the shortages of nurses can to a large part be explained by relatively low pay.

Chapter 5 (by Jo Moriarty) examines shortages and the demand for migrant workers in social care. Over the past ten years, there has been a substantial increase in the proportion of migrant workers employed in social care, most of whom come from outside the European Economic Area (EEA). The chapter argues that this trend should be set within the context of increased demand for social care, created by a combination of demographic changes, government policies aimed at tightening regulation of the sector, and changing public expectations about the nature of care provision. The supply of social care is constrained by public funding arrangements—much of it is funded by local councils—which have resulted in relatively low pay, particularly among those providing direct care. Low pay, unsocial working hours, temporariness of work, a lack of career opportunities, and low status have all been key factors in the intensification of migrants in low-wage jobs in social care. These are, in turn, at least partly a reflection of how the social care sector is organized and funded. Employer demand for migrant workers in this sector is, therefore, another good example of how regulatory and institutional system effects can create a demand for migrant workers that is likely to increase unless wider policies are also changed. The chapter commentary (by Alessio Cangiano) suggests that if the provision of long-term care continues to depend upon large numbers of migrants, their role has to be planned and not an unintentional consequence of poor pay and conditions—and greater coordination between the social care and immigration policies is needed.

The nature and determinants of the demand for low-cost migrant workers in social care show some similarities with the demand for migrant workers in hospitality analysed in Chapter 6 (by Rosemary Lucas and Steve Mansfield). The hospitality workforce is characterized by a reliance on particular marginalized segments of workers. Migrant workers allow employers to manage fluctuating demand, whilst minimizing costs in what is a very diverse sector. Both the main chapter and chapter commentary (by Linda McDowell) suggest that hospitality employers' recruitment decisions can be influenced by a wide range of considerations about the 'ideal' hospitality workers' characteristics and attitudes. Particularly in hotels—which McDowell describes as 'the almost quintessential site for recent studies of the segmentation of labour, of migrant workers, and of precarious work'—new issues, for example, about embodiment and personal style become important elements in deciding who is employed and how they are expected to behave. The analysis in the main chapter makes clear that despite numerous initiatives having been directed at hospitality employers over the past few decades in periods of both growth and recession, embedded recruitment and employment patterns—including a relatively heavy and increasing reliance on migrant workers—have remained. Any change from this scenario would necessitate a major paradigm shift in management philosophy and would require employers to reassess the reasoning behind their demand for particular sectors of the labour market and their stereotypical assumptions of the labour supply available to them.

Chapter 7 (by Andrew Geddes and Sam Scott) critically examines migrant labour demand at the producer-end of the UK food industry. It focuses on the labour-intensive parts of the food production system (horticulture) as this is where shortages (albeit seasonal) are greatest in magnitude. This industry has experienced considerable intensification over recent decades, associated with the concentration of power amongst a relatively small number of transnational food producers and retailers—a key point also made in the chapter commentary (by Ben Rogaly). For labour-intensive employers, this process has manifested itself in a turn towards, and increasingly a dependence upon, low-wage migrant workers (principally from Poland, Lithuania, and Portugal). Rogaly relates the preference of many employers for migrant workers to the supermarket discourse about the importance of 'quality' in production. The main chapter maps the various dimensions of the sector's dependence on migrant workers and assesses the extent to which it is inevitable. Geddes and Scott argue that the use of low-wage, and mainly temporary, migrant labour functions as a hidden 'subsidy' to employers. There are other options available to farmers and food processors in the UK but, from the individual employer's perspective, the easiest response to falling profit margins is to cut labour costs and raise productivity by importing workers eager for employment (however intense this employment may have become). Geddes and Scott point out that debates about the need for migrant workers in this sector cannot be separated from analyses of the short, medium, and long-term consequences of removing the immigration subsidy to the UK food industry.

Chapter 8 (by Paul Chan, Linda Clarke, and Andrew Dainty) examines the interrelation between migrant worker employment, skills, and employment practices in the UK construction sector, in particular discussing how far demand for migrant labour is fuelled by an inappropriate or inadequate skills base among domestic workers. The chapter highlights the difficulties of assessing skills in construction, the low-skills-low-wage route adopted by the industry, and the lack of regulation of the UK construction labour market. The chapter commentary (by Howard Gospel) describes construction as a good example of a systemic labour market trap into which a sector can fall over a long period of time. According to Gospel, this trap comprises extensive failures to train, which in turn lead to a reliance on a strategy of recruitment and poaching. Easy access to migrant workers, the commentary argues, leads to a further reliance on them which, in turn, means that neither national nor migrant labour are trained and the system of skill formation stands in danger of further deterioration. Gospel argues that, under the current system, construction employers pursue 'production' strategies (which involve recruiting and training labour only for their own immediate use) rather than 'investment' strategies (which would involve training labour for the longer-term good of the industry). The main chapter argues the need for tighter labour market regulation to ensure equal treatment of workers and for a more sophisticated deployment and development of skills that go beyond the quantitative measures that have dominated public and corporate policy in this area. A key recommendation is for the industry to shift from current modes of skills reproduction and employment practices towards upgrading the quality of the workforce and the development of a comprehensive vocational education and training (VET) system.

Chapter 9 (by Andrew Jones) and the chapter commentary (by Jonathan Beaverstock) examine the role of migrants in the UK's financial services sector. Migrants are very unevenly distributed within this sector, with some sub-industries, especially mid- and lower-order occupations, making relatively little use of migrant workers, partly because of the soft skills required. In contrast, for high-order occupations in certain industries within the UK financial service sector, migration has been an essential and integral part of growth and success. Jones and Beaverstock agree that London's now established place at the forefront of global financial services would not have been possible without significant flows of migrants moving in and out of key occupations in the City of London and (to a lesser extent) the greater south-east. Beaverstock argues that financial services companies recruit 'high' and selected 'mid-order' migrants to bring particular knowledge, skills, judgement, and decision-making and leadership capabilities to the organization, which cannot be obtained from the national labour market. In the financial services industry, he points out, it is often the employee alone who makes money for the firm. Jones suggests that any government measures to restrict migrant recruitment during the current economic crisis are likely to restrict flexibility and competitive capacity of high value-adding specialist financial service sub-sectors concentrated in the City of London. At the same time, the chapter argues that many of the jobs lost in the industry during the current downturn are unlikely to reappear. Jones suggests that the key issue for immigration policy is that this contributes to substantially increasing the available pool of labour to a range of other sectors beyond financial services since financial service sector workers generally have a wide range of transferable soft skills applicable in sub-sectors that include, for example, business services, hospitality, and leisure. Any long-term decline in the demand for workers in financial services may mean that a substantial pool of labour is available that could act as a substitute for migrant labour in other sectors of the UK economy.

Although the empirical analysis is focused on the UK, the insights and the conceptual framework for discussing immigration, skills, and labour shortages developed in this book are of direct relevance to public debate and analysis of the demand for migrant labour in other high-income countries including the US, Canada, Australia, and major EU countries. The concluding Chapter 10 (by Philip Martin) provides a comparative analysis of research and policy approaches to assessing labour shortages and the implications for immigration policy in the UK and the US, with a particular focus on the potential lessons of the UK's Migration Advisory Committee (MAC), whose work has been heavily influenced by the research for this book, for current debates about immigration reform in the US. The analysis reviews US research on labour shortage complaints and the demand for migrant labour in the specific economic sectors discussed in the other chapters of this book. Martin argues that the two key implications of UK research and policy on labour shortages and immigration policy for US debates are the importance of obtaining and reviewing both top-down *and* bottom-up data on labour supply and demand; and of considering the alternatives to migrant workers in response to perceived labour shortages in specific sectors and occupations.

1.4 A Note on Terminology

It is important to be aware of the different and *non-substitutable* definitions of 'migrant', 'worker', and 'employer'. Assessments of research evidence must be sensitive to the different definitions used by different studies. A migrant may be broadly defined either as 'foreign born' (meaning all persons born outside the host country regardless of their citizenship) or as 'foreign national' (persons without citizenship of the host country). The latter comprises two broad groups, those who are settled (i.e. with permanent residence status), and those who do not have long-term residence rights—and who therefore are not necessarily free to move within the labour market. These distinctions are important not only in terms of describing the size and characteristics of the migrant population, but also in terms of their rights in the host country, and in the extent to which their labour market behaviour can be controlled by immigration policy. Similarly, the term 'worker' may refer to different types of workers as classified by law with implications for employment rights. For example, in the UK, employment rights and responsibilities depend on employment status, first, whether a person is self-employed or employed, and, if the latter, whether they are classified in law as a 'worker' or 'employee'. While all workers are entitled to the national minimum wage and health and safety protection, many rights and responsibilities only apply to 'employees', including the right to claim unfair dismissal and the right to a written statement of terms and conditions. There are also different types of 'employer'. These differences go beyond those to do with the size of business or the proportion of labour costs, and in some cases have a direct impact on employment relations. In social care, for example, an employer might be a local authority, a private company, a voluntary sector group, an agency ('employment business'), or a private individual. This has implications for understanding employer demand for labour, and, crucially, for the policy levers that are likely to be effective for one type of employer but that may not work for another.

References

Finch, T., Latorre, M., Pollard, N., and Rutter, J. (2009), *Shall We Stay or Shall We Go? Re-migration Trends among Britain's Immigrants* (London: Institute for Public Policy Research).

Lucas, R. (1988), 'On the Mechanics of Economic Development', *Journal of Monetary Economics*, 22(1): 3–42.

Marshall, R. (2009), *Immigration for Shared Prosperity—A Framework for Comprehensive Reform* (Washington: Economic Policy Institute (EPI)).

Migration Advisory Committee (2008), *Skilled, Shortage, Sensible: The Recommended Shortage Occupation Lists for the UK and Scotland* (London: MAC).

Romer, P. (1986), 'Increasing Returns and Long-Run Growth', *Journal of Political Economy*, 94: 1002–37.

Veneri, C. M. (1999), 'Can Occupational Labour Shortages be Identified using Available Data?', *Monthly Labor Review*, 122(3): 15–21.

2

Migrant Workers: Who Needs Them? A Framework for the Analysis of Staff Shortages, Immigration, and Public Policy

Bridget Anderson and Martin Ruhs

Introduction

Employer demand for migrant workers has become a key feature of labour markets in high income countries. Employers' calls for more migrant workers are typically expressed in terms of 'labour and skills needs' that cannot be met from within the domestic labour force. For example, pre-crisis newspaper headlines in the UK included: 'Farms need migrants or fruit will be left to rot',[1] 'Sainsbury's says immigrants "have better work ethic" than Britons',[2] and 'UK plc needs more skilled migrants'. Even after the current economic crisis began to bite, there were claims that 'Curry houses "need more migrants"'.[3] Assessing such claims is a fundamental and highly contested issue in any labour immigration policy.

This chapter provides a comprehensive conceptual framework for evaluating employer demand for migrant labour and, more generally, for discussing the relationship between labour shortages, immigration, and public policy. It suggests the kinds of questions that might be usefully asked—and sometimes the kinds of answers that might be typically expected—when analysing labour shortages and immigration policy.

---

[1] Timesonline, 28 May 2007.
[2] *Daily Mail*, 8 Oct. 2007.
[3] BBC website, 13 Feb. 2008.

The chapter discusses four key issues that, we argue, are fundamental to the analysis of shortages, immigration, and public policy: (i) the characteristics, dimensions, and determinants of employer demand for labour (*What are employers looking for?*); (ii) characteristics of and segmentations in labour supply (*Who does what?*); (iii) employers' recruitment practices and use of migrant labour (*How and whom do employers recruit?*); and (iv) immigration and alternative responses to perceived staff shortages (*A need for migrant labour?*).

Labour demand, supply, recruitment practices, and the alternatives to immigration change over time, most notably between periods of economic growth and crisis. Our conceptual analysis of the four fundamental issues above thus includes discussion of the potential effects of the changing economic environment and recognizes, albeit in a limited way, the importance of nuancing arguments with reference to different types of employers. Although our analysis is necessarily broad, we recognize that employers differ, not only across sectors and occupations but also in terms of the nature of employment relations, type of firm, and size of business: for example, a labour user may not be the employer per se; a firm with a huge human resources department is in a very different position from a sole owned business, and so on.

Our discussion draws on a small but rapidly increasing multi-disciplinary and international body of research on employers' attitudes, incentives, and recruitment decisions vis-à-vis migrant labour, as well as more long-standing research on skills, labour supply, and staff shortages. The analysis is grounded in economics but also includes discussion of theories and insights from other disciplines such as sociology, geography, and politics.

There are two key interrelated themes of this chapter. The first is that labour demand and supply are not generated independently of one another. Instead, there is a *dynamic* and *mutually conditioning* relation between labour demand and supply. Employer demand for labour is malleable, aligning itself with supply: 'what employers want' can be critically influenced by what employers 'think they can get' from different groups of workers, and at the same time, labour supply adapts to the requirements of demand. Secondly, the persistent and in many sectors increasing employer demand for migrant workers can, to a significant degree, be explained by 'system effects' that 'produce' certain types of domestic labour shortages. System effects arise from the institutional and regulatory frameworks of the labour market and from wider public policies (e.g. welfare and social policies), many of which are not ostensibly to do with the labour market. Most of these system effects are outside the control of individual employers and workers and are heavily (but not exclusively) influenced by the state. System effects are interdependent and dynamic and, together with the overall macroeconomic environment, have important impacts on the behaviours and incentives of employers and workers. For example, in the UK, labour demand and supply are critically shaped by the recent changes in both welfare benefits and immigration regimes which interrelate with changing economic and labour market circumstances, including the dramatic shifts of 2008–9.

The interdependence between labour demand and supply, and the effects of dynamic regulatory, institutional, and policy systems that produce domestic labour shortages are, we will argue, key to understanding employer demand for (migrant) labour during economic growth and crisis. They have important but rarely discussed implications for the analysis of staff shortages and indeed for immigration policy and public policy more generally.

2.1 Characteristics, Dimensions, and Determinants of Employer Demand: What Are Employers Looking For?

Understanding what employers are looking for 'from the bottom up' requires a critical examination of employers' claims about why they need particular types of workers. This needs to be contextualized within the broader social, political, and institutional frameworks within which labour markets are embedded. It brings to the fore the socially contingent nature of job allocation and more broadly the social and political construction of labour markets and their interrelation with institutions that are exogenous to the relationship between the employer and worker or jobseeker (Granovetter 1985; Peck 1996). Such an approach involves understanding the particularities of how job structures and job designs are shaped, and how very heterogeneous forms of demand are determined in particular times and places. There is no one-size-fits-all approach as labour markets operate differently, depending, for example, on the sector, occupation, type, and size of firm and on the extent of labour market segmentation (see Leontaridi 1998; Peck 1996).

When examining the nature of employer demand for labour, it is important to consider the context of national labour markets and economy. In the 20 years in the UK pre-dating the 2008 recession there has been a shift in: who is in work (for example, there has been a growth of female employment and prime-age male inactivity); wages and employment relations (for example, the decline of trade union membership and increase in wage inequality); and in the kind of work performed and skills required (for example, job polarization with rises in Goos and Manning's (2007) 'lousy' and 'lovely' jobs and a decline in 'middling' occupations). A long period of economic growth did not eradicate labour market inequalities in the UK and the recession beginning in 2008 risks exacerbating them (Rogers 2009: 304). Whilst the long-term impacts are hard to predict, by mid-2009 it was clear that in the UK young people aged 18–24 were particularly hard hit. However, unlike previous recessions, when migrant and ethnic minorities have tended to be first to be laid off and first to be taken on during the recovery, employment rates for these groups have been relatively stable (EHRC 2009).

Many low-skilled jobs have moved to low-waged economies, and there has been an expansion of service sector jobs, some of which have been associated with de-skilling and the proliferation of 'McJobs' in low-skilled and low-waged service occupations (Lindsay and McQuaid 2004; Talwar 2002). At the same time, the growth of computerization has had a major impact on the tasks performed. As the price of computer technology has declined, labour supply is re-allocated from routine to non-routine analytic and interactive tasks, and this is most marked in industries and occupations that have adopted computer technology rapidly (Autor et al. 2003). Thus many occupations now comprise non-routine tasks that demand 'flexibility, creativity, generalized problem-solving capabilities, and complex communications' (Autor et al. 2003: 1284) that cannot (yet) be substituted for by computers.

In the remainder of this section, we distinguish between the kinds of characteristics ('skills' broadly understood) required by employers that are related to the tasks and type of work to be done and those that are related to the employment conditions and relations of the job that is being made available (including whether the work is full- or part-time, temporary or permanent). This is for the purposes of analysis only. As shall be seen, these two aspects of employer demand are closely related and sometimes interchangeable.

2.1.1 *Employer Demand: 'Skills'*

Although commonly used in academic, public, and policy discourse, 'skills' is a very vague term both conceptually and empirically. It can refer to a wide range of qualifications and competencies whose meaning in practice is not always clear.[4] Research has long pointed out that the notion of 'skill' is socially constructed and highly gendered (Cockburn and Ormrod 1993; Peck 1996; Phillips and Taylor 1980). Skills can require years of specialized training, or a one-day course. Some skills, such as basic literacy and numeracy, are supposed to be 'produced' by national educational systems and require long-term state investment, others may be obtained through further education (i.e. a combination of state and individual investment), and others may be firm or industry specific (as in the financial service or information technology sector), in which case they may be principally the responsibility of employers. These systems are usually interdependent—for example, an IT worker may have to have demonstrated numerical competency and have a good degree to qualify for further training paid for by an employer. As Wickham and Bruff (2008) discuss, skills shortages and employers' responses to them 'are the result of specific relationships between the system of production and employment on the one hand and the system of education and training on the other' (p. 31).

Some 'skills' are credentialized (e.g. National Vocational Qualifications (NVQs), professional qualifications, and apprenticeships), but what is and is not credentialized changes and jobs can shift from being classified as 'low-skilled' to 'skilled' and vice versa without necessarily changing in their content (Chan et al., Chapter 8; Moriarty, Chapter 5, both in this volume). The adequacy of NVQs and other formal qualifications to capture skills requirements is regarded with scepticism across many sectors, and the existence of sufficient numbers of people with the right formal qualifications does not guarantee the absence of recruitment difficulties. This is evident in employer demand for *experience* (Bach, Chapter 4; Jones, Chapter 9; Lucas and Mansfield, Chapter 6, all in this volume).

The limitation of formal qualifications as a measure of skills becomes most apparent when one considers 'soft' skills not captured through formal qualifications. They cover a broad range of competences, transferable across occupations (rather than being specialized) from 'problem solving' to teamworking, and they are exactly those skills identified by Autor et al. (2003) as increasingly required as a result of technological change. They can also be crucial complements to 'hard' skills, particularly when formal qualifications have an overly narrow focus (Chan et al. 2008).

---

[4] The National Employer Skills Survey (NESS) 2007 identified 13 different types of 'skill' that employers said were lacking: technical and practical skills; oral communication skills; customer handling skills; problem-solving skills; teamworking skills; written communication skills; management skills; literacy skills; numeracy skills; office/admin skills; IT professional skills; foreign language skills; and general IT user skills (Learning and Skills Council 2008: 10).

Soft skills are often said to be particularly important in sectors where social relations with customers, clients, and/or service users are important to the delivery and *quality* of the work. Certain 'skills' may be necessary to make sure the job is done in a way that contributes to a good service experience, rather than simply to complete the task. For example, the quality of care delivered in both health and social care sectors is affected by the soft skills of those providing care, with some service users actively expressing a preference for personal qualities over formal qualifications (Bach, Chapter 4; Moriarty, Chapter 5, this volume; Cangiano et al. 2009).

At the same time, 'skills' can also be used to refer to attributes and characteristics that are related to employer control over the workforce. Soft skills can shade into 'personal characteristics' and attitudes and what Payne (2000) calls the 'fudging of skill with behaviour' (Belt and Richardson 2005; Jackson et al. 2005; Keep and Mayhew 1999). Employers may find certain qualities and attitudes desirable because they suggest workers will be compliant, easy to discipline, and cooperative (Jackson et al. 2005; Keep and Mayhew 1999; Martin and Grove 2002; Payne 2000; Warhurst and Nickson 2007).

The fuzziness of 'skill' is further exacerbated by its application to demeanour, accent, style, and even physical appearance, at times being applied to situations where a worker 'looks and sounds right' (Nickson et al. 2001; Warhurst and Nickson 2007). There is a growing literature on the importance of physical bodies to work, organizations, and employment relations (see Wolkowitz 2006 for a review). It has long been recognized that certain types of bodies (most obviously, gendered, racialized, and aged) are considered more suitable for certain types of work and that bodies may be used as signifiers for certain attributes, for example, stamina, or laziness (Martin and Grove 2002; Pettinger 2005; McDowell 1997; Warhurst and Nickson 2007; Wolkowitz 2006; Anderson 2000). As skills soften, these signifiers may assume greater importance for those occupations which have less regulation regarding formal qualifications and where employers consequently have greater discretion in recruitment (see the discussion in Section 4).

2.1.2 *Employer Demand: Controlling Work Time and Worker-Effort*

As well as whether a worker has the required 'skills', however understood, an employer must assess whether they will tolerate particular employment relations and conditions. Some of these may be regarded as deriving from the nature of the work: in some interactive service occupations, relations with customers and clients may be inherently 'stressful and emotionally draining' (Lucas and Mansfield, Chapter 6, this volume); 'unskilled' labour in construction, care, or agriculture, may be extremely physically demanding. The temporal configuration of jobs, that is, how time is allocated within work (for example, part-time, full-time, and shift work), and how time is allocated around work, that is, whether work is temporary or permanent, may also be shaped by factors which are not within individual employers' control, such as technology, by the phasing of service requirements and demand, and by sectoral particularities. For example, some care users need 24-hour care, which means that somebody has to work a night shift (Moriarty, Chapter 5, this volume).

However, perceived 'intrinsic' employment conditions may be subject to change, with employers and workers playing an important role. Although constrained by broader socio-economic factors, employers can and do shape employment relations and conditions, usually with a view to profitability, with consequences for the characteristics and attitudes that are required of workers. This is evident at times of economic recession when employers can reduce or increase overtime or shift from full- to part-time employment (Rogers 2009; Geroski and Gregg 1997).

CONTROLLING THE PERIOD OF EMPLOYMENT

Control over the period of employment is an important factor in employer demand. In a flexible labour market, where relations between workers and employers are weakened, conflicts over labour mobility may be heightened, with employers wanting ease of hire and fire but also retention, and workers seeking to balance labour mobility with job security (Anderson 2010).

One increasingly common way for employers to control the period of workers' employment, and in particular to facilitate flexible and short-term employment, is through using 'agency workers'. Numbers have rapidly increased since the restructuring recession of the 1980s, particularly in agriculture and food processing. Agency workers are often not directly employed by the 'labour user', but by an employment business (or 'labour providing agency'). They are associated with temporary work, although in 2008 one in four agency workers in the UK had been in the same job for over a year, and over half for six months or more (TUC Commission on Vulnerable Employment 2008). Agency workers have significantly fewer rights than those who are directly employed: they can be hired on lower hourly rates and on worse terms and conditions, and do not have rights to benefits such as overtime and sickness pay. They are also less likely to be members of a trade union (it should be noted, however, that some workers prefer agency working, sometimes as a means of avoiding the problems of being a permanent staff member or as a response to declining conditions in permanent jobs (Bach 2008)).

The prevalence of agency work in certain sectors has important implications for employer demand: first, the generator of the demand for labour (the labour user) is not the same as the 'employer', and secondly, the labour user is shaping the workforce principally through choosing to employ a workforce with a particular employment status rather than by direct selection of individual workers. Migrants are disproportionately likely to be agency workers (Jayaweera and Anderson 2009; Geddes and Scott, Chapter 7, this volume).

Retaining workers can be extremely challenging for some occupations, and sometimes 'recruitment problems' are in fact the result of high labour turnover (Devins and Hogarth 2005). Some employers do not perceive high turnover to be a problem. Lucas and Mansfield (Chapter 6, this volume) helpfully distinguish between seasonality and unpredictability. In some sectors, labour turnover may be to do with the nature of the work, such as with construction projects, or certain types of seasonal agricultural work where employers actively avoid long-term employment relationships as they are not profitable, though even in these situations an employer seeks to retain labour for the period for which it is needed. Retention is more generally a cause for concern in sectors like social care where trust and familiarity are at a premium or where employers invest in training. Employers' strategies on retention of workers may be partly a function of the characteristics of labour supply: they may not regard it worth investing in training for segments of the labour market that are perceived as 'transient', such as students and some migrants, which in turn may affect job satisfaction and turnover.

CONTROLLING WORKER-EFFORT

Good employment relations are important for worker-effort, which is difficult for employers to control. As Peck (1996: 34) puts it: 'With any one hiring decision, they [employers] may be recruiting either a future employee of the year or a future shop-floor agitator'. This issue is ever more prominent as the proportion of autonomous jobs comprising non-routine tasks increases. Employers may prefer workers who monitor their own performance and describe them as having a good 'work ethic' (Champlin and Hake 2006; Johnson-Webb 2002; Karjanen 2008). They may attempt to exercise control over work-effort by opting for particular types of employment status or offer non-wage benefits to facilitate good or better employment conditions and relations (Moriarty, Chapter 5, this volume).[5]

The discussion makes clear that employers have discretion and their common claims of 'labour and skills shortages' and migrants' superior 'work ethic' must be critically interrogated. At the same time, however, employers are clearly working within constraints (that are susceptible to different degrees of influence) that shape their decisions. Skills shortages, for example, emerge in part from a relation between types of education and training, and systems of employment. Recruitment decisions to 'buy in' rather than 'train up' help ensure this relation persists, but they may be the only profitable solution in certain types of economies and institutional frameworks, at least in the short term (Wickham and Bruff 2008). This indicates that there is a broad range of institutional and non-institutional mechanisms that lay out the parameters of the relation between employers and workers. These include trade union membership, employee participation in decision-making, managerial strategies, and non-wage benefits, as well as the more formalized legal relation between worker and employer. The specificities vary between sectors, occupations, and type of employer. There is, therefore, a need to consider the constraints within which employers are operating, some of which are outside their control. Furthermore, the mutually constitutive relation between demand and supply means that part of the answer to 'What are employers looking for?' lies in the characteristics of and segmentations in labour supply.

2.2 Characteristics of and Segmentations in Labour Supply: Who Wants to Do What?

The (potential) workforce is highly diverse, has different frames of reference, and is differently motivated to participate in the labour market. In considering segmentations in supply, we will, for illustrative purposes, focus on the motivations and constraints of the unemployed and inactive as examples of different groups in the labour market. This is of particular

---

[5] Sometimes what are presented as non-wage benefits by employers may not be so perceived by workers. The provision of accommodation in agriculture, hospitality, health and social care may be considered by employers as a means of helping employees save on transport and housing costs. However 'living in' is often not actively wanted by employees, while there are advantages to the employer of housing workers at or close to their work (Low Pay Commission 2006).

relevance at the time of writing, given the growth in unemployment due to the economic crisis. There are of course other labour pools with different motivations and constraints, including students (Curtis and Lucas 2001; Hofman and Steijn 2003; Lucas and Mansfield, Chapter 6, this volume) and migrants (discussed in Section 3). We then discuss mismatches of demand and supply, with a particular focus on expectations and geography.

2.2.1 *Potential Pools of Labour: The Unemployed and Inactive*

The discussion that follows is necessarily generalized and principally serves to illustrate the issues that might impinge on whether individuals of equivalent qualifications put themselves forward for jobs. Importantly, labour pools are not homogeneous or discrete groups and the unemployed or inactive are segmented by, for example, gender, race, class, age, and immigration status.

Over the past 20 years, unemployment in the UK declined from 1.9 million in 1990 to 1.3 million in 2007. However, the current economic downturn is rapidly expanding the pool of unemployed workers. By the end of July 2009, unemployment was 2.47 million, up from 1.6 million in early 2008. By August 2009, the claimant count had also risen to 1.61 million, the highest level since May 1997.[6] The unemployment rate and claimant count was particularly high for those in lower paid elementary occupations. For example, 37 per cent of those who previously worked in elementary administrative occupations were claiming Jobseeker's Allowance (JSA) (TUC 2009). These increases raise the important and open question whether (fear of) increased competition for jobs and long-term unemployment means some people are more likely to take up jobs at wages and employment conditions that they would not find acceptable during times of high employment and economic growth. In the UK, there is no systematic evidence yet on this question.

Inactivity rates among prime-age men in the UK have risen by a factor of five since the early 1970s (Faggio and Nickell 2005; Tomkins 2008), stabilizing at about 7.85 million before the downturn. Though popularly presented as a problem to do with laziness and 'sick note Britain', the factors underlying this shift are recognized to be less to do with laziness and more to do with changes in the labour market and the operation of the benefit system, as well as a significant increase in the incidence of chronic illness

---

[6] See <http://www.statistics.gov.uk/StatBase/tsdataset.asp?vlnk=430&More=Y>, accessed on 20 Sept. 2009.

and disability. Faggio and Nickell (2005) argue that unskilled men with chronic health problems were particularly vulnerable when the market for low-skilled labour weakened. Skills often deteriorate during periods of unemployment or inactivity, and what may well be required are upgraded technological skills. As Warhurst and Nickson (2007) point out, it is often those most in need of paid work who are in practice the least likely to possess the social, attitudinal, and aesthetic skills in demand. While at the outset of recession the inactivity rate remained stable, by July 2009 it had risen to 7.99 million, the highest figure since comparable records began in 1971.[7]

The categorization of workers as unemployed or inactive is itself subject to state laws and policies, and therefore the size of these labour pools may shift as a result of regulatory changes. For example, from October 2008 Incapacity Benefit for claimants with a long-term illness or disability began to be phased out in favour of the Employment Support Allowance, which has considerably greater conditionality. Thus many of those who previously might have been classed as 'inactive' will become 'unemployed'. A similar process is under way for lone parents, who are transferring from Income Support to JSA. While these changes are promoted as a means of encouraging people to take up employment, the operation of the benefit system can also make jobseekers reluctant to apply for certain jobs, particularly if they are temporary or low-waged or both. For example, the lack of flexibility of the benefits system can act as a disincentive to taking on seasonal work (Geddes and Scott, Chapter 7, this volume). It is not yet clear how the government's welfare reforms (conceived in a time of boom), in particular the phasing out of income support and the greater conditionality for those who are claiming JSA, will impact on this. However, it is clear that the implementation of the benefit system is an important factor in structuring the decisions of jobseekers.

2.2.2 Mismatches: Expectations and Geography

The differing frames of reference and constraints of (potential) jobseekers are important factors in understanding mismatches between demand and supply, in terms of expectations and geography. One cannot assume that *anybody* will be able or want to do any low-skilled work *anywhere*.

---

[7] See <http://www.statistics.gov.uk/cci/nugget_print.asp?ID=12>, accessed 29th September 2009.

MISMATCHES IN EXPECTATIONS

Unsocial hours, low wages, temporariness, lack of opportunities for promotion or personal development, as well as the low status of work can all prevent jobseekers from applying for particular positions (Belt and Richardson 2005; Devins and Hogarth 2005; Lindsay and McQuaid 2004). Differences in expectations between workers and employers are recognized as increasingly important, especially the jobseeker's presentation of skills on the one hand and the employer's 'fundamentally unattractive employment propositions' on the other (Adams et al. 2002).

Issues raised by 'hard-to-fill vacancies' in areas of unemployment are in part a subset of why particular groups of people 'choose' to do (or not do) certain types of jobs, which is in turn related to broader socialization as it affects both workers and employers. Jobs are not simply about earning money but have a social meaning. People who want a long-term engagement with the labour market may be reluctant to consider entry-level jobs because they may be looking for work that offers prospects of promotion, or that is consistent with their particular skills and experience (Lindsay and McQuaid 2004; Tomkins 2008). Those who have caring responsibilities may want work close to home and be limited in the hours they can work. Jobs are also gendered and racialized. The prevalence of feminized jobs in the service sector can be a real problem for older male jobseekers. Thus a male ex-steelworker may not put himself forward to clean private households, even though he might be perfectly capable of doing so. Moreover, should he do so, he may find employers reluctant to take him on (Anderson 2007; Lindsay and McQuaid 2004; Lucas and Mansfield, Chapter 6, this volume). These are complex social processes that cannot be reduced to individuals' simply 'refusing' to take a job.

GEOGRAPHICAL MISMATCHES

Spatial mismatch and geographical immobility have long been recognized as features of the UK labour market (Adams et al. 2002; Collier 2005). This is reflected in the other chapters in this book dealing with specific sectoral labour markets in the UK. However, the extent of regional differences is not uncontested (Jackman and Savouri 1999). As Dickens et al. (2000) point out, there has always been greater variation in unemployment *within* regions than there has been *between* regions, that is, the local area matters (though of course what 'local' means can in turn be heavily contested). The housing market plays an important role in shaping internal labour mobility and regional labour markets, high house prices can prevent movement if not accompanied by expected earnings growth (Murphy et al. 2006), and difficulties in selling can also restrict mobility. House price affordability is a particular problem in rural areas and is acknowledged as an important factor in the labour markets for food processing, agriculture, and social care (Geddes 2008; Moriarty et al. 2008; Scott 2008).

Answering the question 'Who wants to do what?' is not then simply a matter of mapping individuals' preferences and opportunities. Potential workers are differentially constrained and have different frames of reference. Mismatches in the labour market are unlikely to be addressed by an exclusive supply-side approach. Our discussion and other research suggest that reducing mismatches requires consideration of broader labour market processes and institutions, including recruitment processes, job structures, and designs and employer demand more generally (also see Collier 2005; Gore 2005).

2.3 Immigration and Labour Demand: How and Whom Do Employers Recruit?

Faced with a segmented and highly diverse pool of labour, how and *whom* do employers recruit? To discuss this question, we first briefly review employers' use of national and other stereotypes in the recruitment of workers. This is followed by a discussion of the implications of 'what employers want' (as reviewed in Section 2.2) for 'whom employers recruit', given their perceptions of the different types of workers within the available pool of labour. Given this chapter's concern with the demand for migrant labour, we focus on why and how employers use workers' *nationality* as a proxy for determining the suitability of different groups of workers to do particular types of jobs.

2.3.1 *Discrimination and Stereotyping in Recruitment*

The suitability of workers for specific jobs is sometimes determined *categorically*, based for example on gender, age, race, and/or nationality of the job candidates rather than on individual merit (Duncan and Loretto 2004; Waldinger and Lichter 2003). Employers can draw on socially meaningful stereotypes or their own experiences generalized to explain the behaviour of particular nationalities. This may be because of individual prejudices on the part of the person recruiting or because they have incomplete information about the personal characteristics and attributes of individual applicants (Moss and Tilly 2001). Recruitment based on the grounds of race, gender, age, disability, or sexuality has been extensively described (see e.g. Blackburn et al. 2002; Creegan et al. 2003; Duncan and Loretto 2004; Gersen 2007). There is substantially less attention paid to recruitment based on *nationality*. The migration literature does suggest, however, that the nationality of workers (somewhat artificially considered as distinct from 'race') can be an important category and criterion for hiring workers and this has been found to be the case in low-waged sectors in the UK and other economies (Karjanen 2008: 102; Anderson et al. 2006: 60; Anderson 2007: 70; Matthews and Ruhs 2007: 92; Preibisch and Binford 2007: 112). In their analysis of employers' recruitment practices in California, Waldinger and Lichter (2003) suggest that employers have a 'cognitive map' that includes a variable 'hiring queue' which orders job candidates by racial and ethnic origin.

While there is some evidence that nationality and/or country of origin does figure as a proxy for selecting and recruiting workers, its significance is likely to vary with the job and job requirements under consideration. How national stereotypes operate is complex and often not reducible to simple individual prejudices, but is related to how employers respond to, and perpetuate, wider structural imbalances and inequalities in local and global labour markets (Baumle and Fossett 2005).

2.3.2 *Factors Affecting National Stereotyping and Employers' 'Hiring Queue'*

The remainder of this section explores the potential factors that may encourage employers to engage in 'national stereotyping' in the recruitment of labour, that is, to develop ordered (but variable) preferences for particular groups of workers based on their nationality and/or their status as migrants more generally. Although listed separately, many of the factors discussed below are overlapping and interconnected. It is important to bear in mind that these stereotypes are gendered and racialized, that is, an expressed preference for 'Filipinos' might indicate a preference for Filipino *women*, or for Czechs might indicate *non-Roma* Czechs, and so on. Moreover, when employers talk of the advantages of hiring migrants, they are often referring to relatively recent arrivals, rather than the foreign-born or the settled. Indeed the attitudes and characteristics of migrants may converge, or be perceived to converge, to those of local workers over time.

WORKERS' EXPECTATIONS ABOUT WAGES AND EMPLOYMENT CONDITIONS

Migrants, especially recent arrivals and those intending a temporary stay, often operate with a 'dual frame of reference' (Piore 1979). Research suggests that employers are typically acutely aware of the economic and other trade-offs that migrants are willing to make by tolerating wages and employment conditions that are poor by the standards of their host country but higher than those prevailing in their countries of origin (for the UK, see e.g. Anderson et al. 2006; for the US, see Waldinger and Lichter 2003). This is not confined to the lowest-paying occupations and sectors in the labour market (Bach, Chapter 4, this volume). The differences in reservation wages (i.e. the minimum wage that workers are prepared to work for) and expected minimum employment conditions between migrants and equivalent locals,[8] and between different groups of migrants, can be expected to have an important impact on 'whom' profit-maximizing employers recruit. Saucedo (2006) argues that when setting pay rates and employment conditions for particular jobs, employers effectively choose the ethnic composition of their workforce. In the UK, some employers openly acknowledge that the wages and employment conditions they offer for low-skilled work are considered unacceptable to most local workers (Moriarty et al. 2008: 203; Geddes and Scott, Chapter 7, this volume).

'WORK ETHIC AND PRODUCTIVITY'

Existing studies often highlight employers' comments about migrants' perceived superior 'attitude' and 'work ethic' when compared to local workers (Anderson et al. 2006; Dench et al. 2006; House of Lords 2008). In the US, Barbara Ellen Smith found that the greatest conflict between African American and Latino workers arises from 'the acceptable intensity of work effort' (Smith 2006, cited Gordon and Lenhardt 2008; see also Karjanen 2008)—that is, what might be essentialized as 'work ethic'. Among the UK sectors reviewed in this book, migrants' superior work ethic appears to be most commonly mentioned by employers offering low-paying jobs in agriculture, food processing, hospitality, and social care.

The term 'work ethic' can capture a range of factors related to employers' subjective needs and job requirements. There are a variety of reasons why certain groups of migrants are perceived to possess a 'better work ethic' than other workers. Many explanations stem, again, from migrants' different

---

[8] 'Locals' is a diverse and segmented group, and may also include 'foreign-born'.

frame of reference and their consequent greater willingness to do the job *on the employer's terms* (Waldinger and Lichter 2003) compared to domestic workers. Some refer to employers' beliefs that migrants are less likely to be trade union members (Champlin and Hake 2006; Rodriguez 2004). However, there may also be other factors such as the absence or smaller size of family and social networks, which may make them more likely to live on-site or work anti-social or long hours (Preibisch and Binford 2007).

Gordon and Lenhardt (2008) have argued that certain groups of migrants may accord a different 'citizenship value' to low-waged work than do citizens. This too may be a factor shaping intensity of work effort or 'work ethic'. For migrants there are 'citizenship pay offs' of higher status in the country of origin, the value of remittances resulting from favourable exchange rates and pricing, as well as short-term financial pressures resulting from migratory processes. This compares with African Americans who are economically rooted in the US:

The very different stances many African Americans and new Latino immigrants have with respect to work and citizenship—African Americans' desire to control work pace and conditions in order to ensure a modicum of dignity and respect within the United States, and immigrants' incentive to do whatever the boss asks in order to achieve greater economic and social status outside this country—sets up a clash when they meet in the workplace. (Gordon and Lenhardt 2008: 301)

Employers' assessments of the suitability of workers may also be based on perceived cultural traits and characteristics. For example, in the social care sector, some migrants may be seen as having a 'more caring ethos' than other workers (Moriarty et al. 2008: 28). In some instances, perceived cultural capital seems to be more related to *productivity* (Geddes and Scott, Chapter 7, this volume; Park 1999: 229).

IMMIGRATION STATUS

Employers may develop a preference for migrants because of the characteristics and restrictions attached to their immigration status (Bloomekatz 2007; Anderson 2007). In most high-income countries, immigration policies are characterized by a multitude of different types of status. Each status (such as work-permit holder, student, working-holiday maker, and dependent) is associated with different rights and restrictions in and beyond the labour market. These restrictions, which cannot be imposed on citizens, may give rise to a specific demand for particular types of migrant workers.

Some employers, especially those finding it difficult to *retain* workers in certain jobs, may prefer workers whose choice of employment is restricted, as is usually the case with recent arrivals and migrants on temporary visas. Immigration requirements can make it difficult for migrants to change jobs. From the employer's perspective, the employment restrictions associated with particular types of immigration status may make migrants the more 'suitable' and easier to retain in jobs that offer low wages and poor employment conditions (Anderson 2010). For example, the UK's National Farmers' Union (NFU) recently argued that migrants from outside the European Economic Area (EEA) who are employed on temporary Seasonal Agricultural Worker Scheme (SAWS) permits 'provide a source of labour *that is guaranteed to remain on the farm* during the crucial harvest period' (National Farmers Union 2007; emphasis added). Immigration requirements can also prohibit family reunion, meaning the worker is more available to work difficult shifts or more likely to live in than might otherwise be the case.

Because of their very limited rights, illegally resident migrants may be perceived as displaying a better 'work ethic' and be willing to accept worse employment conditions than citizens or migrants who are legally resident. In practice, the research evidence on the impact of illegal status on wages and employment conditions is mixed (for a review, see Ruhs 2009). Importantly, to actively 'choose' to illegally employ migrant labour or to employ migrants on a particular legal immigration status, employers need to know *both* the conditions governing a particular immigration status and the immigration status of the migrants they employ. Both these assumptions, but particularly the latter, need not always apply. However, it is often employers' and workers' *perceptions* of vulnerability, as well as actual legal vulnerability, that drive employers' preferences for recruiting 'certain' types of migrant labour (Bloomekatz 2007: 104).

OVERQUALIFIED WORKERS AND 'NATIONAL' SKILLS

Because of their different frame of reference, new migrants may be prepared to accept jobs whose skill requirements are significantly below their actual skills and qualifications, creating 'high quality workers for low-waged jobs', who may well be more attractive employees than the available British workforce (Anderson et al. 2006; Drinkwater et al. 2008; Lucas and Mansfield, Chapter 6, this volume).

In some cases, employer demand for particular groups of migrant labour may reflect a demand for specified skills or knowledge related to particular countries, including foreign language skills. In a globalized economy, in both high and low-skilled sectors, employers may value the knowledge and contacts migrants bring from their countries of origin (Jones, Chapter 9;

Moriarty, Chapter 5; Lucas and Mansfield, Chapter 6, all in this volume; Somerville and Sumption 2009). Whether or not these specialized skills which are related to particular countries or regions can be taught to, and acquired by, local workers, and consequently, whether certain products, trade links, and services can only be provided by workers from particular countries is more contested in low-skilled than in high-skilled occupations such as financial services (Jones, Chapter 9, this volume). The demand for migrant labour in ethnic cuisine restaurants is a case in point. Employers in these restaurants frequently seek migrant workers, arguing not only that they have learned the culinary skills and traditions in an authentic environment (see e.g. Guild of Bangladeshi Restauranteurs, cited in Lucas and Mansfield, Chapter 6, this volume), but that they have the knowledge of customs and language used in the workplace (Gordon and Reich 1982; Rodriguez 2004). In practice, demand for certain groups of migrants can stem from considerations that go beyond the need for certain 'national skills' and 'cultural knowledge'. For example, Matthews and Ruhs' (2007) study of hospitality businesses in Brighton, UK suggests that the preference for migrant labour sometimes reflects a preference for workers whose choice of employment is restricted by their immigration status. Whilst it is the case that formalized skills are not necessarily sufficient as a measure of quality of work and, in this case, chefs trained to the same NVQ level may indeed produce meals of a different quality (though the question remains how this is or is not related to cultural capital), immigration status may also facilitate employer control over workers. Nationality may then be a proxy for cultural capital, skills sets, and immigration status, all at the same time.

RECRUITMENT CHANNELS: MIGRANT NETWORKS AND AGENCIES

The advantages of recruiting migrants include obtaining a 'self-regulating' and 'self-sustaining' labour supply (Rodriguez 2004). This is largely because of migrant networks which employers can use to control and regulate the flow of labour. Saucedo (2006) identifies network hiring as a key element sustaining US employers' preferences for migrants over domestic workers. Similar processes have been observed in the dominance of white males in employment in the construction sector (Chan et al., Chapter 8, this volume). In the UK, recruitment through migrant networks is thought to be a very common practice among employers with a migrant workforce (see e.g. Anderson et al. 2006; Lucas and Mansfield, Chapter 6, this volume).

Companies with a demand for a flexible workforce may make use of employment agencies to help find suitable workers. Since employment agencies often have significant numbers of migrant workers on their books, they can play an important role in impacting on the national composition of the workforce (Geddes and Scott, Chapter 7; Moriarty, Chapter 5, this volume).

MIGRANT WORKERS FOR MIGRANT JOBS?

The prevalence and relative importance of national stereotyping in recruitment of labour will vary across employers and jobs, and as we have noted, in practice, stereotypes based on nationality or migrant status interact with other stereotypes about, for example, gender, race, age, and class. They may mean that employers make 'trade-offs' between perceived advantages and disadvantages of employing particular groups. For example, an employer may perceive recently arrived Polish workers as having a superior 'work ethic' but poor English language skills, and reach a decision regarding whether to hire such workers by weighing up the perceived costs and benefits. How and to what extent national stereotyping impacts on the recruitment of workers is an empirical question that cannot be addressed without in-depth research of employers' labour demand and recruitment incentives, and the perceived and real characteristics of the local and migrant labour supply in particular occupations, sectors, and regions of the UK.

There may not always be an obvious answer to what is considered 'fair' or 'unfair' discrimination (Waldinger and Lichter 2003) in the recruitment of workers. Overt prejudice-based discrimination and stereotyping in employment is illegal in most liberal democracies. However, employers in the UK are required to 'discriminate' by nationality in that they must give preferential access to employment to British citizens and EEA nationals on the grounds of citizenship (the 'community preference rule'). Moreover, employers typically regard using nationality as a proxy for assessing individual characteristics as a matter of efficiency and profit maximization, rather than the manifestation of prejudice (for a review of 'statistical discrimination', see e.g. Baumle and Fossett 2005; Gersen 2007). It seems clear, however, that migration status and country of origin are one way that employers differentiate amongst the potential workforce.

'What employers want' is partly influenced by the characteristics and qualities different types of workers are perceived to be able to provide to the employer, hence the notion that labour demand and supply are 'mutually conditioning'. This raises the possibility that employers develop a specific demand and preference for migrant workers (or particular groups of migrant workers) over domestic workers (and/or other migrant groups), or even offer jobs with requirements that non-migrants will be unable or unwilling to meet (compare Saucedo 2006). This may already be happening in sectors like agriculture and food processing. In their survey of farmers in the UK, Geddes and Scott (Chapter 7, this volume) find that recruiting British workers is not seen as a viable option any more as they are considered 'part of the problem' rather than the solution.

2.4 Immigration and Alternative Responses to Perceived Staff Shortages: A Need for Migrant Labour?

In theory, at an individual level, employers may respond to perceived staff shortages in different ways. These include:

- increase wages and/or improve working conditions to attract more citizens who are either inactive, unemployed, or employed in other sectors, and/or to increase the working hours of the existing workforce; this may require a change in recruitment processes and greater investment in training and up-skilling;
- change the production process to make it less labour intensive by, for example, increasing the capital and/or technology intensity;
- relocate to countries where labour costs are lower;
- switch to production (provision) of less labour-intensive commodities and services;
- employ migrant workers.

Of course, not all of these options will be available to all employers at all times. In exploring the feasibility and net impacts of alternative responses (which, in practice, vary across sectors and occupations), one must also consider the systemic and social constraints operating on employers (and workers).

RAISING WAGES AND IMPROVING EMPLOYMENT CONDITIONS AND RELATIONS

Economics emphasizes the role of prices in bringing labour supply and demand into equilibrium. In the basic textbook model of labour economics, labour shortages are temporary and eventually eliminated by rising wages. So a key question is how different local labour pools react to increases in relative wages (for a recent review, see e.g. Evers et al. 2008).

Elasticities of labour supply with respect to wages can differ across different groups of workers, but also across sectors and occupations. A wage increase of x per cent may be sufficient to significantly increase domestic labour supply in sector y but not in sector z, perhaps because sector z is associated with difficult employment conditions or considered 'low status'. Although most economists agree that rising wages will trigger an increase in domestic labour supply, there is debate about the magnitude of the supply elasticities in practice.

Improving employment conditions, employment relations, and job quality may encourage the unemployed or inactive to apply for particular jobs (Devins and Hogarth 2005). For employers, to draw from this labour pool may require mechanisms of support to compensate for the effects of long-term unemployment or inactivity and the constraints of caring re-sponsibilities, as well as recognizing workers' longer-term aspirations and expectations of employment. In some instances, it may be feasible for employers to encourage a shift from part-time to full-time, or temporary to permanent employment or vice versa. Employers may be able to adjust workforce roles, making certain types of jobs more accessible to those who have not participated in long-term training, for example, as with the NHS cadet schemes cited by Bach (Chapter 4, this volume).

However, employers in labour-intensive industries are often reluctant to raise wages and improve conditions because of concerns about profitability and even about being priced out of the market. In the UK, agriculture, food processing, construction, hospitality, and social care are currently heavily reliant on low-cost employment. In agriculture and food processing, low wages are partly the result of industrial re-structuring which led to increased cost pressures and the emergence of a significant secondary workforce, much of which is seasonal and low-paid (Geddes and Scott, Chapter 7, this volume). According to Scott (2008), labour costs represent 5–10 per cent of the retail cost of fresh produce, and higher wages and/or improving employment conditions will most likely result in further con-solidation and loss of market share of some farmers to cheaper domestic and foreign producers because they are 'squeezed' by the large retailers in the supply chain.

Similar pictures emerge in construction and hospitality. Chan et al. (Chapter 8, this volume) argue that the 'low-cost, low-quality employment road trodden in many areas' makes it unlikely that employers will consider significant wage increases at present. Lucas and Mansfield (Chapter 6, this volume) make a similar argument for the hospitality sector, arguing that a change in this low-pay, high-labour, churn scenario 'would necessitate a major paradigm shift in management philosophy'.

Employers of workers providing services for the public sector may find it impossible to raise wages to attract more domestic workers due to budget constraints and regulatory requirements. According to the UK Home Care Association, pay rates in the UK's social care sector are heavily influenced by what local councils, which make up 80 per cent of the purchasers of care services, are willing to pay (UK Home Care Association 2008; reported in House of Lords 2008: 37). Moriarty (Chapter 5, this volume) points out that the regulatory requirements for minimum staffing may be a further reason why providers of care services may find it difficult or impossible to increase pay. The implication is that raising wages would require higher taxes or a re-organization of how social care is provided and regulated.

TRAINING

Where staff shortages are partly or primarily the result of a lack of skills among the domestic workforce, one obvious response is that employers and government should invest in training and up-skilling the domestic workforce. There can be a tension between employers' and government's incentives to invest in the training of domestic workers on the one hand, and recruiting fully trained and experienced migrant workers on the other hand. As highlighted in the House of Lords Report on Immigration (2008), there is a risk, at least in theory, that immigration reduces training pro-grammes and incentives for local workers. Although plausible in theory, and illustrated by anecdotal evidence, there appears to be little systematic empirical research on this issue.

Kent's identification, cited by Lucas and Mansfield (Chapter 6, this volume) of a 'sector paradox' in hospitality that one-third of employers are not engaging in any staff training although two-thirds recognize the business benefits of training, is not limited to this sector. In construction, for example, the need for more training is widely recognized across the industry, yet there is a serious shortage of work placements for trainees (Chan et al., Chapter 8, this volume).

Investing in training will not necessarily solve employers' short-term requirements, for which they must select from the current labour pool, particularly if they require later career stage, experienced, skilled workers, rather than newly trained graduates (Khoo et al. 2007). Ensuring sufficient training places is not enough to deal with perceived shortages because of attrition before, during, and after training. At the same time, oversupply in the short term can equally risk newly qualified trainees leaving and exacerbate longer-term shortages (Bach 2008). Training can be a risky investment for employers, and free-riding and poaching of trained labour can be a serious problem (Chan et al., Chapter 8; Lucas and Mansfield, Chapter 6, both in this volume). Investing in training as a response to *anticipated* demand is also a risk.

Where the work is highly specialized and training lengthy, improving supply has to begin early in the education and training process. This raises the question of who should be responsible for training. The state, employers, and workers all play a different role depending on sector and occupation, and the relation between these different actors can be crucial. Greater cooperation between employers and training providers has been recognized as important in both hospitality and construction sectors. Industry fragmentation, particularly size of business, can have an impact on training as small providers may find training more onerous and be disproportionately affected by poaching (Chan et al., Chapter 8, Lucas and Mansfield, Chapter 6, both in this volume). Skills mismatch can continue even after training courses end if, for instance, there are poor links between employers and training organizations. However, attempts to link training, placement, and employer demand more closely have faced a number of challenges, including a lack of interest from employers (partly because of the 'free-rider' problem) and limited post-employment support (Gore 2005; McQuaid and Lindsay 2005; Warhurst and Nickson 2007). Other research has also found that a lack of recognition of the specific challenges faced by segments of the workforce and, importantly, the quality of some of the jobs that ex-trainees are moving to, has resulted in continuing labour force turnover (Belt and Richardson 2005; Devins and Hogarth 2005). Employers' involvement, not just in providing short-term training but also in ensuring long-term career progression, appears to be of crucial importance.

Thus immigration may not only be a solution to employers' reluctance to invest in training their workforce in very specific skills, but also a more general response to a breakdown between the system of production and employment on the one hand and education and training on the other (Wickham and Bruff 2008: 303).

ADOPTION OF NEW TECHNOLOGIES

Where it is technically possible to change the labour intensity in the production process, employers' choice of technique can be expected to depend in part on the available factor supplies. Employers who face a relatively abundant supply of labour can be expected, *ceteris paribus*, to adopt more labour-intensive production technologies than employers operating in an environment of relative labour scarcity. Although there is limited systematic empirical research on this issue, there are a few empirical examples which suggest that immigration can have an impact on employers' choice of technique, including the adoption of new production technologies (Lewis 2004, 2005; Martin et al. 2006). However, the costs of technology are borne by the employer and are fixed. If demand is unstable, this might mitigate against technological changes, and it may be more profitable to use labour as the variable factor of production where the costs of being idle are carried by the worker.

While the relative abundance of low-skilled labour may slow the adoption of new technology, the availability of skilled labour may have the opposite effect of encouraging the adoption of skill-complementary technology (Durbin 2004), and changes to production technology may not necessarily result in a decrease in the *proportion* of migrants in the sector. Mechanization may reduce the demand for labour, but its social impacts might mean that the remaining jobs are less desirable (for example, because they involve more isolated work roles, or are de-skilled and standardized) and therefore less likely to be attractive to nationals (Geddes and Scott, Chapter 7, this volume). Also, they might require an increased supply of skilled labour not immediately available from the national workforce (Chan et al. 2008).

The potential and cost-effectiveness of introducing new technology or new production processes that are less labour intensive can be difficult to assess in practice, especially when the dominant industrial strategy has been based on low-cost employment. Chan et al. (Chapter 8, this volume) suggest that the UK's construction industry has seen a lot of rhetoric about new technology as part of the solution to the industry's skills needs, but there has been little evidence of significant changes to production processes and strategies to date. In agriculture, some fragile crops such as fruit are less amenable to mechanization than others. Capital intensification may further require significant investment which would favour large producers over smaller ones (Geddes and Scott, Chapter 7, this volume). Moriarty (Chapter 5, this volume) refers to evidence from other countries suggesting that assistive technology can reduce care costs and can be acceptable to older people. It can, however, take a long time to implement new methods of telecare. In occupations where the labour process involves significant social interaction, such as front-line occupations in hospitality, social care, and financial services, the scope for automation is likely to be more limited than in other occupations.

PATH DEPENDENCE IN THE EMPLOYMENT OF MIGRANTS

There seem to be 'path dependencies' in the employment of migrants in the sense that once their workforce includes a substantial share of migrants, it may be difficult and costly for employers to switch to alternative responses. In other words, immigration targeted to address short-term shortages may help to sustain the conditions (such as relatively low wages, poor conditions, little training of domestic workers, low propensities for employers to adopt new technologies, and importantly, low status) that encourage shortages of domestic workers in the long run (House of Lords 2008; Wickham and Bruff 2008). There is a supply-side element to path dependence: it can combine with migratory patterns driven by cumulative causation to ensure a ready supply of new arrivals—through family reunion, if not through labour market programmes (Massey 1990; Dobson et al. 2009). Moreover, in the same way that jobs done by men can become 'women's jobs' (Goldin 1994: 302), jobs previously done by (white) citizens can become 'migrant jobs' and therefore lower status. The converse, however, is much more difficult and it is not easy for jobs to regain social status once they have been performed by stigmatized groups, even if pay and conditions improve (Gordon and Lenhardt 2008: 301).

These processes can lead to what Cornelius and others have called a 'structural embeddedness' of the demand for migrant workers in the economy (Cornelius 1998). This 'structural embeddedness' is a consequence of the long-standing and mutually constitutive nature of supply and demand. It can also be related to wider labour market developments such as: labour market segmentations, where specific types of workers are matched and become associated with particular types of jobs; economic restructuring (Champlin and Hake 2006; Johnston 2007); and the emergence of 'dead-end' jobs and a 'low-skills equilibrium', where 'a self-reinforcing network of societal and state institutions interact to stifle the demand for improvements in skill levels' (Finegold and Sosicke 1988: 22; also see Keep and Mayhew 1999; Payne 2000).

However, the discussion above suggests that it is necessary to move beyond an analysis that focuses on path dependence and to consider the importance of system effects, that is, how demand for, and supply of, particular types of labour is generated by institutions and regulations within and outside the labour market. These system effects—which are heavily influenced by the state—interact with other social factors (gender, race, age, etc.) to produce and reproduce a situation where specific types of workers seek, are matched, and become associated with particular types of jobs.

39

2.5 Conclusion

In conclusion, we discuss what the conceptual discussion in this chapter means for public debates about 'labour and skills shortages' and the implications for public policies—including labour immigration policies—in practice.

DEFINING 'SKILLS' AND 'SKILLED' JOBS

The UK and many other high-income countries are operating skills-based labour immigration policies, that is, admission policies that select migrants based on their skills. As this chapter has shown, defining and assessing skills and skill requirements in particular jobs has become an increasingly complex and difficult issue for policy-makers to address. There is a tension between the notion of 'skills' as technical and formally measurable and the more conceptually equivocal use of the term that has come to characterize not just employers' expressions of demand for labour, but debates and policies in employment, education, and training more generally.[9] This suggests that the design of a skills-based immigration policy needs to take a flexible approach to defining skills or skill requirements for certain jobs that goes beyond the use of formal measures, and accounts for some of the changing labour demands and work requirements that are characteristics of a globalizing economy with significant and growing service sectors and increasing use of technology. At the same time, however, it is important to be aware that employers play an important role in defining the competencies and attributes that are 'needed' to do particular jobs. In some occupations, the 'work ethic' and soft skills demanded by employers are partly or largely a reflection of employer preference for a workforce over which they can exercise particular mechanisms of control and/or that is prepared to accept wages and employment conditions that do not attract a sufficient supply of British or other EEA workers.

The implication is that an immigration policy that adopts a more flexible approach in assessing issues related to skills must do so critically. In particular, it must be accompanied by enforcement of labour standards. Policy needs to ensure that the workers with the soft skills which employers say are 'needed' can be and are employed on terms that do not undermine the wages, health and safety, and other protections of the previously existing labour force.

[9] There are clear differences between occupations. The skill requirements of medical doctors, for example, can be more easily identified and measured than those of social care workers.

ANALYSING AND RESPONDING TO STAFF SHORTAGES

An obvious but important first step in assessing staff shortages and the implications for the employment of migrant workers is the definition of the borders of the 'local' labour market. At a micro level the question of what is 'local' is highly relevant, both in terms of how far 'local' workers might be expected to travel, and also more generally in appreciating the specificities of local labour markets. While national-level data may not show up a shortage, this does not mean that employers in particular regions do not experience a shortage of specific types of labour. However, as far as policy in most countries is concerned, 'local' is generally taken to mean citizens and it is widely accepted that in this sense 'local' workers should be given preferential access to jobs in the national labour market. In other words, as far as policy is concerned, employer demand for migrant labour should be a *residual* demand. In the UK and other EEA countries, the pool of 'local' workers includes all EEA nationals (i.e. it includes certain foreign nationals). From a UK policy point of view, non-EEA immigration as a response to staff shortages can only be justified if there is a shortage of EEA workers (and not just of British workers).

The supply of labour is highly segmented in terms of gender, race, ethnicity, class, nationality, and immigration status. Taking a disaggregated view of the labour supply is therefore critical, while at the same time it is important to consider the role of employers' recruitment procedures in contributing to labour market mismatch and in selecting or excluding certain groups. As this chapter has shown, some employers in some sectors use nationality as a criterion for selecting workers. This may lead to the development of a preference for recruiting certain nationalities of migrant workers (including non-EEA workers) over available British and/or other EEA workers. The acceptability of this preference from a policy point of view critically depends on the underlying reasons. Analysis of the micro-foundations of perceived staff shortages can shed light on the factors underlying particular employer preferences in specific sectors and occupations. There is significant variation in employer preferences and labour demands across different sectors, occupations, and types of employers. As is the case with assessing employers' skill requirements, awareness of minimum wages and other standards in the labour market will be key to assessing how immigration policy should respond to employer demand for specific groups of migrant workers.

A key argument of this chapter is that to assess shortages and discuss alternative policy responses it is necessary to recognize that employer demand and labour supply are interrelated and mutually conditioning. Many employers could, in principle, pursue a number of responses to staff shortages, including, for example, raising wages and improving employment conditions, more investment in training of local workers, and adoption of labour-saving production processes and technology. The reasons employers do not currently pursue these alternatives include the availability and characteristics of the migrant labour supply which impacts on labour demand by affecting labour costs as well as job structures and designs and, consequently, the attributes and characteristics that employers require to do certain jobs and occupations. 'What employers want' can be critically influenced by what employers 'think they can get' from different types of available workers.

SYSTEM EFFECTS

However, there are also important 'system effects', many of which are outside the control of individual employers (and workers). These effects can discourage or make it difficult for employers to pursue alternative responses to staff shortages other than recruiting migrants. System effects stem from the institutional structure and regulatory framework of the British labour market (characterized *inter alia* by deregulation and flexibilization, and the decline of trade union membership), as well as from wider welfare and public policies (for example, long-term restructuring in certain sectors, the provision or lack of public training programmes, the operation and incentives created by the benefits system, and the need for effective provision of public services given budget constraints). These systems are heavily (but not exclusively) influenced by the state. They can constrain and impact upon the incentives underlying employers' choices about how to respond to perceived staff shortages (as well as impacting on the behaviour of workers). Employers and workers act within certain systems (i.e. in response to given regulatory and institutional structures and wider economic and social policies). Some systems may encourage the emergence and entrenchment of shortages of domestic workers. Conversely, the availability of low-cost migrant workers may in some cases become an important factor in sustaining certain systems of production and welfare state provision.

For example, in the UK's construction sector, immigration appears to have reduced employers' incentives to invest in training and labour-saving technology, at least in the short run (see the discussion in Chan et al. 2008: 33). However, private construction employers' incentives to train are also critically influenced by the wider labour market and economic environment. A high proportion of construction workers are self-employed under a special arrangement for the purposes of taxation, even though, in terms of the practicalities of their working lives, they are effectively employed. This has had a significant impact on private employers' incentives to train and to offer training placements, so it is not simply the availability of migrants that has reduced training in the sector, but rather the structuring of the sector itself (Chan et al. 2008).

The provision of some public services in the UK is currently based on a model of low-cost employment which creates a persistent demand for migrant workers. For example, raising wages to attract more domestic workers in the social care sector is constrained by the fact that the main client is the public sector, where there are limited budgets and strict regulatory requirements about minimum staffing. Moreover, sectoral interdependencies mean changes in one sector may also affect other sectors in unanticipated and unintended ways. For example, leaving vacancies unfilled in the social care sector is likely to have knock-on effects for the health sector (Moriarty et al. 2008). Encouraging employers to access an 'inactive' female labour pool may have a knock-on effect on demand for paid care. Thus system effects interact with other constraints on workers' and employers' options, including not just the cost of care but also the price of housing, the workings of the benefit system, the gendered nature of labour markets and the status of jobs. As we have emphasized throughout this chapter, we need to analyse labour markets as social institutions, and therefore to understand the behaviour of employers and workers in social as well as economic terms. They are embedded in social structures and motivated as social beings, and it is social actors that interact with systems, rather than simply rational competitive individuals.

The existence and impacts of system effects, the mutually conditioning relation between labour supply and demand, and the social as well as economic nature of labour markets have important implications for public policy debates about the feasibility and desirability of reducing, or at least slowing, the growing dependence of many occupations and sectors in high income countries upon migrant workers. They suggest that expecting employers who currently make heavy use of migrant labour to change their behaviour and pursue alternatives to immigration, without changing some of the wider regulatory, institutional, and policy contexts, is unlikely to work. For changes in employment and recruitment patterns to be sustainable and to genuinely work in the interests of workers, employers, and consumers or clients, changes in immigration and other labour supply-side policies are unlikely to be sufficient. As shown in this chapter, the employment of migrant workers may be symptomatic of issues that do not essentially derive from immigration policy. Policy changes must involve changes to the regulations and wider institutional and social structures ('systems') that 'produce' domestic labour shortages and encourage a heavy use of migrant workers in the first place. If avoiding the employment of additional migrant workers is a policy priority, the implications of a range of other policies (such as achieving a higher level of food self-sufficiency in the UK, announced by DEFRA in August 2009, or the personalization agenda in social care) must explicitly deal with immigration consequences that are currently overlooked—hence the emphasis in this chapter and throughout the book on the need to think critically about the relationship between shortages and *public* policy as broadly understood rather than just immigration policy.

To give an example, it is useful to return to the debate about shortages and the role of migrant workers in the UK's social care sector. Raising wages and improving conditions and job status in the sector would help attract more resident workers, but it would also raise the cost of care and thus require an increase in public funding available to the sector. This would necessitate a re-allocation of existing public expenditure, an increase in taxes, and/or a re-organization of the provision of social care in the UK. There is a clear trade-off between providing social care at low cost and the share of resident workers employed in the sector. It is possible that the economic costs to resident workers due to the competition and lower wages in the care sector are outweighed, at least in the short term, by the benefits of lower prices for consumers of care services and, in the case of publicly funded care, the taxpayer. Whether or not this is the case, and whether the UK's social care sector should continue to rely on low-cost migrant labour in the long run or move to a system that involves higher wages, are important questions for analysis and public debate. At present, immigration debates and discussions about reforming the UK's social care sector are largely disconnected and have, so far, failed to explicitly recognize that the UK state has created system effects that, if left unchanged, imply an ever increasing demand for low-cost migrant workers.

ECONOMIC INSTABILITY AND THE DEMAND FOR MIGRANT LABOUR

A key question for research is the impact of economic shocks, such as the recession that began in 2008, on the process of migrant labour intensifications in different occupations and sectors. Can recession become a 'tipping point' which fundamentally transforms some of these interrelated systems and processes and the consequent demand for migrant workers? The analysis in this chapter suggests that there are reasons to be sceptical.

First, although the economic downturn implies an overall reduction in aggregate labour demand, impacts on shortages and the demand for migrant workers can be expected to vary significantly across sectors and occupations. Some jobs, for example in the health sector, are likely to prove relatively 'recession-resilient' because shortages are structural rather than cyclical due to, for example, insufficient investment in skills or poor forward planning (see Migration Advisory Committee 2009). Secondly, it is far from certain that the demand for non-British migrant workers can be expected to decline faster than that for British workers. It is entirely possible that, at least in some sectors and occupations, employer requirements for good 'work ethic', including willingness to accept lower wages and employment conditions, will intensify during the downturn with a consequent relative increase in the demand for migrant labour. Thirdly, deteriorating economic conditions may affect employers' recruitment methods, specifically the use of agency workers, which leads to an increase in the relative demand for migrants. The recession of the 1980s marked the growth in the use of agency labour which, as has been discussed, is an area where migrants have tended to cluster.

A fourth point is that it is possible that the economic downturn affects some regulatory, institutional, and policy systems that lead to an increase rather than a decrease in the demand for workers in certain sectors and occupations. The most obvious example relates to declining public spending and the consequent pressures to provide certain public services that are already based on a relatively low-cost model at even lower rates. Carers, nurses, and teachers are examples of occupations where much of the labour demand is generated by the public sector and where declining budgets and the inability to raise or increase wages to attract more British workers can be expected to directly raise the demand for migrant workers. In its recent review of Tier 2 of the UK's points-based system for managing labour immigration (MAC 2009), the Migration Advisory Committee (MAC) recommended granting applicants an extra five points if they are to be employed in key occupations in the public sector, a reflection of an explicit recognition that migrants are 'needed' to maintain the current models for the provision of certain public services.

Finally, in regard to labour supply, the incentives and behaviour of workers during an economic downturn may differ significantly between citizens and migrants. Citizens are often reluctant to take up jobs that have come to be seen as low status 'migrant jobs', and governments in the past have not appreciated the extent to which these jobs are shunned by citizens even during times of economic crisis and rapid increases in unemployment

(Dobson et al. 2009). Moreover, for migrants who are not eligible for public benefits, or who are required to have work in order to remain in the UK, the pressures to take up low-waged jobs or to remain in employment whatever the costs are significant and often greater than they are for citizens.

But won't many migrants return home in response to a deteriorating economic environment in the host country? Some surely will but the 'buffer theory' of labour migration, under which migrants are a 'conjunctural shock absorber' (Böhning and Maillat, 1974, cited in Dobson et al. 2009: 5) who can be expected to return home at times of recession, leaving jobs for citizens, is clearly open to question. This is partly because the economic conditions of sending states are key to migrants' decisions to return or remain, and often exercise greater influence than the economic conditions of receiving states (Somerville and Sumption 2009; Rogers 2009). During an economic downturn that is global, incentives to return may be small even if economic conditions in the host country are rapidly deteriorating. Moreover, migration is a social as well as an economic process, and inflows and settlement are not only driven by employment. This is why Dobson et al. (2009: 2) argue that 'total net immigration is likely to remain more stable than most people think over the course of the current economic downturn'.

NO ESCAPE: THE POLITICAL ECONOMY OF SHORTAGES AND LABOUR IMMIGRATION POLICY

Is immigration the best answer to addressing shortages in the labour market? Discussion of this key policy issue must clearly begin with an empirical analysis of the feasibility and net benefits (i.e. benefits minus costs) of the various alternative responses to staff shortages for individual employers. It must go beyond employers' interests and also consider the costs and benefits to other groups (including citizen workers), as well as to the wider economy and society of the receiving country and to migrants and their countries of origin. Many of the costs and benefits of immigration are not only economic but also social and not easily susceptible to measurement, but they are no less important for that.

As shown in this chapter, the employment of migrant workers may be symptomatic of issues that do not essentially derive from immigration policy but are related to broader regulatory, institutional, and policy systems that may not significantly change during the economic downturn. Whether or not it is desirable to change these systems to reduce the UK economy's growing dependence on migrant workers is an inherently normative question. So, for example, farmers might respond to restrictions on immigration by switching from fruit and vegetable production to growing wheat, which is more susceptible to technological innovation. The question then becomes, as one of Sam Scott's respondents put it, 'Does the UK government want a fresh fruit and vegetable industry in this country?' (Scott 2008: 59). Viewed this way, the questions that a selective immigration policy raises are not too dissimilar from those of industrial policy.

As the analysis in this chapter and book shows, social science research can make important contributions to a more evidence-based and analytical approach to assessing shortages and discussing the implications for labour immigration policy. However, although research can make trade-offs more clear, it cannot and should not provide one 'right' answer to the question of whether immigration, raising wages, or other alternatives are the best answer to perceived staff shortages. Addressing this question requires open political debate about the objectives and (often competing) interests that labour immigration policy should serve—issues that high-income countries rarely discuss in an explicit and structured way.

References

Adams, J., Grieg, M., and McQuaid, R. W. (2002), 'Mismatch in Local Labour Markets in Central Scotland: The Neglected Role of Demand', *Urban Studies*, 39(8): 1399–416.

Anderson, B. (2000), *Doing the Dirty Work? The Global Politics of Domestic Labour* (London: Zed Books).

——(2007), 'A Very Private Business: Exploring the Demand for Migrant Domestic Workers', *European Journal of Women's Studies*, 14(3): 247–64.

——(2008), 'Written evidence', in House of Lords Select Committee on Economic Affairs (2008).

——(2010), 'Migration, Immigration Controls and the Fashioning of Precarious Workers' Work', *Employment and Society*, 24(2): 300–17.

——Ruhs, M., Rogaly, B., and Spencer, S. (2006), *Fair Enough? Central and East European Migrants in Low-Wage Employment in the UK* (London: Joseph Rowntree Foundation).

Autor, D. H., Levy, F., and Murnane, R. (2003), 'The Skill Content of Recent Technological Change', *Quarterly Journal of Economics*, 118(4): 1279–333.

Bach, S. (2008), *Staff Shortages and Immigration in the Health Sector. A Report Prepared for the Migration Advisory Committee* (London: MAC).

Baruch, Y. (2001), 'Employability: A Substitute for Loyalty?' *Human Resource Development International*, 4: 543–66.

Baumle, A., and Fossett, M. (2005), 'Statistical Discrimination in Employment: Its Practice, Conceptualization, and Implications for Public Policy', *American Behavioural Scientist*, 48(9): 1250–74.

Belt, V., and Richardson, R. (2005). 'Social Labour, Employability and Social Exclusion: Pre-employment Training for Call Centre Work', *Urban Studies*, 42(2): 257–70.

Blackburn, R. M., Browne, J., Brooks, B., and Jarman, J. (2002), 'Explaining Gender Segregation', *British Journal of Sociology*, 53(4): 513–36.

Bloomekatz, R. (2007), 'Rethinking Immigration Status Discrimination and Exploitation in the Low-Wage Workplace', *UCLA Law Review*, 54(6): 1963–2010.

Böhning, W., and Maillat, D. (1974), *The Effects of the Employment of Foreign Workers* (Paris: Organisation for Economic Co-operation and Development).

Cangiano, A., Shutes, I., Spencer, S., and Leeson, G. (2009), *Migrant Care Workers in Ageing Societies: Research Findings in the United Kingdom* (Oxford: COMPAS).

Champlin, D., and Hake, E. (2006), 'Immigration as Industrial Strategy in American Meatpacking', *Review of Political Economy*, 18(1): 49–69.

Chan, P., Clarke, L., and Dainty, A. (2008), *Staff Shortages and Immigration in Construction: A Report Prepared for the Migration Advisory Committee* (London: MAC).

Cockburn, C., and Ormrod, S. (1993), *Gender and Technology in the Making* (London: Sage).

Collier, W. (2005), 'Unemployment Duration and Individual Heterogeneity: A Regional Study', *Applied Economics*, 37: 133–53.

Cornelius, W. (1998), 'The Structural Embeddedness of Demand for Mexican Immigrant Labour: New Evidence from California', in M. Suarez-Orozco (ed.), *Crossings: Mexican Immigration in Interdisciplinary Perspective* (Cambridge, Mass.: Harvard University Press).

Creegan, C., Colgan, F., Charlesworth, R., and Robinson, G. (2003), 'Race Equality Policies at Work: Employee Perceptions of the "Implementation Gap" in a UK Local Authority', *Work, Employment and Society*, 17(4): 617–40.

Curtis, S., and Lucas, R. (2001), 'A Coincidence of Needs? Employers and Full-Time Students', *Employee Relations*, 23(1): 38–54.

Dench, S., Hurstfield, J., Hill, D., and Ackroyd, K. (2006), 'Employers' Use of Migrant Labour', Home Office Online Report.

Devins, D., and Hogarth, T. (2005), 'Employing the Unemployed: Some Case Study Evidence on the Role and Practice of Employers', *Urban Studies*, 42(2): 245–56.

Dickens, R, Gregg, P., and Wadsworth, J. (2000), 'New Labour and the Labour Market', *Oxford Review of Economic Policy*, 16(1): 95–113.

Dobson, J., Latham, A., and Salt, J. (2009), *On the Move? Labour Migration in Times of Recession: What Can We Learn from the Past?* (London: Policy Network).

Drinkwater, S., Eade, J., and Garapich, M. (2008), 'Poles Apart? EU Enlargement and the Labour Market Outcomes of Immigrants in the UK', *International Migration*, 47(1): 161–90.

Duncan, C., and Loretto, W. (2004), 'Never the Right Age? Gender and Age-Based Discrimination in Employment', *Gender, Work & Organization*, 11(1): 95–115.

Durbin, S. (2004), 'Workplace Skills, Technology Adoption and Firm Productivity: A Review', New Zealand Treasury Working Paper 04/16.

Equality and Human Rights Commission (EHRC) (2009), *Monitoring the Impact of the Recession on Various Demographic Groups* (London: EHRC).

Evers, M., De Mooij, R., and Van Vuuren, V. (2008), 'The Wage Elasticity of Labour Supply: A Synthesis of Empirical Estimates', *De Economist*, 156(1): 25–43.

Faggio, G., and Nickell, S. (2005), 'Inactivity among Prime Age Men in the UK', Centre for Economic Performance Discussion Paper 673.

Finegold, D., and Sosicker, D. (1988), 'The Failure of Training in Britain: Analysis and Prescription', *Oxford Review of Economic Policy*, 4(3): 1–15.

Geddes, A. (2008), *Staff Shortages and Immigration in Food Processing. A Report Prepared for the Migration Advisory Committee* (London: MAC).

Geroski, P., and Gregg, P. (1997), *Coping with Recession: UK Company Performance in Adversity* (Cambridge: Cambridge University Press).

Gersen, J. E. (2007), 'Markets and Discrimination', *New York University Law Review*, 82: 689–737.

Goldin, C. (1994), 'Understanding the Gender Gap: An Economic History of American Women', in P. Burstein (ed.), *Equal Employment Opportunity: Labor Market Discrimination and Public Policy* (Chicago: University of Chicago Press).

Goos, M., and Manning, A. (2007), 'Lousy and Lovely Jobs: The Rising Polarisation of Work in Britain', *Review of Economics and Statistics*, 89(1): 118–33.

Gordon, D. R., and Reich, M. (1982), *Segmented Work, Divided Workers: The Historical Transformation of Labor in the United States* (Cambridge: Cambridge University Press).

Gordon, J., and Lenhardt, R. (2008), 'Rethinking Work and Citizenship', *UCLA Law Review* 55: 1161–238.

Gore, T. (2005), 'Extending Employability or Solving Employers' Recruitment Problems? Demand-Led Approaches as an Instrument of Labour Market Policy', *Urban Studies*, 42(2): 341–53.

Granovetter, M. (1985), 'Economic Action and Social Structure: The Problem of Embeddedness', *American Journal of Sociology*, 91: 481–510.

Hofman, W. H. A., and Steijn, A. J. (2003), 'Students or Lower-Skilled Workers? "Displacement" at the Bottom of the Labour Market', *Higher Education*, 45(2): 127–46.

Home Office (2008), *Skilled Workers under the Points-Based System (Tier 2): Statement of Intent* (London: Home Office).

House of Lords, Economic Affairs Select Committee (2008), *The Economic Impact of Immigration*, House of Lords, UK.

Human Resources and Social Development Canada (2006), *Looking-Ahead: A 10-Year Outlook for the Canadian Labour Market (2006–2015)*, Human Resources and Social Development Canada.

Jackman, R., and Savouri, S. (1999), 'Has Britain Solved its Regional Unemployment Problem?', in P. Gregg and J. Wadsworth (eds.), *The State of Working Britain* (Manchester: Manchester University Press).

Jackson, M., Goldthorpe, J., and Mills, C. (2005), 'Education, Employers and Class Mobility', *Research in Social Stratification and Mobility*, 23(1): 3–33.

Jayaweera, H., and Anderson, B. (2009), *Migrant Workers and Vulnerable Employment: A Review of Existing Data* (London: TUC).

Johnson-Webb, K. (2002), 'Employer Recruitment and Hispanic Labor Migration: North Carolina Urban Areas at the End of the Millennium', *The Professional Geographer*, 54(3): 406–21.

Johnston, D. (2007), 'Who Needs Immigrant Farm Workers? A South African Case Study', *Journal of Agrarian Change*, 7(4): 406–21.

Jones, A. (2008), *Staff Shortages and Immigration in the Financial Services Sector. A Report Prepared for the Migration Advisory Committee* (London: MAC).

Karjanen, D. (2008), 'Gender, Race and Nationality in the Making of Mexican Migrant Labor in the United States', *Latin American Perspectives*, 35(1): 51–63.

Keep, E., and Mayhew, K. (1999), 'The Assessment: Knowledge, Skills and Competitiveness', *Oxford Review of Economic Policy*, 15(1): 1–15.

Khoo, S., McDonald, P., Voigt-Graf, C., and Hugo, G. (2007), 'Global Labor Market: Factors Motivating the Sponsorship and Temporary Migration of Skilled Workers to Australia', *International Migration Review*, 41(2): 480–510.

Learning and Skills Council (2008), *Employers Skills Survey 2007: Key Findings* (London: Learning and Skills Council).

Leontaridi, M. (1998), 'Segmented Labour Markets: Theory and Evidence', *Journal of Economic Surveys*, 12(1): 103–9.

Lewis, E. (2004), 'How did the Miami Labour Market Absorb the Mariel Immigrants?', Working Paper No. 04-3 (Philadelphia: Federal Reserve Bank of Philadelphia).

——(2005), 'Immigration, Skill-Mix and the Choice of Technique', Working Paper No. 05-8 (Philadelphia: Federal Reserve Bank of Philadelphia).

Lindsay, C., and McQuaid, R. W. (2004), 'Avoiding the "McJobs": Unemployed Job Seekers and Attitudes to Service Work', *Work, Employment and Society*, 18(2): 297–394.

Low Pay Commission (2006), 'National Minimum Wage', *Low Pay Commission Report* (London: Low Pay Commission).

Lucas, R., and Mansfield, S. (2008), *Staff Shortages and Immigration in the Hospitality Sector. A Report Prepared for the Migration Advisory Committee* (London: MAC).

McDowell, Linda (1997), *Capital Culture: Gender at Work in the City* (Oxford: Blackwell).

McQuaid, R. W. and Lindsay, C. (2005), 'The Concept of Employability', *Urban Studies*, 42(2): 197–219.

Martin, L., and Grove, J. (2002), 'Interview as a Selection Tool for Entry-Level Hospitality Employees', *Journal of Human Resources in Hospitality and Tourism*, 1(1): 41–7.

Martin, P., Abella, M., and Kuptsch, C. (2006), *Managing Labor Migration in the Twenty-First Century* (New Haven: Yale University Press).

Massey, D. (1990), 'Social Structure, Household Strategies and the Cumulative Causation of Migration', *Population Index*, 56(1): 3–26.

Matthews, G., and Ruhs, M. (2007), 'The Micro-foundations of Labour Shortages: Deconstructing Employer Demand for Migrant Labour in the UK's Hospitality Sector', working paper available at website: <http://www.compas.ox.ac.uk/changingstatus>.

Migration Advisory Committee (MAC) (2009), *Analysis of the Points Based System* (London: MAC).

Moriarty, J., Manthorpe, J., Hussein, S., and Cornes, M. (2008), *Staff Shortages and Immigration in the Social Care Sector. A Report Prepared for the Migration Advisory Committee* (London: MAC).

Moss, P., and Tilly, C. (2001), *Stories Employers Tell: Race, Skill and Hiring in America* (New York: Russell Sage Foundation).

Murphy, A., Muellbauer, J., and Cameron, G. (2006), 'Housing Market Dynamics and Regional Migration in Britain', Department of Economics Discussion Paper No. 275, University of Oxford.

National Farmers Union (2007), Evidence submitted to the House of Lords Select Committee on Economic Affairs Inquiry into the Economic Impact of Immigration. See House of Lords (2008).

Nickson, D., Warhurst, C., Witz, A., and Cullen, A. M. (2001), 'The Importance of Being Aesthetic: Work, Employment and Service Organisation', in A. Sturdy, I. Grugulis, and H. Wilmott (eds.), *Customer Service: Empowerment and Entrapment* (London: Palgrave).

O'Connor, P., and Murphy, J. (2004), 'Research on Information Technology in the Hospitality Industry', *International Journal of Hospitality Management*, 23: 473–84.

Park, E. (1999), 'Racial Ideology and Hiring Decisions in Silicon Valley', *Qualitative Sociology*, 22(3): 223–33.

Payne, J. (2000), 'The Unbearable Lightness of Skill: The Changing Meaning of Skill in UK Policy Discourses and some Implications for Education and Training', *Journal of Education Policy*, 15(3): 353–69.

Peck, J. (1996), *Work-Place: The Social Regulation of Labor Markets* (New York: Guilford Press).

Pettinger, L. (2005). 'Gendered Work Meets Gendered Goods: Selling and Service in Clothing Retail', *Gender, Work and Organization*, 12(5): 460–78.

Phillips, A., and Taylor, B. (1980), 'Sex and Skill: Notes towards a Feminist Economics', *Feminist Review*, 6: 79–88.

Piore, M. J. (1979), *Birds of Passage: Migrant Labour and Industrial Societies* (Cambridge: Cambridge University Press).

Preibisch, K., and Binford, L. (2007), 'Interrogating Racialized Global Labour Supply: An Exploration of the Racial/National Replacement of Foreign Agricultural

Workers', *The Canadian Review of Sociology and Anthropology/La Revue Canadienne de Sociologie et d'Anthropologie*, 44(1): 5–36.

Rodriguez, Nestor (2004), '"Workers Wanted": Employer Recruitment of Immigrant Labour', *Work and Occupations*, 31(4): 453–73.

Rogers, A. (2009), *Recession, Vulnerable Workers and Immigration* (Oxford: COMPAS).

Ruhs, M. (2009), 'The Impact of Acquiring EU Status on the Earnings of East European Migrants in the UK: Evidence from a Quasi-natural Experiment', mimeo (Oxford: COMPAS).

——and Anderson, B. (2010), 'Semi-compliance and Illegality in Migrant Labour Markets: An Analysis of Migrants, Employers and the State in the UK', *Population, Space and Place*, 16(3): 195–212.

Saucedo, L. (2006), 'The Employer Preference for the Subservient Worker and the Making of the Brown Collar Workplace', *Ohio State Law Journal*, 5: 961–1022.

Scott, S. (2008), *Staff Shortages and Immigration in Agriculture. A Report Prepared for the Migration Advisory Committee* (London: MAC).

Smith, B. (2006), 'Across Races and Nations: Social Justice Organising in the Transnational South', in H. Smith and O. Furuseth (eds.), *Latinos in the New South: Transformations of Place* (Aldershot: Ashgate).

Somerville, W., and Sumption, M. (2009), *Immigration in the United Kingdom: The Recession and Beyond* (London: Equality and Human Rights Commission).

Talwar, J. P. (2002), *FastFood, FastTrack: Immigrants, Big Business and the American Dream* (Boulder, Colo.: Westview).

Taylor, Andrew (2008), 'Fears Spark Shift to Temp Workers', *Financial Times*.

Tomkins, R. (2008), 'On Your Bike', *Financial Times Magazine*.

TUC Commission on Vulnerable Employment (2008), *Hard Work, Hidden Lives: The Short Report of the Commission on Vulnerable Employment* (London: Trades Union Congress).

TUC (2009), *Recession Report 11*, Sept. (London: Trades Union Congress).

Veneri, C. M. (1999), 'Can Occupational Labour Shortages be Identified using Available Data?' *Monthly Labor Review*, 122(3): 15–21.

Waldinger, R. D., and Lichter, M. (2003), *How the Other Half Works: Immigration and the Social Organization of Labor* (Berkeley, Calif.: University of California Press).

Warhurst, C., and Nickson, D. (2007), 'A New Labour Aristocracy? Aesthetic Labour and Routine Interactive Service', *Work, Employment and Society*, 21(4): 785–98.

Wickham, J., and Bruff, I. (2008), 'Skills Shortages are Not Always What they Seem: Migration and the Irish Software Industry', *New Technology, Work and Employment*, 23(1): 30–43.

Wolkowitz, C. (2006), *Bodies at Work* (London: Sage Publications).

York Consulting (2008), *A Review of Labour Shortages, Skills Shortages and Skill Gaps. A Paper Prepared for the Migration Advisory Committee* (London: MAC).

Migrant Workers: Who Needs Them? A Commentary

Ken Mayhew

In contemplating acceptable or desirable rates of immigration, any government will have a number of economic and non-economic considerations in mind. The chapter by Anderson and Ruhs is concerned with the former and specifically with what employers need and with when that need justifies the use of migrant labour. It provides a judicious and comprehensive analysis of the issues involved. These comments, which take a largely UK perspective, are designed to highlight some of the main points raised.

In the UK, the Migration Advisory Committee (MAC) is required to 'provide independent, evidence-based advice to government on specific sectors and occupations in the labour market where shortages exist which can sensibly be filled by migration' (MAC website). The UK receives migrants from other EU states and from countries outside the EU. Of course, the authorities have much less discretion in regulating movements of the first group than of the second. This could create complications. For example, there might be sectors into which there had been an inflow of workers from post-2004 EU countries to meet reported shortages of labour. However, had employers contemplated filling these vacancies with non-EU nationals, the MAC would not have regarded this as justifiable, perhaps because it believed it would have been more appropriate to raise wage rates in order to attract local applicants. One wonders whether this in turn might 'pollute' judgements about what is desirable or not in terms of flows of non-EU migrants into other sectors. In other words, how easy is it in practice to maintain a 'case-by-case' basis for making judgements?

The chapter rightly argues that the meaning of the term 'skill' has widened significantly in recent years. This is well illustrated by exploring what is meant when employers report that they have 'skill gaps'—defined as perceived deficiencies in the 'skills' of their current workforce. It turns out that most of the deficiencies relate to 'soft' skills like attitudes to work, problem solving, the ability to operate effectively in teams, and the willingness to be flexible. Thus, the term 'skill' now seems to extend to include personal characteristics and attitudes. For example, case studies conducted in 2006 for *Low Wage Work in the UK* show that some employers valued central European workers because they had a stronger work ethic or were more compliant. A food processing company reported:

Of course, if they are coming from Eastern Europe, wages are so poor there that the attraction of what is a considerable wage, not for living standards here, but what can be taken home, means that they want to work, and that's incredible, people who are coming here who are intelligent, who really want to work even though the job may be repetitive and boring. (Lloyd et al. 2008: 229)

Similar remarks were even made by employers in this sector whose operations were located in areas of high unemployment.

This becomes highly relevant when we turn to the issue of 'skill shortages'—the inability to recruit workers into particular types of jobs. Older readers would immediately associate the term with relatively high level and usually certified skills possessed by the likes of engineers and nurses. Yet, in fact, the term now extends to the inability of an employer to fill any category of vacancy. A reported skill shortage could mean that workers with the relevant skills, as defined in the old-fashioned way, are simply not available, but it could also mean a whole variety of other things. Amongst these are the possibilities that the employer is not willing to pay enough, is incompetent at conducting the recruitment process, or is offering working conditions which are unacceptable. Now that the meaning of skill has become so wide, and if one accepts that any job requires some 'skill', however limited, then the inability to fill that job could be described as a skill shortage.

Therefore, any official body charged with disentangling the meaning of shortage in any given instance has a potentially complex and politically charged job to do. These complexities are well reflected in the chapter. There are two sorts of difficulties. The first is identifying the precise nature of the shortage. The second is deciding what role, if any, immigration should play in addressing it.

Initially, the first task might seem the simpler of the two. However, the comments made above strongly suggest that the task is far from straightforward. It is not establishing that employers might be finding it hard to recruit that is the problem so much as diagnosing why. Yet, the diagnosis is crucial in taking a view about whether immigration is the solution. For example, let us suppose that employers correctly report that they cannot find recruits with a particular technical skill and that it is judged that national aggregate demand exceeds national aggregate supply. In this case, immigration would seem to be the obvious solution. However, it might be the case that this shortage is the consequence of inadequate training by employers. Socially, the better solution in the medium term might well be to take steps to stimulate work-based training rather than to import the skills from abroad. Indeed, doing the latter could impose a moral hazard on employers and encourage them not to train for the future, thus extending the dependence on immigrants into the indefinite future.

To give a second example, relating to the hotel sector, from *Low Wage Work in the UK*. In 2003, a work permit system was introduced to counter 'shortages' in less skilled occupations in the UK. In the following year nearly 75 per cent of these permits were issued for the catering and hospitality sector. When, in 2005, the hospitality sector was excluded from the scheme, there were outcries from employers in the sector who claimed that migrants were essential because British workers were not prepared to do the jobs. Our case studies concentrated on London and Glasgow. It was only in London that migrants were being used in large numbers. What was so different between the labour and product markets in the two cities that made migrants apparently so essential in one location but not in the other?

These examples illustrate two vital points. The first is that the authorities should not make their decisions on a purely static basis. They need to have regard to longer-term impacts. The second and related point is that employer demand for immigrants depends upon the structure and institutions of the labour market and indeed of product markets as well as on the competitive strategies of firms. If these structures, institutions, and strategies are thought to be inadequate or sub-optimal, then the use of immigrants may embed such inadequacies. In this context, we have used the example of a possibly inadequate training system.

Another illustration relates to the commonly held view that something needs to be done about the bottom end of the UK labour market—that there are too many low-paid, badly designed jobs, offering poor working conditions. The study referred to above was part of a comparative project investigating the incidence of low pay in five different European countries—the UK, Denmark, France, Germany, and the Netherlands. It found that the greater the 'inclusiveness' of the pay-setting institutions (broadly defined) of a country, the smaller the incidence of low pay. In other words, different labour market institutions do make a difference.

Thus, in the early to mid 2000s, the stocks of immigrants were very similar in the UK, Denmark, and the Netherlands, and yet the lower reaches of these countries' labour markets were affected very differently. The UK has less inclusive pay-setting institutions than either Denmark or the Netherlands. Accordingly, bottom-end pay appears to have been affected more than in the other two countries.

The UK has a National Minimum Wage. The level of this relative to median earnings is critical. When it was first introduced in 1999, it was set at a very low level. Though it has been substantially up-rated since then, it remains low compared to, for example, the French national minimum. The presence of a significant pool of labour which is prepared to work for low wages would be likely to intensify political pressures to keep it low. This is one possible example of how pay-setting institutions might be affected in the medium term by decisions about immigration. Another example would be the UK's welfare-to-work policies, which put great emphasis on getting people back into work even at very low rates of pay. If this leads individuals to be in poverty, a generous in-work benefits system kicks in to support them. Thus, any policies that keep pay low could have major public expenditure implications.

These examples illustrate the difficulty of constructing and implementing migration policy in isolation from labour market policy as a whole. Some commentators go as far as to argue that anything which keeps pay low hinders the declared policy aim of moving a greater proportion of UK production to the high value-added end. It does this by encouraging the continuation of low-spec production dependent simply on price and therefore cost advantage. Whilst this might be overstating the case, it does underline the point made by Anderson and Ruhs about system dependence.

References

Lloyd, C., Mason, G., and Mayhew, K. (eds.) (2008), *Low Wage Work in the UK* (New York: Russell Sage).

Migration Advisory Committee (MAC), website: <http://www.ukba.homeoffice.gov.uk/aboutus/workingwithus/indbodies/mac/>.

3

The Changing Shares of Migrant Labour in Different Sectors and Occupations in the UK Economy: An Overview

Vanna Aldin, Dan James, and Jonathan Wadsworth

3.1 Introduction

One of the more significant developments in the UK over the past 15 years has been the large rise in the numbers of immigrant population. By 2008, 13 per cent of the working age population had been born overseas, up from 7.5 per cent in 1993 at the end of the last recession and the 7 per cent share observed in the mid-1970s (see Figure 3.1). The addition to the UK working-age population over this period caused by the rise in the number of working-age immigrants, from 2.3 to 5.4 million, is about the same as that stemming from the increase in the UK-born working age population caused by the baby-boom generation reaching adulthood in the previous decade (up from 29.5 to 32.3 million).

It seems pertinent, therefore, to determine which sectors of the economy have made increasing use of immigrant labour over the past decade. In this chapter, we set out some facts on the occupational and sectoral distribution of UK immigrants in order to help inform the detailed discussions in the chapters that follow. We also attempt to unravel the reasons why some sectors have made use of this increasing pool of immigrant labour, and others less so. These trends have stimulated renewed interest among policy-makers and academic researchers concerned with the effects of immigration. For policy purposes it is important to know how and where immigrants are employed, how this

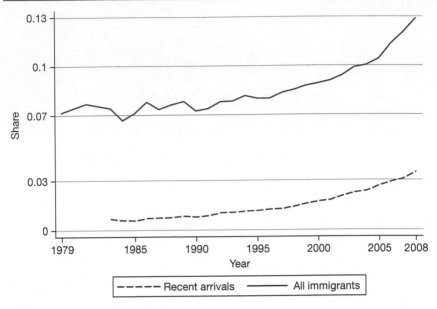

Figure 3.1 Immigration to the UK

Note: Share describes the proportion of those born outside the UK in the total working-age population, including students. Recent arrivals are those who have been in the UK for five years or less.

Source: Labor Force Survey (LFS).

process changes with time or across policy regimes, and whether these patterns benefit immigrants and the wider economy.

3.2 Stocks and Flows

3.2.1 *Defining Immigrants*

All data in this chapter derive from the publicly available Labour Force Survey (LFS) files held at the UK Data Archive. The LFS is the most comprehensive available source of information about the stock of immigrants in the UK, their characteristics, and where and how they are employed in the labour market.

For the analysis in the chapter we define migrants by country of birth, that is, those born outside the UK. Defining immigrants in a way that satisfies all purposes is difficult. Using a definition based on foreign-born individuals will include some UK citizens who happened to be born abroad, while a definition based on a count of foreign-nationals living in the UK

Table 3.1 Stock of working-age population by country of birth and nationality, 2008

		By nationality (thousands)	
		UK	Non-UK
By country of birth (thousands)	UK	32,448	51
	Non-UK	1,998	3,260

Note: Working age defined as females aged 16 to 59 and males aged 16 to 64.
Source: LFS (2008).

will exclude those who have come to the UK and gained British citizenship. This is likely to under-estimate the numbers of immigrants. This is evident in the overall numbers: while in the UK there were 5.3 million working-age foreign-born individuals in 2008, there were only 3.3 million working-age foreign nationals (Table 3.1). One advantage of using country of birth is that estimates are likely to be less sensitive to policy changes over time, for example, in the rules determining how individuals acquire British citizenship. By the same token, those defined as immigrants by country of birth are not necessarily subject to immigration policy. It is also possible to define immigrants by how long they have been in the UK, but this is clearly sensitive to the period chosen. By way of example, in 2008, around 30 per cent of those born outside the UK had come to the UK since 2004.

3.2.2 *Background*

The stock of immigrants in the UK is influenced both by the UK's relative economic performance and also by immigration policy. The composition of earlier waves of immigrants, after the First World War, was greatly influenced by the UK's links with its former colonies. Before 1962, any Commonwealth or Irish citizen had right of entry. The Commonwealth Immigrants Act of 1962 introduced a voucher scheme, and the principle of right of entry to Commonwealth citizens was abolished in 1972 (Dobson et al. 2001). At this time, the existing work permit system was extended to all citizens outside of the EEC, Denmark, and Norway. This system was skewed toward skilled workers in short supply, although channels that allow migrants to come in temporarily to work, often in lower skilled jobs, such as working holiday-makers, also existed. The work permit system was subject to periodic modifications, until being replaced by a points-based entry system in 2008. Since the UK became a member of the EU, there has been an unrestricted right of entry to any citizen of the European

Table 3.2 Working-age immigrants in the UK by area of birth, 2008

	All immigrants (millions)	Recent immigrants (millions)	Median years in country
Non-EU	4.0	0.98	12
EU of which	1.4	0.65	5
A8	0.6	0.47	3
A13	0.6	0.15	15
Irish Republic	0.2	0.03	27

Note: A8 consists of Czech Republic, Estonia, Hungary, Latvia, Lithuania, Poland, Slovakia, and Slovenia. A13 comprises Austria, Belgium, Denmark, Greece, Finland, France, Germany, Italy, Luxembourg, the Netherlands, Portugal, Spain, and Sweden. Working age defined as females aged 16 to 59 and males aged 16 to 64. Recent migrants defined as having come to the UK in the last five years.

Source: LFS (2008).

Union member states.[1] As a result, the composition of UK immigrants has swung away from the Commonwealth toward individuals born in the member states of the EU (Table 3.2). The increase in the stock of immigrants has been driven by an increase in the number of new immigrants entering the UK, rather than any increase in the average length of time immigrants have been in the UK. In 2008, over a quarter of all immigrants had been in the UK for less than five years, up from the 10 per cent share observed in the 1980s. In contrast, the average (median) duration of stay for working-age immigrants fell from 16 years in 2002 to 10 years in 2008. Rising immigration is now also common to many other OECD countries, where the average share of migrants in the labour force has increased from 4.3 per cent to 7.2 per cent between 1995 and 2005 (OECD 2006). Relative economic performance has been shown to be a driver of migration in the context of the UK (Mitchell and Pain 2003; Hatton 2005). However, Dobson et al. (2009) review historical data to suggest that although inflows may drop in times of recession, the extent to which migrant stocks adjust to the business cycle may be dampened by a variety of factors.

3.2.3 *Immigrants in the UK Labour Market*

Historically, unemployment rates of immigrants have on average been higher (and conversely employment rates lower) than for UK-born individuals, and for immigrants, both these variables tend to be more sensitive to the economic cycle.[2] As Figure 3.2 shows, the employment rate for male

---

[1] Though this right of entry does not yet extend to an unrestricted right to work for citizens of the latest EU member countries, Bulgaria and Romania.

[2] For more discussion of this, see Dustmann et al. (2003 and 2006).

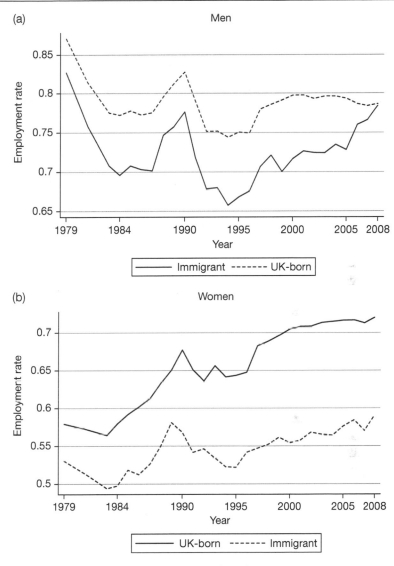

Figure 3.2 Employment rates: immigrant and UK-born

Notes:
a) Men
b) Women
Male employment rate is the proportion of males aged 16 to 64 in employment.
Source: LFS (1979–2008).

immigrants dropped by 12 percentage points during the recession of the early 1990s, while that of UK-born dropped by eight percentage points. Some of this was due to differential levels of age, education, and regional location between the UK-born and immigrant populations, but some of this differential could be observed among individuals in the same region with the same level of education. However, during the last decade, rising immigration coincided with a narrowing of the employment gap between immigrants and the UK-born, so that by 2008 the differential among men had been eliminated. This reflects both increasing employment rates within national groups, but also a substantial compositional effect arising from immigration of those from the 'A8' countries[3] (see Table 3.3), who have very high employment rates in comparison with other immigrants and UK-born. Certainly the immigrant population, on average, is more skilled than in the past and this will help explain the differential performance. Note that the pattern of employment among women is rather different. Until the end of the last recession, employment rates for women evolved in a similar way to that of men, falling more among immigrants during the recession. However, during the recovery, the employment rate among UK-born women rose more than the employment rate among immigrant women. So, in contrast to the trends observed for men, there was divergence in

Table 3.3 Top ten working-age migrants in the UK by country of birth, 2008

All migrants		Recent migrants	
Country	Per cent of all migrants	Country	Per cent of recent migrants
India	8.7	Poland	23.8
Poland	8.3	India	9.4
Pakistan	6.9	Pakistan	4.2
Ireland	4.4	France	2.8
Germany	4.1	China	2.7
South Africa	3.4	United States	2.7
Bangladesh	2.9	Lithuania	2.5
United States	2.4	Australia	2.2
Nigeria	2.4	South Africa	2.1
Kenya	2.3	Slovakia	2.1
Others	54.2		45.5

Note: Working-age defined as females aged 16 to 59 and males aged 16 to 64. Recent migrants defined as having come to the UK in the last five years.

Source: LFS (2008).

[3] A8 countries refer to the eight Central and Eastern European countries that joined the European Union in 2004: the Czech Republic, Estonia, Hungary, Latvia, Lithuania, Poland, Slovakia, and Slovenia.

employment rates between immigrant women and the UK-born. This contrasting experience by gender again suggests that the explanations for differential immigrant labour market performance are far from simple.

3.3 Where Are Immigrants Employed?

Employment in any given industrial sector is the result of employers with requisite demands coming together with individuals with requisite skills looking to work in that sector. The reasons why employers choose to recruit immigrant labour are many and varied and the subject of the subsequent chapters in this book. However, the net result of this matching process can be seen in the sectoral pattern of employment. Occupations are a significant feature of the structure of employment within industries, so it is also important to consider the occupational pattern of immigrant employment. The Labour Force Survey (LFS) allows a detailed disaggregation of employment patterns by three-digit occupation and two-digit industry, according to official classifications.[4] Comparisons over time are hampered by periodic changes to the official industrial and occupational classifications. The analysis in this chapter begins in 2002 with the introduction in the LFS of the most recent occupational classification: the Standard Occupational Classification (2000), alongside the existing 1992 Standard Industrial Classification.

3.3.1 *Industrial Sectors*

According to the LFS estimates outlined in Table 3.4, in 2002, the (two-digit) industry that had the highest share of immigrants in its workforce was clothing manufacturing, where 19 per cent of the workforce was born outside the UK. Similarly, around one in seven of the hotel and restaurant workforce were born abroad (the full list of industries and immigrant shares over time is given in Table 3.A1 in the Appendix). In contrast, in 2002, tobacco manufacturing and recycling industries employed few immigrants among their workforces. Over time, as the average share of immigrants in

---

[4] Even so, to enable an acceptable sample size of immigrants in each sector at this level of disaggregation, the LFS has been pooled across four quarters in the analysis that follows. Some care needs to be taken with the point estimates of the immigrant shares. The standard errors vary across occupations of different sizes with a median of around 0.6 points. No standard error is greater than ± 2 points. The standard errors associated with the industry shares, available on request, are in a similar range. This suggests that changes and/or differences of the order of 1.5 percentage points are likely to be statistically significant.

Table 3.4 Industry distribution of immigrants

Top 5 by workforce share	2002 I	2008 II	Top 5 by share among immigrants	2002 III	2008 IV
1.	Clothing manufacturing (19%)	Clothing manufacturing (28%)		Health & social work (14%)	Health & social work (15%)
2.	Hotels & restaurants (16%)	Hotels & restaurants (22%)		Retail trades (10%)	Other business activities (9%)
3.	IT (15%)	Recycling (22%)		Other business activities (9%)	Retail trades (9%)
4.	Research & development (14%)	Food manufacturing (21%)		Hotels & restaurants (8%)	Hotels & restaurants (8%)
5.	Private households (13%)	Private households (21%)		Education (8%)	Education (7%)

Bottom 5 by workforce share	2002 I	2008 II	Bottom 5 by share among immigrants	2002 III	2008 IV
1.	Tobacco (0.1%)	Forestry (1%)		Fishing (0.01%)	Forestry (0.01%)
2.	Recycling (0.1%)	Tobacco (4%)		Coal (0.01%)	Coal (0.01%)
3.	Fishing (0.6%)	Metal manufacture (5%)		Tobacco (0.01%)	Tobacco (0.01%)
4.	Coal (1.8%)	Coal (5%)		Forestry (0.01%)	Fishing (0.02%)
5.	Wood processing (2.4%)	Fishing (6%)		Leather manufacture (0.06%)	Leather manufacture (0.05%)

Source: LFS.

employment rose from 8.2 per cent in 2002 to 13.3 per cent in 2008, the estimated share of immigrants in the workforce rose in all but one industrial sector (Figure 3.3). By 2008, few sectors had workforces comprised of less than 5 per cent migrants. Clothing manufacture and hospitality sectors retained their dominance. Tobacco and coal remained among the industry sectors making least use of immigrant labour. The nascent recycling industry began to make much more use of immigrant labour between 2002 and 2008, such that it moved from the bottom five immigrant sectors to the top five. Food processing also increased the share of immigrants among its workforce significantly over the same period, by around 13 percentage points. The sectors where use of immigrant labour changed little include forestry (−1.6 percentage points), motor vehicle retail (+0.2 percentage points), paper manufacture (+0.8 percentage points), and the petroleum and nuclear sector (+1.0 percentage point).

However, the size of these two-digit sectors varies considerably and so the estimates of the industry shares and their movements over time will be influenced, to an extent, by sector size. Panels III and IV of Table 3.4 therefore report the share each industrial sector accounts for among all employed immigrants in the UK labour market (Table 3.A1 in the Appendix also gives the share of every two-digit industry in total employment). The health and social work sector employs one in seven of all immigrants in the UK. This sector remained the largest employer of immigrants between 2002 and 2008. The other major employers of immigrants are the retail sector, other business activities,[5] hospitality, and education. In contrast, the small size of many of the production sectors, allied to their low use of immigrant labour, again renders them toward the bottom of the rankings.

3.3.2 Occupation

Table 3.5 repeats this exercise using occupation rather than industry. The full list of occupations and immigrant shares is given in Table 3.A2 of the Appendix. For 2002, not withstanding a few notable exceptions, a relatively clear pattern emerges: the higher the skill level of the occupation, the greater the share of migrants employed in that occupation. Healthcare and research professionals were the occupations with highest migrant shares; science professionals and information and communication technology professionals also had high migrant shares. Food preparation trades

---

[5] This is a rather heterogeneous two-digit sector comprising the law, architecture, industrial cleaning, security, and photography.

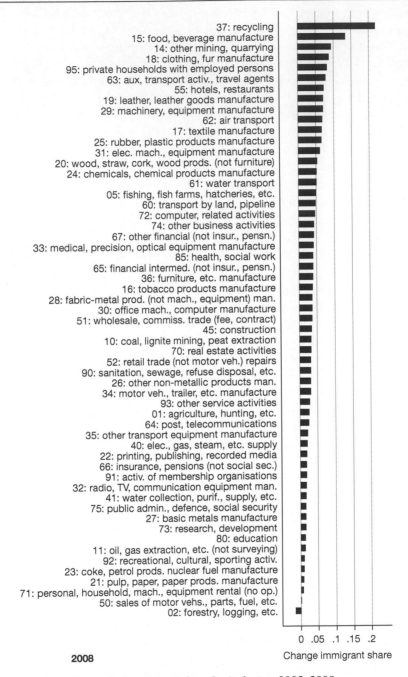

2008

Change immigrant share

Figure 3.3 Change in immigrant share by industry, 2002–2008

Table 3.5 Occupational distribution of immigrants

Top 5 by workforce share	2002 I	2008 II	Top 5 by share among immigrants 2002 III	2008 IV
1.	Health professionals (25%)	Elementary process ng (29%)	Functional managers (5%)	Sales assistants (5%)
2.	Research professionals (20%)	Health professionals (28%)	Sales assistants (5%)	Healthcare related (4%)
3.	Food preparation (17%)	Food preparation (26%)	Teachers (5%)	Functional managers (4%)
4.	Hospital managers (16%)	Process operatives (25%)	Healthcare associates (4%)	Elementary personnel (4%)
5.	Artistic & literary (16%)	Research professionals (21%)	Elementary personnel (3%)	Healthcare associates (4%)

Bottom 5 by workforce share	2002 I	2008 II	Bottom 5 by share among immigrants 2002 I	2008 II
1.	Animal care (2%)	Personal services n.e.c (1%)	Personal services n.e.c. (0.1%)	Personal services n.e.c. (0.1%)
2.	Elementary agricultural (2%)	Agricultural trades (4%)	Animal care (0.1%)	Animal care (0.1%)
3.	Agricultural trades (3%)	Animal care (4%)	Farm managers (0.1%)	Farm managers (0.1%)
4.	Welding (4%)	Farm managers (4%)	Librarians (0.1%)	Librarians (0.1%)
5.	Farm managers (4%)	Protective services (6%)	Legal associates (0.1%)	Legal associates (0.1%)

Source: LFS.

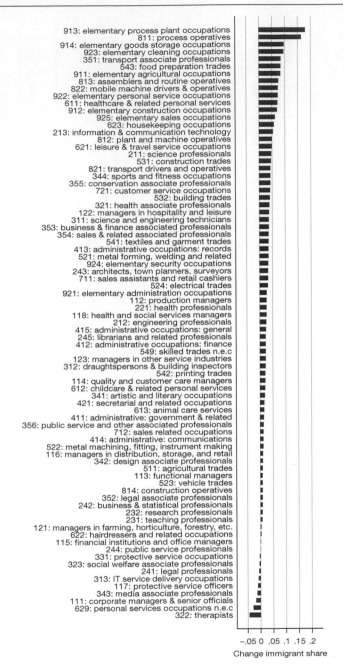

Figure 3.4 Change in immigrant share by occupation, 2002–2008

and elementary security occupations were lower skilled occupations with relatively high migrant shares. However, most occupations with low migrant shares were also less skilled. This partly reflects the demand for skilled workers and a relative shortage of supply of skilled native-born workers, but also that immigration policy for individuals originating from outside the European Union is skewed towards the entry of skilled workers. In 2008, the pattern is less clear, with certain manual or less skilled occupations showing relatively high migrant shares.

This is reflected in the percentage point growth in the immigrant share of labour in Figure 3.4. The occupations that have experienced the largest increase in immigrant share are all less skilled occupations. This change probably reflects the arrival of a new set of immigrants from the accession countries, increasing the available supply in certain manual occupations. Manacorda et al. (2006) note that many immigrants appear to be in occupations that are less skilled than their level of educational attainment would suggest. One hypothesis is that immigrants are using these more basic occupations as a transition step toward different careers or to gain UK work experience, and that employers may have incentives to hire and retain 'overqualified' workers if they are more productive in these jobs than other employees (see Chapter 2 by Anderson and Ruhs, this volume).

The destination sectors of new arrivals are mirrored in these sectoral changes over time. The recycling and food and drinks industries show the greatest increases in the share of immigrants in their workforces. Elementary processing became the occupation with the highest share of immigrants by 2008. Around 20 per cent of elementary processing jobs are filled by immigrants who have been in the UK for less than five years (see Table 3.A2). Similarly, some 15 per cent of process-operative jobs are filled by recent immigrants.

3.4 Explaining Why Some Industries Make More Use of Immigrant Labour than Others

3.4.1 Approach

In order to begin to try to understand why certain industries have made much more use of immigrant labour than others, we look at some characteristics of those industries with high or rising immigrant shares in comparison to those with low or static immigrant shares. It is important to recognize that sectors that have been able to utilize the increasing pool of migrants in the UK labour market since 2002 may behave differently from sectors that have historically been high users of immigrant labour. The analysis of the 'rising' sectors is therefore, to some extent, specific to the pattern of recent immigration, in particular the large inflows of immigrants from the 'A8' countries. Pay, occupational structure, and organization of work, such as part-time working and self-employment, could all potentially affect the extent to which industries can make use of the growing pool of migrant labour. Characteristics of the labour supply such as gender, age, and region, although not the focus of this analysis, could also explain why some sectors make more use of immigrant labour than others.

We illustrate the analysis by comparing the top and bottom five sectors with respect to both the level of and the change in the immigrant share. To recap, from Figures 3.3 and 3.A1, the high utilization industry sectors were hotels, recycling, food processing, clothing, and private households. The top five rising sectors differ only in the replacement of mining for the hotel sector. Low utilization sectors were forestry, tobacco, metal manufacture, coal, and fishing. The static sectors were forestry, motor vehicle sales, rental services, paper manufacture, and the petroleum and nuclear sector. Examining the top and bottom five is somewhat arbitrary, but allows us to examine different effects at the top and bottom of the distribution. Certain factors may act at only one end of the distribution, and thus may be able to explain why some sectors cannot make use of migrant labour, even if the same factor does not explain why other sectors have made much more use of migrant labour. Following descriptive analysis of each of the factors in isolation, we use regression analysis to analyse these factors in combination across the whole of the labour market.

3.4.2 Pay

If immigrants have lower reservation wages than the rest of the population, it may be that firms are able to recruit at lower wages than otherwise. The data in Table 3.6 are set out to examine whether the sectors that made more use of immigrant labour are low-paying sectors. The table indicates that industries with the greatest increases in immigrant usage and those with least change tend to be relatively low-wage sectors, with the exception of the nuclear and petroleum sector. Since the choice of top and bottom five is arguably not illustrative of the entire sectoral distribution, we tested the correlation between wages and immigrant shares across all sectors. No correlation was found between change in immigrant share and the average hourly wages across all two-digit industrial sectors. Similarly, there is no

Table 3.6   Hourly wages by industry, 2008

	Hourly wage (£)			
	Mean	10th percentile	Median	90th percentile
Whole economy	12.50	5.60	10.00	21.60
Rising immigrant share	9.20	4.50	7.50	15.50
Static immigrant share	9.80	4.80	8.20	16.50
High immigrant share	7.40	4.10	6.00	12.00
Low immigrant share	11.40	5.60	9.60	16.80

Note: Hourly wages rounded to 10 pence.

Source: LFS.

correlation between the *level* of the immigrant share and the average hourly wage across all two-digit sectors.[6] This suggests that differences in usage of immigrant labour are probably not explained by recourse to the hypothesis that immigrants have lower reservation wages than other workers. Figure 3.A3 in the Appendix graphs the industry immigrant share against the industry average wage. A regression line summarizing the correlation between immigrant share and wages is superimposed on the data. The figure makes it clear that immigrant labour is used extensively in some, but not all, low-paying sectors, and also in some, but not all, high-paying sectors.

3.4.3 *Occupational Structure*

If a simple wage story appears not to be the explanation for the differences in immigrant utilization, it may be that the job requirements vary across industries, so that differences in the set of occupations within sectors may help explain why some sectors are willing and able to make more use of immigrants than others. Table 3.7 sets out the occupational distribution amongst both high and low immigrant-share industries. These data suggest that industrial sectors with growing immigrant-shares sectors appear to offer relatively more unskilled manual jobs. Most of the immigrants in the high-share sector are also employed in unskilled manual jobs. This contrasts with the distribution of immigrants across the whole economy, which is less skewed towards unskilled jobs. However, the low and static-share sectors are also relatively more manual and less skilled than the

---

[6] The correlation between the change in industry immigrant share and the industry average hourly wage in 2008 across 57 two-digit sectors was −0.23, not significantly different from zero at the 95% level. Similarly, the correlation between the 2008 immigrant share and the industry average hourly wage in 2008 was −0.09, not significantly different from zero at the 95% level.

Table 3.7 Occupation distribution within industry by immigrant share, 2008

	Per cent				
	Whole economy	High share	Low share	Rising share	Static share
Managers	15.8	17.8	13.9	12.8	20.9
Professionals	13.0	1.8	6.6	4.9	3.2
Associate prof.	14.6	2.7	6.8	5.2	6.5
Admin.	11.3	4.6	6.9	6.0	11.0
Skilled manual	11.0	15.1	33.2	17.1	28.6
Personal services	8.4	4.4	0.1	7.8	0.2
Sales	7.5	3.7	0.1	1.9	11.0
Processing ops.	7.2	10.0	22.6	28.4	11.4
Elementary	11.2	39.9	10.0	16.0	7.2

Source: LFS.

economy-wide average, so again a simple story that high immigrant sectors are those that have a greater need for less skilled manual labour does not necessarily follow.

3.4.4 *Part-Time Working and Self-Employment*

Perhaps different patterns of work, for example, the incidence of part-time working or self-employment, explain some differences in the use of immigrant labour. Table 3.8 shows that any differences in the *changing* use of immigrant labour are probably not due to differences in the incidence of part-time working or self-employment across sectors. Both rising and static immigrant utilization make relatively little use of part-time working compared to the economy as a whole. Similarly, the incidence of self-employment is somewhat higher than average in both rising and static immigrant utilization sectors. However, the high immigrant-share group, where the hotel and restaurant sector accounts for the majority of employment, does make extensive use of part-time working.

Table 3.8 Part-time working and self-employment by sector, 2008

	Per cent				
	Whole economy	High share	Low share	Rising share	Static share
Part-time	24.7	38.1	7.9	19.2	11.5
Self-employed	12.7	12.1	14.4	14.5	15.0

Source: LFS.

Table 3.9 Probit estimates of the chances of immigrants working in given sector, 2008

	I	II	II	IV	V
Low immigrant	−0.069*	−0.067*	−0.067*	−0.067*	−0.046*
utilization industry	(0.006)	(0.007)	(0.007)	(0.007)	(0.004)
High immigrant	0.115*	0.106*	0.113*	0.125*	0.108*
utilization industry	(0.004)	(0.004)	(0.004)	(0.006)	(0.006)
Controls					
Occupation	No	Yes	Yes	Yes	Yes
Part-time	No	No	Yes	Yes	Yes
Self-employed	No	No	Yes	Yes	Yes
Wage	No	No	No	Yes	Yes
Age	No	No	No	No	Yes
Region	No	No	No	No	Yes
Gender	No	No	No	No	Yes

Note: Coefficients are marginal effects and they measure the percentage point difference (divided by 100) of an immigrant working in the given sector relative to the mean. Heteroskedastic robust standard errors in brackets. * denotes statistically significantly different from zero at 95% confidence level. Sample size 205, 497.

Source: LFS.

3.4.5 *Summary of Factors*

The extent to which the factors outlined above can explain differences in immigrant utilization can be summarized in a regression format that controls simultaneously for other potential explanations of the differences in immigrant utilization. The idea is to take the 2008 LFS sample of individuals in work and look to see whether an immigrant is still more likely to work in the high utilization sectors than native-born workers, net of controls for age, gender and region, occupation, part-time working, and self-employment. The estimates are based on a probit regression of a dummy variable for immigrant status on the set of controls. The coefficients reported in Table 3.9 are the estimated coefficients on two dummy variables, denoting whether the individual works in either the five low or the five high immigrant-share sectors outlined in the earlier tables. Each column represents a different regression model where the set of controls is allowed to vary. The coefficients can be interpreted as the probability of observing an immigrant working in the featured sectors relative to UK-born workers, compared to the probability of observing an immigrant working relative to UK-born workers in any other sector.

Column I of Table 3.9 gives the raw percentage differences in the chances of an immigrant working in the high and low utilization sectors.[7]

---

[7] The equivalent estimates for the rising and static share sectors are given in Table 3.A3. The implications from these estimates are broadly similar to those drawn from inspection of Table 3.9.

Compared to UK-born workers, immigrants are some 11.5 percentage points more likely to work in the high utilization sectors and some 6.9 percentage points less likely to work in the low utilization sectors. When controls for differences in the incidence of one-digit occupation across sectors are added, (column II), the estimates are little changed. This suggests that any difference in occupations taken up by immigrants compared to UK-born workers does not explain the differential concentration of immigrants in certain sectors. When controls for the incidence of self-employment and part-time working are added (column III), the estimates are little changed. Similar results are obtained when the industry average wage is added (column IV). So differences in these forms of working or average pay are unlikely to underlie the behaviour we observe. Likewise, differences in age, gender, or region of residence of the worker make little difference to the estimated coefficients, so again these factors are unlikely to help explain the differences in immigrant utilization. Researchers interested in looking for explanations may need to explore other areas and, as done in the subsequent chapters of this book, use qualitative and in-depth analysis of issues that cannot be captured in a purely quantitative approach.

3.5 Conclusions

There seems to be little doubt that certain sectors have been more willing or able to make use of the increased supply of labour brought on by the large-scale immigration experienced in the UK over the last 15 years. This is not simply a matter of certain sectors being able to hire more immigrants while at the same time offering low pay, since the sectors that made least use of the growing pool of immigrant labour are also low paid. Neither occupational structure, nor part-time working or self-employment appears to help explain why certain industries have not made use of the growing pool of immigrant labour.

The findings presented here are tentative, but do not appear to support simple hypotheses about why some industries use immigrant labour. The findings are also specific to a period which experienced a substantial increase in the immigrant labour force as a result of the accession of eight Eastern European countries in 2004. Explanations may differ from previous periods when inflows were influenced by a combination of colonial links, employer demand, and immigration policy. In light of this, we look to the more detailed sectoral analysis contained in the following chapters as the basis for future statistical research.

APPENDIX: ADDITIONAL TABLES AND FIGURES

Table 3.A1 Share of immigrants by industry

Industry (2 Digit 1992 SIC)	2002 All immigrants	Recent immigrants	Industry share	2008 All immigrants	Recent immigrants	Industry Share	Mean hourly wage
01: agriculture, hunting, etc.	0.039	0.011	0.012	0.065	0.038	0.013	8.2
02: forestry, logging, etc.	0.029	0.001	0.001	0.013	0.006	0.001	9.8
05: fishing fish farms, hatcheries	0.006	0.001	0.001	0.055	0.022	0.001	9.4
10: coal, lignite mining	0.018	0.009	0.001	0.051	0.017	0.001	13.3
11: oil, gas extraction, etc.	0.104	0.033	0.003	0.116	0.048	0.003	22.9
13: mining of metal ores	0.391	0.043	0.001	0.250	0.100	0.001	28.1
14: other mining, quarrying	0.047	0.001	0.001	0.141	0.023	0.001	10.8
15: food, beverage manufacture	0.081	0.023	0.017	0.214	0.129	0.014	11.3
16: tobacco products manufacture	0.001	0.001	0.001	0.038	0.038	0.001	20.3
17: textile manufacture	0.086	0.013	0.005	0.152	0.039	0.003	9.5
18: clothing, fur manufacture	0.193	0.015	0.003	0.280	0.061	0.002	9.5
19: leather, leather goods manufacture	0.074	0.018	0.001	0.145	0.048	0.001	11.0
20: wood, straw, cork wood products	0.024	0.003	0.003	0.077	0.055	0.003	9.8
21: pulp, paper, paper products manufacture	0.082	0.010	0.004	0.090	0.026	0.003	11.9
22: printing, publishing recorded	0.066	0.008	0.014	0.085	0.021	0.012	13.9
23: cock, petrol products, nuclear fuel	0.089	0.045	0.002	0.099	0.033	0.002	18.9
24: chemicals, chemical products manufacture	0.066	0.018	0.012	0.117	0.038	0.009	17.3
25: rubber, plastic products manufacture	0.061	0.007	0.008	0.126	0.057	0.006	11.2
26: other non-metallic products manufacture	0.032	0.001	0.005	0.064	0.021	0.004	12.2
27: basic metal manufacture	0.035	0.001	0.005	0.050	0.019	0.004	13.0

28: fabric-metals manufacture	0.038	0.006	0.014	0.075	0.027	0.012	11.8
29: machinery eqt. manufacture	0.050	0.006	0.016	0.120	0.053	0.013	12.2
30: office machinery, computers	0.078	0.023	0.004	0.114	0.030	0.002	18.5
31: elec. machinery, equipment	0.064	0.012	0.008	0.125	0.034	0.005	13.3
32: radio, TV, communication	0.084	0.019	0.005	0.101	0.040	0.002	13.8
33: medical, precision, optical	0.069	0.018	0.005	0.111	0.032	0.004	13.6
34: motor vehicle, trailer, etc. manufact.	0.078	0.012	0.011	0.109	0.048	0.008	12.7
35: other transport eqt. manufact.	0.050	0.003	0.009	0.072	0.020	0.009	15.0
36: furniture, etc. manufacture	0.064	0.016	0.008	0.104	0.048	0.006	10.5
37: recycling	0.001	0.001	0.001	0.219	0.109	0.001	9.9
40: elec., gas, steam, etc. supply	0.053	0.012	0.005	0.074	0.014	0.005	15.4
41: water collection, supply	0.050	0.015	0.002	0.066	0.007	0.002	13.8
45: construction	0.045	0.009	0.074	0.079	0.024	0.083	12.8
50: sales of motor vehicles, fuel	0.059	0.013	0.020	0.061	0.019	0.018	9.6
51: wholesale, commiss., trade	0.087	0.015	0.026	0.123	0.044	0.024	11.8
52: retail trade (not motor vehicle)	0.074	0.012	0.106	0.105	0.027	0.104	7.9
55: hotels, restaurants	0.157	0.038	0.044	0.230	0.081	0.043	6.9
60: transport by land, pipeline	0.098	0.006	0.024	0.146	0.018	0.023	11.3
61: water transport	0.091	0.008	0.002	0.142	0.033	0.001	13.0
62: air transport	0.110	0.015	0.002	0.178	0.027	0.002	20.1
63: other transport, travel	0.090	0.017	0.020	0.167	0.053	0.021	11.2
64: post, telecommunications	0.080	0.012	0.022	0.105	0.022	0.021	12.7
65: financial intermediaries	0.097	0.030	0.025	0.137	0.039	0.025	19.9
66: insurance, pensions	0.073	0.017	0.005	0.091	0.013	0.003	15.3
67: other financial (not insurance)	0.061	0.018	0.014	0.104	0.028	0.014	18.4
70: real estate activities	0.083	0.006	0.013	0.116	0.014	0.015	13.0
71: personal, household, machinery, eqt. rental	0.064	0.016	0.004	0.070	0.012	0.004	11.8

(continued)

Table 3.A1 Continued

Industry (2 Digit 1992 SIC)	2002 All immigrants	Recent immigrants	Industry share	2008 All immigrants	Recent immigrants	Industry Share	Mean hourly wage
72: computer, related activities	0.147	0.042	0.018	0.192	0.057	0.019	19.8
73: research, development	0.139	0.036	0.004	0.154	0.054	0.003	17.3
74: other business activities	0.102	0.025	0.071	0.145	0.041	0.076	14.7
75: public admin., defence	0.060	0.008	0.070	0.076	0.010	0.073	13.5
80: education	0.080	0.011	0.084	0.094	0.013	0.093	13.0
85: health, social work	0.101	0.020	0.113	0.141	0.031	0.126	11.6
90: sanitation, sewage, refuse disposal	0.040	0.005	0.004	0.071	0.027	0.005	10.7
91: membership organizations	0.088	0.008	0.008	0.105	0.019	0.007	11.6
92: recreational, cultural, sporting	0.083	0.019	0.028	0.093	0.020	0.029	14.3
93: other service activities	0.069	0.013	0.013	0.096	0.037	0.014	7.4
95: private households with employees	0.132	0.070	0.004	0.214	0.101	0.004	7.7

Source: LFS.

Table 3.A2 Share of immigrants by occupation

Occupation (3 digit 2002 SOC)	2002 All immigrants	Recent immigrants	Occ. share	2008 All immigrants	Recent immigrants	Occ. share
111: corporate managers & senior	0.128	0.040	0.004	0.110	0.029	0.004
112: production managers	0.049	0.010	0.021	0.077	0.010	0.023
113: functional managers	0.097	0.022	0.042	0.106	0.017	0.048
114: quality and customer care	0.075	0.010	0.004	0.096	0.021	0.005
115: financial and office	0.082	0.012	0.013	0.084	0.014	0.015
116: managers in distrib., storange	0.079	0.009	0.019	0.090	0.008	0.021
117: protective service officers	0.104	0.029	0.003	0.094	0.009	0.003
118: health and social services	0.090	0.008	0.006	0.117	0.012	0.007
121: managers in farming	0.038	0.022	0.001	0.041	0.007	0.001
122: managers in hospitality	0.163	0.017	0.011	0.202	0.033	0.011
123: managers in other services	0.103	0.008	0.018	0.126	0.006	0.018
211: science professionals	0.147	0.028	0.004	0.195	0.055	0.005
212: engineering professionals	0.081	0.015	0.015	0.107	0.031	0.017
213: info. & communication technol.	0.142	0.046	0.014	0.197	0.067	0.015
221: health professionals	0.251	0.044	0.010	0.278	0.059	0.012
231: teaching professionals	0.087	0.012	0.042	0.094	0.013	0.045
232: research professionals	0.205	0.066	0.002	0.213	0.056	0.003
241: legal professionals	0.128	0.023	0.005	0.123	0.012	0.006
242: business & statistical profs.	0.128	0.039	0.011	0.137	0.029	0.013
243: architects, town professionals	0.076	0.005	0.005	0.109	0.022	0.006
244: public service professionals	0.113	0.012	0.006	0.115	0.009	0.007
245: librarians and related profs.	0.080	0.013	0.001	0.104	0.006	0.002
311: science and engineering technol.	0.059	0.011	0.010	0.096	0.021	0.008
312: draughtspersons & building inspectors	0.076	0.024	0.003	0.099	0.030	0.003
313: IT service delivery	0.113	0.021	0.007	0.105	0.034	0.006
321: health associate profs.	0.142	0.042	0.024	0.182	0.030	0.026
322: therapists	0.135	0.026	0.004	0.091	0.009	0.005
323: social welfare associate profs.	0.096	0.008	0.007	0.091	0.004	0.010
331: protective service	0.060	0.008	0.012	0.057	0.007	0.013

(continued)

Table 3.A2 Continued

Occupation (3 digit 2002 SOC)	2002 All immigrants	Recent immigrants	Occ. share	2008 All immigrants	Recent immigrants	Occ. share
341: artistic and literary	0.156	0.031	0.005	0.176	0.024	0.006
342: design associate profs.	0.095	0.022	0.004	0.105	0.026	0.005
343: media associate profs.	0.118	0.021	0.006	0.105	0.012	0.006
344: sports and fitness	0.051	0.012	0.003	0.094	0.021	0.004
351: transport associate profs.	0.082	0.008	0.002	0.166	0.026	0.002
352: legal associate profs.	0.056	0.011	0.002	0.064	0.011	0.002
353: business & finance assoc. profs.	0.089	0.019	0.015	0.126	0.030	0.017
354: sales & related assoc. profs.	0.071	0.021	0.016	0.108	0.030	0.015
355: conservation associate profs.	0.068	0.014	0.001	0.111	0.022	0.001
356: public service and other assoc. profs.	0.066	0.012	0.015	0.080	0.016	0.017
411: administrative: government	0.048	0.004	0.021	0.063	0.008	0.018
412: administrative: finance	0.081	0.017	0.031	0.104	0.022	0.026
413: administrative: records	0.060	0.010	0.022	0.096	0.022	0.018
414: administrative: communication	0.047	0.007	0.002	0.060	0.005	0.002
415: administrative: general	0.065	0.015	0.024	0.089	0.027	0.023
421: secretarial and related	0.063	0.012	0.033	0.080	0.015	0.026
511: agricultural trades	0.026	0.004	0.010	0.035	0.005	0.011
521: metal forming, welding, repair	0.037	0.006	0.006	0.072	0.023	0.005
522: metal machining, fitting	0.048	0.006	0.016	0.061	0.017	0.011
523: vehicle trades	0.052	0.010	0.010	0.061	0.021	0.009
524: electrical trades	0.046	0.009	0.017	0.078	0.018	0.015
531: construction trades	0.038	0.006	0.029	0.085	0.030	0.032
532: building trades	0.046	0.010	0.008	0.088	0.039	0.009
541: textiles and garment trades	0.090	0.002	0.002	0.126	0.043	0.001
542: printing trades	0.043	0.001	0.003	0.064	0.024	0.002
543: food preparation trades	0.171	0.026	0.012	0.255	0.068	0.011
549: skilled trades n.e.c	0.060	0.012	0.004	0.082	0.025	0.004
611: healthcare & related	0.079	0.017	0.031	0.151	0.047	0.035
612: childcare & related	0.069	0.018	0.023	0.090	0.017	0.028
613: animal care services	0.022	0.002	0.002	0.038	0.000	0.002

621: leisure & travel services	0.097	0.020	0.006	0.147	0.033	0.006
622: hairdressers and related	0.057	0.009	0.007	0.061	0.017	0.008
623: housekeeping	0.111	0.013	0.004	0.168	0.060	0.005
629: personal services	0.041	0.000	0.001	0.013	0.000	0.001
711: sales assistants and retail	0.058	0.016	0.058	0.100	0.026	0.054
712: sales related	0.061	0.009	0.008	0.074	0.016	0.007
721: customer service	0.053	0.015	0.012	0.106	0.031	0.014
811: process operatives	0.035	0.020	0.015	0.250	0.146	0.011
812: plant and machine operatives	0.059	0.004	0.009	0.109	0.054	0.007
813: assemblers and routine operatives	0.094	0.012	0.016	0.170	0.087	0.010
814: construction operatives	0.056	0.002	0.005	0.065	0.017	0.005
821: transport drivers and operatives	0.080	0.004	0.033	0.124	0.021	0.032
822: mobile machine drivers	0.047	0.004	0.006	0.121	0.049	0.006
911: elementary agricultural	0.024	0.011	0.004	0.107	0.092	0.003
912: elementary construction	0.045	0.013	0.007	0.115	0.060	0.008
913: elementary prccess plant	0.114	0.034	0.011	0.293	0.204	0.009
914: elementary goods storage	0.061	0.013	0.014	0.159	0.082	0.014
921: elementary administration	0.070	0.008	0.010	0.098	0.020	0.009
922: elementary personal service	0.097	0.033	0.031	0.169	0.078	0.029
923: elementary cleaning	0.088	0.027	0.025	0.184	0.086	0.024
924: elementary security	0.120	0.019	0.011	0.153	0.031	0.010
925: elementary sales	0.065	0.011	0.006	0.127	0.058	0.006

Source: LFS.

Table 3.A3 Probit estimates of the chances of immigrants working in given sector, 2008

	I	II	III	IV	IV
Static immigrant	−0.051*	−0.045*	−0.046*	−0.047*	−0.039*
utilization industry	(0.003)	(0.004)	(0.004)	(0.005)	(0.005)
Rising immigrant	0.098*	0.088*	0.088*	0.086*	0.081*
utilization industry	(0.006)	(0.006)	(0.006)	(0.009)	(0.009)
Controls					
Occupation	No	Yes	Yes	Yes	Yes
Part-time	No	No	Yes	Yes	Yes
Self-employed	No	No	Yes	Yes	Yes
Wage	No	No	No	Yes	Yes
Age	No	No	No	No	Yes
Region	No	No	No	No	Yes
Gender	No	No	No	No	Yes

Notes: See Table 3.9.

Source: LFS (2008).

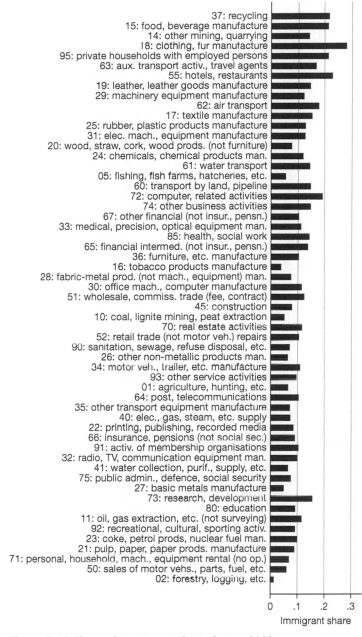

Figure 3.A1 Share of immigrants by industry, 2008

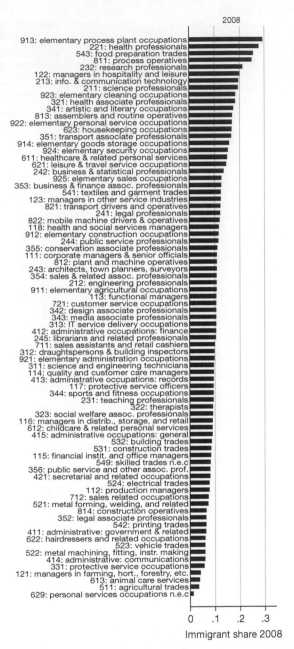

Figure 3.A2 Share of immigrants by occupation, 2008

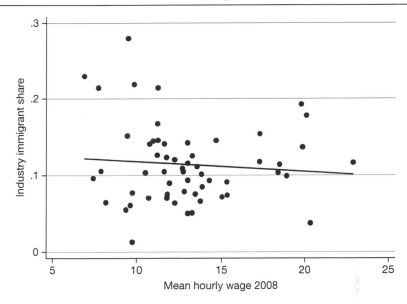

Figure 3.A3 Industry wages and immigrant shares

References

Dobson, J., Koser, K., and Salt, J. (2001), 'International Migration and the United Kingdom: Recent Patterns and Trends', Home Office RDS Occasional Paper 75.

Dustmann, C., Fabbri, F., Preston, I., and Wadsworth, J. (2003), 'Labour Market Performance of Immigrants in the UK Labour Market', Home Office Online Report 05/03, available at: <http://www.homeoffice.gov.uk/rds/pdfs2/rdsolr0503.pdf>.

——Glitz, A., and Vogel, T. (2006), 'Employment, Wage Structure, and the Economic Cycle: Differences between Immigrants and Natives in Germany and the UK', CReAM Discussion Paper No. 09/06.

Hatton, T. (2005), 'Explaining Trends in UK immigration', *Journal of Population Economics*, 18(4): 719–40.

Manacorda, M., Manning A., and Wadsworth, J. (2006), 'The Impact of Immigration on the Structure of Wages in Britain', Centre for Economic Performance Discussion Paper No. 746.

Mitchell, J., and Pain, N. (2003), 'The Determinants of International Migration into the UK: A Panel Based Modelling Approach', NIESR Discussion Paper No. 216.

Organisation for Economic Co-operation and Development (OECD) (2006), *International Migration Outlook: SOPEMI 2006* (Paris: OECD).

4

Achieving a Self-Sufficient Workforce? The Utilization of Migrant Labour in Healthcare

Stephen Bach

4.1 Introduction

Over the last decade ambitious plans to modernize the National Health Service (NHS) were underpinned by international recruitment, ensuring rapid expansion of the NHS workforce (Department of Health 2000). This approach was reiterated by the Wanless (2002) report on NHS funding, which identified staff shortages of doctors and nurses as a key barrier to improved service standards. Since 2002, there has been unprecedented government investment in the NHS with average annual real-term expenditure growth of 7.4 per cent per annum in the five-year period to 2007–8, and the NHS budget in England increased to 90 billion (HM Treasury 2007). A substantial proportion of this investment has been channelled into staff growth. The NHS Plan committed the NHS to employ 7,500 more consultants, 2,000 more GPs, 20,000 more nurses, and 7,500 Allied Health Professionals (therapists). These targets were exceeded, often substantially, by 2006 (Wanless et al. 2007: p. xix).

In 2009, with the UK in the midst of a deep recession, the NHS confronts a much less benign budgetary context, and the period of sustained staffing growth has ended. Workforce expansion was curtailed from 2005 when the NHS confronted financial difficulties, which partly stemmed from staffing growth (Health Committee 2006). The government's emphasis shifted to improving productivity, demonstrating the value for money of the existing workforce, and facilitating new ways of working. The Department of Health suggested that 'NHS workforce capacity has increased to levels where we are now able to see the demand for staff equalling domestic supply' and 'the capacity issue has been addressed' (Department of Health 2007: 31). This altered context enabled the government to avoid the political sensitivity of recruiting health professionals from countries that also confronted shortages and to emphasize 'fair health worker migration policies' in its global heath strategy: 'We will combat the global workforce crisis by becoming more self sufficient in training our own healthcare workers' (Department of Health 2008a: 23).

This statement illustrates that in contrast to many other sectors, the consequences of the migration of health professionals for the *source* country rather than the *destination* country has been politically sensitive. In comparison to sectors such as construction, there has been little public disquiet about migrant health professionals *substituting* for UK nationals, partly because the Labour government was elected to address public concerns about an NHS 'in crisis'. Instead, concerns about brain-drain stem from estimates that there is a global shortage of 4.3 million health workers, with acute shortages in sub-Saharan Africa (World Health Organization 2006). The global political profile of health worker shortages has risen dramatically in recent years, culminating in the 2008 Kampala declaration (<http://www.ghwa.org>) and numerous initiatives to develop forms of ethical recruitment (e.g. European Union 2008). The UK government developed guidelines for NHS employers from 1999 which identified the countries that the UK government considered it ethical to recruit from (essentially *not* sub-Saharan Africa), an additional form of soft regulation of health sector labour markets.

This chapter examines the changing labour market context and the contribution of migrant labour to the NHS workforce. It suggests that central government control over the financing and staffing policy of the NHS ensures tight government control over NHS labour markets. In conjunction with establishing immigration rules (i.e. shortage occupations and entry requirements), and influencing licensing requirements of health professionals, the UK government has a capacity to influence the utilization of migrant health professionals in a manner that distinguishes the NHS from other employers that are reliant upon migrant labour.

The main focus in this chapter is on medical and nursing staff—the occupations that have been the priorities of policy-makers and employers. Within the health sector, the term 'overseas' or 'internationally recruited' staff is used frequently. Although this terminology does not distinguish clearly between the individual's country of birth, qualification, and employment, it signifies health professionals that have usually been *actively* recruited since the late 1990s to fill labour shortages, and whose diploma or degree was obtained outside of the UK. In contrast to many other sectors, the predominant source countries have been India, the Philippines, and parts of sub-Saharan Africa, with EEA nationals comprising a relatively small proportion of recent international recruitment activity.

4.2 Overview of the Health Sector

The UK health system is dominated by the National Health Service (NHS), which finances and provides most healthcare in the UK, and employs more than one million staff. The NHS remains a virtual monopoly purchaser of the services of most health sector professionals, especially at the start of their careers, and is the only commissioner of basic level pre-registration education for professionals such as nurses and doctors. Healthcare in the UK remains predominantly publicly funded. In 2006, only 1.1 per cent of the 8.4 per cent of GDP committed to health expenditure was private expenditure (OECD 2009). Consequently, the government has the dominant influence over effective demand for the NHS via its expenditure decisions, and manages domestic labour supply by its control over the commissioning of training places.

The sector employs a large workforce with staff costs comprising around 62 per cent of hospital and community health services expenditure (Review Body of Doctors' and Dentists' Remuneration 2009: 15). In England, 1.3 million staff are divided between more than 150 main professional groups, comprising a number of different occupational labour markets. The utilization of migrant labour varies considerably between and within key occupational groups. Although the NHS is the dominant employer, independent hospitals also provide acute, cosmetic, and mental health services, but there is less systematic workforce data on the sector. In acute medicine, the independent sector employs only a few hundred Resident Medical Officers (RMOs), often on an agency basis (Independent Healthcare Advisory Services, personal communication). The vast majority of medical consultants are employed by the NHS, who exercise practice privileges in independent hospitals. In 1993, it was estimated that 85 per cent of consultants were NHS employees (Monopolies and Mergers Commission, cited in Laing and Buisson 2007: 145). For registered nurses, almost 9,000 whole-time-equivalent (WTE) qualified nursing staff were employed by independent hospitals and clinics in England, and around 41,000 WTE registered nurses in nursing homes in 2000–1 (Laing and Buisson 2007: 144), although within the whole social care sector the figure is much higher. The social care sector, a less attractive employer than the NHS, has relied heavily on migrant labour and has great difficulties in recruiting nurses to work with older people (Cangiano et al. 2009).

Since 1997, and the move towards political devolution, there has been increased divergence of health policy between each country (i.e. England, Northern Ireland, Scotland, and Wales), and workforce data is collected separately. The health professions, however, remain regulated on a UK-wide basis by the General Medical Council (GMC), Health Professions Council (HPC), and the Nursing and Midwifery Council (NMC), and their registration data is therefore UK wide. There is also a UK-wide pay and career structure termed Agenda for Change, underpinned by an NHS-wide job evaluation scheme. Agenda for Change covers all staff, with the exception of doctors and dentists and some top managers. This chapter concentrates mainly on the workforce in England, where most analysis of the migrant workforce has occurred.

4.2.1 *Policy Challenges: Workforce Implications*

For more than two decades the NHS has been subject to managerial and market-style reforms designed to enhance the efficient utilization of the workforce. The main priority of the first decade of Labour government was to increase the volume of NHS services to bring about reduced waiting times and limit geographical variations in access to services. The establishment of National Service Frameworks (NSFs) for each main service area (e.g. cancer care), and demanding waiting-time targets, required workforce expansion. Government policy also fostered more diversity of provision to encourage competition and enhance patient choice, with provider income more closely linked to the quantity and quality of services delivered. More autonomous Foundation Trusts have been established and Primary Care Trusts are able to use any approved provider and outsource their commissioning to the private sector. The development of GP practice-based commissioning is also stimulating more independent and third-sector involvement in service provision (Iliffe 2008). Although the future contribution of independent providers remains uncertain, it is evident that the sector needs to be more integrated into workforce planning (Laing and Buisson 2007; Wanless et al. 2007).

In 2007–8, following public disquiet about the effectiveness of increased expenditure, the government initiated the Darzi Next Stage Review to set out the direction for the NHS over the next decade (Department of Health 2008b). It signalled a new emphasis on the quality of care as *the* organizing principle for the NHS in England and acknowledged the loss of trust between NHS professional staff and the government. In response to forceful criticisms about the inadequacy of workforce planning (Health Committee 2007), Lord Darzi devoted a separate document to the workforce implications of his proposals, focusing on workforce planning, education, and training matters. His proposals have significant workforce implications, for example, the plan to move to an all-graduate entry profession for nursing by 2015. Revealingly, indicating the policy shift away from internationally recruited health professionals, no mention is made of migrant workers (Department of Health 2008c).

Over the next few years increased demand for healthcare is forecast, stemming from an ageing population, continuing medical and technological innovation, and population expansion (Wanless et al. 2007). The NHS confronts three main workforce challenges. First, a shift in health service delivery from the acute sector to local community settings. Hospitals are becoming more specialized, concentrating on the most complex cases, whilst there is increased emphasis on prevention and managing chronic conditions in the community (Department of Health 2006). This requires an increased primary care workforce, but the balance between GPs and other health professionals is changing, with more work undertaken by nurses and other members of the healthcare team (Department of Health 2007). A major difficulty is ensuring that sufficient staff with the appropriate skill-set are available in the community. This is in the context of a rapidly ageing NHS workforce. Royal College of Nursing (RCN) survey data indicates that 8 per cent of NHS hospital nurses are over 50, but in community settings the figure is 27 per cent, rising to 35 per cent in GP practices (Ball and Pike 2007: 15). GPs are also ageing, with the proportion in England aged 55 and above increasing from 16 per cent in 1998, to 22 per cent in 2008 (Information Centre 2009).

Secondly, these trends reinforce the importance of workforce planning, which in England is undertaken by ten strategic health authorities supported by the national Workforce Review Team (WRT) which identifies workforce priorities (WRT 2008a). There has been forceful criticism of NHS workforce planning, with the Health Committee (2007) concluding:

There has been a disastrous failure of workforce planning. The situation has been exacerbated by constant reorganisation including the abolition of Workforce Development Confederations within 3 years. The planning system remains poorly integrated and there is an appalling lack of coordination between workforce and financial planning. The health service has not made workforce planning a priority. (Health Committee 2007: 3)

One important limitation is that the WRT only considers the NHS in England, excluding other parts of the UK and the independent sector. Concerns have also been raised about the absence of data on internationally recruited staff. The NHS does not record how many international recruits it employs, so there is reliance on registration data, and there is very limited data on outflows abroad, with verification data difficult to interpret. Broader concerns relate to 'short-termism', with health authorities reducing training commissions to reduce deficits, the separation of medical workforce planning from other professional groups, and uncertainties about attrition rates of students in nursing and other professions (Buchan 2007; Health Committee 2007). The Next Stage Review outlined a series of proposals to improve workforce planning, including establishing a centre of excellence (Department of Health 2008c), but to date these measures have not been implemented.

Thirdly, the composition of the workforce is shifting, related to changing workforce roles and new ways of working. The Labour government has been committed to developing more user-centred services, with the reallocation of professional tasks to a wider range of occupational groups (Cabinet Office 2008). A more immediate impetus for change arises from the phased reduction of working hours to a maximum of 48 hours for doctors in training to ensure compliance with the European Working Time Directive. This has led to knock-on effects for other staff, including nurses, whose mandate has been extended (Witz and Annandale 2006). There has been a substantial increase in the employment of assistant occupations such as healthcare assistants, accompanied by locally directed changes to their role (Bach et al. 2008; Thornley 2003). A proliferation of assistant roles in the areas of therapy and midwifery have also been developed to address recruitment and retention difficulties, to encourage new ways of working, and to facilitate access to professional roles (Malhotra 2006). A more diverse workforce structure is emerging, arising from affordability concerns, supply-side difficulties, and attempts to develop more user-centred services. It is certain that as the NHS confronts severe budgetary constraints, employers will seek to employ a more cost-effective workforce and will alter their skill-mix.

Table 4.1   Trends in the NHS workforce, 1997–2007

Year	All medical & dental staff employed within HCHS	Consultants	GPs excluding retainers and registrars	Qualified nursing, midwifery & health visiting staff	Qualified scientific, therapeutic and technical staff (ST&T)
1997	57,099	19,661	26,359	246,011	81,601
1998	58,746	20,432	26,455	247,238	84,560
1999	60,338	21,410	26,558	250,651	86,837
2000	62,094	22,186	26,557	256,276	89,632
2001	64,055	23,064	26,628	266,171	93,085
2002	68,260	24,756	27,833	279,287	98,397
2003	72,260	26,341	27,624	291,925	102,912
2004	78,462	28,141	28,308	301,877	108,585
2005	82,568	29,613	29,248	307,744	113,214
2006	85,975	30,619	30,931	307,447	114,492
2007	87,533	31,430	30,936	307,628	117,107
Percentage increase 1997–2007	53%	60%	17%	25%	44%

Source: Information Centre 2008a, 2008b, 2008c.

4.2.2 The Health Sector Workforce

Detailed data on the NHS workforce in England is published by the NHS Information Centre (Information Centre 2008a, 2008b, 2008c). The NHS Pay Review Body (2008), whose remit covers all NHS staff paid under Agenda for Change, and the Review Body on Doctors' and Dentists' Remuneration (2009), contain detailed information on the workforce, on recruitment and retention, and on morale and pay. In 2007, the NHS in England employed 87,533 full-time equivalent (FTE) medical and dental staff in hospital and community health services (HCHS), an increase of 53 per cent since 1997. The increase in GP numbers from 26,359 to 30,936 was much less marked at 17 per cent. In 2007, the NHS in England employed 893,087 full-time-equivalent (FTE) staff within the non-medical workforce.[1] This represented an increase of 27 per cent since 1997. In contrast to medical staff (consultants and GPs), whose numbers continue to increase slowly, for non-medical staff the trend has been reversed, with staff numbers decreasing by around 2 per cent in 2006, followed by a smaller decrease in 2007 (0.7%). The main trends are shown in Table 4.1.

---

[1] Non-medical staff comprise ambulance staff, administrative and estates staff, healthcare assistants and other support staff, nursing, midwifery and health-visiting staff, scientific, therapeutic and technical staff, and healthcare scientists.

Overall the growth in the workforce has exceeded NHS plan targets by considerable margins. The main characteristics of the workforce comprise:

- *Gender* Women make up 81 per cent of the non-medical workforce and across the NHS this proportion is increasing. For example, women now comprise 39 per cent of all medical and dental staff in England, an increase of 62 per cent since 1997 (Information Centre 2008a) and comprise 42 per cent of the workforce in General Practice.
- *Ethnicity* The proportion of black and minority ethnic (BME) employees in 2007 in the medical and dental workforce in England was 39 per cent (29% in 1997). For the non-medical workforce, ethnic minority backgrounds represented 15 per cent of the workforce, compared to 8 per cent in 1997.
- *Age* The public sector workforce is older than the private sector. Three-quarters of public sector workers are over 35, compared to just over 60 per cent in the private sector, and there are far fewer young workers (under 24) compared to the private sector (Hicks et al. 2005: 23). A similar pattern is evident in the NHS and many professions face increasing levels of retirement, for example GPs (WRT 2008a, 2008b).
- *Part-time employment* The health sector employs a higher proportion of part-time workers (people working less than 30 hours a week) compared to the economy as a whole. LFS data indicates that in 2006–7, the NHS across the UK employed 64 per cent of staff (excluding medical staff) on a full-time basis and 36 per cent on a part-time basis. The lowest level of part-time working was in London (29%) (NHS Pay Review Body 2008: 17).
- *Trade union membership* LFS data for 2008 indicates that trade union membership (57%) was almost four times the level of the private sector (15.5%). In the health and social work industry, which is a broader category than just health, 41 per cent of UK employees were trade union members (Barratt 2009). Workplace Employment Relations Survey data indicates that the health sector has experienced continuous decline between 1980 and 2004 from 85 per cent to 48 per cent in union density, although membership density amongst professionals is much higher than amongst manual and administrative grades (Bach et al. 2009).

4.2.3 *Role of Migrant Labour within the Health Sector*

The international movement of health professionals is not a new phenomenon and a major WHO study concluded that in 1972 about 6 per cent of the world's physicians (140,000) were located in countries other than those of which they were nationals (Mejia et al. 1979). Approximately 86 per cent of all migrant physicians were found in just five countries—Australia, Canada, West Germany, the UK, and the USA. The stock of nurses overseas was estimated to be lower at about 5 per cent, but the main recipient countries were the same as for physicians, with the exception of Australia (Mejia et al. 1979: 399–400). For the NHS, the state's duty to ensure judicious public expenditure resulted in under-investment in the workforce, with insufficient health professionals trained in the UK in the post-war period. This was especially the case for medical staff, who represent a substantial investment for the state, and instead the UK became reliant on non-EEA labour (Raghuram and Kofman 2002).

It is frequently suggested that health professionals such as nurses comprise an increasingly global labour force, with less reliance on historical ties (e.g. Kingma 2006). Whilst increased migration of health professionals is evident (OECD 2007), this can conceal the extent to which nation states continue to exert a powerful influence over the mobility of health professionals. For example, the Philippines has a systematic policy of training nurses (and other occupations) to work abroad, encouraging women to enter nursing to gain employment overseas (Ball 2004). The UK also provides a clear illustration of government influence over health-professional labour markets, with consequences for the utilization of migrant labour (Bach 2007).

The share of migrants in the health sector workforce can be identified in a number of ways. First, Labour Force Survey data provides estimates of the nationality of the UK and immigrant population, disaggregated by occupation (using SOC four-digit occupation codes). As Table 4.2 indicates, almost a third of medical practitioners and approximately a fifth of nurses, dental practitioners, and pharmacists, were born outside the EEA.

Secondly, work permit data indicates that around 3,280 work permits were granted to health professionals (mainly doctors), and 11,110 to associate health professionals (mainly nurses) in 2005. In line with professional registration data (discussed below), there has been a general upward trend amongst doctors being granted work permits since 2000, whilst for nurses there has been a sharp decrease since 2003–4 (OECD 2007), which is related to the removal of nurses from the shortage occupation list. Home Office (2007) data on the A8 countries (the Czech Republic, Estonia, Hungary, Latvia, Lithuania, Poland, Slovakia, and Slovenia) indicates that between May 2004 and December 2006, 530 hospital doctors, 340 dental practitioners, 950 nurses, and 410 nursing auxiliaries/healthcare assistants

Table 4.2 Selected health professions

SOC 2000 4-digit code	Occupation	% employees born non-EEA	% employees born EEA, excluding UK	Estimated number of working-age UK population in this occupation (rounded)
2211	Medical practitioners	32	5	184,000
2212	Psychologists	19	4	23,000
2213	Pharmacists/Pharmacologists	21	5	40,000
2214	Ophthalmic opticians	4	1	13,000
2215	Dental practitioners	20	5	27,000
3211	Nurses	19	3	500,000
3212	Midwives	12	9	37,000
3213	Paramedics	8	2	17,000
3214	Medical radiographers	8	4	25,000
3215	Chiropodists	9	0	10,000
3216	Dispensing opticians	5	8	5,000
3221	Physiotherapists	9	4	32,000
3222	Occupational therapists	5	6	31,000
3223	Speech and language therapists	4	0	14,000

Source: LFS data cited in MAC (2008).

registered in the Work Registration Scheme. Relatively small numbers of health and medical occupation workers are listed in the accession statistics for Bulgaria and Romania. Between October and December 2007, there were 20 approvals of work permits from Romania and five from Bulgaria, but this data is not comprehensive (see Home Office 2008).

Thirdly, professional registration data provides up-to-date information about the country in which the individual qualified (rather than where they were born) and workforce trends. The main disadvantage is that it only provides a proxy measure of employment because it registers intention to work rather than actual employment status.

MEDICAL STAFF

In the 1950s, acute staff shortages encouraged medical staff immigration, mainly from South Asia and especially India (Decker 2001; Kyriakides and Virdee 2003). In the 1970s, foreign-trained doctors comprised about a quarter of the UK workforce (Mejia et al. 1979) compared to around a third at present. GMC registration data (Table 4.3) indicates the proportion of non-UK qualified doctors joining the medical register.

In total, there are more than 231,000 medical practitioners on the GMC register, of which 144,000 (62%) qualified in the UK. Doctors that qualified in India comprise the second largest group, with around 26,500 doctors on the GMC register, over 11 per cent of the total. There are also an estimated 11,000 African doctors registered in the UK, mainly from South Africa (approximately 7,000—3% of the GMC register) and Nigeria (approximately 3,200—1.4% of the register). Other important non-EEA source countries include Pakistan and Egypt (GMC 2009). In terms of the EEA, more than 4,500 registrants are from Ireland and Germany, whilst Poland, Italy, Greece, Spain, and Hungary all have more than 1,000 doctors registered in the UK (GMC 2009). Since 2005, the GMC recorded an increase of around 25 per cent in the number of registered doctors from A8 and A2 countries (Pollard et al. 2008: 36–7).

In England, around a fifth of GPs contracted to the NHS received their primary qualification abroad, divided between the EEA (5%), and elsewhere (16.5%) (Information Centre 2008c). There has been a relatively large increase (from a low base) of EEA-qualified GPs and many of these GPs are providing out-of-hours cover for the NHS. This contrasts with the situation for hospital and community health services (HCHS) medical staff. Not only has there been very rapid growth in non-EEA qualified medical staff, but non-EEA medical staff are concentrated in Staff Grade

Table 4.3 New registrations of doctors in the UK (based on place of primary medical qualification), 1998–2007

Year	1998	1999	2000	2001	2002	2003	2004	2005	2006	2007
UK	4,010 (44%)	4,242 (50%)	4,214 (50%)	4,462 (51%)	4,288 (42%)	4,443 (29%)	4,658 (37%)	5,164 (34%)	5,620 (48%)	6,133 (55%)
EEA	1,590 (17%)	1,392 (16%)	1,192 (14%)	1,237 (14%)	1,448 (14%)	1,770 (11%)	2,419 (19%)	4,103 (27%)	2,994 (25%)	2,446 (22%)
Rest of the world	3,580 (39%)	2,889 (34%)	2,993 (36%)	3,088 (35%)	4,456 (44%)	9,336 (60%)	5,683 (44%)	5,825 (39%)	3,163 (27%)	2,609 (23%)
Total	7,363	8,523	8,399	8,787	10,192	15,549	12,760	15,092	11,777	11,188

Source: GMC, Personal communication.

and Associate Specialist (AS) grades. This data confirms the picture revealed by other studies (Oikelome and Healy 2007). These grades used to be termed 'non-career' grades because they do not incorporate postgraduate training leading to consultant posts. UK qualified doctors are reluctant to enter these grades, as are non-UK qualified doctors, but the latter are disproportionately employed in these grades. They were reformed in 2008, closing the AS grade to new entrants and establishing the grade of 'specialty doctor' with improved salary prospects. These measures are intended to boost morale and motivation amongst these non-consultant career grade doctors (NHS Employers 2008). NHS Trusts have also created trust-grade posts to meet service needs, which have non-standard terms and conditions. These posts, which are often filled by migrants, are not protected by national terms and conditions of employment, and so such terms and conditions incorporated may be worse (BMA 2007).

NURSES

In the 1950s, severe nurse shortages led to recruitment from the Commonwealth and former colonies, which continued until the late 1960s (Carpenter 1988). The Nursing and Midwifery Council (NMC) provides annual statistics on the number of nurses and midwives on the register, together with the numbers entering and leaving the register. In 2008, there were 676,547 nurses on the register (NMC 2009). Until 1998, there was a sharp fall of around 35 per cent in the number of new entrants to the register from UK sources, before increasing by more than 40 per cent during the last decade. It was in this intervening period that overseas registrations filled the shortfall.

As Figure 4.1 indicates, active recruitment by the NHS and independent sector from the late 1990s led to a sharp rise in registration from non-EEA qualified nurses. In the peak year of 2001–2, the number of non-EEA nurse registrants exceeded those from the UK, with only 47 per cent of new entrants qualified in the UK compared to almost 90 per cent UK-qualified in the early 1990s. The key source countries have been India, the Philippines, and Australia (Table 4.4). Active overseas nurse recruitment was curtailed from around 2005, and this was reflected in a sharp decline of non-EEA registrations. This decline stemmed from the expansion of UK-educated nurse training and other policy reforms. In 2006, Bands 5 and 6 posts (registered nurses start on Band 5) were removed from the Home Office shortage occupation list. In 2007, the NMC raised the English-language requirements and the shift to the points-based system further

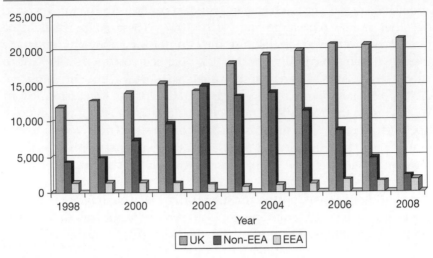

Figure 4.1 Admissions to the UK Nurse Register from the UK, EEA, and non-EEA countries, 1998–2008

discouraged international recruitment (RCN 2008). Overall these changes signalled to overseas nurses that there was less access and fewer opportunities available in the UK labour market.

It should be noted from Figure 4.1 that the number of EEA registrations (excluding the UK) remains relatively low and has been around 1,000–1,500 for the last few years. In 2008 around a quarter (456) of EEA registrations were from Poland (NMC 2009). Considering the expansion of the EEA and the volume of immigration from the EEA in other sectors, this is an important distinguishing feature of the health sector, and in general, outflows of nurses (and to a lesser extent doctors) from Estonia, Poland, and Lithuania have been lower than anticipated (Buchan and Perfilieva 2006). Language barriers are an important reason for difficulties in gaining registration. In addition, uncertainties about the level of nurse training in many A8 countries makes it difficult for nurses to gain recognition for their qualifications because they are not compliant with EU directives, although this will alter over time (Hasselhorn et al. 2005; Zajac 2004). Some nurses also report difficulties in obtaining the requisite documentation about their qualifications from their home country (Charlton 2004). Consequently, many accession state nurses are working as healthcare assistants. For example, the independent sector organization Westminster Health Care initially recruited 200 Polish citizens to work in care assistant roles (Cole 2005).

Table 4.4   Overseas (non-EEA) trained nurses registered per annum in the UK, 1999–2008

Country	1999	2000	2001	2002	2003	2004	2005	2006	2007	2008
India	30	96	289	994	1,830	3,073	3,690	3,551	2,436	1,020
Australia	1,335	1,209	1,046	1,342	920	1,326	981	751	299	262
Philippines	52	1,052	3,396	7,235	5,593	4,338	2,521	1,541	673	249
Nigeria	179	208	347	432	509	511	466	381	258	154
Nepal	—	—	—	—	71	43	73	75	148	117
New Zealand	527	461	393	443	282	348	289	215	74	62
China	—	—	—	—	—	—	60	66	80	52
Zambia	15	40	88	183	133	169	162	110	53	
Zimbabwe	52	221	382	473	485	391	311	161	90	49
Pakistan	3	13	44	207	172	140	205	200	154	42
Ghana	40	74	140	195	251	354	272	154	66	38
USA	139	168	147	122	88	141	105	98	21	35
South Africa	599	1,460	1,086	2,114	1,368	1,689	933	378	39	32
Canada	196	130	89	79	52	89	88	75	31	24
Kenya	19	29	50	155	152	146	99	41	37	19
Total*	3621	5945	8403	15,064	12,730	14,122	11,477	8,709	4,830	2,309

Notes: Listed by 15 most numerous source country registrations in 2008. Aggregate individual country figures do not equal total non-EEA initial registrations as some countries are omitted from this table.

Source: NMC Statistical Register, various years.

The data indicates that the UK has been heavily reliant on migrant labour, with a large stock of doctors and nurses that received their qualifications outside the EEA. The data on new registrations also indicates a greater capacity to regulate the flow of overseas health professionals into the UK than in many other sectors, with significant fluctuations in recent years. It is not only that there is less scope for skilled workers to be employed as an irregular migrant in the health sector, particularly in the NHS, because of professional registration and other (e.g. language) requirements, but also because of the tight regulation of effective demand and supply exercised by the state.

4.3 Employer Demand

As discussed in Chapter 2 of this book, Piore (1979), amongst other researchers, suggests that migration stems from the structural demand for migrant labour by employers within advanced industrial economies. Migrant labour has specific advantages for employers that arise primarily from the attributes of jobs that migrants fill, rather than simply the wages that they are paid. First, migrants often fill jobs that are dirty, difficult, dangerous, and demeaning. These jobs are not always low-paid, but they are usually low-status, with few opportunities for advancement. Even in high-status professions like medicine there are certain unpopular specialties or particular grades that lie outside the main career structure and that are hard to fill. The British Medical Association (2007) has noted that migrant workers usually fill these posts. Secondly, employers are reluctant to raise wages to alleviate shortages because of the impact on the overall wage structure, with higher-paid workers seeking to restore wage differentials. As Piore (1979: 33) argues, 'the hospital administrator cannot envisage paying more to orderlies without paying more to nurses'. Moreover, migrant wage expectations are initially framed by the labour market in their country of origin, reducing their wage expectations, especially if they envisage a temporary stay abroad.

The renewed reliance on internationally recruited health professionals in the late 1990s can be linked directly to government policy. Although NHS trusts are formally separate from employers, tight control over employment policies is retained by central government (Bach 2004). As noted earlier, the NHS Plan for England established ambitious targets for workforce expansion in response to widely acknowledged shortages amongst key occupational groups. International recruitment was the preferred strategy to ensure rapid workforce growth because of the expense and lengthy lead times involved in increasing the numbers of domestically trained nurses and doctors (Health Committee 2007).

The Department of Health established an institutional infrastructure to facilitate recruitment activity. An NHS Director of International Recruitment was appointed, supported by International Recruitment Co-ordinators, with the number of staff recruited internationally comprising a key performance target. These coordinators and staff, located in embassies in Spain and elsewhere, aided NHS trusts in their recruitment efforts. Financial support was made available, enabling managers to travel to the Philippines in particular, to recruit batches of 50–100 nurses at a time. The Department of Health actively marketed the NHS through its website, providing information about the cost of living and pen portraits of nurses, who extolled the virtues of nursing in the UK. It also established a series of bilateral agreements with specific governments (India, Indonesia, Spain, Philippines, South Africa, and most recently in 2005, China) that were willing to allow the UK to recruit because they had a surplus or viewed migration as an important source of remittance income.

Finally, the government eased immigration rules and their implementation. For those outside the EEA, the work permit system has been the basis of the system, with the granting of a work permit linked to employer sponsorship and skill level. The number of work permits was not subject to annual quotas, but the Home Office published a National Shortage Occupation list. If jobs were not on the shortage list, in most circumstances employers had to undertake a resident labour market test, demonstrating that they had advertised their post for at least one week and provide reasons why they rejected applications from resident workers (Salt and Millar 2006). This system provided a considerable degree of flexibility because the number of work permits allocated and the various channels used could all be adjusted. Hatton (2005) notes a large increase in immigration (not simply accounted for by EEA expansion) in the 1990s, indicating a significant relaxation of immigration policy. Moreover, individual employers had considerable informal influence over favoured candidates' applications because employers built up relationships with case workers at Work Permits UK (Salt and Millar 2006: 19).

In December 2004, almost 70 specialist healthcare occupations were included in the Home Office healthcare shortage occupation list, including consultant medical staff in a number of specialist areas, salaried GPs and dentists, nurses, midwives, dieticians, biomedical scientists, pharmacists, clinical psychologists, occupational therapists, and language therapists.

This list signalled that the UK was seeking non-UK-qualified health professionals. By comparison, in June 2008, only medical consultants in a number of specific specialties were included in the shortage list, as were registered nurses at Band 7 or 8, but not entry-level registered nurses.

The government has continued to regulate the movement of health and other skilled professionals by the establishment of the Migration Advisory Committee (MAC), an integral element of the Labour government's shift to a points-based immigration system. The MAC was established to provide independent advice to government on where skilled labour market shortages exist that can sensibly be filled by migration from outside the EEA. To fulfil this role, the MAC establishes and updates shortage occupation lists for skilled occupations, categorized as Tier 2 (MAC 2008). Although other routes exist to recruit skilled (Tier 2) labour from non-EEA countries (e.g. intra-company transfers), in healthcare, employers' scope to recruit skilled migrant labour is influenced strongly by the presence or exclusion of an occupation on the shortage occupation list. The MAC has recommended that particular hard-to-recruit medical consultant posts in specialties such as psychiatry, obstetrics and gynaecology, and paediatrics are placed on the shortage occupation list, but has been much more sceptical about nurse shortages and recommended only that nurses employed in operating theatres and critical care are placed on the shortage list (MAC 2009a). In contrast to the openness of government policy towards non-EEA health professionals in the late 1990s, a much more restrictive approach has emerged over recent years.

Although it is early to assess the impact of the MAC, it has encouraged a more systematic analysis of skill shortages and the utilization of migrant labour. For the government, the points-based system and shortage occupation list provide flexibility to adjust upwards or downwards the number of migrants eligible to enter the UK. At present, health professions are reviewed on a six-monthly basis. This creates considerable uncertainty for migrants and employers, however, who are confronted with the prospect of changes to immigration rules on a regular basis. Anomalies can also arise because the MAC understandably relies primarily on objective data on skills, earnings, and qualification levels to assess requirements for each tier, but this may capture imperfectly the skills of non-EEA applicants because of the manner in which points are allocated to different criteria within the points-based system. Difficulties can occur when job qualifications or earnings are established at a lower level than those required to ensure eligibility for a specific tier of the points-based system. Tier 2 is essentially a graduate-based category, but nurses, including non-EEA nurses, frequently gain a diploma rather than a degree, and are relatively low-paid, precluding them from gaining sufficient points to be eligible for Tier 2. The MAC (2009b) has responded to this concern by recommending that key public service occupations be awarded additional points. A similar difficulty arises for non-EEA medical staff with medical degrees from the UK or elsewhere, because medicine is categorized as a bachelor's (BSc) qualification, when a master's degree is necessary to be eligible for Tier 1. Whilst it may be possible to address these anomalies, the risk is that it will create precedents which may, over time, erode the coherence of the points-based system.

EMPLOYER REQUIREMENTS AND THEIR DEMAND FOR MIGRANT LABOUR

Virtually all health professions require degree-level qualifications, with professional requirements governed by the individual regulatory body. These requirements focus on technical expertise and English-language competency, usually gauged by a combination of educational attainment, experience in appropriate training posts, demonstration of technical proficiency in supervised posts, and evaluation by (practical) examination. Other criteria to gain registration usually focus on 'good character' and 'good health'.

In addition to professional registration, the main approach of the NHS to identify and encourage skill acquisition is grounded in the Knowledge and Skills Framework (KSF), implemented as part of the Agenda for Change pay modernization process. The KSF is based on an annual developmental review process and this leads to the generation of an agreed Personal Development Plan (PDP) for each staff member. The national NHS staff survey indicated that implementation of the KSF has lagged behind other elements of pay modernization (Healthcare Commission 2008: 11–12). Managers suggest that it is too complicated and time-consuming and that because salary increments are virtually automatic, the KSF is of limited value. Apart from technical proficiency, the relative importance of soft skills to the delivery of effective healthcare has been much debated (Grugulis 2007). Overall, the main focus in the sector is on technical proficiency, but employers are also interested in the possession of appropriate experience, good communication skills, and practical ability.

In recruiting employees that demonstrate these skills, there is little evidence that NHS employers have a *positive* preference for migrant workers, with few mentions of 'work ethic' and other points that are often discussed in relation to some other sectors, such as hospitality and agriculture.

Nonetheless, there are a range of benefits that have accrued to employers in recruiting migrant health professionals. The primary motivation of employers has been to address skill shortages and fill vacancies. Geographical locations with the highest vacancy rates for nurses have made the greatest use of non-UK-trained nurses. London has a disproportionate number of non-UK-trained nurses and in conjunction with the south-east, employs approximately 40 per cent of those in the UK (Batata 2005). Employers, especially in the independent sector, indicated that international recruitment was a relatively straightforward and cost-effective method to address their staffing requirements compared to other recruitment and retention initiatives (Buchan 2003: 22).

A second motivation has been to recruit to unpopular specialties, grades, and shift patterns. The use of migrant health professionals to work in unpopular specialties and localities is widely documented. In medicine, it has been the specialties of elderly care, accident and emergency, and psychiatry that have been viewed as lower status and which have employed the greatest proportion of non-EEA-qualified doctors (Decker 2001). The sub-consultant career grades which do not ensure the financial rewards or status of consultant posts are dominated by non-EEA-qualified doctors (BMA 2007). A survey of Staff and Associate specialists indicated that they worked longer hours and had less autonomy than their UK-qualified contemporaries (Oikelome and Healy 2007). Overseas doctors struggle to gain the same training as is provided to their indigenous counterparts. For some doctors this arises because of a lack of understanding of the structure and organization of training, for many others it reflects the view that overseas doctors' careers and training needs are systematically ignored (Unwin 2001; BMA 2004). It has also been noted that non-EEA staff fill particular organizational slots. Amongst nurses, the RCN (2007) reported that internationally recruited nurses were much more likely to work permanent nights, whilst O'Brien (2007) emphasized that non-EEA nurses were expected to undertake less technical direct-care duties.

Finally, employers may be able to exert tighter managerial control over migrant health professionals, not least because employees are often effectively tied to their current employer because of their work permit status or for other reasons, such as the provision of accommodation. Although the sector is highly unionized and the NHS uses a national structure of pay and conditions, limiting the scope for the worst forms of exploitation, a common experience amongst overseas nurses has been the lack of recognition of their skills and previous experience. This has encouraged a feeling that their competence as a nurse is being questioned (RCN 2003; Smith et al.

2006). This lack of recognition can result in a sense of injustice because the tasks allocated and the pay received does not correspond to experience. Because of their dependence on their employer for their work permit and to gain their professional registration, nurses feel insecure and anxious during their adaptation (Winkelmann-Gleed and Seeley 2005: 959). In some cases, employers, especially in parts of the independent sector, have not provided adequate training to enable nurses to gain registration enabling them to be employed on lower-paid (HCA) grades (RCN 2003). Consequently, the use of migrant labour may provide additional flexibility and a higher level of dependence on the employer.

4.4 Labour Supply

In aggregate terms, the NHS workforce is in greater balance and is moving towards self-sufficiency to a greater extent than in the past decade. There has been significant expansion in the number of UK-trained health professionals, with a 12 per cent expansion in the number of nurses in training between 2003/4 and 2005/6, reflected in the number of initial NMC UK registrants (Figure 4.1). The number of medical school places has expanded and it is estimated that the number of medical school graduates in England will rise from 4,091 in 2004 to 6,062 in 2011 (WRT 2008b). Although the main focus has been on increasing training commissions, attempts have also been made to attract staff back into nursing. The Department of Health has undertaken a series of campaigns to encourage returners via 'Return to Practice' courses, but data is not collected on how many returners subsequently take up and remain in NHS employment (Buchan et al. 2003).

This improved labour supply is reflected in NHS vacancy data. In comparison to sectors such as hospitality, even during periods of widespread shortages, NHS vacancy figures remain relatively low, usually below 5 per cent, although there are substantial variations by occupation and region. Healthcare is a highly interdependent labour process, however, and the absence of small numbers of specialist staff (e.g. theatre nurses, anaesthetists) can have significant knock-on effects for health-service delivery. Moreover, there is much debate about the validity of NHS vacancy data, which has been criticized because it only records information on posts that have been vacant for three months or more and does not capture the use of agency staff or the freezing of posts (NHS Pay Review Body 2008: 40–2).

In March 2008, the three-month vacancy rate for medical and dental consultants was 0.9 per cent, compared to 4.7 per cent in 2003 and

3.3 per cent in 2005. The estimated long-term vacancy rate for GPs was 0.3 per cent. For qualified nursing and midwifery staff, the 2008 rate was 0.5 per cent, compared to 1.9 per cent in 2005 (Information Centre 2008d). Both review bodies concluded in 2008 that there were no overall problems with recruitment and retention amongst their remit groups, although there were some difficulties with particular specialisms and in specific regions.

Several other labour supply risks have been highlighted (Bloor et al. 2006; RCN 2008; WRT 2008a, 2008b). First, although the numbers of UK-quali-fied health professionals have increased, *attrition* rates amongst students are high. Data released to the *Nursing Standard* indicated that in 2006, 26 per cent of nursing students left their courses early, which has been partly attributed to high levels of student debt (Waters 2008). Secondly, in specific occupations, supply-side uncertainties remain. Amongst GPs, the WRT concluded: 'in the light of retirement, other turnover and participation trends we will need more GPs and other primary care staff' (WRT 2008a: 4). Concerns about GP supply relate to reductions in GP registrar posts, plans to lengthen GP training, insufficient training posts to maintain supply, an increase in retirees, and the increased proportion of GPs that are seeking part-time employment.

Amongst nurses, forecasts indicate a levelling off of supply and then a fall in nurse numbers (partly because of the ageing workforce). International recruitment from outside the EEA has sharply decelerated. It is often more experienced nurses (Band 6 and above) rather than newly qualified nurses that the NHS has difficulty recruiting and retaining. Particular specialties, such as theatres and paediatrics, are often mentioned as confronting re-cruitment difficulties. Overall, the contribution of non-UK registered nurses to recent health sector workforce growth cannot be overstated, with more than 90,000 new registrants (around 45 per cent of all new entrants to the NMC register). This flow has been jeopardized by the alterations in work permit regulations (RCN 2007). It is uncertain if the inflow from the EEA can substitute for non-EEA nurses in terms of numbers or desired employer competencies.

4.5 Alternatives to Migration

Since around 2003–4, there has been a shift in government emphasis towards 'self-sufficiency', and a variety of measures have been taken to reduce reliance on overseas recruitment. The NHS has made concerted efforts to become an employer of choice (Department of Health 2004), with numerous initiatives to improve working lives, promote work–life balance, boost the remuneration of staff, and increase staff numbers. Measures to recruit and retain older workers and encourage workers to remain in employment beyond conventional retirement age have also been utilized. Nonetheless, uncertainty remains about the state of employment relations. The 2007 NHS annual staff survey indicated that staff exhibit reasonable levels of job satisfaction, have strong support from their managers, and had access to flexible working options. Almost two-thirds of staff, however, worked additional hours (paid and unpaid), 3 per cent of staff experienced discrimination (12 per cent amongst black and minority ethnic staff), and only a quarter of staff thought their trust valued their work (Healthcare Commission 2008). The NHS Pay Review Body (2008: 74) also reported a decline in morale. Research on 'what matters to staff in the NHS' identified widespread frustration. Many staff 'see the NHS serving a business agenda driven by financial considerations and irrelevant targets. This frustration, it appears, is driving a feeling of alienation' (Department of Health 2008b: 22). Other studies have pointed to the growth of agency nursing as being partly linked to the deterioration of permanent jobs (De Rutyer 2008; Tailby 2006).

RAISING WAGES

Cumulatively, Agenda for Change, the new GP contract, and the revised consultant contract have contributed to a significant increase in the NHS paybill. In 2005–6 the average pay of consultants was 109,974, an increase of 27 per cent in three years (National Audit Office 2007). For GPs, pre-tax take-home pay in England increased by 58 per cent from 72,011 in 2002–3 to 113,614 in 2005–6 (NAO 2008). The impact of Agenda for Change is harder to assess because it covers all non-medical staff and therefore there are 'winners' and 'losers', with the implementation process generating many grading appeals. The NHS Pay Review Body (2008: 113) concluded that:

On comparative earnings, there is no evidence that our remit group has done better than average in recent years when compared to other, similar, workers, notwithstanding the introduction of AfC. AfC has led to significant above average pay increases for some groups within our remit, but this is not the case for our remit group as a whole.

The NHS also has the opportunity to target wage increases on a national or local basis. At trust level, local agreements existed prior to Agenda for Change (Bach 2004), and many of these agreements have been continued, for example, using local pay supplements to boost recruitment and retention. Agenda for Change includes provisions for the establishment of recruitment and retention premia to address labour market difficulties amongst specific occupational groups and high-cost area supplements. The NHS Review Body (2008: 57–8) has been cautious about using these provisions, but it has proposed a bonus payment (golden handcuffs) for newly qualified pharmacists that remain in the NHS for five years. The Treasury has expressed interest in making public sector wages more sensitive to local labour markets and some evidence suggests that the competitiveness of nurses' pay does vary between geographical locations (Elliott et al. 2007).

NEW WAYS OF WORKING AND NEW ROLES

The government has been critical of professional role demarcations and has emphasized new ways of working. There has been very substantial change in nursing with the establishment of new specialist career paths and the growth of new roles such as assistant practitioners. Employers have been encouraged to use fully the talents of their unregistered workforce. In general, the response of professionals is more positive when they view assistants as complementary to their own role rather than as a potential threat and substitute to their own job (Bach et al. 2007). The NHS has made concerted attempts to increase the utilization of non-registered health workers. The most high-profile cases include the enhanced role of healthcare assistants, the development of maternity support workers (NHS Employers 2007), and the use of support workers in the therapy and scientific professions (e.g. Ford 2004). It is not straightforward, however, for many of these groups to become registered professionals, and uncertainties remain as to whether support workers reduce the workload of registered professionals (Bridges and Meyer 2007; McKenna et al. 2007). Overall there is sustained interest in altering the skill-mix in the health sector.

WIDENING AND EXTENDING LABOUR SUPPLY

The NHS has promoted 'grow your own' strategies to widen the pool of potential applicants for professional roles (Malhotra 2006). Cadet schemes have been used to increase recruitment into nursing or similar training by encouraging young people with few formal academic qualifications to pursue nursing or an Allied Health Professional career. It is estimated that well-established schemes encourage about 60 per cent of cadets to progress into pre-registration nurse training, whilst many others remain as HCAs

(Norman et al. 2008). The NHS has also moved towards electronic recruitment through NHS Jobs. Although this creates difficulties for HR in dealing with the volume of applicants, it has also extended the reach of NHS recruitment. Ashford and St Peter's Hospitals NHS Trust filled six hard-to-fill radiography posts with overseas workers recruited via NHS Jobs (Suff 2006).

At least 3,000 refugees living in the UK are health professionals and these skills are an under-utilized resource because only about 20 per cent are practising their profession. The main obstacles include the protracted registration process, the high cost of clinical attachments, lack of UK experience, and unfamiliarity with the structures in the sector (King's Fund 2004). The NHS, the BMA, and the RCN have taken a variety of initiatives to publicize the problems faced by refugee nurses and doctors, to lobby for government action, and assist them in gaining registration and finding employment. The ROSE website is a key resource for refugee health professionals. The RCN was involved in establishing the Refugee Nurses Task Force and the BMA convenes the Refugee Doctor Liaison Group.

OFFSHORING

Because of the nature of healthcare as an interactive, face-to-face, service, there is little scope for offshoring direct patient care services. Some patients do seek treatment abroad (e.g. dentistry) because of the cost, or to circumvent waiting times in the UK. Several NHS trusts (e.g. The George Eliot Hospital, Nuneaton) have offshored the typing of medical notes and other secretarial work to India and South Africa, but large-scale offshoring of medical services is not an immediate prospect.

4.6 Conclusions

The health sector has a long history of employing migrant health professionals. It reflects the historical under-investment in the sector's workforce and the scope to encourage doctors in particular, but also nurses, to come to the UK to complete their *training*, and work in the NHS. Historically, migrant workers gained access to training and ultimately gained citizenship, although at a cost in terms of being channelled into the least popular specialties and locations and experiencing widespread discrimination.

After 1997, the Labour government actively sponsored a new phase of international recruitment. A combination of unprecedented increases in NHS expenditure, limited domestic supply, and short-term targets to increase the NHS workforce, led the government to encourage nurses and medical staff to come to the UK. The emphasis was on attracting *qualified* staff, with less attention placed on training, with a code of ethical recruitment and bilateral agreements developed which were intended to forestall accusations of brain drain. By easing immigration rules and establishing an infrastructure to facilitate international recruitment—alongside the government's capacity to shape NHS employment policy—the outcome was a rapid expansion of migrant health professionals employed in the UK health system. The UK case therefore demonstrates the potential in a highly regulated and centralized health system for international recruitment to make an important contribution to achieving government workforce targets.

Since 2005, the public policy and labour market context have altered and the period of rapid expansion of the NHS workforce has ended. The UK has moved towards greater self-sufficiency in its health sector workforce and the shortages that existed in recent years have receded. This altered labour market context has also enabled the UK government to argue that the UK promotes fair migration policies which do not aggravate global workforce shortages (Department of Health 2008a). This altered policy context has not been perceived as 'fair' to those migrant health professionals in the UK whose employment prospects have altered radically because of changes in UK immigration rules. An especially contentious change was the removal of permit-free training for International Medical Graduates (IMGs) who are not UK or EEA nationals. Until this change, IMGs training or working in the UK did not require a work permit, but on 7 March 2006 the government announced that permit-free status would be rescinded from 3 April, with detrimental consequences for IMG employment. In the aftermath of this controversy, attempts are being made to ensure that non-EEA doctors can undertake short-term clinical training in the UK under the auspices of the Medical Training Initiative. Similar concerns have been expressed by overseas nurses about unforeseen shifts in government policy, with many non-EEA nurses facing the prospect of removal from the UK when their current work permit ends.

Some of these difficulties stem from poor workforce planning, exemplified by the difficulties surrounding medical training posts in 2007 (see Health Committee 2008), and exacerbated by political short-termism and the sharp economic downturn. The quality of data and of NHS workforce planning expertise has been uneven and there has been little sense of ownership of workforce planning. In particular, there is little information about health professionals leaving the UK—verification data, for example, is very hard to interpret. Better monitoring and recording of the emigration of health professionals would be an important first step towards developing a better-informed understanding of migration trends in the sector. The record of workforce planning and its integration with financial planning is very poor and the NHS has responded poorly to fluctuations in supply and demand for health services. At present, the health sector context is becoming more volatile, with a wider range of providers and more market-orientated funding. There is uncertainty about the potential workforce consequences of the Next Stage Review and the capacity of the government to fund its service plans. In this context, the risk is that international recruitment can generate expectations amongst overseas health professionals about their future employment prospects that cannot be fulfilled, whilst at the same time the NHS needs to safeguard against expanding domestic capacity beyond the capacity of the health sector to absorb this domestic labour supply.

The sharp economic recession that emerged during 2007–8 is also impacting on the healthcare workforce. The NHS, as a sheltered non-market sector, is less exposed to fluctuations in global economic conditions than other industries considered in this volume. In tandem with most other OECD countries, health expenditure as a proportion of GDP has increased over the last 50 years and the size of the workforce has expanded greatly. Despite these trends, the health sector is not immune from the economic crisis and is most affected by public expenditure decisions. Underpinning the increase in migrant labour employed in the NHS since 1997 has been the unprecedented growth of the NHS budget. This period has ended and the decline in the public finances will result in a marked slowdown in the rate of growth of healthcare expenditure and may result in static or declining expenditure. Nurses and doctors, however, remain integral to the delivery of effective healthcare and for the reasons explored in Section 4.2.1, demand for healthcare and health professionals can be expected to increase. The government, however, is seeking economies which include reducing training commissions. Consequently, as the economy recovers, it can be anticipated that shortages will re-emerge and the claims of 'self-sufficiency' will look increasingly hollow.

References

Bach, S. (2004), *Employment Relations and the Health Service: The Management of Reforms* (London: Routledge).

——(2007), 'Going Global? The Regulation of Nurse Migration in the UK', *British Journal of Industrial Relations*, 45(2): 383–404.

Bach, S. Forth, J., and Givan, R. (2009), 'The Public Sector in Transition', in W. Brown, A. Bryson, J. Forth, and K. Whitfield (eds.), *The Evolution of the Modern Workplace* (Cambridge: Cambridge University Press), 307–31.

——Kessler, I., and Heron, P. (2007), 'The Consequences of Assistant Roles in the Public Services: Degradation or Empowerment?' *Human Relations*, 60(9): 1267–92.

—— —— ——(2008), 'Role Redesign in a Modernised NHS: The Case of Health Care Assistants', *Human Resource Management Journal*, 18(2): 171–87.

Ball, J., and Pike G. (2007), 'Holding On: Nurses' Employment and Morale in 2007' (London: RCN), available at <http://www.rcn.org.uk/__data/assets/pdf_file/0004/78763/003181.pdf>.

Ball, R. (2004), 'Divergent Development, Racialised Rights: Globalised Labour Markets and The Trade of Nurses: The Case of the Philippines', *Women's Studies International Forum*, 27: 119–33.

Barratt, C. (2009), *Trade Union Membership 2008* (London: Department for Business, Enterprise and Regulatory Reform (BERR)).

Batata, A. (2005), 'International Nurse Recruitment and NHS Vacancies: A Cross-Sectional Analysis', *Globalization and Health*, available at <http://www.globalizationandhealth.com/content/1/1/7>.

Bloor, K., Hendry, V., and Maynard, A. (2006), 'Do We Need More Doctors?' *Journal of the Royal Society of Medicine*, 99: 281–7.

Bridges, J., and Meyer, J. (2007), 'Policy on New Workforce Roles: A Discussion Paper', *International Journal of Nursing Studies*, 44(4): 635–44.

British Medical Association (2004), *Career Barriers in Medicine: Doctors' Experiences* (London: BMA).

——(2007), 'Memorandum by the British Medical Association', Evidence to the House of Lords Select Committee on Economic Affairs.

Buchan, J. (2003), *Here to Stay? International Nurses in the UK* (London: RCN).

——(2007), *Nurse Workforce Planning in the UK: A Report for the Royal College of Nursing.* (London: RCN), available at <http://www.rcn.org.uk/__data/assets/pdf_file/0016/107260/003203.pdf>.

——Finlayson, B., and Gough, P. (2003), *In Capital Health? Creative Solutions to London's NHS Workforce Challenges* (London: King's Fund).

——and Perfiliava, G. (2006), *Health Worker Migration in the European Region: Country Case Studies and Policy Implications* (Copenhagen: WHO).

Cabinet Office (2008), *Excellence and Fairness: Achieving World Class Public Services* (London: Cabinet Office), available at <http://www.cabinetoffice.gov.uk/media/cabinetoffice/strategy/assets/publications/world_class_public_services.pdf>.

Cangiano, A., Shutes, I., Spencer, S., and Leeson, G. (2009), *Migrant Care Workers in Ageing Societies: Research Findings in the United Kingdom* (Oxford: COMPAS).

Carpenter, M. (1988), *Working for Health: The History of COHSE* (London: Lawrence and Wishart).

Charlton, J. (2004), 'Low Take-up of Nursing Posts by New EU States', *Personnel Today*, 24 Aug.

Cole, A. (2005), 'Multinational Medicine', *Health Management* (Dec./Jan.): 18–19, available at <http://www.ihm.org.uk>.

Decker, K. (2001), 'Overseas Doctors: Past and Present', in N. Coker (ed.), *Racism in Medicine: An Agenda for Change* (London: King's Fund).

Department of Health (2000), *The NHS Plan: A Plan for Investment, a Plan for Reform*, Cm 4818-I (London: The Stationery Office).

——(2004), *Delivering HR in the NHS Plan 2004* (London: Department of Health).

——(2006), *Our Health, Our Care, Our Say: A New Direction for Community Services* (London: Department of Health).

——(2007), *The Government Response to the Health Select Committee Chapter on Workforce Planning*, Cm 7085 (London: Department of Health).

——(2008a), *Health is Global: A UK Government Strategy 2008–13* (London: Department of Health).

——(2008b), *High Quality Care for All: NHS Next Stage Review* (London: Department of Health).

——(2008c), *A High Quality Workforce: NHS Next Stage Review* (London: Department of Health).

De Ruyter, A., Kirkpatrick, I., Hoque, K., Lonsdale, C., and Malan, J. (2008), 'Agency Working and the Degradation of Public Service Employment: The Case of Nurses and Social Workers', *International Journal of Human Resource Management*, 19(3): 432–45.

Elliott, R., Ma, A., Scott, A., Bell, D., and Roberts, E. (2007), 'Geographically Differentiated Pay in the Labour Market for Nurses', *Journal of Health Economics*, 26: 190–212.

European Union (2008), *Green Paper on the European Workforce for Health* (Brussels: Commission of the European Communities).

Ford, P. (2004), 'The Role of Support Workers in the Department of Diagnostic Imaging—Service Managers' Perspectives', *Radiography*, 10: 259–67.

General Medical Council (2009), *List of Registered Medical Practitioners—Statistics* (London: GMC).

Grugulis, I. (2007), *Skills, Training and Human Resource Development: A Critical Text* (Basingstoke: Palgrave Macmillan).

Hasselhorn, H.-M., Muller, B., and Tackenberg, B. (2005), 'NEXT [Nurses Early Exit Study] Scientific Chapter', available at <http://www.next.uni-wuppertal.de/EN/index.php?articles-and-reports>.

Hatton, T. (2005), 'Explaining Trends in UK Immigration', *Journal of Population Economics*, 18: 719–40.

Health Committee (2006), *NHS Deficits: First Report of Session 2006–07, Volume 1* (London: The Stationery Office), available at <http://www.publications.parliament.uk/pa/cm200607/cmselect/cmhealth/73/73i.pdf>.

——(2007), *Workforce Planning: Fourth Chapter of Session 2006–07, Volume 1*, HC-171-1 (London: The Stationery Office).

Health Committee (2008), *Modernising Medical Careers: Third Report of Session 2007–08, Volume 1*, HC-25-1 (London: The Stationery Office).

Healthcare Commission (2008), *National NHS Staff Survey 2007: Summary of Key Findings*, available at <http://www.cqc.org.uk/_db/_documents/National_NHS_staff_survey_2007_summary_of_key_findings_200804183620.pdf>.

Hicks, S., Walling, A., Heap, D., and Livesey, D. (2005), *Public Sector Employment Trends 2005*, available at <http://www.statistics.gov.uk/pdfdir/pse1005.pdf>.

HM Treasury (2007), *Meeting the Aspirations of the British People: 2007 Pre-Budget Report and Comprehensive Spending Review*, Cm 7227, available at <http://www.hm-treasury.gov.uk/pbr_csr07_repindex.htm>.

Home Office (2007), *Accession Monitoring Report, May 2004–December 2006* (London: Home Office).

——(2008), *Bulgarian and Romanian Accession Statistics, October–December 2007* (London: Home Office/Department for Work and Pensions).

Iliffe, S. (2008), *From General Practice to Primary Care: The Industrialisation of Family Medicine* (Oxford: Oxford University Press).

Information Centre (2008a), *NHS Hospital and Community Health Services: Medical and Dental Staff England 1997–2007* (Leeds: The Information Centre for Health and Social Care).

——(2008b), *NHS Hospital and Community Health Services Staff: Non-Medical Staff England 1997–2007* (Leeds: The Information Centre for Health and Social Care).

——(2008c), *General and Personal Medical Services England 1997–2007* (Leeds: The Information Centre for Health and Social Care).

——(2008d), *Vacancies in the NHS England: 31st March 2008* (Leeds: The Information Centre for Health and Social Care).

——(2009), *General and Personal Medical Services England 1998–2008* (Leeds: The Information Centre for Health and Social Care).

Kingma, M. (2006), *Nurses on the Move: Migration and the Global Health Care Economy* (Ithaca, NY: Cornell University Press).

King's Fund (2004), *Refugee Doctors* (London: King's Fund).

Kyriakides, C., and Virdee, S. (2003), 'Migrant Labour, Racism and the British National Health Service', *Ethnicity and Health*, 8(4): 283–305.

Laing and Buisson (2007), *Laing's Healthcare Market Review* (London: Laing and Buisson).

McKenna, H., Thompson, D., and Watson, R. (2007), 'Health Care Assistants—An Oxymoron?' *International Journal of Nursing Studies*, 44: 1283–4.

Malhotra, G. (2006), *Grow Your Own: Creating the Conditions for Sustainable Workforce Development*, available at <http://www.kingsfund.org.uk/publications>.

Mejia, A., Pizurki, H., and Royston, E. (1979), *Physician and Nurse Migration: Analysis and Policy Implications* (Geneva: WHO).

Migration Advisory Committee (2008), *Skilled, Shortage, Sensible: The Recommended Shortage Occupation Lists for the UK and Scotland* (London: MAC).

——(2009a), *Skilled, Shortage, Sensible: First Review of the Recommended Shortage Occupation Lists for the UK and Scotland: Spring 2009* (London: MAC).

——(2009b), *Analysis of the Points Based System: Tier 2 and Dependants: August 2009* (London: MAC).

National Audit Office (2007), *Staying the Course: The Retention of Students in Higher Education* (London: NAO).

——(2008), *NHS Pay Modernisation: New Contracts and General Practice Services in England*, HC 307 (London: NAO).

NHS Employers (2007), *The Future of the Medical Workforce: Position Paper*, available at <http://www.nhsemployers.org/medicalworkforce>.

——(2008), *Contract Proposals for Specialty Doctors and Associate Specialists*, available at <http://www.nhsemployers.org/sas>.

NHS Pay Review Body (2008), *Twenty-Third Report 2008*, available at <http://www.ome.uk.com/NHSPRB_Reports.aspx>.

Norman, I., Normand, C., Watson, R., Draper, J., Jowell, S., and Coster, S. (2008), 'Calculating the Costs of Work-Based Training: The Case of NHS Cadet Schemes' *International Journal of Nursing Studies*, 45(9): 1310–18.

Nursing and Midwifery Council (2009), *Statistical Analysis of the Register 1 April 2007 to 31 March 2008* (London: NMC).

O'Brien, T. (2007), 'Overseas Nurses in the National Health Service: A Process of Deskilling', *Journal of Clinical Nursing*, 16(12): 2229–36.

OECD (2007), 'Immigrant Health Workers in OECD Countries in the Broader Context of Highly Skilled Migration', in *International Migration Outlook: Sopemi 2007 Edition* (Paris: OECD).

——(2009), *Total and Public Expenditure on Health*, website: <http://dx.doi.org/10.1787/537826662388>.

Oikelome, F., and Healy, G. (2007), 'Second-Class Doctors? The Impact of Professional Career Structure on the Employment Conditions of Overseas and UK-Qualified Doctors', *Human Resource Management Journal*, 17(2): 134–54.

Piore, M. (1979), *Birds of Passage: Migrant Labor and Industrial Societies* (Cambridge: Cambridge University Press).

Pollard, N., Latorre, M., and Sriskandarajah, D. (2008), *Floodgates or Turnstiles? Post-EU Enlargement Migration Flows to (and from) the UK* (London: IPPR).

Raghuram, P., and Kofman, E. (2002), 'The State, Skilled Labour Markets, and Immigration: the Case of Doctors in England', *Environment and Planning A*, 34: 2071–89.

Review Body of Doctors' and Dentists' Remuneration (2009), *Thirty Eighth Report 2009* (London: OME).

Royal College of Nursing (RCN) (2003), '"We Need Respect": Experiences of Internationally Recruited Nurses in the UK', prepared by H. Allan and J. Aggergaard, available at <http://www.rcn.org.uk/__data/assets/pdf_file/0008/78587/002061.pdf>.

——(2007), 'Memorandum by the Royal College of Nursing', Evidence to the House of Lords Select Committee on Economic Affairs (London: House of Lords).

Royal College of Nursing (RCN) (2008), *An Incomplete Plan: The UK Nursing Labour Market Review 2008* (London: RCN).

Salt, J., and Millar, J. (2006), 'International Migration in Interesting Times: The Case of the UK', *People and Place*, 14: 2.

Smith, P., Allan, H., Henry, L., Larsen, J., and Mckintosh, M. (2006), *Valuing and Recognising the Talents of a Diverse Healthcare Workforce*, available at <http://portal.surrey.ac.uk/reoh>.

Suff, R. (2006), 'A Healthy Future for Online Hiring in the NHS', *IRS Employment Review*, 856, available at <http://www.xperthr.co.uk>.

Tailby, S. (2005), 'Agency and Bank Nursing in the UK National Health Service', *Work Employment and Society*, 19(2): 369–89.

Thornley, C. (2003), 'What Future for Health Care Assistants: High Road or Low Road?' in C. Davies (ed.), *The Future Health Workforce* (Basingstoke: Palgrave Macmillan).

Unwin, L. (2001), 'Career Progression and Job Satisfaction', in N. Coker (ed.), *Racism in Medicine: An Agenda for Change* (London: King's Fund).

Wanless, D. (2002), *Securing Our Future Health: Final Report* (London: Treasury).

——Appleby, J., Harrison, A., and Patel, D. (2007), *Our Future Health Secured? A Review of NHS Funding and Performance* (London: King's Fund).

Waters, A. (2008), 'Nursing Student Attrition is Costing Taxpayers £99 Million a Year', *Nursing Standard*, 22(31): 12–15.

Winkelmann-Gleed, A., and Seeley, J. (2005), 'Strangers in a British World? Integration of International Nurses', *British Journal of Nursing*, 14: 954–61.

Witz, A., and Annandale, E. (2006), 'The Challenge of Nursing', in D. Kelleher, J. Gabe, and G. Williams, *Challenging Medicine*, 2nd edition (London: Routledge).

Workforce Review Team (2008a), *WRT Assessment of Workforce Priorities Summer 2008* (Winchester: NHS Workforce Review Team).

——(2008b), *Workforce Risk Assessment 2008–2009: Report on Stakeholder Event London, 11 December 2007* (Winchester: NHS Workforce Review Team).

World Health Organization (2006), *World Health Report 2006—Working Together for Health* (Geneva: WHO).

Zajac, M. (2004), 'Free Movement of Health Professionals: The Polish Experience', In M. McKee, L. MacLehose, and E. Nolte, *Health Policy and European Union Enlargement* (Buckingham: Open University Press).

The Utilization of Migrant Labour in Healthcare: A Commentary

Robert Elliott

The UK health service has long depended on migrants. As early as the 1950s migrants were an important part of the UK medical workforce. The chapter by Bach records that in the 1970s around a quarter of the medical workforce in the NHS had been trained abroad. By 2007, around a third of medical practitioners and over a fifth of nurses working in the NHS may have qualified abroad. Buchan and Seccombe (2004) reveal that half the increase in the number of nurses registering in the UK between 1997 and 2003 came from abroad. Migrants have clearly been an important source of supply to the medical and nursing professions in the UK over a number of decades.

Though health is a devolved power within the UK and the approach to delivering health, both in terms of the organization and funding of hospitals and the emphasis on medical and non-medical interventions to improve health has differed between the four territories (England, Scotland, Wales, and Northern Ireland), they have in common a history of dependence on health professionals trained abroad. Health professionals working in the four countries are also covered by common pay and grading structures.

Until recently the NHS workforce was subject to little detailed analysis. Only recently have labour economists turned to the analysis of specific occupational labour markets in the health sector; prior to that the focus of economists in health was on economic evaluation of drugs and medical procedures. The study of the organizations and workforce that deliver health was neglected. Accordingly, prior to the chapter in this volume there has been no detailed analysis of the migration of health professionals to the UK. This commentary discusses a key question raised by the chapter:

Why has there been this persistent demand for migrants in the UK's health sector and how has it changed recently?

Some simple explanations can be offered, and the first is the level of pay offered to some UK health professionals. It seems reasonable to conclude that pay is likely to provide a large part of the explanation of the shortage of nurses, but it is not the explanation for the shortage of locally trained medical professionals.

Research shows that the wages of nurses have been too low to attract sufficient numbers of locally trained applicants to the profession. Nickell and Quintini (2002) revealed a decline in the relative earnings of nurses as measured by their ranking in the occupational wage distribution over the period 1975 to 1999. Makepeace and Marcenaro-Gutierrez (2007), using LFS data, showed that nurses were under-paid relative to otherwise identical employees in the private sector, though the magnitude of disadvantage fell over the period 1997–2003. Both studies analyse a period before the introduction of Agenda for Change (AfC), which aimed to reform the nursing pay structure, though Bach reports AfC is not judged to have improved relative earnings.

The same study by Makepeace and Marcenaro-Gutierrez revealed that Medical Practitioners were substantially better paid than otherwise identical professionals in the private sector, and the magnitude of the advantage increased over the period 1997–2003. The new consultants' contract, introduced in 2004, substantially increased this advantage.

The wage structures for nurses and doctors provide a further part of the explanation of health professionals' migration. The pay structures of both doctors and nurses are national and allow for some, but not substantial, spatial variation in pay. As a result, the competitiveness of the pay of nurses and doctors varies between regions and this matters for nurses. Research has shown that where pay is less competitive, nursing vacancies are higher (Elliott et al. 2007 and forthcoming). Migrants have filled nursing vacancies in those regions where nurses' pay is least competitive. Migrants have also provided a supply of GPs to otherwise hard-to-fill posts in deprived inner-city areas, and they are disproportionately represented in the least attractive medical specialities.

However, the scale of medical professionals' migration cannot be explained by the existence of some hard-to-fill vacancies. Given the attractiveness of pay, we would expect a ready supply of applicants to even the least attractive specialities and locations. Rather, the shortage of medical professionals is explained by, until very recently, a persistent shortage of training places. The direct costs of training medical practitioners are high and are borne by the state. It is not difficult to understand why policy-makers might have preferred migration to increasing the number of training places; the former results in lower expenditure. Further, the number of training places was historically determined through agreement with the medical profession. Restricting training places restricts supply to the profession and is likely to exert upward pressure on wages. It would appear that a set of perverse incentives was at work. I know of no study that has sought to explain the persistent deficiency of medical training places and that has recognized the incentives that confront the medical profession and their employers, the NHS.

In the last decade, there has been substantial additional public funding for the health service in the UK and some of this has been channelled into training more doctors and nurses. The additional funding follows the recommendations of the Wanless Report and has resulted in an increase in both the number of nurses and doctors employed and the number of training places. Indeed, the increase has been on such a scale that, as Bach reports, self-sufficiency is now claimed. But in the initial phase of the expansion, the number of migrants employed increased. The lead-times involved in both increasing and delivering from the additional training places were such that migrants were the only source of additional supply.

One striking feature of migration into the NHS is that with the exception of the recent recruitment of nurses from the Philippines and Spain and some doctors from the EU to provide out-of-hours cover in some regions of the UK, migrants have come from Commonwealth countries. This pattern of migration is very different from that in other sectors and occupations. Medical and nurse training contains a large formal and general component. Medical and nursing skills are transferable and can be sold in many countries. The Commonwealth countries had very similar structures of training and qualification to those in the UK, and the institutions delivering and accrediting training had often been established along identical lines to those in the UK. Moreover, the educational systems employed English as the common language, thus the recognition and accreditation of skills was greatly simplified. Common institutional structures may also mean shared knowledge of ways of doing things and perhaps shared values. These are all important attributes for the delivery of effective healthcare, which requires skills and competencies that go beyond the 'simple' application of technical skills.

The migration of health professionals provokes controversy. It is both more widely accepted as necessary than many other types of migration, but it also raises concerns that it is unethical. It is argued that it depletes capacity in source countries, depriving some of the lowest-income countries of the skills they need to deliver even the most basic health services. But the picture is more complicated. In many countries, the health sector is publically funded, and inadequate funding of the health service means there are insufficient job opportunities for health professionals trained in such countries. Moreover, training as a health professional is viewed as providing a passport to mobility and thus there is an incentive for individuals in these countries to invest in training in numbers which exceed the requirements of the local economy. Until there is greater investment in the health service of the sending countries, it seems likely that health professionals will continue to migrate.

In the UK, the recent increase in expenditures on the health service and increased training places seem likely to have reduced substantially the short-term demand for substantial medical migration. However, implementation of the European Working Time Directive is expected to result in a cut in doctors' hours of work and a requirement for more staff if the same levels of service are to be provided. There is also a change in the composition of the General Practitioner workforce, with more women entering the workforce and a greater number choosing to work part-time. For both these reasons, the size of the medical workforce will need to expand if service levels are to be maintained, and if numbers are expanded, the NHS may once again turn to migration as the solution as tighter financial regimes lead to reductions in expenditure on training.

A significant proportion of the qualified nursing workforce does not work in the NHS, finding the attractions of working in the private sector greater than those of working in the NHS. The current recession has reduced these outside opportunities and more nurses would therefore be expected to seek NHS employment, diminishing the demand for migrants. Working in the opposite direction in the longer run is the proposal by Darzi to make nursing a graduate entry career by 2015. If this is to be realized, it will require an upward adjustment in nurses' pay to induce sufficient numbers to bear the additional costs of this training. If such an adjustment does not occur, we will again see resort to migration.

One final consideration is the permanence or otherwise of health professionals' migration. Historically, migrants to the NHS have revealed little enthusiasm for returning to the country in which they trained. This attachment of migrants to the NHS will mean the career aspirations of migrants will need to be addressed.

References

Buchan, J., and Seccombe, I. (2004), 'Fragile Future? A Review of the UK Nursing Labour Market in 2003', *Labour Market Review*, Royal College of Nursing.

Elliott, R. F., Bell, D. N. F., Scott, A., Ma, A., and Roberts, E. (2007), 'Geographically Differentiated Pay in the Labour Market for Nurses', *Journal of Health Economics*, 26: 190–212.

——Sutton, M., Ma, A., Skåtun D., Morris M., Rice N., and McConnachie, A. (2010), 'The Role of the Staff MFF in Distributing NHS Funding: Taking Account Of Differences in Local Labour Market Conditions', *Health Economics*, 19: 532–48.

Makepeace, G., and Marcenaro-Gutierrez, O. (2007), 'The Earnings of Workers Covered by Pay Review Bodies: Evidence from the Labour Force', *Office of Manpower Economics*.

Nickell, S., and Quintini, G. (2002), 'The Consequences of the Decline in Public Sector Pay in Britain: A Little Bit of Evidence', *Economic Journal*, 112, F107–F118.

5

Competing with Myths: Migrant Labour in Social Care

Jo Moriarty[1]

5.1 Introduction

Around two million people are employed in the social care sector across the UK. They provide a wide range of services within people's own homes or in communal settings such as care homes, supported housing, and sheltered housing. Their work includes offering practical help and support to older people, people with disabilities (including mental health problems and learning disabilities), and unpaid carers. They also assist children and families defined as being in 'need', for example, through family support schemes, fostering and adoption services, or in residential settings.

Over the past ten years, there has been a substantial increase in the proportion of migrant workers employed in social care, most of whom come from outside the European Economic Area (EEA) (Cangiano et al. 2009). This chapter will argue that this trend should be set within the context of increased demand for social care, created partly by demographic changes and partly by government policies aimed at tightening regulation of the sector and changing public expectations about what sort of care will be provided. These have led to the boundaries between health and social care becoming increasingly blurred. However, the supply of social care is

[1] I should like to acknowledge the support of my colleagues Jill Manthorpe, Shereen Hussein, Michelle Cornes, and Martin Stevens for commenting on this chapter and for access to unpublished data. Thanks to Skills for Care for access to the NMDS-SC. The Social Care Workforce Research Unit receives funding from the Department of Health. The views expressed in this chapter are those of the author and not necessarily those of the Department of Health.

constrained by funding arrangements which have tended to limit levels of pay in the sector, particularly among those providing direct care to people using services and their families.

In contrast with health or education, the term 'social care' is not widely understood (IPPR/PricewaterhouseCoopers 2009; Platt 2007) and this is thought to influence the status of work in the sector (Platt 2007). Assumptions that work in the sector is simply replicating unpaid care in the home doubly devalue the nature of the work because unpaid care is itself devalued, and it is assumed that the only skills that are needed are those of domestic labour (Moss et al. 2006). This is one of the myths about the sector which has led to a failure to appreciate the sorts of skills and personal qualities that are desired by employers and by people using services. More specifically, the way in which these skills and personal qualities are measured by the points-based system for migration (Secretary of State for the Home Department 2006) means that decisions about which occupations should appear on the shortage list, and excluding unskilled workers from entry, are likely to remain controversial. Major changes to—and increasing divergence in— the provision of social care across the UK, combined with likely constraints on future public expenditure, make it difficult to predict what will happen in the future. However, many of the recruitment and retention difficulties reported in social care are long standing and reflect issues beyond the availability or non-availability of migrant workers.

5.2 Overview of the Sector

Historical anomalies in funding have meant that people's support needs have been divided into 'social needs' and 'health needs', although the divisions between the two have never been clear-cut (Glasby 2007). Crucially, while health care is 'free at the point of delivery', social care is means-tested and it is funded by a complex mix of government grants to local councils, local taxation in the form of council tax, and an individual's own resources, including, controversially, their housing assets (Poole 2009). In Scotland, people in residential care receive a contribution designed to cover the costs of their personal and nursing care (Dickinson et al. 2007).

5.2.1 Key Features

In common with health care (Bach, Chapter 4 in this volume), the majority of social care continues to be publicly funded. In 2007–8, councils with social services responsibilities in England spent 20.7 billion, of which around three-quarters was spent on services for adults and a quarter on services for children (Information Centre for Health and Social Care 2009). However, the past 30 years have seen a move away from publicly provided and funded services towards services that continue to be mainly publicly *funded*, but are generally *provided* by the private and voluntary sectors (Glasby 2005; Harris 2003). The overwhelming majority of the workforce is employed in the private sector with less than a fifth of the workforce being directly employed by councils (Eborall and Griffiths 2008), and most of these are social workers rather than people who provide care on a day-to-day basis. As with hospitality (Lucas and Mansfield, Chapter 6 in this volume), although employers include large national and multinational chains, the sector is dominated by small businesses. In England alone, there are over 35,000 establishments arranging or providing adult social care, of which 58 per cent are 'micro establishments' employing between one to ten people (Eborall and Griffiths 2008). In addition, there are another 50,000 people receiving Direct Payments who receive funds from which they purchase support directly from workers themselves (Eborall and Griffiths 2008).

In practice, a distinction is often made between occupations which make up the 'direct care workforce', that is those providing support to a person or persons on a daily basis (such as care assistants or childminders), who comprise the majority of the workforce, and professional staff (social workers, occupational therapists, and other staff who have undertaken training leading to a professional qualification), whose role is primarily to act as 'gatekeepers' for other services. Some social care settings, such as care homes, may also employ nurses. However, while social workers and occupational therapists are generally employed in the public sector, with associated advantages in terms of levels of pay and other benefits, such as occupational pension schemes, it would be wrong to see this as evidence of the operation of a dual labour market (Doeringer and Piore 1971) in which there are 'good' jobs and 'bad' jobs. There is considerable overlap between roles, with most social workers having worked in care work, before beginning social work qualifying training (Balloch et al. 1999; Evaluation of Social Work Degree Qualification in England Team 2008; Harris et al. 2008). There is also an increasing number of intermediary occupations (Hudson 2007) in social care, such as 'care co-ordinators' or 'care navigators', filled by people who may have vocational rather than professional qualifications.

5.2.2 *Definitional and Data Quality Issues*

Widespread interest in social care workforce planning is comparatively recent and existing information has been 'compromised severely by the lack of high quality, systematically collected workforce intelligence' (Evans and Huxley 2009: 255). Recent years have seen considerable improvements in the quality of published data, largely attributable to the development of the National Minimum Data Set for Social Care (NMDS-SC) by the Sector Skills Council in England, Skills for Care (2007), with plans to develop similar systems in other parts of the UK. Nevertheless, as Table 5.1 (discussed below) will show, the level of detail in publicly available data varies across the four UK countries. Although social care workers in adult services in England comprise the largest single group in the workforce and more data are available on them than any other group, there are important variations across different sectors (e.g. children and older people), and across the different UK Government Office Regions (GOR).

The workforce is divided between those employed in the statutory, private, and voluntary sectors, those employed by individuals in receipt of Direct Payments and personal budgets, and those employed by people who fund the costs of their care from their own resources. The size of this latter group is unknown and they are not picked up in routinely collected social care statistics such as the SSD01 return annually completed by local councils (Information Centre for Health and Social Care 2008).

The frequency of part-time working means that information on the workforce is often presented in terms of headcounts and not as whole-time equivalents (WTE), and the number of people holding more than one job is thought to create a certain amount of double counting. For example, interviews with agency care workers revealed that some people were registered with more than one temporary employment agency and that they often combined this work with a part-time permanent post in order to increase the number of hours they worked each week (Cornes et al. 2009).

Since the pioneering work of Simon and Owen (2005), it has been increasingly common to extrapolate information on the social care workforce from general surveys of the population using the four-digit Standard Occupational Classification (SOC) codes. However, as with the financial sector (Jones, Chapter 9 in this volume), the extent to which different social care occupations fit existing SOC codes is variable as job titles change over time and new jobs are introduced. The sector itself has argued that existing codes may need updating (Skills for Care & Development 2009) to take account of new job roles. It has also suggested that the code 6115 (care assistants and home carers)

Table 5.1 Estimated size of the social care workforce in the UK

Service	Estimated numbers in each sector					
	Private sector	Voluntary sector	Local sector	NHS	Direct payments	Total
Adult services England						
Residential care	456,000	129,000	50,000	—		635,000
Domiciliary (home) care services	271,000	35,000	44,000	—	152,000	503,000
Day-care services	8,000	32,000	27,000	—		67,000
Community including NHS and the organization of care	22,000	35,000	90,000	62,000		208,000
workers not directly employed (e.g. agency, 'bank' staff, students, and volunteers)	48,000	34,000	11,000			93,000
Subtotal adult services England	805,000	265,000	221,000	62,000	152,000	1,505,000

	Private sector	Voluntary sector	Local Authority	Other statutory sector	Foster carers	Total
Children's services England						
Subtotal children's services England	36,000	32,300	60,085	2,955	37,000	168,340
Scotland						
Children and adult subtotal			56,837	—		138,000
Wales						
Children's services subtotal			26,392*			19,058
Adult services subtotal						69,715
Northern Ireland						
Children and adult subtotal			5,128	—		40,140
Estimated UK total						1,969,785

Note: *Separate figures not available.

Sources: England: Commission for Social Care Inspection (2009); Children's Workforce Development Council 2008. Scotland: Scottish Executive (2006); Scottish Government (2008). Wales: Care Council for Wales (2006); Statistics for Wales (2007). Northern Ireland: Department of Health, Social Services and Public Safety (2006); Department of Health, Social Services and Public Safety (2008). Because of rounding, individual components may not sum up to the totals provided.

is too broad including senior care workers who may have responsibilities for supervising a team of care workers as well as workers with specialist skills needed to support people with very complex needs, such as people with dementia or people receiving palliative care. Until protection of the title social worker (Care Standards Act 2000), it was possible for people without a social work qualification but working in a related field to describe themselves as social workers and there are some concerns (Commission for Social Care Inspection 2009) that where information is based on self-report, some people who do not hold a social work qualification may be recorded as social workers under the code 2442.

Finally, there is the vexed question of what constitutes a 'migrant worker'? Definitions vary according to the data source used and include the length of a person's intention to stay, his or her country of birth, or nationality (Robinson 2002). In the social care sector, the term 'migrant worker' encompasses a broad group of people including those entering the UK under the points-based system, people who have acquired leave to remain or British citizenship, refugees, students, and those allowed to move to the UK for reasons of family reunification (Cangiano et al. 2009). Indeed, this report suggested that, with the exception of senior care workers, most migrant workers in social care have entered through *non-labour* migration entry channels.

5.2.3 *Size and Composition of the Workforce*

Table 5.1 draws together recent estimates of the size of the social care sector to suggest that almost two million people work in social care in the UK. This represents between 6–7 per cent of the 29.6 million people thought to be economically active (Office for National Statistics 2009). Over 80 per cent of social care workers are women (Eborall and Griffiths 2008), so the sector's importance for women's paid employment is even greater.

The composition of the social care workforce differs substantially from that of the labour force as a whole. Occupational segregation by gender is very marked (Eborall and Griffiths 2008), although there are some signs that more men have joined the sector in recent years (Skills for Care 2008). Segregation by age and ethnicity is less apparent. Although social care is often presented as a 'greying workforce', with a high proportion of workers in their fifties (Manthorpe and Moriarty 2009), there is a reasonable spread of workers among those aged 20–50 (Skills for Care 2008). The proportion of staff from a minority ethnic group (remembering that this will also include British citizens born in the UK as well as migrant workers) varies by region and sector. In some sectors, almost a fifth of staff are from a black or minority ethnic group, but, at 10 per cent, the proportion employed by local councils is closer to that within the population as a whole (Eborall and Griffiths 2008).

Part-time working in the sector is common, particularly because many women combine paid employment with caring for family members (McFarlane 2001; Hall and Wreford 2007). Occupations in which women (especially those working part-time) predominate are over-represented among low-paid workers. In 2008, the Low Pay Commission estimated that social care accounted for around 14 per cent of all jobs in the low-paying sectors (Low Pay Commission 2008). The median hourly pay for a care worker is £6.56, although pay rates vary by region and by employer (Skills for Care 2009). In this context, it is important to note that recent migrants are disproportionately employed in the private sector rather than in local authorities or voluntary organizations, where terms and conditions are generally better (Cangiano et al. 2009).

Over the past ten years, the proportion of migrants in the social care workforce has risen substantially. In 1998, just 8 per cent of care workers were foreign born, compared with 18 per cent in 2008 (Cangiano et al. 2009). Table 5.2 presents a summary of the social care workforce in the UK drawn from the Labour Force Survey, using the four-digit SOC codes (Cangiano et al. 2009). It shows an estimate of the overall numbers within each occupation and the proportion who were born outside, and who moved to, the UK, within the past ten years. Using this definition, the proportion of migrant workers varies by occupation, but, excluding nurses—many of whom will work in the NHS—it is highest amongst childminders and care assistants and lowest amongst youth and community workers. As mentioned earlier, Table 5.2 also shows that the proportion of migrant workers in social care is higher than in the UK labour force as a whole.

5.3 Key Policy Developments

Since the Labour government came to power in 1997, 'few areas of state activity have been more visibly subjected to New Labour's modernisation agenda than the personal social services' (Scourfield 2007: 127). However, only the key developments will be reported here.

5.3.1 *Regulation of the Sector and Impact on Illegal Working*

As with health care, social care is highly regulated with different bodies assuming responsibility for differing aspects of regulation across the UK.

Table 5.2 Estimates of the UK and foreign-born workforce in selected care-related occupations in the UK using Labour Force Survey data (October–December 2008)

SOC Code	Occupation	Numbers in 1,000s			% Born outside UK
		UK born	Born outside UK	Total	
2442	Social workers	87	14	100	14
3211	Nurses	417	122	538	23
3231	Youth and community workers	111	8	118	6
3232	Housing and welfare officers	160	16	176	9
6111	Nursing auxiliaries and assistants	40	191	232	17
6115	Care assistants and home carers	595	135	730	18
6122	Childminders and related occupations	95	23	118	19
	All workers in UK labour force	25,539	3,807	29,346	13

Note: Where totals differ from the sum of the UK born/Born outside UK columns, this is because of rounding.

Source: Cangiano et al. (2009: p 58).

For this reason, although there is evidence of some illegal working in the sector (Leppard 2008), it would appear to be less prevalent than in other sectors such as construction (Chan et al., Chapter 8 in this volume) or hospitality (Lucas and Mansfield, Chapter 6 in this volume). A small-scale study (Moriarty and Manthorpe 2008) suggested that the most frequent example of illegal working was holders of student visas working beyond their permitted hours. However, an important caveat is that very little is known about the extent of unregulated employment of migrant workers in private arrangements with individuals and families. In particular, there is some evidence that migrant domestic workers are increasingly expected to provide care for children and adults (Cangiano et al. 2009; Kalayaan and Oxfam 2008).

All social care workers wishing to work in a care home, day centre, home care or recruitment agency in Wales, England, and Northern Ireland, whatever their immigration status, need to apply for a Criminal Records Bureau (CRB) check, with additional assessments for people wanting to work with children and vulnerable adults through the Independent Safeguarding Authority (ISA). Similar legislative arrangements apply in Scotland. Some employers have reported delays in receiving results from these checks, with the result that applicants have gone on to take up employment in another sector. One employer taking part in an ongoing Longitudinal Study of the Adult Social Care Workforce funded by the Department of Health joked: 'Anybody who wants to work in care should put their name down at birth!'

Depending upon the UK country in which they work, social workers also need to register with one of the four UK councils. Employers and service users are able to check to ensure that the person they employ, or who is assessing them, is on the register. Plans to extend these registers to other types of care worker exist, but the pace at which this has taken place has differed across the UK.

In addition, other bodies—the Care Quality Commission (CQC), Office for Standards in Education, Children's Services and Skills (Ofsted), Care and Social Services Inspectorate Wales (CSIW), and the Scottish Commission for the Regulation of Care (SCRC)—inspect and regulate care service providers. Employers have to ensure that minimum standards are met in terms of staffing and qualifications. However, the situation may change in England following the CQC's consultation on replacing minimum standards with 'essential common quality standards' spanning health and social care (Care Quality Commission 2009).

5.3.2 *Personalization of Care*

The UK was later in introducing 'cash for care' schemes than some other European countries (Glendinning et al. 2004; Ungerson 2003) and initially, funds received through the Independent Living Fund or Direct Payments were only designed to cover the costs of personal care, such as assistance with washing or dressing. However, in 2005, the Department of Health invited local councils in England to take part in a pilot of individual budgets, whereby resources from the different funding streams for which an individual was eligible (including local authority social care, housing-related support services, adaptations, and equipment budgets) were brought together into a single sum that could be spent according to the preferences of that person (Glendinning et al. 2008). For example, service users might choose to employ someone to accompany them to a football match rather than attend a day centre (Manthorpe et al., forthcoming). In 2007, the Department of Health (HM Government 2007) announced that individual budgets—renamed personal budgets—would be expanded to all parts of England as part of a wider policy aimed at 'transforming social care' and responding to the twin challenges of demographic pressures and increased expectations about what support should be. The implications of this for the social care workforce are as yet unknown. Personal assistants currently appear to earn more than their counterparts in care homes or home care agencies (IFF Research 2008). Although this study did not report on immigration status, it did appear that proportionally few personal assistants were from a minority ethnic group. It will clearly be important to monitor the impact of personal budgets on workforce composition.

5.3.3 *Devolution*

Devolution has led to increasing divergence in social policy between the four countries of the United Kingdom (UK) (Birrell 2009), and the results of research suggesting variation in the uptake of Direct Payments across the UK (Davey et al. 2007) exemplifies ways in which the emphases in social care policy differ somewhat across the four UK countries. However, unlike social care, immigration remains a 'reserved' power over which the three devolved administrations have little control. This has led to policy differences in which, for example, the Scottish government has argued that UK policies aimed at controlling and decreasing the supply of migrant labour are unsuited to Scotland's labour market needs, especially in the more remote rural regions where migrant workers have become a source of recruitment in the care sector (de Lima and Wright 2009).

5.4 Employer Demand

As highlighted in the introduction to this book (Anderson and Ruhs, Chapter 1 in this volume), employer demand is not static. In social care, demand is currently driven by the conundrum of controlling labour costs while simultaneously delivering a more skilled workforce able to meet the increasingly complex needs of service users, including their aspirations for autonomy and self-determination about the sort of support they receive and where.

This raises the question of who constitutes the 'employer' in social care. Is it the state as funder of much social care? Or is it the council who has contracted a provider to supply care? Is it the social care provider? Or is it family members who may be paying for and overseeing the work of the provider? Should it perhaps be the people using services that should be the ultimate arbiters of the sort of help they receive? It is useful to consider the triadic power relationship between employer, worker, and customer (Lucas 2004) in which, as in health care and hospitality, workers have a simultaneous and coterminous relationship with the customer (in this instance, service users and their families) and the organization for which they work. This relationship can create tensions, for example, in the practice of unpaid overtime (Cangiano et al. 2009; Hall and Wreford 2007), or where workers feel that employer demands conflict with their personal and professional values (Postle 2002).

5.4.1 *Controlling Labour Costs*

Demographic changes resulting from increased life expectancy (Jagger et al. 2008; Office for National Statistics 2008), and rises in the prevalence of severe disability (Bajekal et al. 2001), have created increased demand for social care. Faced with both this and central government-imposed ceilings on council tax increases, local councils have sought to ration access by raising the eligibility criteria at which people become entitled to social care (Commission for Social Care Inspection 2008). At the same time, they have sought to impose strict limits on the amount they will pay employers to provide care. Employers have complained that contracts with local councils fail to take sufficient account of inflation, rises in the National Minimum Wage, and increased statutory annual leave entitlements.

Some employers avoid these dilemmas by only providing services to people who can fully fund their own care. Currently around a third of all older people in care homes (Williams 2009) fund their own care, and the number of older people arranging and purchasing their own care is thought to be increasing (Commission for Social Care Inspection 2008). However, for many younger adults born with or acquiring a disability, this is unfeasible given that the lifetime costs of severe disabilities, such as some autistic spectrum disorders, amount to nearly £5 million per person (Knapp et al. 2007). Even those with lesser disabilities find that their employment prospects are so variable (Berthoud 2003) that the potential to use employment income as a way of fully or partially funding their care needs may be limited.

The limited number of people who can afford their own care means many employers are reliant on contracts with local councils. Faced with what are, in effect, reductions in the amount of money they receive, and given that labour costs make up around half the costs of providing home and residential care (Wanless 2006), employers nevertheless cannot reduce staffing levels because of the need to conform to minimum staffing requirements. Instead, the number of workers employed is maintained, but options to encourage retention through cost-of-living increases or performance-related pay are reduced, and levels of pay remain low overall. The Low Pay Commission (2007, 2008, 2009) has repeatedly recommended that commissioning policies should take account of the actual costs of care, as they see this as one of the factors for persistently dampening down pay levels in the sector.

5.4.2 Controlling Work Time and Worker Effort

There are two main ways in which employers have tried to use flexible working practices as a way of controlling expenditure on staffing. The first is through the use of temporary agency workers, particularly on an 'as-and-when' basis (Cornes et al. 2008; Hoque and Kirkpatrick 2008). This solution is also proposed as a way of filling vacancies, particularly when unfilled posts would result in funding being withdrawn (Cornes et al. 2009). It has been suggested that migrant workers are over-represented among agency workers (Jayaweera and Anderson 2008). The second is by only paying workers for the hours they actually work. One national survey of 502 home care workers in England found that only half were paid for their time travelling to the homes of service users and half also had to meet all their travel costs, whether in petrol or on public transport (Hall and Wreford 2007). These could easily wipe out the slightly better hourly pay rates for home care workers and workers in care homes (Skills for Care 2009). Proportionally more migrant care workers seem to be employed in home care or in nursing homes than in care homes (Cangiano et al. 2009), so they may be disproportionately affected by these practices.

As with hospitality (Lucas and Mansfield, Chapter 6 in this volume), employers also need to recruit people who are willing to work unsocial hours. Not only do communal establishments such as care homes, supported accommodation, and sheltered and extra care housing need to be staffed 24 hours a day, but home-based services increasingly need workers to provide care at the weekends and evenings. In some instances, a willingness to work nights is also needed for people requiring palliative care or to provide overnight 'crisis care' when, for example, a family carer is admitted to hospital.

5.4.3 *Skills and Training*

Historically, access to training in the social care workforce has been variable (Balloch et al. 1999), and when the Department of Health introduced the targets that 80 per cent of workers in children's homes should be trained to NVQ Level 3 (Department of Health 2002) and 50 per cent of workers in residential and home care for adults should be qualified to at least NVQ Level 2 (Department of Health 2003a, 2003b), there was some doubt that this would be achieved. Despite initial uncertainties, research suggested that regulation had a positive impact on employers' attitudes and that this model of driving up standards might be replicated in other sectors (Gospel and Thompson 2003).

Considerable investment has also taken place in social work education. In 2001, the government embarked on a series of initiatives aimed at encouraging recruitment to social work and introducing a new social work degree (Department of Health 2001a, 2001b). The first new degree programmes began in 2003–4. This has led to increases in the number of new social workers qualifying each year and broadly positive evaluations from social work educators, students, and service users (Evaluation of Social Work Degree Qualification in England Team 2008). However, debates about the extent to which basic qualifying programmes prepare social workers to work with children and families with complex needs continue (Social Work Task Force 2009). At the time of writing, the government's response to the recommendations of the Task Force is unknown.

In addition to vocational or professional qualifications, employers increasingly need workers with the specialist skills necessary to support people with complex needs, such as enduring mental health problems or severe physical disabilities. For those without vocational or professional qualifications, evidence of basic English literacy is required because of the need to be able to follow and contribute to care plans.

There is also a debate about the extent to which 'skills' can be measured through professional and vocational qualifications and what role 'experience' should play in assessing whether people are skilled (House of Commons Home Affairs Committee 2009). Employers value 'soft' skills, such as the ability to work as a member of a team, reliability, a sense of responsibility, and good interpersonal skills, but not all these qualities are easily defined, as one employer interviewed for the unpublished and ongoing Department of Health-funded Longitudinal Study of the Social Care Workforce suggested when asked what she looked for in selecting applicants:

I wish we had something that we can put [in] a statement out there and say, 'This is what you do', but it is so complex and it is not easily defined, care work. I look for their references being correct. I look for—if they haven't had experience and knowledge—a willingness to learn. I look for their manner and approach. I rely a lot on how I feel...At the end of the day it's, sort of gut instinct, you know, as they say...[Applicants] come in thinking they're going to answer questions and actually, I ask very few questions and I expect them to tell me an awful lot. It's how they talk. It's how they talk about people. I love to hear them talk about the last job that they were in because that tells me an awful lot—not about what they did but how they feel about it.

Furthermore, as interviews with employers suggest (Cangiano et al. 2009; Hussein et al., forthcoming), there are circumstances in which accounts of soft skills, such as 'having a good work ethic' or 'being flexible', can blur into descriptions of personal qualities, or even of stereotypes associated with workers of a certain ethnicity or gender. Stereotyped ideas about patterns of family care prevalent in countries outside the UK may also contribute to myths about whether workers from a particular country are more caring than others.

5.5 Characteristics of and Segmentations in Labour Supply: Who Wants to Do What?

5.5.1 *Direct Care Workforce*

Over 98,000 vacancies for care assistants and home carers were notified to job centres in England between January and June 2008 (Commission for Social Care Inspection 2009). The national vacancy rate of 3.4 per cent for employers covered by the social care Sector Skills Council compares with 2.8 per cent for all sectors and 1.9 per cent for Skills for Health (Skills for Care & Development 2009). Turnover ('churn') rates are 22 per cent (Commission for Social Care Inspection 2009).

Women's increased participation in paid employment (Rubery et al. 1999; Twomey 2002) has affected the direct care workforce profoundly. In part, this is because amongst people below the eligibility age for state retirement benefits, women are disproportionately responsible for providing unpaid care to older family members and to family members with disabilities (Buckner and Yeandle 2005; Hoskyns and Rai 2007; Office for National Statistics 2006). Additionally, there are now fewer women with limited educational qualifications seeking part-time paid employment. This group continues to be the mainstay of the social care workforce, but their numbers are no longer sufficient to meet demand (Cameron et al. 2002; Cameron and Moss 2007).

Migrant workers have played an important role in meeting some of this shortfall. As mentioned earlier, the proportion of migrant care workers rose from 8 per cent in 1998 to 18 per cent in 2008 (Cangiano et al. 2009). Their distribution is very uneven, with London and the south-east being by far the main regions of work, but the south-west, north-west, and West Midlands are other important destinations. This pattern broadly fits in with regional vacancy rates (Commission for Social Care Inspection 2009), but, strikingly, with the exception of the south-west where high levels of retirement migration among the UK population are thought to have created increased needs for care, it also accords with the distribution of black and minority ethnic people in the UK as a whole (Office for National Statistics 2002). In this sense, it accords with evidence that migrants may be attracted to areas in which communities of people from a similar background to themselves already exist. At the same time, there is also evidence that migrant social care workers are now found in areas that historically have not experienced inward international migration, such as Scotland (Workers' Education Association 2008), Wales (Evans et al. 2007), and Northern Ireland (McConkey and Thompson 2008).

The government has suggested that the need for 'unskilled' workers can be met by migration from within the European Economic Area, and in particular from the A8 (Poland, Lithuania, Estonia, Latvia, Slovenia, Slovakia, Hungary, and the Czech Republic), and possibly the A2 (Bulgaria and Romania) accession states. However, among the 'top five sending countries' for migrant care workers, just 13 per cent of those moving to Britain within the past ten years were from Poland. Instead, Zimbabwe, the Philippines, Nigeria, and India accounted for almost 40 per cent of the migrant care worker total (Cangiano et al. 2009).

The scale of international mobility among social workers to the UK has also increased substantially over the past 20 years. One account cites data from the General Social Care Council (GSCC), the regulator for social work and social care in England, showing that the number of international social workers applying to practise in the UK quadrupled over an 11-year period from 227 in 1990–1 to 1,175 in 2001–2 (Batty 2003). It is widely agreed (Evans et al. 2006; Welbourne et al. 2007; White 2006) that this expansion occurred at a time when UK recruitment of social workers was extremely difficult, accentuated by steep declines in the number of students entering social work education.

5.5.2 *Skills Gaps and Labour Shortages*

Table 5.3 uses a method developed as part of a study of international recruitment (Hussein et al. 2008), in which information on source of recruitment is used to identify people 'recruited from abroad'. It is possible to use these data to obtain a proxy measure of the migrant workforce who have been internationally recruited. This should be used with caution because of the high proportion of missing responses and because it captures only a small subset of the migrant workforce, given the much larger numbers recruited on the domestic labour market. With these caveats in mind, Table 5.3 summarizes some of the key differences between workers recruited from outside and inside the UK.

Although the strong gender imbalance in favour of women across all three occupations remains, it can be seen that proportionally more care workers recruited from abroad are men. It is not known whether men recruited from abroad are less likely to see caring as 'women's work', if they choose care work because they feel that their chances of making a successful application for employment are higher, or if employers have specifically chosen to recruit them.

Table 5.3 Comparisons between different types of workers recruited from outside and inside the UK using NMDS-SC data

Characteristics by the type of worker	Recruited from outside UK N.	Recruited from outside UK %	Recruited from within UK N.	Recruited from within UK %	Total N.
Care workers (base n = 120,411)					
Gender					
Men	638	22	14,619	13	15,257
Women	2,252	78	101,156	87	103,408
Ethnicity					
White	1,199	42	88,108	82	89,309
All other ethnic groups	1,639	58	19,449	18	21,088
Works full time					
Yes	2,267	79	48,557	44	50,824
No	591	21	60,752	56	61,163
Highest recorded qualification					
At least NVQ 2 or equivalent	61	48	26,569	72	26,906
At least NVQ 3 or equivalent	137	32	8,307	22	8,529
At least NVQ 4 or equivalent	176	20	2,066	6	2,206
Senior care workers (base n = 18,313)					
Gender					
Men	91	12	2,177	13	2,268
Women	675	88	15,168	87	15,843
Ethnicity					
White	148	20	14,347	86	14,495
All other ethnic groups	602	80	2,290	14	2,892
Works full time					
Yes	730	95	11,362	66	12,092
No	42	5	5,760	37	5,802
Highest recorded qualification					
At least NVQ 2 or equivalent	84	19	4,919	43	4,998
At least NVQ 3 or equivalent	288	65	5,715	50	6,003
At least NVQ 4 or equivalent	68	16	863	8	931
Registered nurse (n = 9,664)					
Gender					
Men	99	11	996	12	1,095
Women	757	89	1,669	89	8,426
Ethnicity					
White	67	8	4,563	57	4,630
All other ethnic groups	763	92	3,414	43	4,177
Works full time					
Yes	752	89	4,023	50	4,775
No	91	11	4,046	50	4,137
Highest recorded qualification Registered nurses will hold minimally either a degree or diploma level qualification					
Base n	4,568		143,820		148,388

Source: Secondary analysis of NMDS-SC (April 2009 dataset).

Consistent with the evidence on sending countries presented earlier, Table 5.3 also shows that people from black and ethnic minority groups are over-represented among workers recruited from abroad, supporting the suggestion that comparatively few people from inside the European Economic Area (EEA) have chosen to work in social care compared with migrants from outside the EEA.

Importantly, given the earlier discussion on the preponderance of part-time working in the sector in the context of employers' needs to run a 24-hour service, Table 5.3 shows that care workers, senior care workers, and nurses recruited from outside the UK were all more likely to work full-time, reflecting the comments made by employers and care managers in a study of the impact of work permit restrictions (Moriarty and Manthorpe 2008) that one of their difficulties with recruitment was the number of staff needed to run a round-the-clock service.

Table 5.3 shows that proportionally more care workers and senior care workers recruited outside the UK held levels of qualifications at NVQ level 3 or above. However, interviews with employers (Moriarty and Manthorpe 2008) suggested that whilst employers recognized that migrants were more likely to hold professional or vocational qualifications, they also felt that there were areas in which some migrant workers were less skilled, for example in their understanding of the importance of promoting autonomy or enabling independence among service users. They were also felt to lack specific knowledge of dementia care. Poor command of English (Smith et al. 2008) has also been mentioned as an issue causing concern among employers and people using services and their families. These skills were usually acquired 'on the job' and employers sometimes welcomed employees whose right to work in the UK was restricted, as opposed to other groups of workers, because they were thought to be more likely to remain with them, thus recouping employers' investment in their training (Moriarty and Manthorpe 2008).

5.5.3 *Attractions of Working in the Sector for Migrant Workers*

One criticism that could be made of the established literature on labour migration is that it fails to take account of non-economic motivations for migrating. This highlights the importance of the growing literature, based largely on qualitative studies, looking at the perspectives of migrant workers themselves. It describes their resourcefulness, but also the difficulties that they face in terms of long working hours, poor remuneration, and racism within their workplaces (Cangiano et al. 2009; Cuban 2008; Datta et al. 2006; McGregor 2007). At the same time, it indicates some of the attractions of care work, and in particular the bonds that it creates in terms of developing social capital and social support (Cuban 2008; Giusta and Kambhampati 2006).

The increases in temporary or 'contingent' working (Carey 2007; Conley 2002; Hoque and Kirkpatrick 2008) have meant that that in some circumstances workers choose to forgo benefits such as an occupational pension, sickness, and holiday leave, in favour of a higher hourly rate of pay. For some migrant workers, this type of working may be viewed as preferable to permanent contracts because, for example, they feel they are more able to take time off should they wish to go home for a holiday, or because they are students for whom it fits in more conveniently with their studies (Cornes et al. 2009).

5.6 Increasing the Potential Pools of Labour

Various alternatives to immigration have been explored as a way of dealing with social care labour shortages. They range from national to local initiatives, all sharing the aim of widening the 'workforce pool' by employing people who have not traditionally been recruited to the sector.

In 2001, the Department of Health launched the first national recruitment campaign for social work and social care (Department of Health 2001b) which involved setting up new websites and a telephone helpline for people considering a career in social care. Unfortunately, the funding has not been available to identify how many people contacting the helpline or website go on to take up a post in social care or social work.

Making the sector more attractive to younger workers has been achieved through removing the limit on people being able to achieve a social work qualification before the age of 22. This has resulted in an increase in younger applicants for social work qualifying programmes and they are less likely to withdraw before achieving a qualification (Evaluation of Social Work Degree Qualification in England Team 2008). For those not considering a career in social work but who want to work in social care, Skills for Care South West (n.d.) has developed the Care Ambassador initiative based on using experienced young social care professionals to act as role models to encourage young people to consider careers in social care.

There are also initiatives directed at encouraging social care workers to achieve a social work qualification (Harris et al. 2008), or people from other occupational backgrounds to change career (Scottish Institute for Excellence in Social Work Education 2006). The Open University has become a substantial provider of social work and social care courses, with a focus on helping people to acquire, or 'top up' existing professional qualifications.

Recognizing that the majority of social care employers are small and medium enterprises that may lack the resources to acquire specialist support for recruitment and retention, the Social Care Institute for Excellence (n.d.) has set up a website aimed at informing employers about best practice in issues such as recruitment and retention. It has also developed a series of e-learning resources which can be used for group or individual learning.

Some but not all of these attempts to increase the pool of labour in social care are integrated with other wider public policy goals, such as efforts to reduce the impact of long-term unemployment upon young people's life chances. The 2009 Budget (HM Treasury 2009) announced the introduction of the Care First scheme, whereby employers will receive a 1,500 subsidy to take on up to 50,000 social care trainees aged between 18 and 24 who have been out of work for 12 months, giving them the skills and experience they need for a permanent career in the sector.

Current funding arrangements mean that social care employers are unlikely to be able to raise wage levels substantially. However, it has been suggested that more attention could be paid to finding other ways of improving employment (Eborall and Griffiths 2008). For example, Leicester Council is reported to have had more success in retaining home care staff by enabling them to be classified as essential car users, giving them access to a car leasing scheme and parking permits (Improvement and Development Agency for Local Government 2007).

Some attempts have been made to respond to labour costs through the greater use of assistive technology and telecare. Assistive technology has been shown both to reduce care costs and to be acceptable to older people (McCreadie and Tinker 2005). However, the study on which this work was based and the cross-national ENABLE project (Löfqvist et al. 2005) has shown that the 'high level' assistive technology needed to impact on labour costs is only currently available to a minority of older people in the UK, and that there are gaps in the provision of even low-level forms of assistance.

Although most of these schemes remain un-evaluated, the potential for telecare is possibly greatest but will also require greatest investment. Improving terms and conditions in the form of car or travel allowances or developing 'grow your own schemes' are likely to produce the greatest benefits in the short term, given that these workers are already in post and will not require basic induction or training. National recruitment initiatives are more expensive than local advertising, but may achieve more in helping to change public attitudes.

5.7 Future Trends and the Impact of the Economic Downturn

Demographic changes have been an important driver of demand for social care labour. Wittenberg et al. (2004) have estimated that to keep pace with demographic pressures over the next 50 years in the UK, residential and nursing home places in the UK need to expand by around 150 per cent, and numbers of hours of home care by around 140 per cent. Work also undertaken by the Personal Social Service Research Unit on behalf of Skills for Care (Eborall and Griffiths 2008) has estimated that by 2025 the size of the workforce required will be between 2–2.5 million workers. This range was based on three different assumptions: the 'base case' (broadly the status quo), 'maximizing choice' (an increase in Direct Payments for all those who wish to receive them), and 'reining in' (reduced access to care and greater use of family care and self-funding).

Government policy objectives have also played a part in increasing demand. Initiatives such as Sure Start have led to an expansion in the children's social care workforce. It is not known how future plans for personalization in social care (HM Government 2007) will alter the workforce, either in terms of its size or in the jobs that they do. While the policy is likely to result in increases in the number of people holding personal budgets, it is important to recognize that this is unlikely to produce substantial reductions in the costs of services (Glendinning et al. 2008).

A series of reports (Commission for Social Care Inspection 2008; Davies 2007; Wanless 2006) has emphasized the unfairness of the current funding system, particularly for older people. Employers in the sector have argued that it has contributed to labour shortages by placing strict limits on the amounts they receive from councils, thus impacting upon the terms and conditions of work that they are able to offer their staff. Although the government (Secretary of State for Health 2009) has issued a green paper outlining possible options for the future funding of adult social care in England, at this stage in the electoral cycle, it is unclear whether any of these will be enacted in legislation.

A key factor influencing the social care sector in the future will be the impact of the economic downturn. It is not clear as yet that job losses in other sectors have led to an increase in applicants seeking work in social care. In the context that some workers from EU states may return home, existing restrictions on the employment of migrant labour from outside the EEA have received criticism (Local Government Association 2009). Early unpublished results from interviews with employers undertaken as part of the Department of Health-funded Longitudinal Study of the Adult Social Care Workforce present a mixed picture, with some employers saying they have seen an increase in applicants, but no increase in the number of suitable applicants, and others arguing that there has not yet been an impact.

What is more certain is that changes in the level of public expenditure will have an impact on social care. Although it has been claimed that the recession offers an opportunity to create new jobs in care work (Mulgan 2009), the majority of commentators argue that cuts in funding are inevitable (Bundred 2009; Chote 2009; Chote et al. 2009). Very few people can afford to fund their own care. The majority of these are older people who are likely to have had their incomes affected by reductions in interest rates. A survey of carers suggested that they had also been affected by the recession and would not be able to afford to subsidize the person for whom they cared (Carers UK 2008). Decisions about public expenditure are likely to be strongly influenced by public opinion and the results of one poll (BBC News 2009) found that just 2 per cent of the public thought expenditure on social care was a priority. There is a risk that existing budgets will be cut to avoid reducing expenditure in other areas. It has been reported that some councils have held reverse e-auctions to run home care services (*Panorama* 2009) and concerns have been expressed that 'corners' might be cut to reduce care costs (Rose 2009). Were these trends to become more widespread, they would be likely to have a considerable impact both on the quality of services and on the working conditions of those who provide them.

References

Bajekal, M., Primatesta, P., and Prior, G. (eds.) (2001), *Health Survey for England 2001: Disability* (London: The Stationery Office), <http://www.archive2.official-documents.co.uk/document/deps/doh/survey01/disa/disa01.htm>, accessed 29 June 2009.

Balloch, S., McLean, J., and Fisher, M. (eds.) (1999), *Social Services: Working under Pressure* (Bristol: Policy Press).

Batty, D. (2003), 'UK Draining Zimbabwe of Social Workers', *Guardian*, 19 Feb.

BBC News (2009), 'Tax and Spending Poll', available at <http://news.bbc.co.uk/1/hi/programmes/the_westminster_hour/8007252.stm>.

Berthoud, R. (2003), 'Disabled People and Jobs', *Benefits*, 11(3): 169–74.

Birrell, D. (2009), *The Impact of Devolution on Social Policy* (Bristol: Policy Press).

Buckner, L., and Yeandle, S. (2005), *We Care—Do You?* (Sheffield: ACE/Carers UK/Sheffield Hallam University).

Bundred, S. (2009), 'Our Public Debt is Hitting Armageddon Levels', *The Times*, 27 Feb.

Cameron, C., Mooney, A., and Moss, P. (2002), 'The Child Care Workforce: Current Conditions and Future Directions', *Critical Social Policy*, 22(4): 572–95.

——and Moss, P. (2007), *Care Work in Europe: Current Understandings and Future Directions* (Abingdon: Routledge).

Cangiano, A., Shutes, I., Spencer, S., and Leeson, G. (2009), *Migrant Care Workers in Ageing Societies: Research Findings in the United Kingdom* (Oxford: COMPAS).

Care Council for Wales (2006), *The Social Care Workforce in Wales—Themes and Trends* (Cardiff: Care Council for Wales).

Care Quality Commission (2009), *Press Release 1 June 2009: CQC Seeks Feedback on Guidance for Registration of all Health and Adult Social Care Services* (London: Care Quality Commission).

Care Standards Act (2000), Chapter 14 (London: The Stationery Office).

Carers UK (2008), *Carers in Crisis: A Survey of Carers' Finances in 2008* (London: Carers UK).

Carey, M. (2007), 'White-Collar Proletariat? Braverman, The Deskilling/Upskilling of Social Work and the Paradoxical Life of the Agency Care Manager', *Journal of Social Work*, 7(1): 93–114.

Children's Workforce Development Council (2008), *The State of the Children's Social Care Workforce: A Statistical Overview of the Workforce Providing Children's and Families Social Care in England* (Leeds: Children's Workforce Development Council).

——(2009), *Early Years Professional Status* (Leeds: Children's Workforce Development Council), available at <http://www.cwdcouncil.org.uk/eyps>, accessed 30 July 2009.

Chote, R. (2009), 'Public Spending: Outlook Grim—With the Threat of Darker Clouds', *The Times*, 19 Mar.

——Emmerson, C., and Tetlow, G. (2009), *Budget 2009: Tightening the Squeeze? IFS Briefing Note BN83* (London: Institute for Fiscal Studies).

Commission for Social Care Inspection (2008), *Cutting the Cake Fairly: CSCI Review of Eligibility Criteria for Social Care* (London: Commission for Social Care Inspection).

——(2009), *The State of Social Care in England 2007–2008* (London: Commission for Social Care Inspection).

Conley, H. (2002), 'A State of Insecurity: Temporary Work in the Public Services', *Work, Employment & Society*, 16(4): 725–37.

Cornes, M., Moriarty, J., Blendi-Mahota, S., Chittleburgh, T., Hussein, S., and Manthorpe, J. (2008), *Working for the Agency: The Role and Significance of Temporary Employment Agencies in the Social Care Workforce: Interim Report* (London: King's College London, Social Care Workforce Research Unit).

—— —— —— —— —— ——(2009), *Working for the Agency: The Role and Significance of Temporary Employment Agencies in the Adult Social Care Workforce: Final Report* (London: King's College London, Social Care Workforce Research Unit).

Cuban, S. (2008), 'Home/work: The Roles of Education, Literacy, and Learning in the Networks and Mobility of Professional Women Migrant Carers in Cumbria', *Ethnography and Education*, 3(1): 81–96.

Datta, K., McIlwaine, C., Evans, Y., Herbert, J., May, J., and Wills, J. (2006), *Work, Care and Life among Low-Paid Migrant Workers in London: Towards a Migrant Ethic of Care* (London: Queen Mary, University of London).

Davey, V., Fernández, J., Knapp, M., Vick, N., Jolly, D., Swift, P., Tobin, R., Kendall, J., Ferrie, J., Pearson, C., Mercer, G., and Priestley, M. (2007), *Direct Payments: A National Survey of Direct Payments Policy and Practice* (London: Personal Social Services Research Unit).

Davies, B. (2007), 'Public Spending Levels for Social Care of Older People: Why We Must Call in the Debt', *Policy & Politics*, 35(4): 719–26.

de Lima, P., and Wright, S. (2009), 'Welcoming Migrants? Migrant Labour in Rural Scotland', *Social Policy and Society*, 8(3): 391–404.

Department of Health (2001a), *Press Release 2001/0154: Radical Reforms to Social Work Training to Raise Social Care Standards* (London: Department of Health).

—— (2001b), *Press Release 2001/0486: Government Launches first ever Social Worker Recruitment Drive* (London: Department of Health).

—— (2002), *Children's Homes: National Minimum Standards, Children's Homes Regulations* (London: The Stationery Office).

—— (2003a), *Care Homes for Older People: National Minimum Standards*, 3rd edn. (London: The Stationery Office).

—— (2003b), *Domiciliary Care: National Minimum Standards* (London: Department of Health).

Department of Health, Social Services and Public Safety (2006), *Personal Social Services: Development and Training Strategy 2006–2016* (Belfast: Department of Health, Social Services and Public Safety).

—— (2008), *Northern Ireland Health and Social Services Workforce Census—March 2007* (Belfast: Department of Health, Social Services and Public Safety).

Dickinson, H., Glasby, J., Forder, J., and Beesley, L. (2007), 'Free Personal Care in Scotland: A Narrative Review', *British Journal of Social Work*, 37(3): 459–74.

Doeringer, P. B., and Piore, M. J. (1971), *Internal Labor Markets and Manpower Analysis* (Lexington, Mass.: Heath and Company).

Eborall, C., and Griffiths, D. (2008), *The State of the Adult Social Care Workforce in England 2008: The Third Report of Skills for Care's Skills Research and Intelligence Unit* (Leeds: Skills for Care).

Evaluation of Social Work Degree Qualification in England Team (2008), *Evaluation of the New Social Work Degree Qualification in England: Volume 1: Findings* (London: Social Care Workforce Research Unit, King's College London).

Evans, S., Baker C., Huxley, P., White, J., and Philpin, S. (2007), *International Recruitment of Social Care Workers and Social Workers in Wales: Final Report* (Swansea: Centre for Social Carework Research, Swansea University).

—— and Huxley, P. (2009), 'Factors Associated with the Recruitment and Retention of Social Workers in Wales: Employer and Employee Perspectives', *Health and Social Care in the Community*, 17(3): 254–66.

—— —— and Munroe, M. (2006), 'International Recruitment of Social Care Workers and Social Workers: Illustrations from the UK', *Hong Kong Journal of Social Work*, 40(1–2): 93–110.

Giusta, M. D., and Kambhampati, U. (2006), 'Women Migrant Workers in the UK: Social Capital, Well-Being and Integration', *Journal of International Development*, 18(6): 819–33.

Glasby, J. (2005), 'The Future of Adult Social Care: Lessons from Previous Reforms', *Research Policy and Planning*, 23(2): 62–70.

—— (2007), *Understanding Health and Social Care* (Bristol: Policy Press).

Glendinning, C., Challis, D., Fernández, J., Jacobs, S., Jones, K., Knapp, M., Manthorpe, J., Moran, N., Netten, A., Stevens, M., and Wilberforce, M. (2008), *Evaluation of the Individual Budgets Pilot Programme: Final Report* (York: Social Policy Research Unit).

—— Davies, B., Pickard, L., and Comas-Herrera, A. (2004), *Funding Long-Term Care for Older People: Lessons from Other Countries* (York: Joseph Rowntree Foundation).

Gospel, H., and Thompson, M. (2003), *The Role and Impact of the Statutory Framework for Training in the Social Care Sector: Research Report 495* (Nottingham: DfES Publications).

Hall, L., and Wreford, S. (2007), *National Survey of Care Workers: Final report. JN 142079* (London: TNS UK).

Hansard (2009), *Written Ministerial Answers, Parliamentary Secretary in the Cabinet Office and Minister for the Third Sector, 27 April 2009: Column 1087W* (London: Hansard).

Harris, J. (2003), *The Social Work Business* (London: Routledge).

—— Manthorpe, J., and Hussein, S. (2008), *What Works in 'Grow Your Own' Initiatives for Social Work? Research Report* (London: General Social Care Council).

HM Government (2007), *Putting People First: A Shared Vision and Commitment to the Transformation of Adult Social Care* (London: Department of Health).

HM Treasury (2009), *Budget 2009: Building Britain's Future* (London: HM Treasury).

Hoque, K., and Kirkpatrick, I. (2008), 'Making the Core Contingent: Professional Agency Work and its Consequences in UK Social Services', *Public Administration*, 86(2): 331–44.

Hoskyns, C., and Rai, S. M. (2007), 'Recasting the Global Political Economy: Counting Women's Unpaid Work', *New Political Economy*, 12(3): 297–317.

House of Commons Home Affairs Committee (2009), *Managing Migration: The Points Based System: Thirteenth Report of Session 2008–09, Volume I, HC 217-I* (London: The Stationery Office).

Hudson, K. (2007), 'The New Labor Market Segmentation: Labor Market Dualism in the New Economy', *Social Science Research*, 36(1): 286–312.

Hussein, S., Manthorpe, J., and Stevens, M. (2008), *International Social Care Workers: Initial Outcomes, Workforce Experiences, and Future Expectations* (London: Social Care Workforce Research Unit, King's College London).

Hussein, S., Manthorpe, J., and Stevens, M. (forthcoming), 'People in Places: A Qualitative Exploration of Recruitment Agencies' Perspectives on the Employment of International Social Workers in the UK', *British Journal of Social Work*.

—— —— —— (2009), *International Social Workers in England: Their Characteristics and Country of Qualification* (London: King's College London, Social Care Workforce Research Unit).

IFF Research (2008), *Research Report: Employment Aspects and Workforce Implications of Direct Payments* (London: IFF Research).

Improvement and Development Agency for Local Government (2007), *Leicester City Council* (London: Improvement and Development Agency for Local Government (IDeA)), available at <http://www.idea.gov.uk/idk/core/page.do?pageId=6588963>, accessed 30 July 2009.

Information Centre for Health and Social Care (2008), *Personal Social Services Staff of Social Services Departments at 30 September 2007, England* (London: Information Centre for Health and Social Care).

—— (2009), *Personal Social Services Expenditure and Unit Costs England, 2007–08* (London: Information Centre for Health and Social Care).

IPPR/PricewaterhouseCoopers (2009), *Expectations & Aspirations: Public Attitudes towards Social Care* (London: Institute for Public Policy Research).

Jagger, C., Gillies, C., Moscone, F., Cambois, E., Van Oyen, H., Nusselder, W., and Robine, J. (2008), 'Inequalities in Healthy Life Years in the 25 Countries of the European Union in 2005: A Cross-National Meta-regression Analysis' *Lancet*, 372 (9656): 2124–31.

Jayaweera, H., and Anderson, B. (2008), *Migrant Workers and Vulnerable Employment: A Review of Existing Data: Report For TUC Commission on Vulnerable Employment*, (Oxford: COMPAS).

Kalayaan and Oxfam (2008), *The New Bonded Labour? The Impact of Proposed Changes to the UK Immigration System on Migrant Domestic Workers* (London: Kalayaan).

Knapp, M., Romeo, R., and Beecham, J. (2007), *Economic Consequences of Autism in the UK Report* (London: Foundation for People with Learning Disabilities).

Leppard, D. (2008), 'Home Office in Illegal Immigrants Cover-Up', *The Sunday Times*, 30 Mar.

Local Government Association (2009), *The Impact of the Recession on Migrant Labour* (London: Local Government Association).

Löfqvist, C., Nygren, C., Széman, Z., and Iwarsson, S. (2005), 'Assistive Devices among Very Old People in Five European Countries', *Scandinavian Journal of Occupational Therapy*, 12(4): 181–92.

Low Pay Commission (2007), *National Minimum Wage: Low Pay Commission Report 2007, Cm 7056* (London: Low Pay Commission).

—— (2008), *National Minimum Wage: Low Pay Commission Report 2008, Cm 7333* (Norwich: The Stationery Office).

—— (2009), *National Minimum Wage: Low Pay Commission Report 2009* (Norwich: The Stationery Office).

Lucas, R. (2004), *Employment Relations in the Hospitality and Tourism Industries* (London: Routledge).

McConkey, R., and Thompson, S. (2008), *New Horizons: Migrant Workers and Services for People with a Learning Disability in Northern Ireland* (Belfast: ARC).

McCreadie, C., and Tinker, A. (2005), 'The Acceptability of Assistive Technology to Older People', *Ageing & Society*, 25(1): 91–110.

McFarlane, L. (2001), 'Managing a Dual Role: Working Carers in Social Services', *Journal of Integrated Care*, 9(4): 26–31.

McGregor, J. (2007), '"Joining the BBC (British Bottom Cleaners)": Zimbabwean Migrants and the UK Care Industry', *Journal of Ethnic and Migration Studies*, 33 (5): 801–24.

Manthorpe, J., and Moriarty, J. (2009), 'Older Workers in Social Care: Undervalued and Overlooked?', in A. Chiva and J. Manthorpe (eds.), *Older Workers in Europe* (Oxford: Oxford University Press).

——Stevens, M., Rapaport, J., Jacobs, S., Challis, D., Wilberforce, M., Netten, A., Knapp, M., and Glendinning, C. (forthcoming), 'Gearing up for Personalisation: Training Activities Commissioned in the English Pilot Individual Budgets Sites 2006–2008', *Social Work Education: The International Journal*, available at <http://dx.doi.org/10.1080/02615470902913175>.

Moriarty, J., and Manthorpe, J. (2008), *An Audit of the Impact of Work Permit Restrictions on the Adult Social Care Workforce* (London: King's College London, Social Care Workforce Research Unit).

Moss, P., Boddy, J., and Cameron, C. (2006), 'Care Work—Present and Future: Introduction', in J. Boddy, C. Cameron, and P. Moss (eds.), *Care Work—Present and Future* (London: Routledge).

Mulgan, G. (2009), 'A Silent Voice: Third Sector can Limit Damage of Recession', Joe Public blog (the *Guardian*), 11 Feb., available at <http://www.guardian.co.uk/society/joepublic/2009/feb/11/voluntary-sector-recession>, accessed 23 Feb. 2010.

Office for National Statistics (2002), *Social Focus in Brief: Ethnicity* (London: Office for National Statistics).

—— (2006), 'Caring & Carers', available at <http://www.statistics.gov.uk/cci/nugget.asp?id=1336>, accessed 19 May 2009.

—— (2008), *News Release: Life Expectancy at Birth is Longest in the South of England* (London: Office for National Statistics).

—— (2009), *Social Trends 39* (Basingstoke: Palgrave Macmillan).

Panorama (2009), 'Britain's Homecare Scandal' (BBC1, television programme, UK), 9 Apr.

Perry, R. W. (2004), 'The Impact of Criminal Conviction Disclosure on the Self-Reported Offending Profile of Social Work Students', *British Journal of Social Work*, 34(7): 997–1008.

Platt, D. (2007), *The Status of Social Care—A Review 2007* (London: Department of Health).

Poole, T. (2009), *Funding Adult Social Care in England: King's Fund Briefing* (London: King's Fund).

Postle, K. (2002). 'Working "Between the Idea and the Reality": Ambiguities and Tensions in Care Managers' Work', *British Journal of Social Work*, 32(3): 335–51.

REC Industry Research Unit (2009), *Nursing & Social Care: REC Sector Profile* (London: Recruitment & Employment Confederation).

Robinson, V. (2002), 'Migrant Workers in the UK', *Labour Market Trends*, 110(9): 467–76.

Rose, D. (2009), 'Care Homes Come under Pressure to Cut Costs', *The Times*, 1 Apr.

Rubery, J., Smith, M., and Fagan, C. (1999), *Women's Employment in Europe—Trends and Prospects* (London: Routledge).

Scottish Executive (2006), *Scotland's Social Care Labour Market: 2nd Report of National Workforce Group* (Edinburgh: Scottish Executive).

Scottish Government (2008), *Staff of Scottish Local Authority Social Work Services, 2007*, available at <http://www.scotland.gov.uk/Publications/2008/06/25090222/3>, accessed 24 Apr. 2009 (Scottish Executive, Edinburgh).

Scottish Institute for Excellence in Social Work Education (2006), *Hooks and Anchors: Recruitment and Retention for the Scottish Social Services* (Dundee: Scottish Institute for Excellence in Social Work Education).

Scourfield, P. (2007), 'Social Care and the Modern Citizen: Client, Consumer, Service User, Manager and Entrepreneur', *British Journal of Social Work*, 37(1): 107–22.

Secretary of State for Health (2009), *Shaping the Future of Care Together, Cm 7673* (Norwich: The Stationery Office).

Secretary of State for the Home Department (2006), *A Points-Based System: Making Migration Work for Britain, Cm 6741* (Norwich: The Stationery Office).

Simon, A., and Owen, C. (2005), 'Using the Labour Force Survey to Map the Care Workforce', *Labour Market Trends*, 113(5): 201–8.

Skills for Care (2007), *NMDS-SC Briefing: Issue 1 Overview—An Oasis in the Data Desert* (Leeds: Skills for Care).

—— (2008), *NMDS-SC Briefing: Issue 5 Age & Gender* (Leeds: Skills for Care).

—— (2009), *NMDS-SC Briefing: Issue 8 Pay* (Leeds: Skills for Care).

Skills for Care & Development (2009), *Shortage Report on Social Care Workers for the Migration Advisory Committee* (Leeds: Skills for Care).

Skills for Care South West (n.d.), 'About Care Ambassadors', available at <http://www.carecareers-southwest.info/care-ambassadors>, accessed 30 July 2009.

Smith, K., Milburn, M., and Mackenzie, L. (2008), 'Poor Command of English Language: A Problem in Care Homes? If So What Can be Done?' *Journal of Dementia Care*, 16(6): 37–9.

Social Care Institute for Excellence (n.d.), SCIE's People Management website: <http://www.scie-peoplemanagement.org.uk/>, accessed 30 July 2009.

Social Work Task Force (2009), *Facing up to the Task: The Interim Report of the Social Work Task Force* (London: Department for Children, Schools and Families).

Statistics for Wales (2007), *Local Authority Social Services—Staff Numbers March 2008* (Cardiff: Local Government Data Unit—Wales).

Twomey, B. (2002), 'Women in the Labour Market: Results from the Spring 2001 Labour Force Survey. A Description of the Patterns of Women's Participation in the Labour Market in Spring 2001', *Labour Market Trends*, 110(3): 109–27.

Ungerson, C. (2003), 'Commodified Care Work in European Labour Markets', *European Societies*, 5(4): 377–96.

Wanless, D. (2006), *Securing Good Care for Older People: Taking a Long-Term View* (London: King's Fund).

Welbourne, P., Harrison, G., and Ford, D. (2007), 'Social Work in the UK and the Global Labour Market: Recruitment, Practice and Ethical Considerations', *International Social Work*, 50(1): 27–40.

White, R. (2006), 'Opportunities and Challenges for Social Workers Crossing Borders', *International Social Work*, 49(5): 629–40.

Williams, C. (2009), 'A Fair Deal for Self Funders', *Community Care*, 29 Apr.

Wittenberg, R., Comas-Herrera, A., Pickard, L., and Hancock, R. (2004), *Future Demand for Long-Term Care in the UK* (York: Joseph Rowntree Foundation).

Workers' Education Association (2008), *Workforce Development and Migrant Workers Research Project* (Paisley: Scottish Social Services Learning Network West).

Migrant Labour in Social Care: A Commentary

Alessio Cangiano

Moriarty's chapter provides a comprehensive and analytical overview of the migrant workforce in social care. It clearly shows how reliance on migrant workers has become a key feature of the care sector, which faces significant difficulties in the recruitment and retention of its workforce. As she points out, low wages, unsocial working hours, temporariness of work, lack of career opportunities, and low status are the main factors responsible for a mismatch between demand for and domestic supply of care workers.

This short commentary complements this picture by shedding more light on the legal entry routes of migrant care workers and their pathways into the social care labour market, discussing the way in which the UK immigration system affects recruitment and retention. The following observations refer to the direct care workforce only—not to social workers, managers, and other workers in professional care roles—and are based on evidence for the UK collected by an international research project on migrants working in care for older people (Cangiano et al. 2009).

The employment of migrant workers in social care is set within the context of restrictive labour immigration channels for non-EU nationals with low formal education and qualifications and restricted access to the labour market for foreign nationals subject to immigration control.[1] Recent changes to immigration policies have also had important implications for the opportunities of migrants to work in the care sector. The current

---

[1] The long-established foreign-born labour force—mostly people with indefinite leave to remain or British nationals—enjoys full employment and welfare rights.

negative economic climate has put even more pressure on the government to cut inflows of new migrants.

After EU enlargement in 2004, nationals of the eight new member states in Central and Eastern Europe (A8 nationals) were allowed to enter the UK and seek employment. In contrast, the 2007 EU enlargement to Bulgaria and Romania meant only restricted access to the UK labour market. There are currently limited opportunities for non-EU workers to obtain a work permit in social care—only senior care workers fulfilling specific requirements are entitled to a visa, formerly under the work permit system and currently through Tier 2 of the new points system (MAC 2008, 2009). Among migrants who enter the UK through non-labour market channels, recognized refugees (not asylum seekers) and spouses enjoy unrestricted access to the labour market, while people on student visas, working holiday maker visas, and other less common immigration statuses can also take up work subject to varying degrees of restriction.

Comprehensive data on the inflows of migrant workers and their immigration status on entry are not available. Labour Force Survey (LFS) data show that migrant care workers who entered the UK in the past decade and took up jobs in the care sector came from both within and outside the EU, the most common countries of origin being Poland (and to a lesser extent other A8 countries), the Philippines, India, and some English-speaking African Countries (e.g. Zimbabwe and Nigeria) (Cangiano et al. 2009). Between EU enlargement in 2004 and March 2009, 23,580 A8 nationals registered as care assistants (Worker Registration Scheme (WRS) data reference). However, WRS registrations as care assistants have been constantly decreasing after the peak reached in 2005 (6,925), down to only 3,000 in 2008 (UKBA, various years). The number of non-EU workers entering the UK on Senior Care Worker visas has decreased even more dramatically since the introduction in 2007 of more restrictive criteria: between 2001 and 2006, over 22,000 Senior Care Worker visas were issued (nearly 6,000 in 2004), compared with 1,005 in 2007 and only five in 2008 (until 31 October, i.e. before the launch of the points-based system) (UKBA 2008).

In the absence of quantitative data on other categories of migrants entering the UK and taking up work in the care sector, some idea of the magnitude of these inflows can be indirectly obtained by comparing total inflows with the above administrative statistics on labour-related entries. Combining LFS data with other data sources, it can be roughly estimated that about 120,000 foreign-born care workers entered the UK between 2000 and 2008 (Cangiano et al. 2009). This estimate, read jointly with the above figures, suggests that most recent migrants working in the care sector entered the UK via non-labour immigration channels.

Data on recruitment methods of care providers also confirm that migrants who are already in the UK represent a major source of care workers. Organizations in the care sector recruit migrants in various ways, mostly within the domestic labour market. Advertising in local newspapers, informal networks, and Jobcentres are the main methods for recruiting foreign-born care workers in the home care sector. A low proportion of employers (less than one in five) use agencies recruiting overseas as the main means to hire migrant care workers.

From a policy perspective, this seems to suggest that the focus on Senior Care Workers and A8 nationals of the debate on migrant workers and labour shortages in the care sector is partly misplaced. In particular, a key implication which is often overlooked is that restricting the immigration channels (or the opportunity to work) for spouses, students, refugees, working holiday makers, or domestic workers can have significant implications for the supply of migrant labour in the care sector.

The focus of the public debate on new migrants tends also to miss another important aspect, that is, the large contribution of the long-established foreign-born workforce to the sector. About 40 per cent of foreign-born care workers currently working in the UK are either British nationals or permanent UK residents (Cangiano et al. 2009). This means that, while the supply of migrant care labour in the short term is affected by the characteristics of legal entry routes, the availability of foreign-born care workers in the medium and long term depends also on the provision of law regulating the settlement of recent migrants. Policies restricting access to full employment and citizenship rights may discourage settlement and reduce the future supply of foreign-born workforce. For example, many overseas trained nurses leave the UK for Australia, New Zealand, the US, and Canada. While knowledge of secondary migration patterns is very scarce, it is not unrealistic to assume that one of the reasons behind their decision to re-migrate may be found in the availability of better opportunities for settlement—this may be the case especially for those who move to Canada. The loss of migrant workers who have acquired skills that they may lack on arrival (e.g. English proficiency, recognized qualifications, and local work experience) may result in a significant waste of resources for the health sector and other industries highly reliant on migrant labour, contributing to exacerbate labour shortages and demand for new migrant workers.

A further implication of the significant reliance of the care sector on migrant workers who are already in the UK is that wages and conditions prevailing in the care labour market affect their availability to take up (and stay in) care jobs in a similar way as for the UK-born workforce. Interviews with recently arrived migrant care workers show that care work is among a limited range of low-paid jobs they were able to access. Their 'willingness' to accept low pay and demanding working conditions was often the result of the difficulty of finding other employment opportunities in the presence of various types of constraints—economic hardship, lack of support from the family, need to send remittances, restrictions attached to their immigration status (Cangiano et al. 2009). Also, LFS data shows that long-established migrant workers, similarly to the UK-born workforce, are more likely to be employed in the better paid and more secure jobs of the public sector, leaving recent migrants concentrated in the less attractive jobs of the private sector. Therefore, the capacity of the (private) care sector to retain migrant workers in the medium and long term also depends on wages and conditions relative to other sectors of the UK labour market.

The current tensions between the high reliance of the care sector on migrant workers and the immigration policy challenges mentioned in this commentary have significant implications also for the future of the care sector, particularly for the provision of long-term care for older people. As pointed out in Moriarty's chapter, demographic trends will have a large impact on the demand for care labour. In the UK, there is currently one care worker in older adult care for every 15 older people, and the projected increase in the number of older people means that, other things being equal, the size of the direct care workforce in the sector will need to grow by 400,000 over the next 25 years if this ratio has to remain at the current level (Cangiano et al. 2009). A key question is therefore the extent to which the expansion of the workforce will continue to rely on migrant workers. It is reasonable to expect that, in the absence of a step change in public funding for older adult care, the contribution of migrant carers will continue to be essential for staffing the sector. Given the current and likely future constraints on the allocation of public resources and the historically low prioritization of social care for older people, the implementation of expensive policies to re-qualify the provision of social care, thereby improving wages and working conditions and considerably reducing the reliance of the sector on new migrant workers, seems an unlikely scenario.

Until recently, changes in immigration policy were undertaken with little awareness of the potential implications for the staffing of the social care sector; while social care policy equally lacked recognition of the role of migrant workers—the recent Adult Social Care Workforce Strategy surprisingly still makes no mention of their current and possible future contribution (Department of Health 2009). If the provision of long-term care continues to depend upon large numbers of migrant workers, their role has to be planned in national policy-making—not to be an unintentional consequence of poor pay and conditions—and greater coordination between social care and immigration policies is needed.

References

Cangiano, A., Shutes, I., Spencer, S., and Leeson, G. (2009), *Migrant Care Workers in Ageing Societies: Research Findings in the United Kingdom* (Oxford: COMPAS).

Department of Health (2009), *Working to Put People First: The Strategy for the Adult Social Care Workforce in England* (Leeds: Department of Health).

MAC (2008), *Skilled, Shortage, Sensible: The Recommended Shortage Occupations Lists for the UK and Scotland* (London: Migration Advisory Committee).

—— (2009), *Skilled, Shortage, Sensible: First Review of the Recommended Shortage Occupations Lists for the UK and Scotland: Spring 2009* (London: Migration Advisory Committee).

UKBA (2008), 'Shortage Occupation List: Questions & Answers', available at <http://www.ukba.homeoffice.gov.uk/sitecontent/documents/workingintheuk/shortageoccupationlistqanda>.

—— (various years), *Accession Monitoring Reports*, joint online reports between the UK Border Agency, Department for Work and Pensions, HM Revenue and Customs, and Communities and Local Government.

6

The Use of Migrant Labour in the Hospitality Sector: Current and Future Implications

Rosemary Lucas and Steve Mansfield

6.1 Introduction

The UK hospitality sector covers a range of different industries including hotels, restaurants, and public houses. There is widespread use of flexible working practices, and people employed are typically seen as a resource or cost. Profit maximization is pursued through the use of hard-line Human Resource Management (HRM) practices. Migrant labour has played an important role in enabling employers to pursue this strategy and has become crucial to hospitality employers seeking low-cost employees who are prepared to work long and unsociable hours. This has led to claims by employers in the sector that the tightening up of immigration laws will have serious and detrimental effects on their long-term ability to staff and run their organizations profitably.

Against this background, and with reference to public policy, the work of the Migrant Advisory Committee (MAC), and the current recession, this chapter will address the nature and determinants of labour demand, available supply, recruitment practices, and the feasibility and desirability of the options employers may have to respond to perceived staff shortages in this sector. We then make recommendations that may inform public policy and employment practice.

The published information used to inform this chapter is drawn from sources that vary in terms of research rigour, reliability, validity, and quality. To illustrate, research reports that have been commissioned independently by official bodies, such as the Low Pay Commission and the Home Office, are informed by as accurate and reliable national and regional data from official statistical sources as is available (also Lucas 2004, drawn from the Workplace Employment Relations Survey (WERS) 1998), but such data may only indicate broad trends. People 1st reports incorporate similar macro data. However, this institution also serves to represent the views of hospitality employers, as does the British Hospitality Association (BHA), and the *Caterer* magazine, such that the presentation and interpretation of the data collected will reflect a particular perspective. Contradictions between employers' intentions and practice will be highlighted as they arise.

6.2 An Overview of the Hospitality Sector

The UK hospitality sector is very diverse in terms of the range of businesses it represents, the types of customers it serves, the occupations within it, and the nature of the people employed within occupational groups (by gender, age, ethnicity, education, race, etc.). This diversity is compounded by the variety within the different industries. Hotels, for example, can range from one star, where the level of service is described as 'friendly and courteous', to five star, where staff will be 'professional, attentive and provide flawless attention to detail' (English Tourism Council 1999). The sector comprises 14 industries, ranging from hotels to contracted-out food and cleaning services, with a combined turnover of approximately £135 billion a year. It employs approximately 1.9 million people in more than 180,000 establishments. Whilst the majority of these are employed in the private sector, approximately 500,000 people provide hospitality services in other sectors, including education and local authorities (People 1st 2006a). Small enterprises employing fewer than ten people account for around 75 per cent of all hospitality businesses, although many of them may be part of a larger organization (Lucas 2004). Workplaces employing over 25 people account for 45 per cent of all employees within the sector (People 1st 2006a).

The workforce of 1.9 million people represents approximately 7 per cent of the overall working population in the UK, with restaurants being the largest employing industry and women comprising 57 per cent of the overall workforce. The workforce relies on segments of marginal workers such as young people, students, women, ethnic minorities, and migrants (Wood, 1997; Nickson 2007; Lucas 2004). Only 56 per cent of employees work full-time, with restaurants, pubs, and clubs employing above average proportions of part-time workers, due to the ad hoc nature of the demand for services.

6.2.1 *Employment Relations*

The employment relationship in hospitality work embodies a triadic power relationship between employers, workers, and customers (Lucas 2004). Employment relations and personnel practices have traditionally been depicted as 'poor' (Lucas 1996; Martin and Gardiner 2007; Hurrell 2005), with harder-line HRM being seen as the predominant approach to the management of people (Head and Lucas 2004; Wickham et al. 2008). In relation to hotel chains and larger establishments employing over 250 people, research has been limited but has come to similar conclusions. Raub et al. (2006) discovered that whilst HR functions were in evidence in many large hotels, they appeared disconnected from the daily activities of the workforce and filled mainly an administrative role.

Current trade union density for the hospitality sector is 5.6 per cent (DTI 2007), well below the national level of 25.8 per cent. The suggested underlying causes for this include the transient nature of the workforce, the number of small establishments, and employer resistance. Nevertheless, research has shown that when factors such as individual and workplace characteristics are controlled for, hospitality employees show a greater propensity to unionize than other private sector workers (Lucas 2009).

The unpredictable nature of demand for goods and services, combined with the search for ways to minimize costs, has led to the development and widespread use of flexible working practices within the industry (Lai and Baum 2005; Lucas 2004; Baum et al. 2007). Whilst the seasonal nature of the industry is more predictable than the short-term demands of, for example, a coachload of customers unexpectedly arriving for lunch, it still presents problems in terms of minimizing staff costs but having enough employees to provide a rewarding experience for the consumer.

Six generic features that characterize the employment relationship can be identified:

1. An unpredictable and ad hoc demand for services. This contributes to the demand for highly flexible jobs, with employers trying to minimize costs whilst still delivering a quality service (Lucas 2004; Lai and Baum 2005).
2. Around half of all jobs involve dealing directly with customers, which may be stressful and emotionally draining (Lucas 2004). In customer service work, control of emotions, behaviour, and appearance are

legitimate managerial strategies (Korczynski 2002; Sandiford and Seymour 2007).

3. The lowest rates of productivity of any sector in the economy, representing inter alia the labour-intensive nature of the work, and the limited extent to which human endeavour can be replaced with technology (People 1st 2006a).

4. Low wages prevail, with the majority of occupational rates being set at or around the National Minimum Wage (NMW) (Low Pay Commission 2007). Low pay is associated with factors such as the high presence of young workers and other marginal groups, and lower skill requirements, although skills may be undervalued.

5. Sectoral staff turnover rates average 31 per cent, with levels of between 90 per cent and 100 per cent per annum having been observed in pubs and restaurants (People 1st 2009). Many hospitality employers do not regard this as problematic, with only 14 per cent regarding this figure as too high. Employers' staffing practices may favour particular segments of marginal workers employed on non-standard, non-permanent contracts that induce high turnover.

6. The number of job vacancies for the sector classified as hard-to-fill is higher than any other sector within the economy. It is currently running at 40 per cent and around 19 per cent are hard-to-fill because of the lack of skilled or suitably qualified applicants (People 1st 2009), with particular concern about the lack of skilled applicants for managerial and chefs' jobs. Firms in rural areas have more problems in filling vacancies than those in urban areas, due to the lack of available labour (People 1st 2005).

6.2.2 *The Role of Migrants*

The major development in terms of the role of migrant workers in recent years has been the influx of workers from A8 countries[1] in Central and Eastern Europe since 2004. Reliable statistics for the number of A8 migrant workers in hospitality are not available because data sources rely on inflows, without measuring out-going migrants (Dench et al. 2006). Information from the Home Office Accession Monitoring Report (2008) shows that during the course of 2007 just over 33,000 workers from the A8 countries registered for work in the hospitality sector, with the highest proportions taking up employment as kitchen assistants or room attendants in hotels. In 2008, the

---

[1] Czech Republic, Estonia, Hungary, Latvia, Lithuania, Poland, Slovakia, Slovenia.

number of applications from A8 workers to work in hospitality fell to 26,995. This comes at a time when the UK government is anticipating that European Economic Area (EEA) workers will fill any 'low skilled' shortages resulting from the changes in immigration laws in November 2008. Moreover, these figures do not account for migrants leaving the sector to take up positions in other sectors or to return home. There is some limited evidence that some employers used Eastern European migrants as a 'safety valve' (Smedley 2007: 26) to manage supposed labour market shortages prior to the recession in 2008. Anderson et al. (2006) note that many Eastern European migrants intend only to stay in the UK for a limited period of time before returning to their home countries, placing the hospitality sector and other sectors in a potentially very vulnerable position. This prompted Skills Minister David Lammy to suggest that British employers should invest in training rather than developing a reliance on migrant workers (*Caterer* 2007). However, as will be shown later in the chapter, due to the changing economic climate in 2008/9 and a large proportion of employers freezing recruitment or shedding staff, migrant workers have proved to be in a far more vulnerable position than their employers.

Traditionally, migrant workers tend to be concentrated in back-of-house functions, such as cooks and kitchen assistants, and elementary occupations where there is little or no interaction with customers (Baum et al. 2007; Anderson et al. 2007), such as room attendants and cleaners. 23.4 per cent of hotel porters are non-British, compared to 8.6 per cent of hotel or accommodation managers (Labour Force Survey (LFS) 2007). They also share commonalities with UK workers in the sector in that they work long hours, receive minimum pay and holiday allowance, and suffer poor employment practices (Wright and Pollert 2006).

However, whilst still being dominant in these occupational groups, as can be seen from Table 6.1, it has become more common to see migrants from A8 countries and developed countries such as Australia and South Africa occupying front-of-house roles. The Labour Force Survey (2006) figure of 18 per cent of the workforce being born overseas is likely to be much higher if we account for illegal working. Students working more than the permitted hours, people who have entered the country illegally, and those who have stayed beyond their visa expiry may not show up in official statistics, and are forced towards the low-skill, low-wage jobs within the sector. Most migrant workers originate from the Middle East and Asia (44%) and Europe (31%). In line with the overall workforce characteristics, the profile of migrant workers shows a dominance of younger people, with 64 per cent being under the age of 39. It is probable that a large proportion

Table 6.1 Employment in the UK hospitality sector by occupation

SOC Code	Occupation	UK born (%)	EEA not A8 (%)	A8 (%)	Non-EEA (%)
1221	Hotel accommodation managers	91.6	3.6	0.2	4.6
1223	Restaurant/catering managers	71.6	7.0	0.9	20.5
4216	Receptionists	92.3	1.7	0.4	5.6
9222	Hotel porters	76.5	10.3	2.0	11.2
9223	Kitchen/catering assistants	85.1	2.7	2.1	10.1
9224	Waiters/waitresses	81.2	4.0	3.3	11.5
9225	Bar staff	92.4	2.9	1.2	3.5

Source: Labour Force Survey (2007).

of them will be international students who are employed on a casual basis to supplement their income during a gap year.

Regional differences are important. McDowell et al. (2006) report that 60 per cent of all workers in London's hotels and restaurants were migrants, while the TUC estimated that 70 per cent of catering jobs in London were carried out by migrants. Although the concentration of migrant labour is still centred on London, the presence of migrant workers has now spread throughout the country, where they are employed in both rural and urban areas (Warhurst et al. 2006). Indeed, in many rural locations where there is a lack of students and young people to fill vacancies within the sector, migrants have become crucial in enabling employers to fill their staffing needs. In short, employers in the sector now rely on migrant workers to cover a range of occupations (McDowell et al. 2006; McKay and Winkelmann-Gleed 2005; Dench et al. 2006; Matthews and Ruhs 2007a).

6.2.3 Recession and Recovery

It can be taken as read that any recession will impact upon employment and employers' needs for particular labour sources within the UK hospitality sector. Given that the majority of services within the sector rely on disposable income and can be seen as luxuries, it is anticipated that many areas of business will face considerably difficulty (Galbraith 2008). Evidence suggests that the impact of a recession varies greatly depending on location and target market. Budget hotels can anticipate an increase in business as customers look to save money whilst still enjoying weekends away, and indeed in 2008 Travelodge announced expansion plans. Tourist destinations in the UK can also benefit from a recession as holidaymakers look for cheaper options. For restaurants, which are the largest employers in the sector, the recessionary impact is mixed. Many smaller, independent, and high-end restaurants are struggling to survive, whereas larger branded chains can benefit from the climate and even expand, creating more jobs (Galbraith 2008). This is due to a reliance on volume sales and being able to offer reduced price deals, such as two-for-one meals or vouchers for repeat visits (BHA 2009).

Although not strictly a result of the recession, the hardest hit industry within the sector has undoubtedly been pubs. The British Beer and Pub Association claimed that by the end of 2008 there were 36 pubs closing every week, a 33 per cent increase on 2007 (BBPA 2009).

As a result of these factors, it is reported that during the period April 2008 to January 2009, the number of people employed in the sector fell at its fastest rate in 12 years (*Caterer* 2009b). Twenty-six per cent of businesses in the sector have frozen recruitment and 23 per cent have reduced their use of temporary workers (People 1st 2009). At the same time, it is estimated that the number of unemployed people seeking work in the sector rose by nearly 30,000 to 75,345, with many coming from a retail and banking background (*Caterer* 2009c), bringing the type of service skills which hospitality employers value. This may be bad news for the most vulnerable employees, such as migrants. Employers who are still recruiting now have more choice and as a result can potentially force down the pay and conditions of those desperate for work.

In the longer term, after a period of recovery, it is anticipated that after replacement demand is taken into account, over a million additional people will be required to work in the sector by 2017 (People 1st 2009). Employers are already being encouraged to target their recruitment towards individuals who are more likely to stay with the business, and to use training to create a more permanent workforce and reduce the high turnover and vacancy rates, rather than employing transient workers such as migrants and young people (People 1st 2009). However, it remains to be seen whether employers will change their employment practices and engage in a more long-term strategic approach to staffing. It seems unlikely given the deeply embedded employment culture noted.

6.3 Employer Demand: What Are Employers Looking For?

As highlighted by Ruhs and Anderson in Chapter 1, employer demand for labour and the subsequent employability of potential applicants is a 'multifaceted concept' (Gore 2005). Employers not only want people with the appropriate skills and attributes but also have perceptions about which groups of workers may have these features, and which do not, such as the unemployed, and workers on government training schemes (Lucas and Keegan 2008; Warhurst and Nickson 2007). A People 1st (2005) report identified the two most important factors in employers' preferences as having previous experience and the right personal attributes. They suggested this 'confirms the view of many employers that they recruit personality and train skills' (p. 34). However, this ignores the dynamic and complex nature of employer demand and the stereotypical perceptions that employers have about the different personalities they believe certain sections of the labour market possess. The issue of personality, though, does becomes important in customer service jobs, where, in effect, 'employees become part of the product' (Warhurst and Nickson 2007: 105) and personality, appearance, and demeanour can have a dramatic impact upon the profitability of the business.

Employers have traditionally been viewed as demanding 'softer' skills from their employees and wanting them to have the 'right' positive attitude (Burns 1997; Pratten 2003). Dealing with customers is seen as an inherent attribute or skill rather than an ability that can be learnt, in contrast to the 'harder' more technical skills of food preparation, operating technical equipment, etc. Employers value enthusiasm, commitment, stamina, and responsibility over previous experience and technical skills (Rowley and Purcell 2001), and prefer the right personality over qualifications (Nickson et al. 2005). These highly valued 'softer' skills have been termed emotional intelligence, whereby an individual has an array of non-cognitive skills which allow them to motivate themselves, be creative, and understand their own emotions and those of others (see Dulewicz and Higgs 2000). Emotional intelligence encompasses attitude, skills, and personality, which are crucial in successful service encounters (Varca 2004). This has been found to be one area where migrants may struggle to compete with UK-born workers due to the subtle difference in attitudes and expectations that different cultures have (Dyer et al. 2008). However, this can be countered by migrants from certain A8 and wealthy nations bringing a level of 'middle classness' (Warhurst and Nickson 2007: 789) to the job, which again employers value.

Recent indications show that employees now have to demonstrate the right aesthetic qualities such as: ' . . . certain capacities and attributes that favourably appeal to customers' visual or aural senses' (Nickson et al. 2005: 198), which then renders a competitive advantage. This is particularly true for front-of-house roles such as receptionists and waiting-on staff. Matthews and Ruhs' (2007b) study of hospitality employers in Brighton found that 'constructions of nationality' (p. 21) tended to have an impact upon the functions assigned to migrant workers. Hence workers from Middle Eastern, Asian, and African countries tend to be concentrated in back-of-house jobs, whereas front-of-house jobs were dominated by migrant workers from the EU, New Zealand, South Africa, and Australia—the latter two nationalities in particular being preferred for bar work. This is further supported by McDowell et al.'s (2007) study of a London hotel, where it became apparent a combination of gender-stereotypical assumptions about nationalities and the qualities attached to them influenced management recruitment decisions. Adib and Guerrier (2003) stated that 'hotels are structured around a range of work roles that carry different expectations about gender, race, ethnicity and class' (p. 414). Research in the US by Kirschenman and Neckerman (1991) found that customer views were also taken into account when recruitment decisions were made and that employers had a hierarchy of ethnic preferences in recruitment decisions, with white natives being at the top and white immigrants being second. This was demonstrated by Adib and Guerrier (2003) whose research into hotel receptionists came to the conclusion that black women may be under-represented in this type of work because they are not perceived to be as sexually attractive to white men as white women are, so in effect creating a business case for discrimination.

Warhurst and Nickson (2007) argue, though, that the interaction between customer and worker has changed, and the interaction process could be defined in three different ways: subordination (when the worker is servile and more 'traditional', attempting to please the customer in any way possible), equivalence, and superordination (whereby the employee acts as superior to the customer). These different types of service relate to the environment and context within which the exchange is taking place. In chic boutique hotels, employees may take on an air of superordination, whereas the reverse could be true in a more traditional dining experience. Each of these settings and types of service require different skills from employees and different aesthetic and emotional qualities are valued by the employer. So within hospitality, issues are further clouded by the customer's expectations and involvement in the service encounter: employers believe customers have a stereotypical idea about the type of person they expect to be served by and so employ staff accordingly. Whether this is indeed true is an area where further research is required.

An apparent state of confusion about what employers actually want is highlighted in the recent National Skills Consultative Document produced by People 1st (2006b). Sixty-three per cent of employers believed their front-of-house staff did not possess the necessary customer service skills to meet their business needs and that young people in general did not have adequate communication skills. The continued dominance of these groups is likely to be a function of flexibility and cost arguments and the fact that students and migrants may be the only available labour prepared to work for the level of pay offered. While it can be argued that this highlights the shortfall of recruiting personality and aesthetic qualities, among other things, it also raises serious questions about employers' approach to training. This is highlighted by Kent (2006), who identifies a 'sector paradox' (p. 5), in that a third of employers are not engaging in any staff training. While nearly two-thirds of them recognize the business benefits of training, one-quarter state that they will not train staff.

6.4 Labour Supply: Who Wants to Do What?

Employer-led research has found that employers have turned to migrant workers to alleviate the recruitment problems created by hard-to-fill vacancies (People 1st 2006b). This was recognized by the government in terms of the 'essential support' (Home Office 2006: 29) that Eastern European migrant workers give hospitality employers. This arises in areas where there are low levels of unemployment or where UK workers either do not want to work for the levels of pay offered or they do not see hospitality as a career opportunity (McDowell et al. 2006). Research from Pantelidis and Wrobel (2008) showed that prior to the recession the proportion of British nationals applying for jobs in hotels in London ranged from 1 per cent to 15 per cent. The majority of employers interviewed in all these research projects claimed they had tried extensively to recruit locally but had limited success and therefore recruited from abroad. How far this attempt at local recruitment is simply to fulfil legal requirements before being able to recruit from abroad, or indeed, was actually attempted at all is unknown and is an important area for research.

One of the solutions suggested has been to change the image that people hold about working in hospitality (Lyon and Sulcova 2009; Pantelidis and Wrobel 2008). However, it can be argued that it is not people's perceptions that are wrong but the reality of working long hours for low pay that results in only individuals with limited options putting themselves forward for employment in the sector. As discussed above, at a time of rising unemployment, hospitality employers can draw upon labour from a wider variety of sources than they have traditionally (Lucas 2004; Canny 2002; Hurrell 2005; Baum et al. 2007).

6.4.1 *Students*

Seventeen per cent of the hospitality workforce are full-time students and nearly a half of the total workforce is aged 30 or under (People 1st 2009). In urban areas, students are a readily available source of labour that is prepared to work for lower rates of pay and work unsociable hours to fund their studies, so in effect there is a 'coincidence of needs' (Curtis and Lucas 2001), where students trade off low pay against flexibility and other perceived gains, such as working with and serving their friends. They can also, like certain migrant groups, bring a range of softer skills and 'middle classness' that many employers value. Additionally, students tend to have little or no knowledge from previous jobs and can be trained from scratch without preconceptions about the jobs they will be performing (Lucas and Keegan 2007, 2008). Therefore, in effect, they can displace lower skilled potential employees, such as the unemployed, by offering better value for money for employers (Warhurst and Nickson 2007).

The introduction of university tuition fees and the cessation of grants means many students have little option but to work. Despite hospitality being a viable employment option during their studies, evidence indicates that many do not see the sector as an attractive proposition once leaving education. The reasons include low pay, low status, and a lack of career progression opportunities, with small and medium-sized enterprises (SMEs) dominating the industry (Martin and Gardiner 2007). After leaving education, students tend to seek alternative employment despite, or maybe even because of, having already experienced employment in hospitality.

During periods of employment growth in the sector, there has been no evidence that migrant workers have been replacing students, as they tended to fill roles that employers felt they were more suited to, such as housekeeping and kitchen assistants. What is more likely to have had an impact on the number of students in employment is the recent decline in the pub, bar, and nightclub industry, which has shed nearly 65,000 jobs in the period December 2007 to December 2008 (People 1st 2009).

6.4.2 *Women Workers*

Fifty-nine per cent of the hospitality workforce is female. Women are targeted by employers because they are prepared to work flexibly and for lower wages, either because the work fits in with family or care obligations (Lucas 2004) or because that is the only work that is available to them. Evidence suggests that women predominate in the workforce for three main reasons. First, many jobs within the service sector are deemed to require softer skills such as empathy, listening, and sensitivity (Varca 2004), which employers stereotypically attribute to women. Secondly, employers perceive the role of women, their inherent skills and attributes, and the range of jobs they can undertake, according to their traditional domestic roles (Lucas 2004). For example, 95 per cent of cleaners within hospitality are women. Thirdly, women fit with many of the aesthetic values that employers hold, particularly in hospitality chains, where an employee identity is established to match the product and the requirement to wear a particular 'uniform', for example, short skirts for females leads to a sexualization of labour. Finally, it is related to the issue of atypical working hours and the need of many women to combine childcare with the part-time work available.

6.4.3 *Older Workers*

One alternative available source of labour is older workers, who are under-represented in the workforce as a whole, with only 14 per cent of all employees in the UK hospitality sector being aged 50 or over (People 1st 2006a). Traditionally, hospitality employers have had a negative impression of older workers (Meyer and Meyer 1988), with the appearance and attitude of younger people being preferred (Lucas and Keegan 2008). There is limited evidence to counter this, although Martin and Gardiner's research on age discrimination in hospitality (Martin and Gardiner 2007) did find a more favourable attitude towards older workers and recommended employing them as a way of reducing high staff turnover (Rowley and Purcell 2001). The ageing profile of customers who have different expectations of the service encounter will place different demands on staff (Furunes and Mykletun 2007). Such customers may be better served by an older worker who has developed more life skills and can be in a better position to empathize with them (Kent 2006).

6.5 Immigration and Labour Demand: How and Whom Do Employers Recruit?

6.5.1 *The Right Attitude and Work Ethic*

The primary reason identified in different studies for employing migrant workers ahead of British is worker attitudes and work ethic (Lyon and Sulcova 2009; Matthews and Ruhs 2007a; Dench et al. 2006; McDowell et al. 2006; Dhalech 2007). Key words such as motivated, reliable, committed, excellent attitude, hardworking, flexible, and superior work ethic emerged in all the studies. As with other sectors covered in this book, especially construction and social care, employers particularly value migrants working longer hours and asking if there were any more shifts they could cover (Dench et al. 2006). Hamilton-Atwell's (1998) summary of work ethic and attitude is doing work diligently without complaining, showing respect for authority, and doing as one is told. This suggests that a good attitude is a lack of willingness to challenge management prerogative, and this influences prospective employers' preference for migrant staff. There is little doubt that hospitality employers view migrant workers far more positively than British ones, with Bob Cotton, the president of the BHA, recently claiming UK workers were unemployable because of their lack of reliability and poor attitude towards work (*Caterer* 2008a). This notion of a right attitude and showing respect for authority towards management can be extended in hospitality to include the customer and the service encounter between guest and employee. Many aspects of this relationship, even down to job titles such as waiting-on and housekeeping, have their roots in the master–servant relationship, and as such 'subordination ranks high among the criteria employers want' (Waldinger and Lichter 2003: 40). So, by recruiting migrant workers, employers get workers who are not only less likely to challenge them but also more likely to treat guests in the manner they expect.

Little research is available as to whether the work attitudes of migrant workers are perceived to change over time and in particular whether they are believed to develop similar attitudes to those of the native-born workforce. Whether employer preferences are for recent arrivals in the UK or for migrant labour regardless of the length of time they have been in the country is unclear (but see Anderson et al. 2006). One could surmise that it depends on a range of factors, including the attitude of the individuals involved, the culture of the organization involved, the legal status of the immigrant, and the attitude of the employer.

6.5.2 *Profit Maximization*

The second reason put forward for employing migrant workers fits with employers' strategy of 'maximising profits in a segmented labour market' (Matthews and Ruhs 2007a: 9). The availability of a migrant labour force means that the labour market becomes even more segmented, as an additional group of marginal workers are employed at rates of pay that do not reflect their skills or qualifications. Migrant workers may accept work and conditions of employment that British workers would not tolerate. There is a mismatch between the skills and qualifications of migrant workers and the roles they are being recruited to fill (Devine et al. 2007; Dustmann et al. 2007; Anderson et al. 2007). This same argument has also been presented for the reliance of the hospitality sector on students. Curtis and Lucas (2001) demonstrate employers' use of full-time students in order to maximize both numeric and functional flexibility and because of the attributes they can bring to the job in terms of 'intelligence, personality, being articulate and able to communicate' (p. 40). Migrants are placed at an unfair advantage in the labour market because they will work for the same level of pay but have more desirable qualities than some non-migrant jobseekers and in effect employers get more for their money.

This is summed up by the research of Cronin and Thewlis (2004) who describe one hotel as reporting that 'one-quarter of its domestic staff were from Eastern Europe . . . not only because they were prepared to work at this rate, while local staff were not, but also . . . the quality of these staff, from a work, service and educational perspective, was considerably higher' (Low Pay Commission 2007). The TUC (2008) has recognized that more productive use could be made of these skills, and are trying to get employers to recognize and utilize the higher-value skills of Eastern Europeans rather than confining them to the lower-skilled jobs.

Employers also perceive that migrant workers will be more flexible within the employment relationship (Anderson 2007). For reasons previously stated, there is a large degree of informality in the management of people within hospitality (Adam-Smith et al. 2003), and employees are expected to be flexible in terms of hours worked and roles undertaken, as well as to cover for sickness absentees or long-term vacancies. Part of this flexibility is undoubtedly facilitated by the fact that a high proportion of migrant workers have accommodation provided for them (Matthews and Ruhs 2007b) and a high proportion live in. They are, in effect, available for 24 hours a day (Lucas 2004), and so fulfil the role of a just-in-time labour supply (Lai and Baum 2005). However, not all employers provide accommodation and there are concerns about the cost and quality of commercial accommodation provided (Low Pay Commission 2007). Another emerging factor is the recruitment of migrant workers on full-time contracts, but in reality, giving them less than full-time hours and using them at peak periods of demand, thereby paying only for work that is actually done (Wickham et al. 2008).

6.5.3 *Recruitment Practices*

Resourcing practices within hospitality have traditionally been viewed as being informal (Marchante et al. 2006). In relation to recruitment and selection, evidence shows there are few systematic approaches and even in large hotels, practices are informal and basic (Lockyer and Scholarios 2004), particularly for non-managerial staff. Recruitment is commonly achieved by word of mouth, or by placing an advertisement in local news-papers, while unstructured interviews are the main selection tool. Although chain hotels were more likely to use standardized application forms, they were only slightly more likely to use sophisticated selection techniques than small hotels (Lockyer and Scholarios 2004). McGunnigle and Jameson (2000: 415) claimed that it was the 'ease and willingness' of management to dismiss employees who did not have the right attitude that had led to a situation where developing more sophisticated recruitment and selection was not seen as necessary.

Employers have been found to prefer students because they frequently make the initial approach to the employer, thereby reducing the cost and effort of recruitment (Lucas and Keegan 2008). The use of established connections within the local labour market and amongst the friends of current employees has also traditionally been popular and both of these factors appear to have been extended to the migrant labour force as well (McDowell et al. 2006), with a large reliance on local migrant networks to fill vacancies that exist.

6.6 Immigration and Alternative Responses: Is there a Need for Migrant Labour?

6.6.1 *Increasing Pay*

One solution to the labour shortages within the hospitality sector that occur during periods of growth is to increase wages. However, since 1999 the NMW (National Minimum Wage) has risen incrementally from £3.60 for 22 year olds and above, and £3.00 for 18–21 year olds to £5.73 and £4.77 respectively, which although not significant in real terms, has resulted in increases for those working in the lowest-paid occupations, including hos-pitality. This does not appear to have had an impact upon the labour shortages within the sector, with vacancies, up until the recession in 2008, still running at a high level. Although the majority of employers supported the NMW, it was starting to have an impact on profits (Denvir and Loukas 2006). In light of the recession, with many areas of the sector experiencing significant difficulties and a downturn in revenue for 2009 of between 10 and 22 per cent (*Caterer* 2009), it is perhaps unrealistic to expect wages to increase. Hotels with high levels of staff turnover are willing to consider any measure to keep staff, except increasing wages, although they acknowledge that they may have to pay more to recruit a replacement (Rowley and Purcell 2001). Chefs are already one of the highest-paid occupational groups, although they represent the biggest proportion of hard-to-fill vacancies (People 1st 2005) because of the lack of applicants who possess the necessary skills.

6.6.2 *The Unemployed*

While it is likely that some of the elementary jobs in the UK could be filled by currently unemployed people (Devins and Hogarth 2005), there does appear to be a mismatch between employers' perceived needs and those of potential applicants. This is particularly true in areas where there are low levels of unemployment, or where UK workers either do not want to work for the levels of pay offered, are unwilling to work in hospitality, or do not see it as a career opportunity. The majority of employers interviewed in research (Matthews and Ruhs 2007b; French and Mohrke 2006) claimed they had tried to recruit locally but had had limited success and therefore had little alternative but to look elsewhere. No specific research has been conducted on hospitality employers' attitudes towards the unemployed, but it is often the case that the long-term unemployed are less likely to have up-to-date technical skills, as well as the social and attitudinal skills that employers demand (Warhurst and Nickson 2007) because they have been out of work for so long. However, government initiatives such as the Local Employment Partnership scheme are trying to address this, with a recent success being the announcement by Jury Inns that they would recruit 200 long-term unemployed workers as part of current expansion plans (*Caterer* 2009c).

As illustrated by Anderson and Ruhs in Chapter 2, it is not simply an issue of retraining sections of the long-term unemployed in order to make them attractive to potential hospitality employers. Issues surrounding geography, socialization, expectations of employers and potential employees, and regulatory systems all contribute to this complex situation.

6.6.3 *Better People Management*

There are clearly barriers to training and up-skilling the domestic work-force, noted earlier, that have little to do with the availability of migrant workers to fill the vacancies within the sector. Employers have traditionally been reluctant to invest in the training and development of workers be-cause it is expected that staff will leave after a short period or will be poached by a competitor offering a slightly better wage. This problem increases when considering migrant labour, with employers feeling that it is seldom worth investing in training because long-term benefits will not be realized as the migrants seek out other avenues. It is not simply a case of migrant workers filling vacancies and therefore employers not having to invest in training, the issues are deeply rooted in the beliefs of employers about the value of training and the types of potential workers they target. Even when the direct costs of training are met by external agencies, uptake within the sector is low. Currently only 6 per cent of employees have attended government-funded training courses, with employers citing a lack of awareness, a confusing system, and problems with access as the major causes for not making greater use of them (Perkins 2006).

People 1st suggest that the problem of labour shortages would be better addressed by focusing on staff retention, with 70 per cent of recruitment being carried out in order to replace staff that had left. However, research has shown that staff leave because of poor management skills, lack of training and development, and lack of career progression (Marchante et al. 2006). It is difficult to envisage how this situation can be resolved when the targeted marginal groups, particularly students, are going to be transient (Lucas and Keegan 2007). Employers accept that high turnover of staff is inevitable due to the nature of the staff they employ and because employees are mobile and will leave if better rates of pay are offered (Rowley and Purcell 2001). Low wages and intensive and anti-social working condi-tions mean that many leave the industry when better opportunities arise. Work intensification then occurs as the vacancies tend to be absorbed by the organization and remaining employees are expected to cover the out-standing vacancies (Adam-Smith et al. 2003). Employees who leave in the early stage of employment may have false expectations about the industry and the nature of the work involved and may have gained an 'over-glamor-ized' view from the multitude of television programmes that present an image that is far removed from the reality of the situation (Rowley and Purcell 2001).

Although some of the staff retention issues may be solved by implementing better systems of people management, it is likely that the sector will continue to be characterized by relatively low pay, long and unsociable hours, intensive work, and poor career progression, making it an unattractive sector to work in for many potential applicants. Employers do not view the turnover and retention rates within the industry as being particularly problematic, reflecting the enduring view of it being 'inevitable'.

6.6.4 *Technology*

Technology within the hospitality sector has a limited impact in relation to the substitution of employees or in making the production process less labour intensive. The main advances have been made in the use of on-line marketing techniques and electronic distribution (O'Connor and Murphey 2004). A central reservation system or guest management system allows for greater efficiency in the allocation of rooms, forecasting demand, and providing after-sales support (Lai and Baum 2005), and an electronic bar management system can provide cost savings in relation to stock, but it cannot socialize with customers or serve drinks with a smile.

Technology has been seen to have an impact in commercial kitchens, where the preparation of the product can be outsourced and technology in the form of microwaves and convector ovens can be used to reheat the meal before it is served, a practice that is not new but is now becoming more widespread, especially in pubs and hotels (Robinson and Barron 2007; Riley 2005). This may create problems with chefs feeling that their work is becoming de-skilled and standardized, such that they prefer to work in restaurants rather than in pubs and hotels (Pratten and O'Leary 2007). On the other hand, the customer-driven requirement for fresher, healthier, locally sourced food moves the emphasis away from the pre-packaged meals back to more traditional freshly prepared ones. This means that meals become more labour intensive to prepare and skilled chefs are required at a time when there does appear to be a shortage of them in the UK.

6.6.5 *Agency Working*

Offshoring work in the hospitality sector is clearly not an option. While the use of employment agencies has become more prevalent within the sector, little is known about their role and relationship with employers. There has been limited research on the use of agency staff within the hospitality sector, and as a result little is known about how widespread their use is and which particular occupational groups are most affected. However, given that employers in general choose to use agency workers because they prove more adaptable, more flexible in terms of response to changing demand and market turbulence, and are cheaper in a number of areas (Markova and McKay 2008: 54), it would be surprising if hospitality employers were not making widespread use of them. In their case-study of London hotels, Lai and Baum (2005) did find that more than half of the housekeeping staff were drawn from agencies and in one particular case this figure rose to 90 per cent. They likened this system to a just-in-time one, whereby costs could be kept down to a minimum, the legal obligations towards employees could be minimized, and managers did not have to worry about hiring and firing decisions. Matthews and Ruhs (2007b) also found evidence that external agencies and variable contracts were used to eliminate labour wastage and 'externalise risk' (p. 24) in hotels, particularly for housekeeping jobs and kitchen porters, as did Wickham et al. (2008), who found that the use of agency workers as low-paid cleaners in hotels was on the increase in Northern Ireland.

6.7 Hospitality and the Points-Based Immigration System

In a recent survey, the BHA and People 1st claimed that 89 per cent of employers felt the new immigration laws would have a detrimental effect on their business (People 1st 2008). At the time of writing, it is too early to test this claim, although similar fears were expressed surrounding the introduction of the NMW, and they subsequently proved unfounded. Initially, the major concern surrounded chefs, particularly those who were deemed to be suitably skilled in 'creating ethnic cuisine' (MAC 2008: 170). Therefore, skilled chefs (where the salary is at least 8.10 per hour) were included in Tier 2 of the points-based immigration system (PBS) following recommendations from the MAC. Based on evidence presented primarily from Bangladeshi and Chinese restaurateurs, the needs of ethnic restaurants in particular were deemed to be 'special' and it was felt that UK and EEA workers did not have the necessary skills to fill the roles. The Guild of Bangladesh Restaurateurs and the Bangladeshi Caterers' Association (BCA) argued that it was essential to bring staff from countries where they had been brought up with the traditions and culture of what is required and have learnt the necessary culinary skills in an authentic environment. However, this does seem to be contradicted by what we know of 'authentic' Indian cuisine which is served in the majority of restaurants. The balti and chicken tikka masala were both invented in the UK and most offerings on the average menu bear only a vague resemblance to food that is eaten in India (Bedell 2002). Moreover, skilled chefs are able to cook food from different countries successfully: British chefs successfully offer French fare and a non-Asian received the UK's Asian Chef of the Year Award in 2007. In reality, reasons for the demand for chefs from outside the EEA are more likely to be related to availability, language, culture, and cost, with UK national chefs being one of the highest-paid groups in the sector and also the hardest to recruit. A report on jobs published in 2009 placed chefs as one of the key permanent and temporary positions where skills were in short supply (Markit 2009).

Following the introduction of the points-based immigration system, it was reported that there was a serious skills shortage, with 7,000 vacancies for chefs in ethnic cuisine restaurants. Independent research on this subject is not available, but reports from owners claim they have no alternatives. They claim attempts to use A8 workers in their businesses have proved unsuccessful, as they usually resign after a short period, reputedly mainly for language reasons (*Caterer* 2008b). In response to this, the government has announced it will supply additional funding for the training of chefs in cooking ethnic food and extra funding for training of members of ethnic communities to NVQ level 3. The problem continues to be that the second-generation Bangladeshi community either do not want to enter the hospitality sector or prefer alternative careers which are better paid and offer better prospects (Guild of Bangladesh Restaurateurs 2008), despite unemployment being at more than 14 per cent (Office for National Statistics 2004). Without methods designed to entice them into working in the sector, the provision of extra training is unlikely to make a significant difference to the numbers making themselves available.

There are many issues regarding this debate which require further research:

- Are the barriers of alleged knowledge, skill, cultural, and traditional practice insurmountable?
- How long do EEA workers stay in the UK? Will employers get a return on their investment in training?
- Is it through choice or necessity that English is not the primary language in many ethnic restaurant kitchens? What are the implications for non-speakers' integration in the work environment?
- Would trained UK/EEA chefs want to work in an environment which is culturally alien to them?

However, the main reason for ethnic cuisine restaurants to be deemed 'special' is that in a very competitive market for chefs, issues of language and culture make them a less attractive proposition and mean employers in this segment of the market face even greater problems in finding suitable applicants than do other hospitality businesses.

6.8 Conclusion: Implications for Analysing Staff Shortages in the Sector

Much of the evidence presented in this chapter has been collected in pre-recessionary times and before the start of a new immigration regime in November 2008. In the absence of longer-term, reliable data, predictions about their potential impacts are necessarily speculative. Nevertheless, it is not disputed that both developments will clearly have an important impact on business activity and employment in the hospitality sector. For example, a significant growth in the number of restaurant and catering managers in the last three years, around one-fifth of whom originate from outside the EEA (LFS 2007, compiled by the Migration Advisory Committee), will be subject not only to recessionary effects but also to the new immigration rules. Combined with the regulatory framework and the economic climate, it is also vital to consider claims made by employers in the sector in relation to skills shortages and a lack of alternatives to migrants being available to them. This bottom-up approach can show, as in the case of ethnic cuisine restaurants, that employer demands may be justified, particularly in the short term, but that strategies are needed for a more viable long-term solution.

In spite of the current mismatch of skills, in terms of what employers want from potential employees and those which the current education system is supplying, skills needs are likely to change. However, as has been illustrated, what counts as a skill is a contentious issue, and is not solely knowledge-based or related to NVQ levels in many hospitality jobs. Indeed, 'skill' as used by employers can have as much to do with personality, gender, ethnicity, age, and nationality as it can with recognized qualifications.

The hospitality sector is an excellent example of the dynamic relationship between labour demand and supply, and demonstrates that focusing policy purely on the supply side is unlikely to be successful. Numerous initiatives have been directed at hospitality employers over the past few decades in periods of growth and recession, yet its employment problems, including high labour turnover, skills shortages, and training deficiencies, have remained enduring realities (see Lucas 1996: 12–15; Lucas 2004). Any change would necessitate a paradigm shift in management philosophy and would require employers to reassess the reasoning behind their demand for particular sectors of the labour market and their stereotypical assumptions of the supply available to them. In this sense, the hospitality sector not only displays generic problems that are associated with other low-paying sectors, such as construction and social care, but is also competing with them for labour (Low Pay Commission 2007).

For the first time in over a decade, hospitality employers are experiencing an increase in the numbers of people 'wanting' to work in the sector and are being urged away from a reliance upon migrants and young people by the government and the Sector Skills Council. However, within the current regulatory and social structures, this is unlikely to prove successful, with employers continuing their reliance on cheaper sources of labour. One of the problems facing policy-makers is the diversity of businesses within the sector, and in forcing employers to improve terms and conditions, they may well force many smaller private operators out of business.

The UK will remain an important international tourist destination for visitors from across the world, and international tourists speaking different languages and having particular cultural requirements will continue to consume the products and services provided by the hospitality sector. The emerging markets of China and Russia present considerable opportunities for attracting international visitors to Britain and it is conceivable that the 'international flavour' of the hospitality and tourism product will grow and that some of this growth will be better served by employing international workers, for example, with appropriate language skills. Nevertheless, there is evidence that current migrants' skills and abilities could be used more productively, a consideration that could also be applied to other groups, including women and younger workers.

The hospitality sector has always employed, and continues to employ, a significant proportion of migrant workers. Many of them may work in jobs that are, in effect, mutually accepted as temporary—for the employer, because of the nature of demand—for workers, because the decision to work in the UK is a short-term one; not all migrants settle. It is unrealistic to expect this to change radically, although both employers and migrants may find themselves in a vulnerable position during periods of economic downturn. Public policy decisions on immigration need to be shaped carefully to take account of these tensions and to ensure that unnecessary barriers to entry into the UK do not exist when it can be proven that there is a genuine need for migrant workers to sensibly fill skill shortages.

References

Adam-Smith, D., Norris, G., and Williams, S. (2003), 'Continuity or Change? The Implications of the National Minimum Wage for Work and Employment in the Hospitality Industry', *Work, Employment & Society*, 17(1): 29–47.

Adib, A., and Guerrier, Y. (2003), 'The Interlocking of Gender with Nationality, Race, Ethnicity and Class: The Narratives of Women in Hotel Work', *Gender Work and Organization*, 10(4): 413–32.

Anderson, B. (2007), 'A Very Private Business: Exploring the Demand for Migrant Domestic Workers', *European Journal of Women's Studies*, 14(3): 247–64.

—— Clark, N., and Parutis, V. (2007), 'New EU Members? Migrant Workers' Challenges and Opportunities to UK Trade Unions: A Polish and Lithuanian Case Study', TUC, London.

—— Ruhs, M., Rogaly, B., and Spencer, S. (2006), 'Fair enough? Central and East European Migrants in Low-Wage Employment in the UK', available at <http://www.compas.ox.ac.uk/changingstatus> (Oxford: COMPAS).

Baum, T., Dutton, E., Kamiri, S., Kokkranikal, J., Devine, C., and Hearns, N. (2007), 'Cultural Diversity in Hospitality Work', *Cross Cultural Management*, 14(3): 229–39.

Bedell, G. (2002), 'It's Curry but Not as we Know it', *Telegraph*, 12 May, available at <http://www.guardian.co.uk/liteandstyle/2002/may/12/foodanddrink.shopping2>.

British Beer and Pub Association (BBPA) (2009), 'One In Ten Beer and Pub Jobs to Go if Tax Rises in Two Weeks' Time', Website: <http://www.beerandpub.com/news-List_detail.aspx?newsId=280>, accessed 8 April 2009.

British Hospitality Association (2009), 'No Respite in Sight for Hospitality Operators', available at <http://www.bha.org.uk/details.cfm?page=news&section=ind-news&codeid=135703>.

Burns, P. (1997), 'Hard-Skills, Soft-Skills: Undervaluing Hospitality's "Service with a Smile"', *Progress in Tourism and Hospitality Research*, 3(3): 239–48.

Canny, A. (2002), 'Flexible Labour? The Growth of Student Employment in the UK', *Journal of Education and Work*, 15(3): 277–301.

Caterer (2007), 'Don't Depend on Migrants, Lammy Warns Employers', 22 Nov., available at <http://www.caterersearch.com/Articles/2007/11/22/317427/dont-depend-on-migrants-lammy-warns-employers.htm>.

—— (2008a), 'BHA Slammed for Suggesting UK Workers are Unemployable', available at <http://www.caterersearch.com/Articles/2008/01/23/318306/bha-slammed-for-suggesting-uk-workers-are-unemployable.htm>.

—— (2008b), 'Immigration Squeeze Hits Ethnic Restaurant Sector', available at <http://www.caterersearch.com/Articles/2008/02/28/319247/immigration-squeeze-hits-ethnicrestaurant-sector.html>.

Caterer (2009a), 'Hotel Predictions for 2009', available at <http://www.caterersearch. com/Articles/2008/12/28/325461/hotel-predictions-for-2009.html>.

—— (2009b), 'Hospitality Jobs amongst Worst Hit by Recession', available at <http:// www.caterersearch.com/Articles/2009/02/06/326076/hospitality-jobs-amongst-worst-hit-by-recession.html>.

—— (2009c), 'Jury Inns Flooded by Job Seekers from Recession Hit Sectors', available at <http://www.caterersearch.com/Articles/2009/03/30/326922/jurys-inns-flooded-by-job-seekers-from-recession-hit-sectors.html>.

Cronin, E., and Thewlis, M. (2004), *Qualitative Research on Firms' Adjustments to the Minimum Wage: Final Report* (London: Low Pay Commission).

Curtis, S., and Lucas, R. (2001), 'A Coincidence of Needs? Employers and Full-Time Students', *Employee Relations*, 23(1): 38–54.

Dench, S., Hurstfield, J., Hill, D., and Akroyd, K. (2006), 'Employers' Use of Migrant Labour, Main Report', Home Office Online Report 04/06 (London).

Denvir, A., and Loukas, G. (2006), *The Impact of the National Minimum Wage: Pay Differentials and Workplace Change*, Research Report for the Low Pay Commission (London: Institute for Employment Studies).

Department of Trade and Industry (DTI) (2007), *Trade Union Membership 2006* (London: Office for National Statistics), available at <http://www.berr.gov.uk/ files/file39006.pdf>.

Devine, C., Baum, T., Hearns, N., and Devine, A. (2007), 'Cultural Diversity in Hospitality Work: The Northern Ireland Experience', *The International Journal of Human Resource Management*, 18(2): 333.

Devins, D., and Hogarth, T. (2005), 'Employing the Unemployed: Some Case Study Evidence on the Role and Practice of Employers', *Urban Studies*, 42(2): 245–56.

Dhalech, M. (2007), 'Mapping of Advice and Support Needs in Cumbria for Migrant Workers', Centre for Local Policy Studies.

Dulewicz, V., and Higgs, M. (2000), 'Emotional Intelligence A Review and Evaluation Study', *Journal of Managerial Psychology*, 15(4): 341–72.

Dustmann, C., Frattini, T., and Preston, I. (2007), 'A Study of Migrant Workers and the National Minimum Wage and Enforcement Issues that Arise', available at <http://eprints.ucl.ac.uk/14329/1/14329.pdf>.

Dyer, S., McDowell, L., and Batnitzky, A. (2008), 'Emotional Labour/Bodywork: The Caring Labours of Migrants in the UK's NHS', *Geoforum*, 39: 2030–8.

English Tourism Council (1999), 'Sure Signs of Where to Stay', available at: <http:// www.fweb.org.uk/dean/visitor/accom/symbols.html>.

French, S., and Mohrke, J. (2006), *The Impact of 'New Arrivals' upon the North Staffordshire Labour Market* (London: Low Pay Commission).

Furunes, T., and Mykletun, R. J. (2007), 'Why Diversity Management Fails: Metaphor Analyses Unveil Manager Attitudes', *International Journal of Hospitality Management*, 26(4): 974–90.

Galbraith, A. (2008), *The Credit Crunch and the Hospitality, Leisure, Travel and Tourism Sector* (London: People 1st).

Gore, T. (2005), 'Extending Employability or Solving Employers' Recruitment Problems? Demand-Led Approaches as an Instrument of Labour Market Policy', *Urban Studies*, 42(2): 341–53.

Guild of Bangladesh Restaurateurs (2008), 'Government Scheme Puts Skids under UK Curry Houses', available at <http://www.gbruk.org.uk/press.htm>.

Hamilton-Attwell, A. (1998), 'Productivity and Work Ethics', *Work Study*, 47(3): 79–86.

Head, J., and Lucas, R. (2004), 'Employee Relations in the Non-Union Hotel Industry: A Case Of Determined Opportunism?' *Personnel Review*, 33(6): 693–710.

Home Office (2006), *Accession Monitoring Report May 04–Sept 06* (London: Border and Immigration Agency).

—— (2008), *Accession Monitoring Report: May 2004–Dec 2007* (London: Border and Immigration Agency).

Hughes, J. (2005), 'Bringing Emotion to Work: Emotional Intelligence, Employee Resistance and the Reinvention of Character', *Work Employment & Society*, 19(3): 603–25.

Hurrell, S. (2005), 'Dilute to Taste? The Impact of the Working Time Regulations in the Hospitality Industry', *Employee Relations*, 27(5): 532–46.

Kent, M. C. (2006). *Knitting with Fog, Assessing Whether the Education System is Meeting the Needs of the Sector* (London: People 1st).

Kirschenman, J., and Neckerman, K. M. (1991), '"We'd Love to Hire them but . . . " The Meaning of Race to Employers', in C. Jencks and P. E. Peterson (eds.), *The Urban Underclass* (Washington: Brookings Independent Press).

Korczynski, M. (2002), *Human Resource Management in Service Work* (Basingstoke: Macmillan).

Lai, P., and Baum, T. (2005), 'Just-in-Time Labour Supply in the Hotel Sector: The Role of Agencies', *Employee Relations*, 27(1–2): 86–103.

Learning and Skills Council (2005), *National Employers Skills Survey* (London: LSC).

Lockyer, C., and Scholarios, D. (2004), 'Selecting Hotel Staff: Why Best Practice Does Not Always Work', *International Journal of Contemporary Hospitality Management*, 16(2): 125–35.

Low Pay Commission (2007), *National Minimum Wage, Low Pay Commission Report*, Cm 7056 (London: The Stationery Office).

Lucas, R. E. (1996), 'Industrial Relations in Hotels and Catering: Neglect and Paradox', *British Journal of Industrial Relations*, 34(2): 267–86.

—— (2004), *Employment Relations in the Hospitality and Tourism Industries* (London: Routledge).

—— (2009), 'Is Low Unionisation in the British Hospitality Industry due to Industry Characteristics?' *International Journal of Hospitality Management*, 28(1): 42–52.

—— and Keegan, S. (2007), 'Young Workers and the National Minimum Wage', *Equal Opportunities International*, 26(6): 573–89.

Lucas, R. E. and Keegan, S. (2008), 'Probing the Basis for Differential Pay Practices of Younger Workers in Low Paying Hospitality Firms', *Human Resource Management Journal*, 18(4): 386–404.

——and Ralston, L. (1996), 'Part-Time Student Labour: Strategic Choice or Pragmatic Response?' *International Journal of Contemporary Hospitality Management*, 8(2): 21–4.

Lyon, A., and Sulcova, D. (2009), 'Hotel Employer's Perceptions of Employing Eastern European Workers: A Case Study of Cheshire, UK', *Tourism, Culture & Communication*, 9: 17–28.

McDowell, L., Batnitzky, A., and Dyer, S. (2006), 'Migrant Workers in a Global City: Ethnicity and Gender in Servicing Work in a Greater London Hotel', Centre for Employment, Work and Finance, Oct.

McGunnigle, P. J., and Jameson, S. M. (2000), 'HRM in UK hotels: A Focus on Commitment', *Employee Relations*, 22(4): 403–22.

McKay, S., and Winkelmann-Gleed, A. (2005), *Migrant Workers in the East of England: Project Report* (Cambridge: East of England Development Agency).

Marchante, A. J., Ortega, B., and Pagan, R. (2006), 'Determinants of Skills Shortages and Hard-to-Fill Vacancies in the Hospitality Sector', *Tourism Management*, 27(5): 791–802.

Markit (2009), *Report on Jobs*, 4 Feb. (Henley on Thames: Markit Economics).

Markova, E., and McKay, S. (2008), *Agency and Migrant Workers: Literature Review* (London: Working Lives Research Institute).

Martin, E., and Gardiner, K. (2007), 'Exploring the UK Hospitality Industry and Age Discrimination', *International Journal of Contemporary Hospitality Management*, 19(4): 309–18.

Matthews, G., and Ruhs, M. (2007a), *The Micro-foundations of Labour Shortages: Deconstructing Employer Demand for Migrant Workers in the UK's Hospitality Sector* (Oxford: COMPAS).

—— —— (2007b), 'Are You being Served? Employer Demand for Migrant Labour in the UK's Hospitality Sector', Working Paper No. 51 (Oxford: COMPAS).

Meyer, R., and Meyer, G. (1988), 'Older Workers: Are they a Viable Labour Force for the Hotel Community?' *Hospitality Research Journal*, 12(2): 361–4.

Migration Advisory Committee (MAC) (2008), *Skilled, Shortage, Sensible: The Recommended Shortage Occupation Lists for the UK and Scotland* (London: Home Office).

Nickson, D. (2007), *Human Resource Management for the Hospitality and Tourism Industries* (Oxford: Butterworth-Heinemann).

——Warhurst C., and Dutton, E. (2005), 'The Importance of Attitude and Appearance in the Service Encounter in Retail and Hospitality', *Managing Service Quality*, 15(2): 195–208.

O'Connor, P., and Murphey, J. (2004), 'Research on Information Technology in the Hospitality Industry', *Hospitality Management*, 23: 473–84.

Office for National Statistics (2004), 'Ethnicity and Identity: Labour Market, Non-white Unemployment' (London: The Stationery Office), available at <http://www.statistics.gov.uk/cci/nugget.asp?id=462>.

Pantelidis, I., and Wrobel, S. (2008), 'London's Hospitality Workforce: Cultural Diversity a Choice or Necessity?' *London Journal of Tourism, Sport and Creative Industries*, 1(1): 13–21.

People 1st (2005), *Recruitment and Retention Survey*, UK Report (London: People 1st).

—— (2006a), *The Hospitality, Leisure, Travel and Tourism Sector, Key Facts and Figures* available at <http://www.people1st.co.uk/key-facts.html>.

—— (2006b), *Skill Needs Assessment for the Hospitality, Leisure, Travel and Tourism Sector*, UK Report (London: People 1st).

—— (2008), *About us*, available at <http://www.people1st.co.uk/about-us>.

—— (2009), *The State of the Nation*, UK Report (London: People 1st).

Perkins, C. (2006), *Counting those Pennies, Government Funded Training Provision: Who, What, Where and How?*, UK Report (London: People 1st).

Pratten, J. D. (2003), 'The Importance of Waiting Staff in Restaurant Service', *British Food Journal*, 105(11): 826–34.

—— and O'Leary, B. (2007), 'Addressing the Causes of Chef Shortages in the UK', *Journal of European Industrial Training*, 31(1): 68–78.

Raub, S., Alvarez, L., and Khanna, R. (2006), 'The Different Roles of Corporate and Unit Level Human Resources Managers in the Hospitality Industry', *International Journal of Contemporary Hospitality Management*, 18(2): 135–44.

Riley, M. (2005), 'Food and Beverage Management: A Review of Change', *International Journal of Contemporary Hospitality Management*, 17(1): 88–93.

Robinson, R. N. S., and Barron, P. E. (2007), 'Developing a Framework for Understanding the Impact of Deskilling and Standardisation on the Turnover and Attrition of Chefs', *International Journal of Hospitality Management*, 26(4): 913–26.

Rowley, G., and Purcell, K. (2001), 'As Cooks Go, She Went: Is Labour Churn Inevitable?' *Hospitality Management*, 20: 163–85.

Sandiford, P. J., and Seymour, D. (2007), 'A Discussion of Qualitative Data Analysis in Hospitality Research with Examples from an Ethnography of English Public Houses', *Hospitality Management*, 26: 724–42.

Smedley, T. (2007), 'Say Hello, Wave Goodbye', *People Management*, 6 Mar.: 25.

TUC (2008), *UK Businesses Missing Out on Migrant Workers' Skills* (London: TUC).

Varca, P. E. (2004), 'Service Skills for Service Workers: Emotional Intelligence and Beyond', *Managing Service Quality*, 14(6): 457–67.

Waldinger, R., and Lichter, M. I. (2003), *How the Other Half Works: Immigrants and the Social Organization of Labour* (Berkeley, Calif.: University of California Press).

Warhurst, C., and Nickson, D. (2007), 'Employee Experience of Aesthetic Labour in Retail and Hospitality', *Work, Employment & Society*, 21(1): 103–20.

—— —— Dutton, E., Commander, J., James, S., and Lloyd, C. (2006), *Low Wage Work in UK Hotels and the Institutional Policy Responses* (London: Russell Sage Foundation).

Wickham, J., Moriarty, E., Bobek, A., and Salamonska, J. (2008), 'Migrant Workers and the Irish Hospitality Sector', Trinity Immigration Initiative, Employment Research Centre, Trinity College Dublin.

Wood, R. C. (1997), *Working in Hotels and Catering*, 2nd edn. (London: International Thomson Press).

Wright, T., and Pollert, A. (2006), *The Experiences of Ethnic Minority and Migrant Workers in Hotels and Restaurants: Strategies and Necessities* (London: Working Lives Institute).

The Use of Migrant Labour in the Hospitality Sector: A Commentary

Linda McDowell

In their admirably clear chapter, Lucas and Mansfield lay out the key dimensions of the contemporary hospitality sector in the UK. As they argue, the sector is characterized by diversity in its structure and in its demand for and supply of labour. The sector is composed of several industries, an extremely large number of sites of employment of various sizes, a labour force that is diverse in its social characteristics, and which is often employed on a seasonal and casual basis and so is hard to organize. Add to this low pay and 'hard' management and the classic picture of the hospitality sector is confirmed as one in which labour is both hard to recruit and to manage. Most workers, especially those employed by agencies, are unlikely to find secure well-paid employment, let alone progression or promotion, and so rates of turnover are high. It is also an industry in which the embodied social attributes of workers matter. The hospitality industry, especially at the top end, aims to entice and enchant its customers, producing an experience that must be repeated in order for organizations to make profits and stay in business in economies increasingly based on the instantaneous satisfaction of desire (Bauman 1998, 2000). Deferred gratification is or must become an alien concept in the type of consumer service-dominated economies that now characterize advanced industrial societies, where every emotional experience increasingly is for sale in the market. While the ideal of enchantment and desire may seem less relevant at the bottom end of the market, where fast food, low-price 'ethnic' restaurants, and chains of bars and pubs dominate, here too the aim is to repeatedly satisfy consumer demands for an enjoyable (and reliable) experience at a low price.

In western economies, then, hospitality is a growing sector for employment (despite the dip during the current recession), and it is also a key location for migrant workers. As Lucas and Mansfield document, the sector has always relied on those with least choice in the labour market and/or those for whom hospitality is merely a way of making some money before taking up a 'real' job. Thus all those discriminated against in the market in different ways—women (especially mothers), people of colour and recent arrivals, and students who in the UK increasingly are in debt and so seek term-time employment—are all found in the hospitality sector in disproportionate numbers. As Lucas and Mansfield show, migrant workers are a central element in this exploitable (and exploited) workforce. Numerous studies of migrant workers have documented the ways in which newcomers with few recognized educational credentials, or skills, are excluded from the better-paid jobs in the primary sector. This tends to crowd migrants into bottom-end jobs in poorly paid sectors of the labour market, often in the types of precarious and/or temporary work that are dominant in the hospitality sector (Vosko 2000). Here and elsewhere in the service sector, class, skin colour, lack of language skills, and low levels of unionization combine to reinforce the disadvantages new entrants to the labour market typically experience. Poor conditions, long or irregular hours, low pay, and discriminatory promotion prospects combine to reinforce their initial segregation. What is interesting here is to ask to what extent this initial segregation is avoidable: studies of the employment trajectories of hospitality workers might be interesting. And, as Lucas and Mansfield show, the composition of this labour force changes over time. East Europeans, for example, especially after EU enlargement in 2004, moved into the hospitality industry in the UK in large numbers. It seems clear that they replaced previous migrant populations, and perhaps 'local' Black and Minority Ethnic (BME) workers, whose skills and personal characteristics may have begun to compare unfavourably with this new migrant population, who were often young, and possessed higher education and perhaps greater language abilities, and were more likely to possess the 'soft' people skills identified by Lucas and Mansfield. There is interesting work to be done here exploring the changing composition of the migrant labour force in hospitality, both at the national scale and in its regional variations.

Although the sector as a whole relies on migrant and other forms of exploitable labour, hotels in particular are notorious employers of cheap, relatively docile, and insecure migrant labour (Waldinger 1992). What is interesting is how, in the broad discipline of labour studies, and especially the sociology of work, hotels have become an almost quintessential site for recent studies of the segmentation of labour, of migrant workers, and of precarious work. Lucas and Mansfield hint at this in their chapter, despite their level of analysis remaining at the aggregate level of labour supply and demand. What is fascinating is that the service sector in general, but hotels in particular, have replaced the assembly-line case-studies of an earlier generation of labour analysts (including classics such as Burawoy 1979, and Beynon 1984, and more recent work, including Hayter and Harvey 1993; as well as feminist analyses of assembly-line labour such as Kondo 1990; Ngai 2005; Wright 1999). Where once the classic worker in this tradition was a brawny manual worker, heroically manning the heavy male-employing industries such as coal, iron and steel, or agriculture (Samuel 1977), and the assembly line in the car plant, workers have now changed their sex, their nationality, their skin colour, and, perhaps, their class alliances. As Lucas and Mansfield note, trade union membership in the hospitality industry is extremely low and the older forms of class solidarity and forms of industrial struggle have melted into air. And so, labour economists, geographers, sociologists, and anthropologists interested in exploring both hyper-exploitation and labour segregation in new service-based economies have turned to the hotel as an ideal site (Savage 2006; Tufts 2006; Waldinger and Lichter 2003), asking a new set of questions about workers and their workplace practices, in which the intersections of class with other social divisions have become significant.

Central among these new questions is the link between labour market segmentation and performativity in the labour market. It is here, as in many of the bottom-end 'servicing' jobs in the now dominant service sector in the UK and the USA, that issues of 'doing gender' and 'doing ethnicity' in forms of interactive or body work (Leidner 1993; McDowell 2009; Wolkowitz 2002) that depends on a personal relationship between the seller and purchaser of a service are perhaps at their starkest. Hotels are organizations that provide both a visible (checking in, waiting on table) and an invisible (cleaning rooms and corridors, providing clean linen) service in which an often sexualized 'service with a smile' is highly valued, if not highly rewarded. Managers, employees, and guests all construct their identities and forge social relationships in the interactions and exchanges that take place in a hotel. Thus, as Lucas and Mansfield note, new questions about gender, nationality, personal style, embodiment, skin colour, weight, bodily hygiene, and language abilities (especially when there is an international client basis) become crucial parts both of the decision to hire categorically distinctive workers and of the performativity of workplace identities in order to produce a particular experience of 'hospitality' for the guests. Lucas and Mansfield helpfully distinguish three different performances that may be found in hotels, bars, restaurants, and the other multiple sites that characterize this industry, adding to the conventional exploration of deference or subordination. Two other useful categories for analysis are equivalence, when there is some performance of equality between service provider and consumer, and the probably less common superior or superordinate performance. As Lucas and Mansfield suggest, we need to know far more about the relationships between workers and clients, although the implications for research methods are complicated. And, as I argued initially, if hotel workers are the seen and unseen objects of the multiple desires and fantasies of managers, clients, and co-workers, desires that are especially significant in the 'enchantment' (Ritzer 1999) of guests that is intended to ensure their return, it is clear that employees are often at risk of sexual harassment (Guerrier and Adib 2000). This is another issue that deserves further exploration. Research is possible, although the methodological implications here too are vexed. In the UK, the Fawcett Society (2009) has, for example, begun to explore not only the sexualization of workers in one of the most seedy parts of the hospitality industry, in lap-dancing establishments, but has also addressed the relationships between hospitality and attracting clients in other industries such as the financial sector. As Lucas and Mansfield have shown, the hospitality sector not only demands attention as a key sector of the British economy, but also because it illustrates and raises so many of the central questions at the heart of any analysis of contemporary patterns of labour supply and demand in service economies.

References

Bauman, Z. (1998), *Work, Consumerism and the New Poor* (Buckingham: Open University Press).

——(2000), *Liquid Modernity* (Cambridge: Polity).

Beynon, H. (1984), *Working for Ford*, 2nd edn. (Harmondsworth: Penguin).

Burawoy, M. (1979), *Manufacturing Consent* (Chicago: University of Chicago Press).

Fawcett Society (2009), *Corporate Sexism: The Sex Industry's Infiltration of the Modern Workplace* (London: Fawcett Society).

Guerrier, Y., and Adib, A. (2000), '"No, We Don't Provide that Service": The Harassment of Hotel Employees by Customers', *Work, Employment and Society*, 14: 689–705.

Hayter, T., and Harvey, D. (1993), *The Factory and the City: The Story of Cowley Automobile Workers in Oxford* (London: Mansell).

Kondo, D. (1990), *Crafting Selves: Power, Gender and Discourses of Identity in a Japanese Workplace* (Chicago: University of Chicago Press).

Leidner, R. (1993), *Fast Food, Fast Talk: Service Work and the Routinization of Everyday Life* (Berkeley, Calif.: University of California Press).

McDowell, L. (2009), *Working Bodies: Interactive Service Employment and Workplace Identities* (Oxford: Wiley-Blackwell).

Ngai, P. (2005), *Made in China: Women Factory Workers in a Global Workplace* (Durham, NC: Duke University Press).

Ritzer, G. (1999), *Enchanting a Disenchanted World: Revolutionising the Means of Consumption* (London: Pine Forge Press).

Samuel, R. (ed.) (1977), *Miners, Quarrymen and Saltworkers* (London: Routledge and Kegan Paul).

Savage, L. (2006), 'Justice for Janitors: Scales of Organising and Representing Workers', *Antipode*, 38: 645–66.

Tufts, S. (2006), '"We Make it Work": The Cultural Transformation of Hotel Workers in the City', *Antipode*, 38: 350–73.

Vosko, L. (2000), *Temporary Work: The Gendered Rise of Precarious Employment* (Toronto: University of Toronto Press).

Waldinger, R. (1992), 'Taking Care of the Guests: The Impact of Immigrants on Services—An Industry Case Study', *International Journal of Urban and Regional Research*, 16.

——and Lichter, M. I. (2003), *How the Other Half Works: Immigrants and the Social Organisation of Labour* (Berkeley, Calif.: University of California Press).

Wolkowitz, C. (2002), 'The Social Relations of Body Work', *Work, Employment and Society*, 16: 497–510.

Wright, M. (1999), 'The Politics of Relocation: Gender, Nationality and Value in the Macquiladoras', *Environment and Planning A*, 31: 1601–17.

7

UK Food Businesses' Reliance on Low-Wage Migrant Labour: A Case of Choice or Constraint?

Andrew Geddes and Sam Scott

7.1 Introduction

A general answer to the question of whether the UK economy needs migrant workers requires the piecing together of numerous sector-specific analyses. The food production sector more than any other demonstrates the need for emphasis on local detail. There is very high variability in labour use because of seasonal rhythms in production, on the one hand, and the daily, weekly, and seasonal patterns of consumer demand on the other. One can distinguish, for example, between highly seasonal (for example, soft fruit and Christmas puddings), seasonal (for example, salad produce and turkey), and year-round activity (for example, dairy and ready-meals). This variability is much more significant than elsewhere in the economy.

For centuries, such variability has meant reliance upon itinerant workers; and for centuries, these workers have been anchored at the very bottom of the labour market. Temporary vacancies are, then, a permanent feature of food production. What has changed, over the last quarter-century in particular, has been the location and scale of the food production system and the origins and composition of the labour used within it. There has also been a shift from primary food production to secondary food processing, with a significant number of jobs moving from the field to the factory.

This chapter examines these geographic, economic, and labour market shifts and their role in constructing what is commonly thought of as an inevitable 'need' for migrant workers (especially young graduate migrants from Eastern Europe). The focus is very much upon the labour-intensive parts of the food production system (horticulture), as this is where shortages (albeit seasonal) are greatest in magnitude.

Section 7.2 provides a general overview in order to contextualize the analysis that follows. Section 7.3 focuses on employer demand and its changing nature over recent decades, before Section 7.4 goes on to examine labour supply and the shift from local to migrant labour. The final substantive section (Section 7.5), is concerned with the role of labour market intermediaries (also known as gangmasters) in matching workers to available work. We conclude by considering the alternatives to the now seemingly inevitable reliance of UK food producers on migrant workers.

7.2 Context

The food production system is made up of an uneven competitive terrain. This was noted in April 2008 when the Competition Commission called for greater monitoring of supply-chain relationships via the introduction of an ombudsman and a new code of practice. Such relationships have seen power concentrate amongst a small number of multinational retailers (Table 7.1) and suppliers,[1] and competitive pressures grow amongst the sub-contracted small and medium-sized enterprises (SMEs) (growers, processors, labour providers) below them.[2] Vorley (2003) characterizes contemporary food production as involving two different 'rural worlds', with power and control draining into the large and transnational retail end of the food system and away from food producers over the past 30 years (see also Gereffi and Korzeniewicz 1994).

Commensurate with this inequality in the economic system, we have seen growing social inequality, with polarization between desirable and undesirable jobs (Goos and Manning 2004; Kaplanis 2007). This has meant that low-paid farm and factory work has 'intensified' (Rogaly 2008): it now pays relatively

---

[1] Supermarket buyers prefer dealing with one or two companies for each food product they provide in order to avoid the inefficiency and complexity of having to negotiate with myriad food producers on a daily, and sometimes hourly, basis. Some 'category managers' are as—if not more—powerful than the supermarkets because of consumers' brand awareness.

[2] Since 2000, the four largest grocery retailers have doubled their number of stores (Competition Commission 2007a: para. 10) such that they now account for three-quarters of total grocery sales in supermarkets and convenience stores in the UK (Competition Commission 2007b: para. 6).

Table 7.1 Market share of the leading supermarkets by till roll sales (%)

Supermarket	Share of till roll sales (%)
Tesco	30.4
Asda	16.5
Sainsbury's	15.9
Morrisons	10.3
Somerfield	5.6
Co-op	4.7
Waitrose	3.7
Iceland	1.6
Aldi	2.3
Lidl	0.2
Netto	0.7

Source: Competition Commission (2007a: 15).

less than in the past and conditions have become worse because of efficiency savings and the monitoring and surveillance associated with this. At the same time, and because of the turn to greater sub-contracting, the opportunities available to workers and unions to improve pay and conditions have declined by virtue of them being one, two, three, or even four steps away from the managers and directors controlling the food production system.

Against this socio-economic context, we have seen temporary labour shortages emerge on farms and in food packing and processing factories, at a time when full-time labour use has been declining. The enlargement of the EU in 2004 and 2007 has allowed workers from the European periphery to fill these vacancies.[3] The jobs on offer have been seen by migrants as relatively appealing compared to the jobs available in their own country. This has meant that employers have been able to source 'better quality' (by which is often meant, more compliant and deferential) workers from abroad than are available to them in the UK.

The dominance of the 'big four' supermarkets may have dramatically reduced the number of food retail outlets and proved a death-knell for the more democratic and diverse local high street (NEF 2004). However, it has underpinned an era of cheap and increasingly sophisticated food, and consumers have voted with their feet, choosing supermarkets over independent high street stores.

---

[3] Some workers come from outside the EU ('third country nationals' (TCNs) subject to UK and EU immigration rules); though with the ending of sector-based schemes for food manufacturing, and the confinement of the Seasonal Agricultural Workers Scheme (SAWS) to migrants from within the EU, it is now very difficult for TCNs to work legally in the UK.

Two of the most visible consequences of the contemporary food supply system, beyond the changes to the high street, have been: the consolidation of farmers and food processors, and the influx of foreign migrant workers into the rural agricultural heartlands of the UK. In terms of the former, profit margins have been squeezed by retailers and category managers (large suppliers dealing directly with the 'big four'), and producers have become amalgamated via acquisitions, mergers, and cooperatives into larger and more specialized industrial operations.

In terms of the latter, the exact ways in which labour savings have been made vary from employer to employer. At a basic level, there has simply been a mass reduction in farm-based labour demand since the 1970s. New crop varieties, more sophisticated machine technology, and larger farms have all contributed to this development. The picture, however, is complex. At the same time as farms were shedding jobs, factories and pack-houses began to supply a more sophisticated consumer market with higher value-added food products such as ready meals and bagged salads.

Beyond the overall reduction in labour demand, employers have also made savings by using the workers they have more efficiently. Once again, new crop varieties and more sophisticated machinery have been key, as has the use of new worker monitoring and surveillance technology, and sophisticated psychological/management techniques to extract extra value from workers. We have also seen the resurgence of the age-old piece-rate and gangmaster systems as workplace regimes intensify (Rogaly 2008).

The situation in the UK is mirrored in the US (Martin 2003; Massey and Liang 1989; Taylor and Espenshade 1987; Taylor and Thilmany 1993). Californian agriculture in particular has been the 'laboratory' for the global agricultural system (Mitchell 1996). Its reliance on migrant labour is long-standing: first on Chinese and Japanese gang-based workers at the end of the nineteenth and beginning of the twentieth century respectively (Fisher 1953; Martin 2003: 28); then on Mexican farm workers (Martin 2003: 36–50). Today it is estimated that 75 per cent of all farm workers in the US are foreign-born (Martin 2003: 1), rising to over 90 per cent in California (Woods 2005: 38), with temporary contract-based labour the most migrant-dense (Vandeman et al. 1991). However, whilst developed-world agriculture does appear to have a universal need for immigrant labour, important differences remain in terms of crop type, seasonality, level of migrant penetration, status of immigrants, and the extent and enforcement of worker protection.

7.3 Employer Demand

7.3.1 *Segmented Labour Markets*

The context outlined above has 'constructed' (see chapter 2 by Anderson and Ruhs in this volume) a specific type of labour demand and, therefore, helps us understand the persistence of labour shortages in UK food production. A dual-labour market system exists whereby employers require a core of permanent staff—some in food production and some in management/clerical roles—alongside a variable workforce.

Segmented labour market theory (Massey et al. 1998; Piore 1979) helps us to understand the rationale behind this. The theory shows how it is possible for firms to offset the costs of an uncertain market—a particular issue with food supply and demand (and made more prominent since the 1980s by supermarkets' highly flexible 'just-in-time' ordering systems)—by passing this uncertainty on to certain groups of workers. They are able to do this by having a segment of their labour force that is employed and deployed on an 'as and when needed' basis. This temporary workforce constitutes the 'secondary labour market' and it is here where the least desirable and most insecure forms of employment are concentrated. Unsurprisingly, it is also here where labour shortages and migrant penetration have been most intense. This is why we talk of labour shortages and immigration in the food sector as 'constructed' rather than inevitable.

Piore characterizes secondary labour as: '...a means of evasion: a sector of the labour market that is not subject to restrictions or lay-off and discharge to which the unstable portion of demand can be transferred' (1979: 39). This is a point that Anderson and Ruhs also make more generally in the first two chapters of this book. It is clear that certain sectors of the UK economy have a more unstable demand base than others and thus a greater propensity to experience cyclical and structural labour shortages and immigration. Migrants have filled these shortages over the past decade and especially (or more visibly) since EU enlargement in 2004.

7.3.2 *Temporal Rhythms*

The secondary labour market thesis is excellent at an abstract level, but on the ground the situation is far more nuanced and dynamic. Four temporal dimensions are particularly noteworthy.

First, the jobs at the bottom of the UK food chain are amongst the least desirable in the UK economy and so turnover is high. Workers, if they can, will use temporary posts as stepping stones to move up or out of the sector and so secondary labour markets function as a 'revolving door': hence the persistence of labour shortages over time. Immigrant labour is especially significant here, as migrants tend to be self-selecting and more skilled than local workers. They will accept a degree of brain-waste as a short-term sacrifice for longer-term career success and so will not want to work in temporary roles indefinitely.

Secondly, the balance between immigrant and local labour will change over time as economic cycles play out and as immigration policies adjust (the two are often but not always related). One key question is whether recessions lead to domestic workers filling vacancies ahead of immigrant workers (who tend to be recruited by employers during economic booms). Amongst other things, the answer to this question depends upon: the location of the unemployed relative to the location of food industry va-cancies; the flexibility of state benefits; employer preferences and preju-dices; changes in migration flows; and changes in immigration policy. Thus, whilst simple labour market theory suggests that rising unemploy-ment will lead to British workers replacing migrant workers, the situation on the ground is more complex.

This was recently illustrated by the 2007–9 UK economic downturn. Evidence showed how EU nationals were returning home (Pollard et al. 2008) and that flows of workers from EU accession states had peaked (Balch et al. 2009). However, there was no substantial evidence to indicate that the food industry's secondary labour markets had become home to newly unemployed British workers. Reasons for a lack of immediate substitution between different groups of workers can be manifold. Local workers gener-ally have more intense social ties than migrants, making it more difficult in both a practical and psychological sense for them to 'get on their bike' to find work. They also have regular fiscal (mortgages) and familial (child and elderly care) commitments that can make the volatile wages and hours of secondary labour markets unworkable and non-viable. Furthermore, it is more difficult for workers to switch welfare state benefits on and off than it is for employers to recruit and lay off secondary labour: coming off welfare benefits and travelling long distances for the possibility—but not guaran-tee—of minimum-wage work is quite a risk.

Thirdly, secondary labour shortages vary over time, depending on the particular production strategy of the food business. It is possible, for instance, to distinguish between labour-intensive (horticulture) and capi-tal-intensive (other arable), and between specialist and generalist food producers. A horticultural specialist, for instance, will have a considerable labour demand, but if he or she is growing a highly seasonal crop then this demand will be ephemeral. In contrast, whilst a horticultural generalist may also have considerable labour demand volatility, he or she will be able to offset some of this by growing crops with different supply and demand patterns. Firms can also address demand volatility by adopting transnational supply strategies. A specialist salad processor, for instance, can keep staff employed all year by importing raw materials during the winter months; without these imports, year-round labour would not be required. Moreover, some producers have operations in a number of countries and move staff between their different bases depending on the growing seasons and product demand-and-supply cycles. This mobility enables them to keep staff (mainly managers) employed on permanent contracts.

Finally, technological innovations have led to changes over time in the demand for labour. Certain crops can now easily be harvested or processed by machine (e.g. wheat), whilst others can, but are more problematic or costly (e.g. lettuce), with some simply too fragile to be automated (e.g. raspberries). Firm size also mediates the speed and scale of technological uptake and scholars have consistently observed how larger firms are quicker to develop and adopt new labour-saving machines, with smaller producers reliant on labour for much longer due to the fixed costs involved in, and economies of scale required from, machine-based production (Ilyukhin et al. 2001; Aly 1989).

Secondary labour demand, then, is shaped by temporal rhythms related to career progression, recession and growth, business mix, and technological innovation and adaptation.

7.3.3 Intensification

In addition, many authors argue that the particular crisis in labour supply that has afflicted UK food producers over recent decades relates to the emergence of a particular period of intensification of work. It has been argued that the economic base of food production (described in Section 7.2, above) has made the work available on farms and in factories worse, both in an absolute and relative sense, and that this intensification is part of a broader polarization of employment in advanced capitalist economies.

There is no doubt that the competitive climate is an issue and that this has led to employers cutting costs, with labour one of the easiest and quickest costs to cut. The Competition Commission (2007a), for instance, reported on the 'standard' tactics used by larger firms to draw value from smaller firms in the food supply-chain: 61 per cent of all supermarket retailers were found to require obligatory contributions to marketing costs; 48 per cent of suppliers reported delays in receiving payment; 48 per cent of suppliers were required to make excessive payments in cases of customer complaints; 37 per cent of suppliers were asked to provide additional packing and distribution services; and 37 per cent of suppliers were requested to make price reductions before or after delivery. The suppliers most exposed to this down-stream pressure invariably have a narrow customer base: possibly just a single supermarket or single category manager; and the supermarkets and category managers will know how vulnerable their clients are and negotiate accordingly.

Rogaly (2008) has argued that this competitive climate has led to an absolute intensification of work (see also Brass 2004). He cites the increased use of gangmasters and piece-rates as particularly symptomatic of this. Other modes of intensification involve employers housing workers on-site and being able to employ them as and when required at very little notice, and employers monitoring workers' movements with greater frequency and with a greater threat of negative consequences for non-compliance.[4]

Another way in which employment has deteriorated is through relative intensification. Even if none of the above had taken place, work in the food industry would still have become less desirable. Newby (1977) showed how food producers' ability to exercise demand over local and national labour markets has declined because of the broader sociological context within which agricultural work is embedded (and through which it derives meaning and value). Most obviously, farm work has become less communal, more isolated, and more impersonal as the scale of farm activity has grown and as the number of workers needed per unit of output has declined. The commensurate decline in the rural working-class and loss of affordable housing for low-paid rural workers have served to further isolate those farm workers that remain. Stripped down to its financial bones, the harshness of agricultural work has become more exposed than ever.

The absolute and relative intensification arguments lie at the heart of the temporary and seasonal labour shortages at the producer end of the UK food industry. Thus, whilst segmented labour market theory tells us why low-wage insecure employment exists, the insights of Rogaly (absolute intensification) and Newby (relative intensification) are more sector-specific, and

---

[4] Although union penetration of the food industry remains low, absolute intensification has been checked to some extent by the national minimum wage, the agricultural wages boards, the Gangmaster Licensing Authority (GLA), and retailer-led supply-chain auditing.

tell us why secondary labour markets have become especially undesirable in farming and food packing and processing.

7.3.4 Current Demand Base

Statistics show that both the number of farm businesses and the number of paid farm labourers has declined considerably since the 1970s, but that for the businesses that have survived, turnover (though not necessarily profits) has increased. Since 1971, for instance, there has been a 65 per cent drop in paid labour use on farms and an associated rise in productivity, up by 52 per cent since 1973 (Defra 2007: 94). Both trends are part of firms' attempts to survive an increasingly competitive and retailer-controlled operating environment (Gereffi and Korzeniewicz 1994).

Data on the exact balance between permanent and temporary staff and between farm and factory work are patchy. The Labour Force Survey (part of the Annual Population Survey) appears to be better at capturing factory work than at recording farm-based employment, which receives better coverage through Defra's annual Agricultural Census. Both surveys, though, suffer from the impossibility of capturing a large, floating, and often non-English-speaking workforce.

In April 2008, in collaboration with the National Farmers' Union (NFU), we surveyed 268 farmers in the UK to look at their labour demand and supply issues.[5] Our aim was to investigate the scaling-up in labour use between low and peak season and to find out who filled this uplift. The results relate largely to the labour-intensive horticultural sector and showed that employment levels grow by around three to five times between low and peak seasons (Table 7.2), with only 16 per cent of the peak season farm workforce now British-born (Table 7.3).[6]

The 268 employers who responded to our April 2008 survey took on an extra 28,206 workers for the peak season, with 30 per cent recruited via gangmasters and 70 per cent directly (Table 7.4). The nationality of those supplied through gangs is shown in Figure 7.1 and is based on data from the Gangmaster Licensing Authority (GLA, the organization in the UK

---

[5] The results must be understood in this context: they were generated through the active involvement and support of employers who, arguably, have a vested interest in maximizing labour supply and particularly the supply of relatively well-educated migrants.

[6] The mean figure in Table 7.2 is higher because of the existence of a small number of very large businesses. These businesses over-emphasize the peak-to-low season uplift and so the median average is considered alongside the mean average because it is much less affected by small but significant outliers.

Table 7.2 Change in employment levels between peak and low season: mean and median averages

	Peak	Low	Difference
Mean	134	29	105
Median	40	9	31

Source: University of Liverpool and NFU survey, 2008.

Table 7.3 Origins of agricultural labour (peak season)

Origin	No.	%
UK	5,632	16
A8[1]	17,280	49
A2[2]	11,132	32
Other	958	3

Notes: [1] A8 refers to eight of the ten countries that joined the EU in May 2004: Poland, Estonia, Latvia, Lithuania, Czech Republic, Slovakia, Hungary, and Slovenia. These eight countries (unlike Malta and Cyprus: the other two Accession States in 2004) were subject to transitional restrictions imposed on a country-by-country basis.
[2] A2 refers to the two countries that joined the EU in January 2008: Bulgaria and Romania. These two countries, like their A8 counterparts, were subject to transitional restrictions imposed on a country-by-country basis.

Source: University of Liverpool and NFU survey, 2008.

Table 7.4 Types of workers (recruitment method and employment status) hired by UK farm businesses to meet additional peak-season labour demand

Recruitment method/ employment status	Proportion (%)	Total workers*
Direct/permanent	3.5%	984
Direct/temporary	65.6%	18,492
Agency/permanent	1.7%	480
Agency/temporary	29.3%	8,250

Note: * The 268 survey respondents took on a total of 28,206 extra workers for the peak season.
Source: University of Liverpool and NFU survey, 2008.

responsible for licensing labour providers in the food production sector). The Polish stand out as the most important nationality, and what is most striking is the fact that a GLA licence is more likely to be held by a gangmaster supplying A8-only[7] (268 businesses) than UK-only (164 businesses) workers (Table 7.5).

[7] Migration from the eight Central and East European (A8) countries that joined the EU on 1 May 2004.

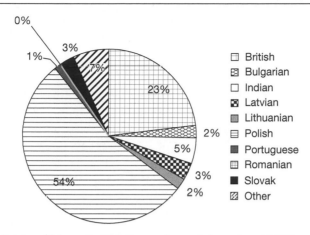

Figure 7.1 Origin of labour in GLA-licensed gang labour (n = 65,311 workers)
Source: Balch et al. (2009).

Table 7.5 Nationalities of workers supplied by GLA-licensed gangmasters

Groups of nationality	Number of businesses
UK only	164
A8 and A2	268
UK + A8	184
UK + A8 + Non-EU	108
UK + A8 + EU 15 + Non-EU	113
Other combinations	266

Source: Balch et al. (2009).

In terms of where this low-to-peak demand uplift is concentrated, Defra data show that the 'general cropping' and 'horticultural' areas of UK agriculture are most significant. Together, these two primary activities account for 47 per cent of all agricultural employment in the UK and a massive 62 per cent of all temporary agricultural employment.

LFS data summarized in the September 2008 MAC report show similar trends for food processing. The 'packing, bottling, canning and filling' category is 40 per cent foreign-born, with an equal reliance on A8 and non-EU migrants. Similarly, around 30 per cent of the workforce in the 'processing of tobacco, food and drink' are foreign-born, with evidence suggesting particular concentrations in food processing rather than the drinks and tobacco sub-sectors. As discussed in Chapter 3 of this book (by Aldin et al.), looking across all LFS occupational categories, the food processing and packing occupations stand out as some of the most migrant-dense of all occupations in the UK. (The LFS shows much more limited migrant labour use in agriculture, but this relates to the sample methodology of the survey.)

For both farming and food packing and processing, there appears to have been a considerable easing of shortages following EU enlargements in 2004 and 2007. However, employers fear future labour supply problems as the impact of this 'migration bonus' diminishes. Our 2008 survey found that 73 per cent of employers reported experiencing recruitment difficulties in their temporary and seasonal positions. This was an issue of both quantity and quality. Nine in every ten employers (91%) cited 'work ethic' as being the reason behind favouring migrants over British workers. This preference, however, is likely to be challenged by both the reduction in arrivals to the UK from the new EU member states and by the recent growth in UK unemployment.

The geographical distribution of migrant workers in agriculture and food processing closely matches the areas of the country associated with labour-intensive food production. Two types of location stand out: areas of high-grade farm land suitable for horticultural activity (farming); and locations near to major transport networks and supermarket distribution centres (food packing and processing). WRS data record where migrants from the new EU member states register to work in terms of both location and sector.

A number of concentrations are evident from WRS data: the Wash (Lincolnshire, Cambridgeshire, and Norfolk); Fife, Perthshire, Kinross, and Angus; Herefordshire and Worcestershire; Kent; West Lancashire; Cornwall; North Lincolnshire and Humberside; West Sussex and Hampshire; and Suffolk. Food manufacturing activities are concentrated along the main arterial roads in England (the M1, A1, M6, and M62 in particular).

7.4 Labour Supply

7.4.1 *Choice*

The supply of labour into a given industry is a function, at the microeconomic level, of the wages being offered relative to other wages in the economy. In the basic textbook model of the labour market, labour shortages arise because wages are lower than the equilibrium wages that would bring demand and supply into balance. In theory, the answer to such shortages is to raise wages and/or improve working conditions, making labour shortages frictional rather than structural.

The persistence of structural labour shortages at the producer end of the UK food supply chain can be explained by employers' inability (and some argue unwillingness) to raise wages and improve working conditions. A demand perspective allows us to understand why this transition has taken place: as we argued above, the evidence shows that wages and conditions have deteriorated in both an absolute and a relative sense in the UK food industry over recent decades (Brass 2004; Newby 1977; Rogaly 2008).

Nevertheless, from a supply perspective, labour shortages can be addressed with different combinations of workers irrespective of the way in which they are constructed and explained. Most obviously, shortages in some areas of the UK economy are more likely to be filled by migrant workers than those in other areas. Of particular note here is the fact that the secondary labour markets of the UK food industry have virtually been no-go areas for would-be British workers, especially since the turn of the century. Labour has instead been supplied from abroad, mostly from the 2004 and 2007 EU accession states.

Our employer survey of April 2008 picked up the supply-side impact of EU enlargement particularly strongly. In the period 2003–6, 44 per cent of respondents felt it had become harder, and 34 per cent felt it had become easier, to find workers. Given that it is in employers' interest to over-report shortages, this 34 per cent figure is actually much higher than we had expected. This becomes even clearer when, from 2007, the survey reveals that only 2 per cent of employers were now finding it easier to attract workers. Clearly, the enlargement of the EU in 2004 opened up new and very valuable labour supply channels to employers recruiting at the very bottom of the UK labour market.

The 'migration bonus' and specific supply patterns associated with it, at one level, reflect the limited choice of employers unable or unwilling to raise wages and conditions and in many cases, actually overseeing a reduction, in an absolute and relative sense, of the quality of the work on offer. At the same time, though, employers have still shown that they are in a position to choose by preferring migrants over British-born workers (especially with regard to their temporary labour vacancies). This is because the quality of migrant workers is perceived to be much higher, linked to the role of farm and factory work as a 'stepping-stone' for foreign nationals from peripheral economies, but as a 'dead-end' for British-born nationals (Waldinger and Lichter 2003).

In essence, different groups of workers exhibit different elasticities of supply for the same work because the 'value' of the work is socially and geographically mediated. Immigrants view farm work as an opportunity both for career advancement and for increasing their families' wealth and status back at home, whilst domestic workers view the same work in a largely negative sense. Employers pick up on this social and geographical mediation, in terms of attitudes, levels of compliance, and productivity, and in turn generalize particular qualities and failings across particular groups of workers. Recruitment preferences reflect these supply-side differences and are particularly pronounced when both immigration barriers (as in the EU) and barriers to labour market entry such as skills, language, and qualifications (as in temporary food production jobs) are low.

Even against a backdrop of acute labour shortages, food industry employers have chosen migrant workers ahead of inactive British citizens. They have also engaged in particular gendered and age-based patterns of recruitment, thereby manipulating the supply of labour even whilst offering relatively low wages and relatively poor employment conditions. In terms of the former, men tend to be in charge of machinery and dangerous tools (e.g. machetes) out in the field, whilst women are preferred for the 'nimble' tasks (e.g. soft fruit picking and packing). Moreover, women are alleged to be better linguists, so in our experience have been more likely than male migrants to move from secondary into primary labour markets, and especially into human resource roles. In terms of age, employers have consistently preferred young migrant workers and the recent industry-wide push to extend the Seasonal Agricultural Workers Scheme (SAWS), which is targeted at students, underlines this.

7.4.2 Constraint

Notwithstanding employers' ability to manipulate the supply of workers at the bottom of the labour market, it is clear that the number of low-wage British workers willing to work in the food industry has declined particularly steeply since the early 1980s. The combination of reduced social and affordable housing, the rise in middle-class 'counter-urbanites', and the growth in university education, has meant that there are simply very few young people available to work in rural areas and market towns; and those who are available have been more attracted to service work. Employers have, therefore, looked to migrant workers out of both choice (they think they can get more for their money abroad) and constraint (the rural working-class is smaller than ever before).

Five post-war shifts are particularly noteworthy with respect to this 'drying up' of the rural working-class:

1. Agricultural workers are no longer in the majority within rural areas as a result of both the influx of counter-urbanites, 'the rural population today is generally older and *more middle-class* than it was 30 years ago'

(Woods 2005: 72), and the long-term decline in total agricultural employment in both absolute terms and relative to other sectors.

2. Farmers have shifted from adopting a paternalistic role with regard to their employees to adopting a *more distant and bureaucratic* role. This has been associated with the development of industrial farming or 'agri-business', which has meant that the largely local and informal systems of social relations structuring agricultural employment have disappeared.

3. There has been an overall shift in the employment base of rural areas away from primary sectors and towards *service sectors*; seven in ten workers living in rural England are now employed in the service sector (Woods 2005: 62). Women, in particular, who once supplied a significant proportion of seasonal labour, have been drawn into the service sector and away from agriculture.

4. Agricultural employment was once judged relative to other local employment opportunities: it is now *judged against a national (even international) hierarchy* of employment. This has meant the loss of local status hierarchies and informal social networks that once structured agricultural employment, with farm work now being judged according to national or international 'attributional' criteria rather than local 'interactional' criteria. We have moved from a situation where farm work had a low 'economic' but high 'social' wage, to a situation where it now has both a low 'economic' and a low 'social' wage (Newby 1977, 1987).

5. Labour market intermediaries have been *formalized* by gangmaster regulation and this has hastened the already declining local informal gang-supply systems. Similarly, workplace formalization has occurred. For instance, a generation ago local women would take their children with them at harvest time: some would work and others would be left at the side of the field to play. This is not possible today: the hours are too irregular and childcare is too expensive to make harvest work viable for this potential labour supply.

Even when there are unemployed British workers, it is difficult for them to take up temporary and seasonal work. Geographically, the inactive population tends to cluster in deprived urban neighbourhoods far away from the main food employers. Furthermore, many recently unemployed people will have fixed and regular outgoings (mortgages, bills, rent) and commitments (family care, voluntary work); foregoing regular benefits in favour of irregular employment and an uncertain income would be a risk.

There are a number of solutions to increasing the supply of inactive British citizens into the food industry's labour markets. Most obviously, workers need to have places to live near to the available work but, ideally, not tied to the employer so as to give them independence. Ways also need to be found to redress the decline in permanent and stable employment in order to make work on farms and in food factories pay. If temporary work must persist, then the interchange between work and benefits needs to be made smoother. Some have advocated a workfare system that would force people into work and this issue has received particular attention in light of the Department for Work and Pensions (DWP's) recent Welfare Reform Bill.[8] Critics argue that the Bill has a compulsory workfare dimension which ignores the fact that few people actively choose to live on £64.30 per week (the unemployment benefit for over 25s in April 2009). They also fear that employers might be tempted to further intensify their work offer because they know that people will be forced to accept whatever is available. Advocates of the Bill refute these 'workfare' allegations.

Practically, it may also be difficult to get the urban unemployed into largely rural labour markets and the costs of this might be better spent on rural affordable housing and encouragement rather than compulsion to work. Moreover, employers[9] can recognize how tough and 'back-breaking' is temporary and seasonal harvest work. Most of the employers we interviewed felt that the intensity of work was too much to be sustained over a full 12-month period, even if the weather allowed, and believed vacancies were best filled by young, fit workers. If there is a significant but older unemployed population in the UK, then the secondary labour market vacancies could prove too physically demanding and possibly debilitating.

7.5 Mediating between Supply and Demand: Labour Market Intermediaries

Approximately one-third of temporary vacancies at the producer end of the UK food industry are filled by workers supplied via labour providers (Table 7.4). For migrants in particular, these intermediaries act as a vital first foothold in the UK labour market (and in many cases, help migrants to move internationally in the first place). In UK food production alone, there are 1,200 licensed gangmasters now supplying temporary (mainly migrant)

[8] This DWP Welfare Reform Bill was published on 14 January 2009. Its main architect was David Freud, an investment banker.
[9] We carried out 30 in-depth employer interviews as part of a Nuffield-funded research project.

workers to farmers and food processors. An estimated further 20–25 per cent of the sector operates under the UK government's radar (Balch et al. 2009).

Exactly how employers recruit workers and the socio-demographic and cultural morphology of this recruitment depends upon a number of factors, most notably: the combination of products being produced, the balance between farm and factory activity, the products' demand and supply cycle, profit margins, and the individual links and preferences of the employer. Direct employment is more common in factories and fields where outputs and demands are less subject to peaks and troughs; it is also more common amongst firms with direct links to major supermarkets and category managers. Agency labour is more common where product supply and demand cycles experience dramatic changes on a daily, weekly, monthly, and seasonal basis. It is also more common when specific time-limited tasks are required. For instance, demand for salads and soft fruit tends to increase over the summer and rise to a particular high when the weather is good, and when this coincides with a Bank Holiday, the peak is further intensified.

Only one-in-four agency workers in UK food production are now British-born (Balch et al. 2009) and so labour market mediation has principally become about matching migrant labour supply to domestic labour demand. Since 2004, the migrants being supplied by labour market intermediaries have mainly come from Poland, the Baltic States, and Portugal. Many appear to use recruitment agencies both to enter the UK and to secure initial employment, as well as accommodation. There is also a strong link between labour market intermediaries and irregular immigration that is not picked up in any of the statistics.

Lengths of agency placements are usually short; 64 per cent of staff are supplied for less than 12 weeks (ibid.). Over time, this insecurity means that workers, where possible, look to more secure direct forms of employment. Thus, whilst most migrant workers will have used a labour market intermediary to secure employment (and accommodation) at some point since arriving in the UK, their propensity to use these intermediaries diminishes over time.

In terms of how labour market intermediaries work, some function as traditional informal local gangs (Brass 2004), whilst others are much more professional, and in some cases, transnational. Table 7.6 summarizes the nine different types of labour market intermediary we encountered during various pieces of research for the GLA into labour use in the UK food industry (Balch et al. 2009; Geddes et al. 2007; Scott et al. 2007). It is clear from this that firms source secondary labour in a range of ways.

Table 7.6 Modes of 'gangmaster' recruitment in the UK food industry

Gang structures and systems	Details	Risk of exploitation or informality
A. Independent familial gang labour	One worker heads a small gang of other workers on an informal basis. This system was common when seasonal labour was sourced locally and corresponds to the traditional use of the term 'gangmaster'. Given the local base of this system, there is some degree of self-regulation.	Medium
B. Independent bureaucratic gang labour	A business supplies workers to a labour user, but without the familial ties of mode A. Unlike mode A, the business will have a number of clients and will not work alongside the labour being supplied.	High
C. In-house gang labour	An employer externalizes recruitment and HR functions by relying on an internal but independent gangmaster. This system is often used by employers to tap into the social networks their migrant workers have in their home country. The in-house gangmaster is usually a migrant worker, given an added degree of responsibility but kept at arm's-length from the main company.	Medium
D. Project-oriented gang labour	Workers are brought in as a specialist team for a specific time-limited task such as slaughtering and bagging turkeys at Christmas or cleaning out animal pens/cages at the end of a production cycle.	High
E. Indirect labour provision	Deployment by an agent to another labour market intermediary. This is quite common in international recruitment where a foreign labour provider supplies workers to a UK labour provider.	Very high
F. Cooperative labour provision	Businesses exchange labour on a kith and kin pro-bono basis. This occurs at a local level and was especially common, alongside mode A, before migrant labour became significant. The system remains prominent in shellfish and in hill-farming communities. Given the local base of this system, there is some degree of self-regulation.	Medium
G. Internal flexible labour provision	A parent company has a number of divisions, including a labour supply unit supplying workers to other units. This is especially common amongst large transnational category managers.	Low
H. External labour networks	An HR manager within a company delivers groups of workers to that company on a regular basis by co-opting external labour clearing agencies. This can involve the use of social networks, recruitment fairs, etc. It is especially common in agriculture, where HR staff are sent abroad to source groups of migrant workers prior to the peak season.	Low
I. Foreign labour providers	Labour is supplied to a UK farm or factory from a gangmaster based abroad.	Very high

Source: Scott et al. (2007: 19–20).

Furthermore, the type of gang structure adopted is likely to tell us something about the risk of worker exploitation and business informality. The important questions to ask with each of the nine methods of labour market mediation in the food industry are why vacancies are filled in this way and why it is not possible or cheaper to recruit directly.

Overall, however, we have also noted a drop in the use of intermediaries over time and a reorientation towards directly sourced labour, even if this labour is temporary. This change most likely reflects the influence of gangmaster licence-based regulation and enforcement, which has made it harder for illegal labour providers to undercut competitors and, therefore, reduced the savings employers are able to gain from using gangmasters.

In terms of the geography of agency labour, gangmasters cluster where labour-intensive horticultural activity is based, and this activity in turn reflects the presence of high-grade farm land. Nonetheless, gangmasters often work hundreds of miles outside their base and are responsible in particular for migrant workers moving across vast swathes of the UK. This mobility most commonly relates to gangmasters based in agricultural heartlands moving workers into businesses located in more peripheral areas of the UK as and when they are needed. An example of this, we encountered, was a Lincolnshire gangmaster supplying migrant workers for a few weeks to pick daffodils in Cornwall, and then later in the season moving workers up to Scotland to pick soft fruit. The more distant a worker is from their home and from their gangmaster, the more vulnerable they generally are.

7.6 Six Alternatives to Migrant Labour

Over the past decade UK reliance on foreign labour in food production has increased dramatically. To some extent this increase may be statistical: EU enlargement enabled employers to source staff legally from a much larger area and reduced dependence upon clandestine, and therefore statistically invisible, forms of migrant labour. However, to a large extent the increase represented the reality during the late 1990s and first part of this century: that farmers and food packers and processors experienced considerable labour shortages and were both unable and unwilling to fill these shortages locally or nationally.

It is important to recognize here that shortages are socially, economically, culturally, and politically constructed and that they need not exist; the fact they have been so prevalent reflects a set of broader structural constraints governing upstream employment in the UK food sector (discussed earlier in

211

the chapter). Moreover, and notwithstanding the constructed nature of labour shortages, one must also recognize that immigration is one of a number of potential solutions to the labour shortages we have observed. As Martin (2003: 6) argues: 'There are alternatives to the farm labour status-quo (immigration) that would make farming profitable, raise farm worker wages, and still keep strawberries and lettuce affordable'. In this section, we will consider these alternatives. There are six main ones and they address either the demand or supply side of the contemporary labour shortages in the UK food industry.

The first potential solution to employers' labour shortages is to substitute foreign nationals with locally or nationally unemployed or inactive work-ers. This is possible when we have the paradoxical situation of shortages in low-wage and relatively low-skilled sectors of the economy, where barriers to entry are low, at the same time as mass unemployment. You simply move inactive British citizens (who could still be foreign-born) into jobs and any labour shortages become short term and frictional rather than long term and structural. This could be done by making benefits as flexible as the work that benefit claimants are asked to go into. It could also be done by increas-ing the amount of affordable rural housing in the UK. Finally, there could simply be an element of workfare-style compulsion. All of these options require absolutely no improvement in the wages and conditions within the food industry. The main problems with this approach are that: the unem-ployed are usually concentrated in deprived urban areas quite some way from food production sites; those who are unemployed or inactive are not always suited to the dirty, dangerous, and demanding work available (e.g. those close to retirement and those on incapacity benefit); employers may still prefer immigrant workers (even if these are 'illegal') because of their perceived superior quality over the British unemployed; and compelling the unemployed to work has practical, moral, and legal issues attached (Bauder 2006, chapter 11). Also, the episodic nature of low-paid work can make it difficult for domestic workers (who are likely to have more social and financial ties and obligations than migrants) to make work pay, and it will probably always be easier to move into and out of secondary labour markets than to move into and out of the benefit system.

A second obvious solution is to improve the work offer: to pay more and/ or to offer better conditions to workers. Simple economic theory tells us that if employers face labour shortages, they need to improve their 'bid' for the available labour. The problem with this solution is as obvious as the solution itself: where does the money come from to support upstream employers to do this? It seems unlikely that cheap food—acting as a deflationary force on the economy and as a means of increasing consumers' sense of affluence—can co-exist with expensive local resources. This said, 2008 saw total income from farming (TIFF) rise dramatically, by 36 per cent in real terms according to Defra, meaning that producers now have the capacity to improve working conditions after years of seeing their incomes decline.

It also evident that 'revolving door'-style recruitment has a number of hidden costs and that paying more for workers in order to ensure their long-term loyalty can actually be more efficient. Firms spend considerable amounts on continuous recruitment and training, as new workers are brought in and leave on a daily, weekly, and seasonal basis, and reducing the number of workers in the secondary labour market will actually reduce these costs. In short, increasing the direct labour bill does not always increase the total outgoings of a business because other indirect costs may be reduced in the process.

In addition, farm and factory labour actually represents a very small proportion of the total retail cost of a given food output. In the United States, Martin (2003: 194), for example, argues that a 40 per cent rise in the wage bill would translate into a mere 2.4 per cent increase in a household's food bill. At present, the 'big four' supermarkets, allied with some of their larger category managers, control the UK food chain and they would simply not entertain this solution, given the importance placed on value and price-based competition. Furthermore, consumers possess very little knowledge regarding how little of their total food bill actually finds its way to farm and factory labourers.

The work offer could also be improved by tying more of the available jobs in the food industry into career paths, and linking initial low-wage work to longer-term career progression. These careers could also be linked to entitlement to affordable social or cooperative housing (as has occurred on a pilot basis in the US; see Woods 2005: 263). The supermarkets might even be persuaded to sponsor one or two of these schemes in areas where housing is least affordable (Cornwall, North Yorkshire, the Lake District).

A third solution is to substitute capital for labour. Evidence from the US (Martin 2003) shows that the food industry is more likely to adopt new technology when labour costs are relatively high, but will not entertain the idea if labour costs are low. Thus, there is a negative correlation between immigration and technological innovation. Mass migration makes the substitution of variable capital (workers) for fixed capital (machines) less likely (Friedland et al. 1981, chapter 4; Martin 2003: 192–6). However, given the large technological shifts in agriculture that have taken place, stopping immigration will not guarantee further large-scale technological innovation, and even if it did, there would be a time-lag between immigration stopping and new machinery being used in place of migrant workers.

New technology can replace the jobs once done by humans (e.g. planting, harvesting, watering, cutting, cleaning, sorting, preparing), or it can change the nature of the job being done (e.g. new crop types, waist-high shelf-based picking systems, greenhouse growing to prolong the season). There are barriers to new technology. There is the obvious problem of fragile versus robust crops. Potatoes, for example, are simply much easier to harvest by machine than soft fruits like raspberries and cherries. There is also the problem of the growing season: it makes more sense to invest in machinery for crops with a longer growing season because the longer the machine is idle, the less cost effective it is. Finally, even within a particular crop, there will be variation. In the fresh herb sector, for instance, the consistency of drilled crops (like parsley and coriander) makes them much more amenable to mechanization than less consistent herbs (like mint, rosemary, and thyme). Similarly, in the lettuce sector, tightly growing varieties (like iceberg) can more easily be harvested by machine and are less weather dependent than fragile baby-leaf varieties.

A fourth solution, which would feed into the above, is for farmers to continue scaling up production. The larger the farm, the less labour per unit output is required and the more viable it is to substitute labour for capital. In other words, continued shifts from family to factory farming will have a 'demand easing' effect and continue the long-term trend of a declining farm workforce. In the UK, the average size of farm needed to support a full-time occupier has doubled every decade since the war (Newby 1987: 190).

A fifth solution would be that shortages could be addressed by employers recruiting workers from overseas—the example we have focused on in the chapter. This solution is a classic case of 'supply easing'. From 2004, immigrants have been readily available from the new EU member states (principally Poland). The question for the future is if such flows will continue, and how they will be received in light of local unemployment. Moreover, if they do dry up, will employers look to other 'illegal' sources of labour supply, such as clandestine migrants (common in the US and Southern Europe) and local 'cash casuals' (who work as and when required whilst still claiming benefits)?

The sixth solution is for food production, especially labour-intensive branches of UK agriculture, to move overseas. In other words, rather than bringing cheap labour to the farms and factories, the farms and factories could move to where the cheap labour is located. This is already a policy of

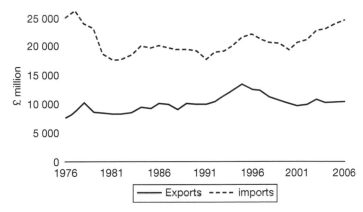

Figure 7.2 UK food imports and exports, 1976–2006
Source: Defra (2007: 67).

some of the larger UK food producers (with bases in Spain, Portugal, Poland, and the Ukraine, amongst other countries), but it raises the politically sensitive question of the extent to which the UK should be self-sufficient in an increasingly uncertain world. Figures show that from 1996 to 2006, UK self-sufficiency fell from 84 to 72 per cent (but it is still higher than in the 1950s), with the gap between agricultural imports and exports rising, following a period of contraction (Figure 7.2). The self-sufficiency debate has recently risen to prominence via Defra's new 'food security' agenda (announced on 10 August 2009). Food is a tradable commodity and, assuming the UK remains an open international trading nation, 100 per cent self-sufficiency is not what is needed (especially given the UK does not have a comparative advantage in all food types). What is at issue is the rising cost of food imports as the world population grows and the extent to which both UK producers (combining migrant and domestic labour and home-based and foreign production) and UK consumers (changing diets, buying more local produce, throwing less food away) can minimize these costs.

7.7 Conclusion

Labour shortages were a general feature of the UK economy until mid-2008 when the current recession hit. The 12 years of economic growth the UK had experienced up to this point saw both the number of jobs increase, and immigrants move in to fill the resultant vacancies at both the bottom and top of the UK labour market. Had immigration not occurred, it is likely that growth would have been slower. At the very least, low-wage food producers would not have seen such cost savings and productivity increases, as they would have been reliant on 'poorer quality' domestic workers, or they would have had to reverse the long-term intensification of farm and factory work and improve pay and conditions to attract staff of a suitable calibre.

In this sense, labour shortages, especially in an era of open EU borders and persistent domestic unemployment, constitute both a genuine constraint on business and a business profit-maximizing strategy. Employers offer the lowest possible wages and poor working conditions (physically tough, repetitive, dangerous, and/or insecure) for the maximum possible worker input, knowing that they will struggle to attract workers. This struggle is especially evident in the food industry where product supply and consumer demand patterns are so varied and uncertain and where the whole economic system is inherently skewed towards the large transnational supplier and retailer. Employers also know that migrant workers are the best source of labour for filling the secondary labour markets that are created as a result of these pressures and that these labour markets work best with a constant supply of new workers.

There are at least five other main options, however, beyond the use of migrant labour, each with a distinct set of (politicized) pros and cons attached. The question is whether individual employers are in a position to develop some or all of these alternatives and, if not, then whether it is in the national interest to help them do so. The answer to this rests on: the attitude towards low-status immigration and the revolving-door employment with which it is associated; whether or not such immigration should function as a de facto industry subsidy to keep food prices low and to avoid excessive reliance on imports from poorer countries; and, finally, what the short, medium, and long-term consequences of removing the immigration subsidy to the UK food industry would be.

References

Aly, N. (1989), 'A Survey on the Use of Computer-Integrated Manufacturing in Food Processing Companies', *Food Technology*, 43(3): 82–7.

Balch, A., Brindley, P., Geddes, A., and Scott, S. (2009), *Gangmasters Licensing Authority: Annual Review 2008 Main Report* (Nottingham: Gangmasters Licensing Authority/Defra).

Bauder, H. (2006), *Labour Movement: How Migration Regulates Labour Markets* (Oxford: Oxford University Press).

Brass, T. (2004), 'Medieval Working Practices? British Agriculture and the Return of the Gangmaster', *The Journal of Peasant Studies*, 31(2): 313–40.

Competition Commission (2007a), *Groceries Market Investigation: Emerging Thinking* (London: Competition Commission), available at <http://www.competition-commission.org.uk/inquiries/ref2006/grocery/index.htm>.

—— (2007b), *Working Paper on Buyer Power* (London: Competition Commission), available at <http://www.competition-commission.org.uk/inquiries/ref2006/grocery/index.htm>.

Department for Environment, Food and Rural Affairs (Defra) (2007), *Agriculture in the United Kingdom 2007* (London: Defra/National Statistics).

Friedland, W., Barton, A., and Thomas, R. (1981), *Manufacturing Green Gold* (Cambridge: Cambridge University Press).

Geddes, A., Scott, S., and Nielsen, K. (2007), *Gangmasters Licensing Authority Evaluation Study: Baseline Report* (Nottingham: Defra).

Gereffi, G., and Korzeniewicz, M. (eds.) (1994), *Commodity Chains and Global Capitalism* (London: Greenwood Press).

Goos, M., and Manning, A. (2004), *Lousy and Lovely Jobs: The Rising Polarization of Work in Britain* (London: London School of Economics).

Ilyukhin, S., and Haley, T. (2001), 'A Survey of Automation Practices in the Food Industry', *Food Control*, 12(5): 285–96.

Kaplanis, I. (2007), *The Geography of Employment Polarisation in Britain* (London: IPPR).

Martin, P. L. (2003), *Promise Unfulfilled: Unions, Immigration and the Farm Workers* (Ithaca, NY: Cornell University Press).

Massey, D., Arango, J., Hugo, G., Kouaouci, A., Pellegrino, A., and Taylor, J. (1998), *Worlds In Motion: Understanding International Migration at the End of the Millennium* (Oxford: Clarendon Press).

——and Liang, Z. (1989), 'The Long-Term Consequences of a Temporary Worker Program: The US Bracero Experience', *Population Research and Policy Review*, 8(3): 199–226.

Mitchell, D. (1996), *The Lie of the Land: Migrant Workers and the California Landscape* (Minnesota: University of Minnesota Press).

New Economics Foundation (NEF) (2004), *Clone Town Britain: The Loss of Local Identity on the Nation's High Streets* (London: NEF).

Newby, H. (1977), *The Deferential Worker: A Study of Farm Workers in East Anglia* (Harmondsworth: Penguin).

——(1987), *Country Life: A Social History of Rural England* (London: Wiedenfeld and Nicolson).

Piore, M. J. (1979), *Birds of Passage: Migrant Labour and Industrial Societies* (Cambridge: Cambridge University Press).

Pollard, N., Latorre, M., and Sriskandarajah, D. (2008), *Floodgates or Turnstyles?* (London: Institute for Public Policy Research).

Rogaly, B. (2008), 'Intensification of Workplace Regimes in British Horticulture: The Role of Migrant Workers', *Population, Space and Place*, 14: 497–510.

Scott, S., Geddes, A., Nielsen, K., and Brindley, P. (2007), *Gangmasters Licensing Authority: Annual Review* (Nottingham: Gangmasters Licensing Authority/Defra), available at <http://www.gla.gov.uk>.

Taylor, J., and Espenshade, T. (1987), 'Foreign and Undocumented Workers in California Agriculture', *Population Research and Policy Review*, 6(3): 223–39.

——and Thilmany, D. (1993), 'Worker Turnover, Farm Labor Contractors, and IRCA's Impact on the California Farm Labor Market', *American Journal of Agricultural Economics*, 75(2): 350–60, available at <http://www.jstor.org/action/showPublication?journalCode=amerjagriecon>.

Vandeman, A., Sadoulet, E., and de Janvry, A. (1991), 'Labor Contracting and a Theory of Contract Choice in California Agriculture', *American Journal of Agricultural Economics*, 73(3): 681–92, available at <http://www.jstor.org/action/showPublication?journalCode=amerjagriecon>.

Vorley, B. (2003), *Food Inc. Corporate Concentration from Farm to Consumer* (London: UK Food Group/International Institute for Environment and Development).

Waldinger, R., and Lichter, M. (2003), *How the Other Half Works: Immigration and the Social Organization of Labour* (Berkeley, Calif.: University of California Press).

Woods, M. (2005), *Rural Geography* (London: Sage).

UK Food Businesses' Reliance on Low–Wage Migrant Labour: A Commentary

Ben Rogaly

Introduction

The chapter by Geddes and Scott (Chapter 7; henceforth G&S) makes a signifi-cant contribution to knowledge about changes in the main workforces in UK agriculture, food packing and food processing in the nineties and noughties. This is based on survey work and in-depth interviews with employers, and a major programme of evaluation and review of the regulator of labour-providing intermediaries in the sector,[1] colloquially known in the UK as 'gang-masters'. We learn much, for example, about the geography of employment in food production, about employers' different recruitment strategies, and about the different kinds of gangmasters involved. Whilst attempting to convey national trends, the authors rightly emphasise the diversity of employment regimes in food production, and pepper the text with specific examples to show how this makes for variations in the demand for workers.

In common with the other chapters in this book, G&S were asked to consider both demand for and supply of labour and to reflect on possible alternatives to the widespread employment of migrant workers in the sector.[2] In this commentary, my focus will be on discussing and adding to

---

[1] Although the sector is referred to here in the singular for convenience, agriculture and food processing are usually analysed separately. Treating them together, as the authors have been asked to do here, is particularly challenging.

[2] G&S choose country of birth rather than nationality to distinguish between migrants and UK workers.

the descriptive and analytical material in G&S, rather than the normative, policy-focused sections of the chapter.

Clearing the Ground

Two points of clarification are in order regarding the descriptive evidence presented in G&S. First, although commonly used in immigration analysis and debates, it can be misleading to use, as G&S (and many other authors) occasionally do, the term 'local workers' to describe food production workers born in Britain. This is because the term 'local' can also suggest that workers' accommodation is close to their places of work. Much of the chapter's description of the declining inclination of British-born workers to seek employment in agriculture is based on evidence from secondary literature on the reduced affordability and supply of rural housing. But temporary agricultural workers, whether or not they are British-born, do not necessarily live in the countryside. There is considerable evidence that large numbers of food production workers live in built-up areas (in both towns and cities) and either drive themselves or are transported to work (Frances et al. 2005; Grieco, 1996; Hickman et al. 2008; Taylor and Rogaly 2004; Anderson et al. 2006). Thus British-born workers are not necessarily *local*, and local workers are not necessarily *British-born*. The location of agricultural workers' accommodation and the degree to which it is connected to an employment relation (whether to a food-producing company or a labour contractor) have varied across time and space and can make a critical difference. In nineteenth-century rural England, for example, farmers' and landowners' 'encouragement of localism' enabled them to legitimate their dominance of village society, through making it seem natural that they should be leaders (Newby 1977: 52). Moreover, for some contemporary horticultural employers, the requirement for workers to live on site, and thus be available during a season at short notice at exactly the times needed, was a key means of labour control and lay behind their lobbying for the continuation of the Seasonal Agricultural Workers' Scheme (Rogaly 2008).

Secondly, G&S correctly state that existing large-scale surveys have failed to enumerate the number of people employed in the sector across the years, because of the temporality of production. It follows that summaries of national statistics which suggest a decline in that workforce must be viewed critically. Large-scale temporary employment, especially for crop harvesting, food packing, and food processing, cannot convincingly be said to be in long-term decline when commoditized forms of packaging and processing (for example, for ready meals) have expanded, along with the growth of supermarket retailing. The size of the temporary labour force in the food production sector remains unknown. Similarly, many food production businesses would not fall into the categories of small or medium enterprises, nor of sub-contractors. Importantly, however, in spite of the growing concentration of businesses involved in horticultural production, which G&S rightly draw readers' attention to, the majority of businesses in that sub-sector remained very small until at least five years ago (Key Note 2004).

Explaining Change in Labour Supply and Demand

Evidence from earlier studies can be used to support G&S's explanation of why migrants were found to be willing to work in food production in spite of intensified workplace regimes. Migrant workers making temporary trade-offs to work in low-paid intensive work, in the expectation of labour market mobility to follow, was a key finding in a survey of hundreds of Central and Eastern European workers in four sectors, including agriculture, carried out in 2004 (Anderson et al. 2006). The latter study also involved a survey of employers across the same sectors, which similarly to G&S, found that 'work ethic' was the most commonly given reason why employers in these sectors preferred migrants of particular nationalities (ibid.: 78). G&S also found that migrants were seen by food production employers as more desirable workers, more evidence for which can be found in Rogaly (2008: 500), who links this directly to the supermarket discourse of quality in production:

the supermarket governance of the chain through the language of 'quality' fed through into a demand by growers for particular 'qualities' in the workforce. In particular, workers were sought who would be reliable, flexible and compliant. For the growers we interviewed, all these 'qualities' were seen as more likely to be found in foreign workers. (Rogaly 2008: 500)

In the same work, it was tentatively suggested that the manifestations of intensification of workplace regimes could be found in three areas: the increased demand for foreign nationals by horticultural employers, a change in the kind of gangmaster companies operating in the sub-sector (p. 502), and the use of piece-rates to increase the work required to earn the Agricultural Wages Board minimum hourly rate and its daily equivalent (pp. 504–6).[3]

---

[3] In my article, migrants were defined by nationality rather than country of birth, and I focused exclusively on horticulture rather than food production as a whole. As G&S point out, I did also suggest that the use of piece–rates had increased.

221

Understanding intensification and its relation to the demand for migrant workers requires an analysis of capitalism. Capital accumulation in agriculture is hampered because of the mismatch of production time and labour time and the slower turnover of capital in relation to other sectors that results. But capitalists can accumulate indirectly through making money out of finance deals, input supply, and processing and retailing (Newby 1987: 193; Henderson 1998; Guthman 2004; Morgan et al. 2006).[4] Moreover, Guthman explains that intensification is one way in which capitalists can overcome obstacles to accumulation in production, including through innovations in labour control (2004: 498).

As Newby's seminal research on rural England makes clear: '[f]rom the eighteenth century onwards English rural society became a capitalist society and a system of agrarian capitalist development was set in train that continues to have a widespread impact upon the nature of rural life today' (1987: 3). Crucially, he also argues that the effect of social and economic change on agricultural workers has 'not nearly [been] so unilinear as is sometimes supposed' (1977: 82). Newby showed how, over a period of 200 years of massive and sometimes rapid change, some workers moved from individualized through more collective labour arrangements and back to a patriarchal existence, living in employer-provided accommodation.

It would be productive analytically to weigh up whether and in what ways agricultural employers use intensification in response to the increasing pressure on price, 'quality', and timeliness of supply that G&S rightly state provides the context for the widespread employment of migrant workers in the sector. Intensification as labour control, in the sense of getting people to work harder within a specified time period for the same money, has a long history in capitalism, and not only in the food production sector (Thompson 1967; Harvey 1990: 231). Harvey brilliantly shows the contradictions that emerge with employment of migrant workers. These include, first, that the free mobility of workers can simultaneously be a requirement of accumulation by capital as a whole, and a brake on accumulation by individual capitalists; and secondly, that labour migration itself can be both liberation for workers suffocated by localism and encouraged by employers to see off worker organizing (Harvey 2006: 236–7, 384)—something which, with notable exceptions, has been all too rare in UK food production.

---

[4] For the nineteenth century, see also Newby (1977: 57).

References

Anderson, B., Ruhs, M., Rogaly, B., and Spencer, S. (2006), *Fair Enough? Central and East European Migrants in Low-Wage Employment in the UK* (York: Joseph Rowntree Foundation).

Frances, J., Barrientos, S., and Rogaly, B. (2005), *Temporary Workers in UK Agriculture and Horticulture: A Study of Employment Practices in the Agriculture and Horticulture Industries and Co-located Packhouse and Primary Food Processing Sectors* (Framlingham, UK: Precision Prospecting for the Department of Environment, Food and Rural Affairs (DEFRA)).

Grieco, M. (1996), *Workers' Dilemmas: Recruitment, Reliability and Repeated Exchange. An Analysis of Urban Social Networks and Labour Circulation* (London: Routledge).

Guthman, J. (2004), *Agrarian Dreams: The Paradox of Organic Farming in California* (Berkeley, Calif.: University of California Press).

Harvey, D. (1990), *The Condition of Postmodernity* (Oxford: Blackwell).

——(2006). *The Limits to Capital*, 2nd edn. (London: Verso).

Henderson, J. (1998), *California and the Fictions of Capital* (Philadelphia: Temple University Press).

Hickman, M., Crowley, H., and Mai, N. (2008), *Immigration and Social Cohesion in the UK* (York: Joseph Rowntree Foundation).

Key Note (2004), *Fruit and Vegetables Market Report* (London: Key Note).

Morgan, K., Marsden, T., Murdoch, J. (2006), *Worlds of Food: Place, Power and Provenance in the Food Chain* (Oxford: Oxford University Press).

Newby, H. (1977), *The Deferential Worker: A Study of Farm Workers in East Anglia* (London: Allen Lane).

——(1987), *Country Life: A Social History of Rural England* (London: Weidenfeld and Nicolson).

Rogaly, B. (2008), 'Intensification of Workplace Regimes in British Horticulture: The Role of Migrant Workers', *Population, Space and Place*, 14(6): 497–511.

Taylor, B., and Rogaly, B. (2004), Migrant Working in West Norfolk (Norwich: Norfolk County Council).

Thompson, E. (1967), 'Time, Work Discipline and Industrial Capitalism', *Past and Present*, 38(1): 56–97.

8

The Dynamics of Migrant Employment in Construction: Can Supply of Skilled Labour ever Match Demand?

Paul Chan, Linda Clarke, and Andrew Dainty

8.1 Introduction

This chapter examines the interrelation between migrant worker employment, skills, and employment practices in the UK construction sector, in particular discussing how far demand for migrant labour is fuelled by an inappropriate or inadequate skills base. It shows the need for tighter labour market regulation to ensure equal treatment of workers and for a more sophisticated deployment and development of skills that goes beyond the quantitative measures that have dominated public and corporate policy in this area. A key recommendation is for the industry to shift from current modes of skills reproduction and employment practices towards upgrading the quality of the workforce and the development of a comprehensive vocational education and training (VET) system. Further recommendations relate to political and legislative instruments that safeguard the welfare of all workers by engaging social partners.

The chapter is structured as follows. We first outline the key features of the construction industry, highlighting the idiosyncratic, project-based nature of the sector. This serves to promote the use of a transient, casualized, and self-employed workforce, thereby eroding the incentive for training investment. It is also argued that current employment practices in the industry create barriers to entry for women and ethnic minorities and favour short-term resourcing strategies such as poaching and recruitment of migrant workers, often through agencies. We then illustrate current trends in migrant employment in construction in the United Kingdom

(UK), before exploring how the reliance on migrant employment is related to a mismatch between demand and supply of skilled labour in the sector. Above all, the chapter highlights the difficulties of assessing skills in construction, the low-skills-low-wage route adopted by the industry, and the lack of regulation of the UK construction labour market, which arguably stems from a lack of industrial democracy and social partnership.

8.2 Key Features of the Construction Industry

8.2.1 *Output, Size, and Structure*

UK construction accounts for approximately 10 per cent of Gross Domestic Product and employs nearly 1.9 million people (BERR 2008a). If a broader view is taken of construction—including the supply chain of producers and suppliers of raw materials, building components, manufacturers, professional services, and labour organizations—the workforce is estimated at around 3 million or, alternatively, using SIC (Standard Industrial Classification) categories 45 and 74.2, at 2.5 million (Pearce 2003; ConstructionSkills 2009).

After a sharp decline in activity in the early 1990s, construction output steadily increased from £60 billion in the mid-1990s, to £83 billion in 2007 (Briscoe 2006a). Repair and maintenance (R&M), including housing improvements, much of which are carried out by small or one-person firms, account for 43 per cent of this output, whilst housing represents 39 per cent. As a proportion of new work, however, housing is 31 per cent, whilst private industrial and commercial output represents 43 per cent and infrastructure 11 per cent. There are significant regional variations in output, with large concentrations in London and the South-East, though there are pockets of high activity in other regions, including in the South-West and the Midlands (BERR 2008a).

The output of the industry is varied, implying also a varied deployment of labour and skills. A critical aspect of this is that the industry tends to be more labour-intensive and unproductive than in other European countries. This is evident from detailed comparative studies of housebuilding sites, which showed that 39 per cent more labour was required to produce 1 square metre in England than compared with Germany, and 50 per cent compared with Denmark (Clarke and Herrmann 2004a). An authoritative analysis of research projects across Europe placed the UK at 55 per cent on its resource-use benchmarking index, compared to 69 per cent for Germany and 72 per cent for Denmark (BWA 2006). The report emphasized the UK's poor record in investment in research and development and training, 'exacerbated by extensive sub-contracting', and the fact that 'low labour rates and efficiency do not go together'. This analysis is supported by a series of reports prepared over the last 50 years which, according to the Comptroller and Auditor General (2001):

... have identified a lack of serious and sustained commitment to education, training, safety and research and in particular the low levels of commitment to serious skills development ... leading to consistently low levels of performance in areas such as cost, time, quality, running costs and fitness for the end user.

The industry includes about 186,000 private contracting companies. Over 93 per cent of these have fewer than 13 employees, and account for only 37 per cent of direct employment and 20 per cent of the value of private contractors' work done (BERR 2008a). Firms employing over 600 account for 18 per cent of employment and 26 per cent of work done. These have significantly declined in number, as have the medium-sized firms. The largest companies are relatively small in global terms, the highest placed UK contractor being eleventh in a league of European contractors based on turnover in 2008 (See Glackin, 2009). An estimated 65 per cent of contractors' output is subcontracted, more than double that in other leading European countries (e.g. Clarke and Herrmann 2004b). It is on the smaller firms, therefore, which compete throughout the work process including as subcontractors, that the productive capacity of the industry largely rests (Bosch and Philips 2003).

The construction industry is the epitome of a project-based industry (Dainty et al. 2007). The term 'temporary multiple organization' (TMO) is often used to describe the unique project team established for every new construction project, comprising an often complex set of inter-organizational relationships (Cherns and Bryant 1984; Bresnen et al. 2004). Moreover, construction is sensitive to the weather and more work is available in the spring and summer than the winter, with implications for migrant workers, particularly as a seasonal pattern for arrivals in the UK is evident from the Worker Registration Scheme (WRS) (Pollard et al. 2008). However, fluctuations in employment throughout the year are not only seasonal. For instance, the surge in employment observed during the second quarter of 2004 coincided very closely with the joining of the European Union by the A8 countries,[1] after which time seasonality in construction employment stabilized (BERR 2008a).

---

[1] The A8 countries refer to the accession countries that joined the European Union in 2004, including the Czech Republic, Estonia, Hungary, Latvia, Lithuania, Poland, Slovakia, and Slovenia.

The project-based nature of construction, together with geographic mobility, can make for an unstable employment regime and require a relatively mobile labour force. Labour is often employed contingently through subcontracting chains or hired by different subcontractors who feed up their supply of workers to larger subcontractors (McKay et al. 2006). Firms—whether regional, national, foreign-based, or international—may rely on labour from outside the localities where the construction site is situated. Thus local labour can be marginalized in terms of employment and training opportunities. Attempts are being made to redress this, though with limited success. For instance, Terminal 5 (T5) and the Wembley Stadium developments sought to impose on employers requirements for the recruitment and training of local labour, thereby engaging with those who are unemployed in the area (GLA 2007).

8.2.2 *Overview of Skills and Qualifications in the Sector*

The industry comprises at least 50 different skilled occupations and numerous professional occupations: 75 per cent of the workforce is in manual occupations, 25 per cent in non-manual (almost half composed of office staff). Its labour-intensive nature and adherence to traditional trades are in contrast with many European countries (Clarke and Herrmann 2007a). It has a high proportion of untrained workers, many of whom, echoing the persistence of a craft system, continue to be classed as labourers. Others pick up some skills informally, and are gradually taken on and paid as tradespeople or classed as plant operatives following a short plant-specific training course. The largest group of manual workers (19.7% of the total operative workforce) is in the wood trades, primarily carpentry and joinery with approximately 270,000 employed, followed by two other traditional trades, bricklayers (7%) and painters and decorators (9.1%). Plant operatives (3%) and other civil engineering operatives (4.1%) constitute a significant and growing part of the manual workforce (ConstructionSkills 2008a).

It is extremely difficult to assess skill levels accurately given the nature of National Vocational Qualifications (NVQs), which underpin the industry's skills framework and have been widely criticized (Callender 1997; Clarke and Winch 2004). They are based on narrowly focused task-based standards whose specification—it has been argued—effectively achieves a Taylorist separation of conception and execution (Steedman 1992; Grugulis 2007). Though at least an NVQ2 would be expected in, for example, bricklaying, and NVQ3 for carpentry, many work their way up from labourer or 'mate' to bricklayer, perhaps attending at the same time day release in a Further

Education (FE) College. Given the low underpinning knowledge required, it is then possible to obtain an NVQ2, and to progress to NVQ3, through the On Site Assessment and Training (OSAT) process under ConstructionSkills. This situation compares with other European countries where qualifications obtained through a formal VET process are becoming a prerequisite to work on site (Clarke and Wall 1998; Clarke 2006).

The proportion of those with the equivalent of at least NVQ2 was estimated at 74 per cent in 2002, having increased from 65 per cent in 2000, whilst the proportion of those with at least the equivalent of NVQ3 was estimated at 46 per cent, having increased from 39 per cent in 2000. This is about half the proportion in Germany (ConstructionSkills 2004; Richter 1998). However, the words 'equivalent' and 'estimated' are important. In 2002, only 7 per cent of the directly employed construction workforce had actually acquired an NVQ2 or above, a figure which had risen to 33 per cent by 2007 (ConstructionSkills 2008a). This represents a situation far removed from the aspiration—increasingly realized in other leading European countries—for a fully qualified workforce in the industry, and signifies both the inadequacy of VET provision and the lack of confidence in the qualifications system by employers.

There have been attempts to better regulate skills, in particular through the Construction Skills Certification Scheme (CSCS), intended to register skilled workers and ensure that certain criteria are met, including the passing of a health and safety test every five years. CSCS is geared to qualify those with experience and skills. In the long term, however, the eventual system is intended to help employers and employees recognize what skills are needed so that they can, in theory, work towards developing these. Under CSCS, those who have attained an NVQ of at least level 2 are recognized as 'skilled' (Clarke 2006). To date 1.55 million cards (see http://www.cscs.uk.com) have been issued and the card is increasingly required for working on sites.

There are at least six Sector Skills Councils (SSCs) overseeing occupations and skills relevant to construction. These include ConstructionSkills, Summit Skills (for building services engineering), Asset Skills (for housing, property, and facilities management), Energy and Utilities Skills, Proskills (for materials, products, and manufacturing), and LANTRA (for the environmental and land-based sector)—reflecting the disjointedness of supply relations. Together with the Engineering Construction Industry Training Board (ECITB), these SSCs form part of the Built Environment Skills Alliance in which ConstructionSkills plays a dominant role, coordinating the construction industry training levy, labour market intelligence, and the sector skills agreement. However, with no single body having responsibility

229

for skills issues within the labour market, policies have arguably led to a complexity of networks of supply provision that severely limits long-term impact (Chan and Moehler 2007 and 2008; Moehler et al. 2008; Lobo and Wilkinson 2007). In a vicious circle, the breadth, informality, and fragmented nature of the sector pose considerable difficulties in defining and delineating it, which in turn leads to multi-agency governance of skills policy (Pearce 2003; Clarke and Herrmann 2004c).

8.2.3 *Employment and Working Conditions*

By 2008, average gross weekly earnings for full-time male employees in construction had reached £608.20. For non-manual workers, however, earnings are higher. There are also significant differences in earnings according to occupation, with bricklayers earning an average £508 per week in 2008, carpenters and joiners £484, and labourers £399 (Office of National Statistics 2009). The earnings differential between skilled and semi-unskilled manual workers has also been widening: labourers earned on average 22 per cent less per week (25% less per hour) than bricklayers, carpenters, and joiners. The increasing differential between skilled workers and labourers is significant with respect to migrants, who—when employed in a manual capacity in the industry—are frequently found as labourers. Earnings recorded are higher than the collectively agreed rates in the Working Rule Agreement (WRA),[2] which were, even in July 2008, still only £309 for a 39-hour week and 775p per hour for the lowest skill level of General Operative, though the highest skill 'Craft' Rate was £402 per week and 1030p per hour (CIJC 2008).

Any wage premium recorded by official statistics masks the sector's long hours. On average, hours for non-manual workers, at 41.4 hours per week, are lower than for manual workers, at 43.7 hours, higher than the average for all sectors of 38.9 hours. These are, however, only average figures; workers on many construction sites work far in excess of this, potentially contravening the maximum of 48 hours per week stipulated by the Working Time Directive (GLA 2007). The continued exercise of an 'opt-out' clause in the enforcement of this Directive means that all workers, not only migrant workers, become vulnerable to exploitation.

The construction industry is characterized by hazardous working conditions. Workplaces can be dangerous and unhealthy, the fatal and major injury

---

[2] The Working Rule Agreement (WRA) covers pay and conditions in the industry and is signed by unions and employers' associations (CIJC 2006).

rate is three times higher than for all industries, and the rate of reported injuries twice as high (HSE 2008). The occupational health team on Heathrow's Terminal 5 found, of the 7,000 workers screened in safety critical occupations, about 25 per cent had medical problems, especially hypertension, and 2,000 lifestyle-related problems (Clarke and Gribling 2008).

Labour arrangements in construction are often casual and divided between those who are directly employed 'on the cards' and those—who may be working side-by-side with directly employed—classified as 'self-employed', including migrants (Briscoe et al. 2000). The self-employed numbered nearly 750,000, or an estimated 48 per cent of operatives in 2007, though even the Labour Force Survey (LFS) does not address the issue adequately (Briscoe 2006b; BERR 2008a). It has been claimed that, of these, approximately 58 per cent are 'bogus' self-employed, in that the worker would be deemed directly employed by normal legal tests, and the remaining 42 per cent 'genuinely' self-employed (Harvey and Behling 2008). The majority of those classified as self-employed possess a special CIS (Construction Industry Scheme) tax certificate issued by the Inland Revenue, which does not require employers to pay National Insurance and allows them to deduct workers' tax at source (Blackman 2007). It is a system unique to the construction sector and subject to considerable criticism due in part to the devastating and long-term impact it has had on training in the industry (Harvey 2001; Clarke and Wall 1998). UCATT (Union of Construction and Allied Technical Trades) estimates the fiscal loss to the Exchequer through 'bogus' self-employment at approximately £1.7bn, the larger part of this through non-payment of National Insurance by the employer (Stewart 2007a; Harvey and Behling 2008). The government has made various attempts to tighten up the system, the latest in April 2008 mandating self-employed persons to demonstrate their genuine status or face automatic tax deductions at point-of-payment. This has had little discernible impact on numbers. Many 'self-employed' come through agencies, with which a large proportion of migrants are also to be found (Forde and MacKenzie, 2007; Fitzgerald, 2007).

Trades unions—UCATT, UNITE (previously AMICUS and TGWU), and the GMB—represent a declining proportion of the workforce, with union density estimated at 15 per cent compared with 26 per cent in 1995 (BERR 2008b). As well as low trade union membership in the industry there is also a fragmented picture with regards to the employers' federations. The Construction Confederation (CC) has been the key body, covering the British Woodworking Federation, the Civil Engineering Contractors Association, the National Federation of Builders, and the Scottish Builders Federation.

However, UK Contractors Group (UKCG), composed of many of the largest contractors, was officially launched on the 5 January 2009 and is aimed at supporting the industry on sector-specific issues whilst leaving more general business issues to the newly formed Construction Council of the Confederation of British Industry (CBI).

A final key characteristic of the construction workforce is its exclusivity and homogeneity, comprising almost entirely white, able-bodied males (GLA 2007). It is important to remember that 'white' in this industry includes significant proportions of Irish and Eastern European migrants. In trade occupations, the proportion of women is as low as 0.3 per cent, whilst those from BAME (Black and Asian Minority Ethnic) groups represent only 2.8 per cent of those employed (Byrne et al. 2005). These trends challenge the efficacy of exhortations made since the 1990s about encouraging diversity in construction and efforts to raise awareness among women and BAME groups about career opportunities in construction (see e.g. Dainty and Bagilhole 2005; Fielden et al. 2000; Mackenzie et al. 2000; Royal Holloway 2002).

To summarize, the industry has been crying out for change, given its high labour intensity, relatively low levels of productivity, and stagnant and traditional division of labour. Employment remains exclusive, overwhelmingly white and male dominated, and dogged by casual and so-called 'bogus' self-employment. These peculiarities help shape the nature of labour demand and supply in the sector.

8.3 Migrant Worker Employment in UK Construction

Until the current recession, many jobs in construction were filled by migrants, especially from Eastern Europe, in numbers significantly higher than official labour market statistics suggest (Chappell et al. 2008). Statistics on migrant workers in construction are extremely patchy and their reliability is limited, especially when disaggregated down to a sub-regional level (Briscoe 2006b; Watson et al. 2006; Dainty et al. 2005; Chan and Dainty 2007). Labour force survey data for 2008 suggest that about 8 per cent of the UK's construction workforce are foreign born, up from just under 5 per cent in 2002. Many commentators have claimed that this represents a gross underestimation, since it does not take into account those who are self-employed or undeclared (Balch et al. 2004; Cremers and Janssen 2006). Lillie and Greer (2007) estimate, based on interviews with unionists and employer association representatives, that the share of migrants operating within the UK sector was as high as 10 per cent.

Among migrants in this sector, East European workers constitute a key group. According to the WRS, the cumulative number of A8 nationals registered to work within the construction and land sector was 30,965 by 2008, with 3 per cent of the total A8/A2 migrant worker population[3] in construction and more than a third of these registering as labourers (Border and Immigration Agency 2008). Other research has also shown the sector to be the most popular for male migrants from Eastern Europe; the construction union UCATT suggested that as many as 350,000 Poles were working in UK construction in 2007 (Bolger 2008; Stewart 2007b). At firm level, one of the largest bricklaying subcontractors in Europe, employing approximately 800 weekly paid operatives, attributed the origins of its workforce as follows: 60 per cent UK, 25 per cent East European, 5 per cent rest of Europe; 5 per cent Caribbean; and 5 per cent Africa (Nuffield 2009).

The proportion of migrants in the industry varies considerably according to region and occupation. A quarterly survey for the National Specialist Contractors' Council, for instance, revealed that 3 per cent of respondents' workforces are made up of Polish workers, a figure varying geographically from 1 per cent in the North East of England to up to 30 per cent in Greater London, the South-East, and East Anglia (Murdoch 2008). This geographic spread corresponds tenuously with data from the Border and Immigration Agency (2008; see also Green et al. 2005; Fitzgerald 2007; Pollard et al. 2008). Industry practitioners reported in a CIOB (Chartered Institute of Building) survey that migrants operated mainly in semi-skilled or labouring positions, and very rarely in management occupations where recruitment was particularly difficult (Campbell 2006). LFS (2005) data confirm higher proportions of migrants, defined as 'foreign born', in lower positions, whether as labourers (8.9%), or in the arguably lesser skilled trades such as painting and decorating (8.2%), though 3,242 migrants are recorded as carpenters and joiners (6.1%), many from non-EEA (European Economic Area) countries. It is significant that, in professional and technical areas of construction and for the more skilled and regulated electrical trades, migrants tend to come from non-EEA countries. For instance, 10.6 per cent of electrical engineers are non-UK born, but 8.2 per cent are non-EEA; 4.1 per cent of electricians are non-UK born, but 2.7 per cent are non-EEA. A similar phenomenon is evident with technicians in the industry. In contrast, only 2.9 per cent of painters and decorators, and 3.5 per cent of

---

[3] The A2 countries refer to the accession countries that joined the European Union in 2007, including Bulgaria and Romania.

building and woodworking labourers are from non-EEA countries, compared with 5.3 per cent and 5.4 per cent respectively from EEA countries.

Sectoral transfers into and out of construction indicate relatively low
barriers to entry (Beaney 2007). Indeed, according to LFS data, the construction sector exhibits the highest level of labour connectivity to other
industry sectors (Beaney 2006). Analysis of migrant labour flows is complicated by the fact that many migrant construction workers enter the UK and
work on a self-employed basis, rendering them invisible in existing statistics (Dench et al. 2006: 22; Anderson and Rogaly 2005). It is also relatively
easy to find work illegally as a migrant worker if there is already a migrant
community working on site (Gribling and Clarke 2006).

Speculations about migrant labour flows continue to dominate the agenda of policy-makers, particularly in light of the recession and disputes at the
Lindsey and other refineries by engineering construction workers (Griffiths
2009a and 2009b). These disputes have concerned jobs being subcontracted to migrant or posted workers rather than to locally sourced workers,
without their terms and conditions of employment being transparent and
equivalent to those in the prevailing collective agreement—as required by
the Posted Workers Directive. The inquiry by the Advisory, Conciliation
and Arbitration Service (ACAS) resulting from the initial Lindsey Oil
Refinery dispute indicates a more complex story. It notes: 'If locally sourced
workers were to be employed [the subcontractor] indicated that they
would only be used on less skilled work or where the work entailed servicing mainstream operations (cranage, riggers, NDT, painting etc)' (ACAS
2009: 3).

The economic downturn has led to concerns about the possibility of a
mass exodus of migrant workers. One projection estimates that, if migrants
from the A8 countries leave, the industry would require approximately
10,000 workers per annum—professional and skilled workers—to fill the
gap (Pollard et al. 2008).

Some concerns have been raised about the health and safety consequences of large numbers of migrant workers in the sector. The rise in
fatalities on UK construction sites in 2006 has been attributed to the large
number of migrants employed, with language barriers contributing to
difficulties in enforcing health and safety policies (Owen 2007). A recent
report indicates that, of 419 deaths of construction workers between 2002
and 2008, 35 were migrants, who represented a rising percentage, from
3 per cent (2 out of 70) in 2002, to 17 per cent (12 out of 72) in 2007/
8 (CCA 2009). Most of these were in London and construction workers
identified came from a wide range of countries, with the largest number

from Poland. Migrant workers are more likely to be employed in sectors and occupations where there are health and safety concerns, and skilled and potentially dangerous work, like scaffolding, may be offered to individuals without experience in the task (McKay et al. 2006). Only 30 per cent of reportable accidents are, however, estimated to be actually reported to the HSE and the record is likely to be particularly poor for a sector such as construction (Davies et al. 2007).

8.4 Labour Demand in the Construction Sector

Considerable effort is expended in forecasting demand for construction labour, on the basis of traditional skill and labour loadings attached to given units of output. ConstructionSkills runs a skills and productivity observatory process across the regions to gather and disseminate labour market intelligence. Given that the demand for labour in construction is sensitive to locality and to differences in work-flow across the regions, it incorporates a 'bottom-up' approach from key stakeholders at regional level (Chan and Dainty 2007; Anumba et al. 2005). Such an approach mitigates some of the shortcomings of disaggregating both regional and local employment and demand statistics from national datasets. Nevertheless, all estimates need to be treated with considerable caution, assuming as they do that a given output equates to a given labour requirement, and that current practices and skill sets can be projected forward (Briscoe 2006a and 2006b).

8.4.1 *Projected Labour and Skills Requirements*

The total annual employment requirement for the sector was previously estimated to be 88,390 between 2008 and 2012 (Table 8.1), though recently released 2009–13 forecasts show a considerable adjustment in demand, suggesting that the industry will be severely affected by the downturn in the short to medium term, and the workforce may not begin to expand until 2011 (ConstructionSkills 2008a and 2009). Nevertheless, a net growth in output of 0.5 per cent per year between 2009 and 2013 is still forecast, equating in employment terms to a growth of around 37,000 per year over the next five years, excluding new entrant trainees. Thus, demand for labour and skills in the medium term is not forecast to be stifled, even during the six quarters of negative growth forecast, and could even be exacerbated should migrant workers from Eastern Europe return to their countries of origin. Yorkshire and the South-West are the only regions

Table 8.1 Average annual employment requirement forecasts, 2008–2012 (nationally and by regions) against first-year entrant figures, 2006–2007

Occupational group	National	First-year entrant figures, 2006–2007	Scotland	North East	North West	Yorkshire and Humber	East Midlands	West Midlands	Wales	East of England	Greater London	South East	South West	Northern Ireland
Senior & executive managers	190		<50	<50	<50	<50	<50	<50	<50	<50	<60	<70	<50	<50
Business process managers	2770		150	70	160	200	140	220	160	420	610	400	140	100
Construction managers	6350		330	170	570	560	350	480	130	910	1090	1320	320	120
Office-based staff (excl. managers)	6420		300	120	590	530	330	340	360	1010	920	1260	390	270
Other Professionals/technical staff & IT	790	4864	<50	<50	70	100	50	100	240	<50	<50	90	<50	<50
Wood trades & interior fit-out	12860	14126	1360	370	1120	970	820	800	800	1290	2060	1750	800	720
Bricklayers and building envelope specialists	10670	9083	710	430	1270	620	550	610	290	1330	1790	1460	1010	600
Painters & decorators	4490	3362	370	170	410	350	170	400	190	730	830	460	330	80
Plasterers & dry liners	1570	2037	70	50	220	100	90	60	70	270	220	280	70	70
Roofers	2020	553	200	80	150	160	80	240	50	350	300	160	160	90
Floorers	840	377	<50	<50	70	<50	<50	60	130	70	170	120	50	<50
Glaziers	1110	10	50	<50	140	70	<50	100	50	170	100	280	70	<50
Specialist building operatives nec*	2210	605	170	80	90	150	130	210	140	360	240	400	170	70
Scaffolders	1200	925	160	80	80	170	<50	90	90	90	170	140	90	<50
Plant operatives	1570	2899	180	90	70	90	70	50	230	280	160	130	130	90

Plant mechanics/fitters	<50	<50	190	<50	110	120	<50	60	<50	200	80	70	331	940
Steel erectors/structural	90	<50	90	170	80	130	50	<50	70	100	<50	110	5	1000
Labourers nec*	<50	160	<50	420	250	250	120	90	220	140	80	180		1940
Electrical trades & installation	230	530	1600	1610	1640	240	790	600	770	950	380	620		9960
Plumbing & HVAC trades	170	300	710	830	590	250	370	230	440	390	150	260		4690
Logistics	<50	<50	50	80	130	150	<50	<50	<50	60	<50	50		650
Civil engineering operatives nec*	<50	140	350	170	270	170	180	90	160	200	100	210	1187	2040
Non-construction operatives														
Maintenance operatives													46	
Total (SIC 45)	2840	4910	11310	12050	4250	10430	5330	4060	5810	7070	2650	5570	40410	76280
Construction professionals & technical staff	140	1070	1830	2880	500	580	860	470	810	1800	420	750		12110
Total (SIC 45 & 74.2)	2980	5980	13140	14930	4750	11010	6190	4530	6620	8870	3070	6320		88390

Note: *nec = not elsewhere classified.

Source: ConstructionSkills (2008a); and 3ERR (2007: 149).

projected to show no growth to 2009, with the strongest demand being in Greater London and the South-East (ConstructionSkills 2009).

8.4.2 *Nature and Types of Skills Required*

The nature of the sub-sector in which construction projects are located plays a part in determining the skills required. Non-residential work, particularly in public buildings (in healthcare and education), is, for example, set to grow in the short term, although the prospects beyond this are less clear (ConstructionSkills 2009). Infrastructure has the best prospects over the next five years, with a projected growth in output of just under 7 per cent per annum, whilst a decline in new-build housing work, especially private, is forecast for a number of regions. Repair and Maintenance (R&M) work (particularly non-housing) may fare better, and given its labour intensity could have an impact on labour demand. Up until the current recession, about 80 per cent of all private and an even higher proportion of social housebuilding firms expressed difficulties in recruiting skilled workers (Clarke and Herrmann 2007b). About 50 per cent of firms had problems recruiting managers, 40 per cent bricklayers, and 33 per cent carpenters, with over 60 per cent of firms reporting at least one hard-to-fill vacancy. Therefore, the question remains as to whether there is adequate capacity to meet the demands associated with medium-term recovery, particularly if workers move to other industry sectors.

Some of the sectors into which construction is divided are significantly more regulated and demanding of formal VET and qualifications than others. The most demanding, and most likely to be covered by highly regulated collective agreements, are the mechanical and electrical (M&E) and engineering construction sectors, concerned with large projects such as power stations and oil refineries. The building sector, incorporating housebuilding and the traditional 'wet' and 'dry' trades such as roofing, carpentry, bricklaying, plastering, painting and decorating, and glazing, is much less regulated, except in certain specialist areas such as exhibition work and shopfitting. The civil engineering sector is perhaps the least demanding in a formal sense, with the wage being still—to all intents and purposes—constructed around the status of the labourer, with 'plus rates' accorded for working in particular areas. Unlike other countries such as the Netherlands and Germany, where a comprehensive civil engineering VET scheme is in place, certification is necessary to operate in Britain on a plant-by-plant basis, obtained by attending short courses of training. Only for certain trades, above all M&E, is NVQ3 a prerequisite; in these areas, workers have usually been through a formal VET scheme of three years (four in Scotland). A formal process of transnational recognition of qualifications, through the European Qualifications Framework (EQF) and the European Credit Transfer System (ECVET), has not yet been established, and the use of European migrant labour, particularly from Eastern Europe, may therefore be lower than for some of the traditional building trades.

Despite recessionary falls in output, skill demands on the sector are persistent and high, especially in particular sub-sectors and managerial and skilled occupations. Given the often low-level and narrow nature of the skills of the existing workforce, the question is, therefore, how far demand for migrant labour is fuelled by an inappropriate or inadequate skills base in construction. In a recessionary period, broad-based and transferable skills may anyway be preferred, facilitating the movement of workers from one site to another. Are these the skills provided by migrants?

8.4.3 *Demand for Migrant Workers in Construction*

Until the recent recession, the Sector Skills Council had a policy to integrate migrant labour as part of its broader skills, training, and qualifications strategy (ConstructionSkills 2008b). Reflecting this, over 50 per cent of construction employers were, by 2005, alluding to looking abroad for the workers they required (Warwick Institute for Employment Research 2006), with implications for the productive capacity of the industry. One reason for this may be the existing craft-based skills structure of the industry, reducing the reflexive nature of skills-in-use (Chan and Cooper 2006; Stasz 2001). This means that employers and workers cope through improvization and there is no holistic reassessment of construction occupations, or of the scope of activities encompassed within each (Mayhew 2003). On large sites, skill requirements are varied and often outside the traditional trades (Clarke and Gribling 2008; Nuffield 2009). Groundworkers, for instance, may have to carry out steel-fixing, plant operation (cranes, forklifts, etc.), scaffolding, paving, drainage, banking, concreting, etc. Though this tends not to happen in practice, such 'multi-skilling' can facilitate labour mobility and relocation of workers from one site to the next, which should go together with a large directly employed workforce.

One of the peculiarities of the British construction industry is that many areas of work such as concreting and groundworks are not classfied as 'skilled areas', though requiring considerable expertise, and are the subject of extensive lobbying by contractors for a recognized NVQ3 scheme of training (Clarke and Wall 1998). Moreover, unlike their counterparts in

Germany or Poland, workers trained in Britain tend to be 'single-skilled', rather than trained for a range of activities, and in social and problem-solving skills. As a result, it can be difficult for contractors to recruit appropriate skills, and migrant workers may be preferred simply because they are more 'multi-skilled', more adept at problem-solving, and possess more transferable skills, attributable in large part to higher levels of education and training than their British counterparts.

Migrant labour may also be preferred for reasons of lower labour costs. The Posted Workers Directive is of crucial importance here. It requires that local employment conditions in the host country should apply when workers are 'posted' to another country, whether employed directly or by an agency or subcontractor. Current UK government policy interpretation of this is that posted workers should not be paid below the minimum wage. There has been much lobbying, particularly by the trade union UNITE, which represents many in the mechanical and electrical trades, that the Directive be applied according to the terms and conditions of the collective agreement and even that there be statutory recognition of this, as well as that workers be required to be directly rather than self-employed. Moreover, migrants are not necessarily posted workers, and may nevertheless be paid less than British nationals. On T5, it was found that the lower wage rate of many East European and German workers was based on their wider range of skills, which meant that they were regarded as 'multi-skilled' and therefore not as 'specialized' as a 'single'-skilled British tradesperson such as a steel fixer (Clarke and Gribling 2008).

The industry, in particular the housebuilding sector, is often synonymous with high cost, low quality, and chaotic working practices. The long hours of work and the renowned failure to implement the Working Time Directive in the sector may also encourage the employment of migrants. Pollard et al. (2008) have suggested that migrant workers work, on average, four hours longer a week than their local counterparts. Studies of construction sites with large concentrations of migrant workers have pointed to excessively long hours (GLA 2007). Fitzgerald (2006) found evidence of poor treatment and abuse of migrant workers in construction in North-East England, with companies at times paying below the minimum wage, and many workers not receiving wage slips or written employment contracts. Migrant workers may also be unaware of their employment and legal rights and of prevailing terms and conditions. RIFT, an organization operating since 1999 for auditing wage and tax payments of migrants in the UK and handling about 3,000 cases per year, reports considerable irregularities in the payment of wages and taxes to migrants in the construction sector (*CLR News* 2007).

In summary, the available data points to relatively high proportions of migrants in the construction industry, consisting of up to 10 per cent of operatives, and varying according to region and trade, with large numbers concentrated in labouring or semi-skilled occupations. There are indications of a preference for migrants because many have a broader range of skills and wider occupational capacity than their British counterparts. Indeed, the high education level, problem-solving abilities, and transferable skills of many migrants are throwing into relief the often narrow and traditional trade-based nature of skills, VET, and NVQ qualifications to be found in the British construction industry. In this regard, their employment can be of positive benefit for the industry, whilst nevertheless disadvantaging further those trained in Britain and seeking to work in the industry, including women and those from BAME groups. Other reasons for employers preferring migrants, however, may include the often lower labour costs involved and the ability to exploit them in terms of pay, working hours, and conditions. The effect of such exploitation can only be negative, in particular for health and safety, and risks accentuating disparities in employment and working conditions between different groups in the industry.

8.5 Labour Supply in the Construction Sector

The supply of skilled labour in construction can be disjointed and fragile, complicated by labour-only-subcontracting (LOSC) and self-employment. As a result, the capacity development of the construction workforce has been largely tactical and ad hoc, epitomized by a lack of investment in training for the industry and a 'fossilization' of existing skill divisions (Clarke 2006). The situation is exacerbated by 'short-term fixes'. The 'poaching' of skilled operatives and supervisors from other firms so typical of craft labour markets is rife, particularly in the housebuilding sector (Clarke and Herrmann 2007b; Marsden 1999). Training largely relies on the goodwill of individual employers, albeit financially supported by the levy and grant system. Nonetheless, there is an acute shortage of opportunities for trainees to obtain the necessary work experience, and employers generally abdicate from responsibility for training, in particular the small construction firms which dominate the sector (IFF 2003; Forde and MacKenzie 2004).

8.5.1 *Recruitment Practices, Training, and Domestic Labour Supply*

Employment practices in construction tend to be informal, with employers preferring to recruit through word-of-mouth, or promoting from within the firm's internal labour market, and paying little regard to strategic 'best practice' models of human resource management (Clarke and Herrmann 2007b; Lockyer and Scholarios 2007). 'Word-of-mouth' practices rely heavily on existing networks so that alternative labour supplies may be overlooked. A longer-term approach to planning, deploying, and developing human resources is claimed to be difficult given the need to deliver projects within a strict time frame and to make sufficient profits (Raidén and Dainty 2006). Informal recruitment practices result, however, in a 'no-outsiders' mentality, as evident in the prevalence of white men in the labour force. A further problem concerning discriminatory recruitment and selection practices is the requirement that workers in recognized skilled trades provide their own tools. An example is given by Clarke and Herrmann (2007b) of a carpentry subcontractor recruiting workers on the basis of their tool kits, valued at as much as £3,500 each, and thus creating a barrier to entry not necessarily connected with actual skills levels.

An important question is whether employers look outside the formal VET system for construction labour, relying on the practice of 'poaching' and on migrant worker employment because of inadequacies in existing provision. Table 8.1 indicates the number of first-year entrants to construction-related courses in Further Education (FE) colleges in 2008. At the time, these appeared grossly inadequate to meet the projected average annual employment requirement. However, numerical estimates tend to mask the quality, nature, appropriateness, inclusiveness, and adequacy of VET provision and to lag behind the needs of the industry. For example, the figure of 40,000 trainees does not take account of drop-out rates from college courses, which stood at over 40 per cent for those in the main building trades, partly because many students struggle with basic numeracy and literacy (FEFC 2001; ConstructionSkills 2004). Compounding this, nearly two-thirds of first-year entrants are based in FE colleges. Many people go to local colleges to do construction courses in order to avoid unemployment, learn a trade, and develop a career. But for such trainees, especially women and BAME groups, the link to work experience and employment is unclear; placements are rare and limited in scope (ConstructionSkills 2005; Byrne et al. 2005).

Good construction training schemes are vastly oversubscribed. However, of the 50,000 applicants for construction apprenticeships in 2007, only

7,200 actually succeeded in being placed with employers in the industry (Blackman 2007). The main problem is that VET provision and qualifications are concentrated in traditional craft areas and reinforce trade boundaries, contributing to a narrowing of skills and knowledge in construction, especially as employers tend to focus on existing practices so that the scope for innovation is limited (Farlie 2004; Brockmann et al. 2008). Compared with trainee rates per trade in other European countries of anything from 8 per cent to 16 per cent, rates of first-year trainees in Britain in the wood trades comprised only 5.5 per cent of those employed in this area, roofers 1.4 per cent, and floorers a shocking 0.9 per cent (ConstructionSkills 2008a; Clarke and Wall 1996). Even for those occupations encompassed by formal VET provision, this has a different form, quality, and scope from other European countries, being much narrower and with only restricted knowledge components (Clarke and Winch 2004). Large areas of construction activity remain without any training provision, including groundworks and concreting, precisely the areas which stood out as areas of high labour intensity in a comparative study of labour deployment on sites, and where many migrants are to be found (Clarke and Herrmann 2004a).

Further indications of the low levels of qualifications and training in the industry are given through apprenticeship completions. In 2006/7, 24,000 apprentices were recruited across England, Scotland, and Wales, the vast majority at Level 2 and concentrated in carpentry, bricklaying, painting and decorating, and plastering. About 20 per cent progressed from Level 2 to Level 3. The apprenticeship achievement rate is about 50 per cent, as many drop out once they have the NVQ, which enables them to obtain the CSCS card. In 2002, only 41 per cent of the workforce had completed an apprenticeship, though significant differences were found between trades, the rate for the building trades being only 45 per cent, for the wood trades 73 per cent, and for machine drivers only 8 per cent (ConstructionSkills 2003). The patchiness of data on the workforce hampers efforts to determine exact levels of the stock of skills.

The disconnection between demand for training places and the provision of work-based experience reflects the industry's indifference to formal qualifications, symptomatic of a low skills equilibrium (Brown et al. 2001). The widespread practice of (bogus) self-employment has tended to erode the incentive for construction employers to engage in training, leading them to place increasing emphasis on on-the-job training and 'learning-by-doing' (IFF 2003). Therefore, numerical quantification of skills shortages and the use of qualifications as a proxy for skills only tell a partial story; there is also the issue of the quality of existing skills and qualifications and of significant areas where VET provision is lacking, of low quality and/or inadequacy to meet the present needs of the sector (Stasz 2001).

8.5.2 *Recruitment and Supply of Migrant Workers*

Migrant workers experience particular issues and different routes to employment in construction when they arrive in the UK. Many are, for instance, compelled by construction employers or their agents to register as self-employed persons (Fitzgerald 2007). Indeed, until the formal accession of these countries, workers from Bulgaria and Romania were routinely issued CIS tax certificates as 'entrepreneurs', thereby unknowingly foregoing benefits such as holiday and sick pay entitlement, and employers' contributions to National Insurance and pension schemes. Researching migrant workers in the construction and food processing industries in the North-West and North-East of England, Fitzgerald (2007) noted five routes to entry, namely: 'On spec' (i.e. arriving in the UK with no firm job offer); through family and friends; direct recruitment (i.e. companies directly recruiting from other countries); direct agency (i.e. recruitment through an agency, based in the UK or overseas); and group recruitment (i.e. a group of companies pool resources to recruit from overseas). Construction workers were also found moving from the North-East to the North-West, signifying secondary movements. The study of T5 found each company had its own way of recruiting, mainly word-of-mouth for manual jobs, though the press and gangmasters were also used and some companies had their own agencies or agencies they regularly worked with. These could specialize in bringing in, for example, German carpenters, Polish groundworkers, Portuguese concretors, etc. (Clarke and Gribling 2008). Firms also rely on workers turning up. One large bricklaying firm interviewed classified about 50 per cent as 'chancers', without the skills to do the work required and released immediately (Nuffield 2009).

Numerous reports have indicated that many migrants are highly qualified, but may be unable to work in areas for which they have been trained and have to settle for a job that requires a lower skill (Green et al. 2005; Pollard et al. 2008; Lucio et al. 2007). For instance, recent research on bricklaying workers revealed an English-speaking, medically qualified bricklayer, and another qualified as a laboratory chemist who was employed by an agency responsible for bringing in workers from the Ukraine (Nuffield 2009). Serious institutional failures and a lack of recognition of their qualifications in the UK, or of proficiency in the English language may, for instance, create barriers to accessing jobs for which they are qualified (Dench et al. 2006).

Some migrant workers attempt to re-train in specific occupational areas and/or to gain proficiency in English in order to move to a more stimulating job. Researchers have found that proficiency in the language narrows the gap between migrant and indigenous workers (Green et al. 2005). Barriers to entry into skilled construction occupations for migrants are also evident. For example, Pollard et al. (2008: 37) observed:

a large discrepancy between the high levels of education that many post-enlargement migrants have and the low-skilled and poorly paid jobs in which the majority are working [...] workers who have higher education qualifications are more likely to be working in elemental professions [...] than those with vocational skills, who are able to find work in skilled trades.

In summary, the lack of industrial democracy and the non-existence of social partnership have contributed to a VET system that is increasingly out of step with the needs of the production system (*CLR News* 2009). Lack of regulation in skill entry requirements and employment conditions has in turn exposed migrant workers to unequal treatment and exploitation. Resolving these problems demands both strong political will and social partnership in the pursuit of a comprehensive VET framework and tighter regulation to ensure equal treatment of all workers.

8.6 Policy Implications

Given the context of the industry, using migrant labour as a 'short-term fix' may simply reinforce employers' apparent reluctance to invest in the training and development necessary for alleviating the industry's ingrained skill problems. Ultimately, a revised VET system is required which recognizes and addresses the structural factors outlined in this chapter. Such a strategy should form a component aspect of any public policy that attempts to 'manage migration', with migrant workers themselves benefiting from a renewed emphasis on training and development within the sector. However, without such a policy shift, migration could obscure the true extent of skills requirements whilst providing a disincentive for domestic workers to acquire new skills.

Years of deregulation, privatization, and taxation policy have resulted in large-scale self-employment, undermining managerial control and encouraging low-skill, low-wage strategies (Harvey 2003). This in turn has increased the informality of the labour market, further undermining training and skills development within the sector (Cremers and Janssen 2006). The result is that it is impossible to gain an accurate picture of the size of the industry's labour market, where and how people are employed, and the extent of skills availability. Without better data, it is difficult to understand the role and importance of non-EEA migrant workers or to assess the appropriateness of current migration policy with respect to meeting the industry's skills needs.

The construction industry has been highly criticized with regard to its employment practices and industrial relations climate. Underlying this criticism is a fundamental tension: too often construction relies upon informal and casualized employment practices which provide low barriers to entry for those wanting to work within the sector. Yet it also maintains an exclusionary culture which mitigates against the entry of those who cannot conform to its norms and stereotypes (Dainty et al. 2007). As the industry employs an increasingly diverse range of workers, including migrants, it is important for employers to facilitate their integration. Implementation of the Posted Workers Directive to ensure the principle of host country conditions, that is, according to the terms and conditions laid down in collective agreements and not just the minimum wage, would help to establish more equal pay and conditions in the sector. The implementation of the Agency Workers Directive, requiring equal treatment for those employed through agencies, many of whom are migrants, and the extension of the Gangmasters Licensing Act, would also significantly improve conditions in construction for all workers (Donaghy 2009).

Reward in the industry tends to be contingent on individual performance and this, coupled with the low-cost, low-quality employment road trodden in many areas, holds back the possibility of significant wage rate increases. The use of migrant labour can represent a further attempt to deflate wage rates and the costs associated with the direct employment of domestic workers, especially those associated with VET. Increasing wage rates could, however, have an impact on the attractiveness of working in the industry and hence help to alleviate skills shortages in the longer term.

Unequal treatment and discrimination lie at the heart of the problems of social relations of production in the industry. Effective implementation of equal treatment legislation would not only improve the participation and position of women and BAME groups and help to break down the exclusivity of the sector, but also facilitate the integration of migrant workers. Currently, the industry relies on informal practices and procedures, for instance in terms of the recruitment and selection of workers, which favours the appointment of 'likes', is relatively indifferent to qualifications, and instead prioritizes experience (Beck et al. 2003). What is needed instead are formal and transparent procedures for the recruitment and selection of different groups of workers, whether women, those from BAME groups, or migrants, and including more objective criteria such as qualifications and VET. Equal treatment of all groups would help prevent the inequalities in pay and conditions which currently exist, with migrant workers undertaking similar work to non-migrants but paid at different—even at labourers'—rates. One key problem to be addressed in this respect is that construction workers are at a higher risk of accidents than in any other industry in the UK (GLA 2007). Ensuring the safety, health, and welfare of migrant workers is a key priority in the short term.

Whilst migrant labour has been effective in filling some skills 'gaps', the regulatory implications for the industry are of crucial importance. On larger sites, undeclared labour has often been associated with the employment of migrant workers (Gribling and Clarke 2006). Informing migrant construction workers of their rights and construction employers of their responsibilities is one short-term measure to combat this. Other measures would be to make the main contractor ultimately responsible for all employees on site (main contractor liability), and to restrict the subcontracting chain to prevent further exploitation down the chain, to facilitate direct rather than 'bogus' self-employment and at the same time to keep track of and ensure the availability of statistics related to all those employed on site, according to gender and ethnicity. Regulation has been introduced in the Spanish construction industry, for instance, to control supply relations and curtail the extent of subcontracting by restricting it to three tiers (Ministerio de Trabajo e Inmigración 2006).

Influential reports, such as Egan (1998) and Barker (2004), have emphasized the benefits of the industry, embracing new techniques and innovative technologies in a bid to improve productivity and performance in the construction and housing sectors respectively. Advancement takes time, particularly in housebuilding and in the repair and refurbishment sector, which do not lend themselves to the application of many innovative methods, especially those involving off-site fabrication. However, there is little evidence of modern and innovative methods having a significant impact (Chan and Dainty 2007). New technologies and innovation in the construction process also create their own skills requirements (see e.g. Venables et al. 2004), involving much greater precision, and have therefore been further restricted by the lack of a comprehensive VET system that transcends the boundaries of the 'biblical trades'. The cumulative effects have arguably been to undermine the industry's capacity to translate research into innovation (Gann 2001). Thus, despite the rhetorical claims of the potential of technology substitution as an espoused panacea for the industry's skills needs, there is little evidence of this being the case.

8.7 Conclusions

In light of the evidence presented within this chapter, the optimal longer-term response is to develop an improved and comprehensive VET system, supported with measures to manage the integration of migrant workers into the sector and to regulate the labour market. These would have the potential to secure the productive capacity of the industry and ensure a solid skills infrastructure for the future. The importance of VET as a counter-balance to migrant labour exploitation cannot be overstated. A structured long-term VET policy, meeting the needs of both the demand and supply sides, is the only sustainable solution to coping with the variability of the production process (Arkani et al. 2003). It is also a policy which may be increasingly forced on the government as VET gradually ceases to be an area of no competence with respect to European policy-making.

The construction industry has come to rely on 'poaching' labour trained and educated at considerable expense elsewhere, in particular in the East European countries. This constitutes a form of social dumping, which is in the long term unsustainable, especially as many from Eastern Europe return to their country of origin. With the implementation of the EQF and ECVET, the disparity between skill levels in construction in Britain and other countries is increasingly obvious, including through European Commission implementation projects for the construction industry, for instance in the area of bricklaying (Brockmann et al. 2009). This disparity and the capacity of the industry for recovery are key concerns with the current recession. If the existing labour force does not have the skills needed, from both numerical and qualitative perspectives, this implies that a reliance on recruiting skilled labour from elsewhere will continue. Thus, if a comprehensive VET system remains elusive, construction is likely to remain a significant employer of migrant labour in the future.

In the immediate short term, specific measures can be taken with respect to training and inclusion. These include channelling funding to encourage employers to establish work experience schemes and take on more trainees, implementing clauses on training and employment conditions in local authority planning agreements, providing well-equipped training workshops and special training sites, and changing the current funding regime, which does little to encourage upskilling and career development, as full funding is only secured at NVQ2. Unemployed persons seeking employment opportunities with construction firms could also be empowered through improving the assessment of unemployment benefit and requiring employers to work closely with the local Jobcentre Plus and the Department of Work and Pensions.

It has been shown in other European countries that, managed effectively, migrant workers can be a force for positive change. For example, Pereira (2007) reveals that in Switzerland, working with migrants has strengthened the trade union's role as a representative of all workers and has led to considerable improvements in terms of the knowledge, expertise, and know-how of workers. In this respect, the fact that many migrants are well educated, with transferable skills, and now with considerable experience in the industry, is likely to be critical in improving the skills base and establishing an effective VET programme.

References

ACAS (2009), *Report of an Inquiry into the Circumstances Surrounding the Lindsey Oil Refinery Dispute*, available at <http://www.acas.org.uk>; accessed 6 Mar. 2009.

Anderson, B., and Rogaly, B. (2005), *Forced Labour and Migration to the UK* (Oxford: COMPAS with the Trades Union Congress), available at <http://www.tuc.org.uk/international/tuc-9317-f0.pdf>.

Anumba, C., Dainty, A. R. J., Ison, S. G., and Sergeant, A. (2005), 'The Application of GIS to Construction Labour Market Planning', *Construction Innovation: Information, Process, Management*, 5(4): 219–30.

Arkani, S., Clarke, L., and Michielsens, E. (2003), 'Regulation for Survival: Training and Skills in the Construction Labour Market in Jersey, Channel Islands', *Journal of Vocational Education and Training*, 55(3): 261–80.

Balch, A., Fellini, I., Ferro, A., Fullin, G., and Hunger, U. (2004), 'The Political Economy of Labour Migration in the European Construction Sector', in: M. Bommes, K. Hoesch, U. Hunger, and H. Kolb (eds.), *Organisational Recruitment and Patterns of Migration* (Osnabrück, Germany: für Migrationsforschung und Interkulturelle Studien (IMIS), Universität Osnabrück).

Barker, K. (2004), *Review of Housing Supply* (London: Office of the Deputy Prime Minister).

Beaney, W. D. (2006), 'An Exploration of Sectoral Mobility in the UK Labour Force: A Principle Components Analysis', unpublished M.Sc. thesis, Newcastle Business School, Northumbria University.

Beaney, W. D. (2007), 'A Principal Components Analysis of Labour Sectoral Transfers', in D. Boyd (ed.), *23rd Annual ARCOM Conference*, 3–5 Sept. 2007 (Belfast: Association of Researchers in Construction Management), Vol. 1: 233–42.

Beck, V., Clarke, L., and Michielsens, E. (2003), 'National Report UK: Overcoming Marginalisation: Obstacles to Inclusion in Strongly Segregated Sectors', Final Report to the European Commission, TESR 5 programme.

Blackman, B. (2007), 'Regulating the Situation for Migrants in the British Construction Industry', *CLR News No 4/2007* (European Institute for Construction Labour Research).

Bolger, M. (2008), 'Migrant Labour: What Happens When the Poles Go Home?' *Building*, 24 Oct., available at <http://www.building.co.uk/story.asp?sectioncode=627&storycode=3125647>; accessed 5 Mar. 2009.

Border and Immigration Agency (2008), *Accession Monitoring Report: May 2004–Dec 2007* (Home Office), available at <http://www.ukba.homeoffice.gov.uk/sitecontent/documents/aboutus/reports/accession_monitoring_report/report14/may04-dec07.pdf>; accessed 5 May 2008.

Bosch, G., and Philips, P. (2003), *Building Chaos: An International Comparison of Deregulation in the Construction Industry* (London: Routledge).

Bresnen, M. J., Goussevskaia, A., and Swan, J. (2004), 'Embedding New Management Knowledge in Project-Based Organizations', *Organization Studies*, 25(9): 1535–55.

Briscoe, G. (2006a), 'The Accessibility and Usefulness of Construction Labour Market Statistics', *Construction Information Quarterly: Special Issue on Construction Labour Markets*, 8(3): 119–23.

—— (2006b), 'How Useful and Reliable are Construction Statistics?' *Building Research and Information*, 34(3): 220–9.

—— Dainty, A. R. J., and Millett, S. J. (2000), 'The Impact of the Tax System on Self-Employment in the British Construction Industry', *International Journal of Manpower*, 21(8): 596–613.

Brockmann, M., Clarke L., and Winch C. (2008), 'Knowledge, Skills, Competence: European Divergences in Vocational Education and Training—the English, German and Dutch Cases', *Oxford Review of Education*, 34(5): 547–67.

—— —— —— (2009), 'Bricklaying Qualifications, Work and VET in Europe: Context Report England', Leonardo project, unpublished report, University of Westminster.

Brown, P., Green A., and Lauder H. (2001), *High Skills: Globalization, Competitiveness and Skill Formation* (Oxford: Oxford University Press).

Business Enterprise and Regulatory Reform (BERR) Department (2007), *Construction Statistics Annual 2007* (London: BERR).

—— (2008a), *Construction Statistics Annual 2008* (London: BERR).

—— (2008b), *Trade Union Membership 2008* (London: BERR).

BWA (Bernard Williams Associates) (2006), 'Benchmarking of Use of Construction (Costs) Resources in the Member States', Final Report.

Byrne, J., Clarke, L., and van der Meer, M. (2005), 'Gender and Ethnic Minority Exclusion from Skilled Occupations in Construction: A Western European Comparison', *Construction Management and Economics*, 23(10): 1025–34.

Callender, C. (1997), *Will NVQs Work? Evidence from the Construction Industry*, Report by the Institute of Manpower Studies (IMS) for the Employment Department Group.

Campbell, F. (2006), *Skills Shortages in the UK Construction Industry: Survey 2006* (Ascot: Chartered Institute of Building).

Centre for Corporate Accountability (CCA) (2009), *Migrants' Workplace Deaths in Britain*, jointly published with Irwin Mitchell Solicitors.

Chan, P., and Cooper, R. (2006), 'Talent Management in Construction Project Organisations: Do You Know Where Your Experts Are?', *Construction Information Quarterly*, 8(1): 12–18.

—— and Dainty, A. R. J. (2007), 'Resolving the UK Construction Skills Crisis: A Critical Perspective on the Research and Policy Agenda', *Construction Management and Economics*, 25(4): 375–86.

—— and Moehler, R (2007), 'Developing a 'Road-Map' to Facilitate Employers' Role in Engaging with the Skills Development Agenda', in D. Boyd (ed.), *23rd Annual ARCOM Conference*, 3–5 Sept. 2007 (Belfast: Association of Researchers in Construction Management), Vol. 1, 409–18.

—— —— (2008), 'Construction Skills Development in the UK: Transitioning between the Formal and Informal', in *Proceedings of the CIB W55/W65 Joint Conference: Transforming through Construction*, 15–17 Nov. 2008 (Dubai, UAE).

Chappell, L., Sriskandarajah, D., and Swinburn, T. K. (2008), *Building a New Home: Migration in the UK Construction Sector* (London: Institute for Public Policy Research).

Cherns, A. B., and Bryant, D. T. (1984), 'Studying the Client's Role in Construction', *Construction Management and Economics*, 2: 177–84.

Clarke, L. (2006), 'Valuing Labour', *Building Research and Information*, 34(3): 246–56.

—— and Gribling M. (2008), 'Obstacles to Diversity in Construction: The Example of Heathrow Terminal 5', *Construction Management and Economics*, 26(10): 1055–65.

—— and Herrmann, G. (2004a), 'Cost versus Production: Labour Deployment and Productivity in Social Housing Construction in England, Scotland, Denmark and Germany', *Construction Management and Economics*, 22: 1057–66.

—— —— (2004b), 'Cost vs. Production: Disparities in Social Housing Construction in Britain and Germany', *Construction Management and Economics*, 22 (June): 521–32.

—— —— (2004c), 'The Institutionalisation of the Skills in Britain and Germany: Examples from the Construction Sector', in C. Warhurst, I. Grugulis, and E. Keep (eds.), *Skills that Matter* (Oxford: Palgrave).

—— —— (2007a), 'Divergent Divisions of Labour', in A. Dainty (ed.), *People and Culture in Construction* (London: Taylor & Francis).

—— —— (2007b), 'Skills Shortages, Recruitment and Retention in the House Building Sector', *Personnel Review*, 36(4): 509–27.

Clarke, L. and Wall, C. (1996), *Skills and the Construction Process: A Comparative Study of Vocational Training and Quality in Social Housebuilding* (Bristol: Policy Press in association with Joseph Rowntree Foundation).

—— —— (1998), *A Blueprint for Change: Construction Skills Training in Britain* (Bristol: Policy Press).

—— and Winch, C. (2004), 'Apprenticeship and Applied Theoretical Knowledge', *Educational Philosophy and Theory*, 36(5): 509–21.

CLR News (2007), *Labour Migration*, No. 4 (European Institute for Construction Labour Research).

—— (2009), *Employee and Trade Union Involvement in VET*, No. 1 (European Institute for Construction Labour Research).

Comptroller and Auditor General (2001), *Modernising Construction: Report by the Comptroller and Auditor General* (London: National Audit Office), available at <http://www.nao.org.uk/publications/nao_reports/00-01/000187.pdf>; accessed 10 May 2008.

Construction Industry Joint Council (CIJC) (2006), *Working Rule Agreement June 2006 to June 2009* (London: CIJC).

—— (2008), *Pay and Conditions from 2009* (London: CIJC).

ConstructionSkills (2003), *Skills Foresight Report 2003* (Bircham Newton).

—— (2004), *Skills Foresight Report 2004* (Bircham Newton).

—— (2005), *Trainee Numbers Survey* (Bircham Newton).

—— (2008a), *Blueprint for UK Construction Skills 2008 to 2012* (Kings Lynn: Construction Skills).

—— (2008b), *Sector Skills Agreement: Our Challenges*, available at <http://www.constructionskills.net/sectorskillsagreement/ourchallenges/qualifyingtheworkforce/integratingmigrantlabourtobridgeskillgaps/index.asp?subpage=theidea>; accessed Apr. 2008.

—— (2009), *Blueprint for UK Construction Skills 2009 to 2013* (Kings Lynn: Construction Skills).

Cremers, J., and Janssen, J. (2006), 'Shifting Employment: Undeclared Labour in Construction', *CLR Studies*, 5 (Rotterdam: Antenna).

Dainty, A. R. J., and Bagilhole, B. M. (2005), 'Equality and Diversity in Construction', guest editorial in *Construction Management and Economics*, 23(10): 995–1000.

—— Ison, S. G., and Root, D. S. (2005), 'Averting the Construction Skills Crisis: A Regional Approach', *Local Economy*, 20(1): 79–89.

Dainty, A., Green, S., and Bagilhole, B. (2007), *People and Culture in Construction: A Reader* (Oxon: Taylor & Francis), 26–38.

Davies, J. C., Kemp, G. C., and Frostick, S. P. (2007), *An Investigation of Reporting of Workplace Accidents under RIDDOR using the Merseyside Accident Information Model*, RR528 (Norwich: HMSO for the Health and Safety Executive).

Dench, S., Hurstfield, J., Hill, D., and Akroyd, K. (2006), *Employers' Use of Migrant Labour: Summary Report*, Mar. (London: HMSO).

Donaghy, R. (2009), *One Death is Too Many: Inquiry into the Underlying Causes of Construction Fatal Accidents* (London: HMSO).

Egan, J. (1998), *Rethinking Construction* (London: DTI).

Farlie, V. (2004), 'Are Apprenticeships any longer a Credible Vocational Route for Young People, and can the Supply Side Respond Effectively to Government Policy, and Address the Needs of Learners and Employers?', *Nuffield Review of 14–19 Education and Training*, Working Paper 28, available at <http://www.nuffield14-19review.org.uk/files/documents52-1.pdf>.

FEFC (Further Education Funding Council) (2001), *Construction in Further Education: National Report from the Inspectorate 2000–1* (London: FEFC).

Fielden, S. L., Davidson, M. L., Gale, A. W., and Davey, C. (2000), 'Women in Construction: The Untapped Resource', *Construction Management and Economics*, 18: 113–21.

Fitzgerald, I. (2006), *Organising Migrant Workers in Construction: Experience from the North East of England* (Newcastle: TUC North).

—— (2007), *Working in the UK: Polish Migrant Worker Routes into Employment in the North East and North West Construction and Food Processing Sectors* (London: TUC).

Forde, C., and MacKenzie, R. (2004), 'Cementing Skills: Training and Labour Use in UK Construction', *Human Resource Management Journal*, 14(3): 74–88.

—— —— (2007), 'Getting the Mix Right? The Use of Labour Contract Alternatives in UK Construction', *Personnel Review*, 36(4): 549–63.

Gann, D. (2001), 'Putting Academic Ideas into Practice: Technological Progress and the Absorptive Capacity of Construction Organisations', *Construction Management and Economics*, 19: 321–30.

Glackin, M. (2009), 'Europe's Top 100 Contractors and Materials Firms', *Building*, 23 Jan, available at <http://www.building.co.uk/comment/europes-top-100-contractors-and-materials-firms/3131842.article>; accessed 15 July 2010.

Greater London Authority (GLA) (2007), *The Construction Industry in London and Diversity Performance* (London: Greater London Authority).

Green, A., Owen, D., and Wilson, R. (2005), *Changing Patterns of Employment by Ethnic Group and for Migrant Workers*, Report by Warwick Institute for Employment Research (Coventry: Learning and Skills Council).

Gribling, M., and Clarke, L. (2006), *Undeclared Labour in the Construction Industry: Country Report Great Britain* (Brussels: European Institute for Construction Labour Research).

Griffiths, S. (2009a), 'Wildcat Strikes Spread over Use of Foreign Workers', *Building*, 3 Feb.

—— (2009b), 'Union Threatens Strike over Foreign Labour Use', *Building*, 19 Feb.

Grugulis, I. (2007), *Skills, Training and Human Resource Development: Critical Text* (Basingstoke: Palgrave Macmillan).

Harvey, M. (2001), *Undermining Construction: The Corrosive Effects of False Self-Employment* (London: The Institute of Employment Rights).

—— (2003), 'The United Kingdom: Privatization, Fragmentation, and Inflexible Flexibilisation in the UK Construction Industry', in G. Bosch and P. Philips, *Building Chaos: An International Comparison of Deregulation in the Construction Industry* (London: Routledge), 188–209.

Harvey, M., and Behling, F. (2008), *The Evasion Economy: False Self-Employment in the UK Construction Industry* (London: UCATT Report).

HSE (Health and Safety Executive) (2008), 'Work-Related Injuries and Ill Health in Construction', available at <http://www.hse.gov.uk/statistics/industry/construction/>.

IFF Research (2003), *The Effect of Employment Status on Investment in Training* (London: IFF for CITB and Department for Education and Skills).

Labour Force Survey (LFS) (2005), (Office of National Statistics).

Lillie, N., and Greer, I. (2007), 'Industrial Relations, Migration, and Neoliberal Politics: The Case of the European Construction Sector', *Politics and Society*, 35(4): 551–81.

Lobo, Y. B., and Wilkinson, S. (2007), 'New Approaches to Solving the Skills Shortage in the New Zealand Construction Industry', *Engineering, Construction and Architectural Management*, 15(1): 42–53.

Lockyer, C., and Scholarios, D. (2007), 'The "Rain Dance" of Selection in Construction: Rationality as Ritual and the Logic of Informality', *Personnel Review*, 36(4): 528–48.

Lucio, M. M., Perrett, R., McBride, J., and Craig, S. (2007), *Migrant Workers in the Labour Market: The Role of Unions in the Recognition of Skills and Qualifications*, Research Paper No. 7, Dec. (London: TUC).

McKay, S., Craw, M., and Chopra, D. (2006), *Migrant Workers in England and Wales: An Assessment of Migrant Worker Health and Safety Risks* (London: Report for HSE by Working Lives Research Institute, London Metropolitan University).

Mackenzie, A., Kilpatrick, A. R., and Akintoye, A. (2000), 'UK Construction Skills Shortage Response Strategies and an Analysis of Industry Perceptions', *Construction Management and Economics*, 18(7): 853–62.

Marsden, D. (1999), *Theory of Employment Systems: Microfoundations of Societal Diversity* (Oxford: Oxford University Press).

Mathiason, N., and Mead, K. (2008), 'A High Cost in Builders' Lives', *Observer*, 11 May, available at <http://www.guardian.co.uk/business/2008/may/11/construction.tradeunions1>.

Mayhew, K. (2003), 'The UK Skills and Productivity Gap', talk given to the CIHE/AIM colloquia, 30 Oct.

Ministerio de Trabajo e Inmigración (2006), *Ley 32/2006 reguladora de la subcontratación en el Sector de la Construcción* (Madrid: MTIN), available at <http://empleo.mtin.es/es/Guia/leyes/L3206.html>.

Moehler, R., Chan, P., and Greenwood, D. (2008), 'The Interorganisational Influences on Construction Skills Development in the UK', in A. R. J. Dainty (ed.), *24th Annual ARCOM Conference*, 1–3 Sept. 2008 (Cardiff: UK, Association of Researchers in Construction Management), Vol. 1, 23–32.

Murdoch, I. (2008), *NSCC State of Trade Report 2008: Quarter 1* (Newcastle upon Tyne: Northumbria University).

Nuffield (2009), 'A European Skills Framework: Cross-National Equivalence of Vocational Qualifications', Final Report to the Nuffield Foundation, Kings College London.

Office of National Statistics (2009), *Housing and Construction Statistics* (London: ONS).

Owen, E. (2007), 'Shock Rise in Site Deaths down to Language Barrier', *New Civil Engineer*, 22 Mar., 11.

Pearce, D. (2003), *The Social and Economic Value of Construction: The Construction Industry's Contribution to Sustainable Development* (London: nCRISP).

Pereira, M. (2007), 'Supporting Migrants in Switzerland: The Role of Trade Unions', *CLR News: Labour Migration*, 4/2007: 43–9.

Pollard, N., Latorre, M., and Sriskandarajah, D. (2008), *Floodgate or Turnstiles? Post-EU Enlargement Migration Flows to (and from) the UK* (London: Institute of Public Policy Research (IPPR)).

Raidén, A. B., and Dainty, A. R. J. (2006), 'Human Resource Development in Construction Organisations: An Example of a "Chaordic" Learning Organisation?', *The Learning Organisation*, 13(1): 63–79.

Richter, A. (1998), 'Qualifications in the German Construction Industry: Stocks, Flows and Comparisons with the British Construction Sector', *Construction Management and Economics*, 16(5): 581–92.

Royal Holloway (2002), *Retention and Career Progression of Black and Asian People in the Construction Industry*, EMI Research Report No. 15, prepared for the CITB (London: University of London).

Stasz, C. (2001), 'Assessing Skills for Work: Two Perspectives', *Oxford Economic Papers*, 3: 385–405.

Steedman, H. (1992), 'Mathematics in Vocational Youth Training for the Building Trades in Britain, France and Germany', NIESR Discussion Paper, No. 9 (London).

Stewart, D. (2007a), 'False Self-Employment Costs £2.5bn a year', *Building*, 19 Mar.

—— (2007b), 'Third of Eastern European Migrants work in Construction', *Building Magazine*, 29 May.

Venables, T., Barlow, J., and Gann, D. (2004), *Manufacturing Excellence—UK Offsite Capacity*, Innovation Studies Centre (London: Constructing Excellence).

Warwick Institute for Employment Research (2006), *LMI Future Trends: Construction*, available at <http://www.guidance-research.org>; accessed 5 May 2008.

Watson, D., Johnson, S., and Webb, R. (2006), 'Employer Perceptions of Skills Deficiencies in the UK Labour Market: A Subregional Analysis', *Environment and Planning A*, 38(9): 1753–71.

The Dynamics of Migrant Employment in Construction: A Commentary

Howard Gospel

Construction is a good example of a systemic labour market trap into which a sector can fall over a long period of time. This trap comprises the following: extensive failures to train which leads to a reliance on a strategy of recruitment and poaching; with accessibility to migrant workers which in-turn leads to a further reliance on these easy sources of labour; this further means that neither indigenous nor migrant labour are trained, and the system of skill formation stands in danger of further deterioration. Chapter 8 of this book, by Chan, Clarke, and Dainty, admirably charts this vicious cycle. This comment will mainly focus on the training aspects of the construction industry and migrant labour.

The construction sector in the UK is characterized as follows. On the employers' side, big firms have been in long-term decline as direct employers of labour and are now increasingly 'hollowed out', becoming essentially project tendering, design, and management organizations. This means that they do not themselves employ many, or indeed often any, construction workers, who instead are employed by medium and smaller sized firms. In practice, as the chapter shows, the industry has come to be dominated by small and medium enterprises that act as subcontractors, and by one-man firms on a self-employment basis. All these firms operate in a demand situation, marked by strong seasonality and cyclicality and by work that is split up and scheduled into complex parts, making labour deployment difficult. Labour is taken on and laid off as demand changes in a much more acute way than in most other industries.

On the labour side, employment is therefore often indirect and casual. Some areas (such as electrical and mechanical) are highly skilled; other areas (such as ground work) can often be low skilled. In the UK, the division of labour tends to be on traditional lines, especially in the so-called 'biblical trades' (carpenters, bricklayers, etc.), with tight job boundaries and with most workers single- rather than multi-skilled. In many parts of the industry, it is possible to enter with few, or even no, formal qualifications. A number of studies have suggested that the UK industry has lower levels of labour productivity compared to many of its European counterparts. Some evidence also suggests that in many cases the timeliness and quality of build is also lower.

In most of the industry, the regulatory framework is not particularly extensive. There are, of course, statutory and quasi-statutory regulations in areas such as health and safety that cover all parts of the industry. But, in terms of wages and working conditions, much of the sector is little regulated by collective bargaining—union membership is low, as is membership of employers' organizations, and national agreements set only minimal terms and conditions which do not always regulate what goes on at the workplace.

The skill formation system reflects many of the characteristics outlined above. Vocational education and training is partly regulated via a compulsory levy system, whereby firms either train or pay into a fund from which they can then draw if they subsequently train. Though this existed previously in other industries, it is now confined to construction. However, firms can still manage to evade the levy system which also, according to its critics, is cumbersome and ineffective in setting quality standards and achieving quantity outcomes. In this context, employers are reluctant to take on and train many, or often any, young apprentices to the requisite skill levels. Rather, they prefer to recruit outsiders and poach from other firms. Where further training is needed, firms go in for informal up-grade training on the job. This has some advantages, in terms of training for needs and not over-training, but it has the disadvantage that the stock of skilled workers is low relative to high levels of demand. In other words, it might be argued that construction employers pursue 'production' strategies (which involve recruiting and training labour only for their own immediate use) and not 'investment' strategies (which would involve training labour for the longer-term good of the industry).

For their part, trade unions have wanted to regulate the industry more effectively, but they have been notorious in having problems both recruiting and retaining members. Historically, their concern about skills was with restricting the quantity of labour in the sector, as much as with the quality of training. Paradoxically, perhaps, as their appreciation of both quantity *and* quality has increased, their power to influence outcomes has simultaneously declined.

The chapter shows how migrant labour in recent years, especially from the East European countries, fits into this context. Migrant labour is not the cause of the low skills configuration in the sector. As shown, the causes are longer term and lie deeper. Does migrant labour alleviate or contribute to the skills 'problem' in the sector? The chapter suggests ways in which it may contribute to the problem: it provides an easy option for employers and, in so far as it may depress wages, it may constitute a disincentive for indigenous labour to enter the sector. On the other hand, many of the migrant workers are well skilled, and can both reduce skill shortages (the difference between skills required and outside skills in the market) and skills gaps (the difference between inside skills deployed and skills which should ideally be deployed). In turn, migrant workers can benefit, in terms of jobs, wages, and opportunities to learn and progress. Equally, however, they can themselves be victims of the system, easily taken on and laid off, underpaid for their skills, and themselves not given the opportunity for more formal training. Of course, this is not to mention the pros and cons in terms of the effects on home countries per se of the outflow of their skilled labour.

The chapter nicely analyses these dilemmas, set in an economic and institutional context. However, a number of further points may be registered. First, it would appear that not all big firms behave in the way described above. There are some exceptions and it would be good to have more research on their employment and training policies, including the proportion of migrant labour they hire. Equally, not all parts of the country are so much influenced by the advantages and some of the challenges caused by migrant labour. Of course, it is not surprising that London is a prime example of the trap we have described. But, it would appear that in parts of the North and in Scotland, skill shortages and gaps are not so acute. Secondly, one part of the sector, namely electrical contracting, has a more effective vocational education and training system. This would seem to be attributable in small part to greater statutory regulation, but also in larger part to greater industry self-regulation. A question here is as to whether such arrangements could be extended to other parts of the sector. Thirdly, the chapter, and the book as a whole, touch on a range of policy options for dealing with issues raised, such as increasing employer liability, raising wages, and better implementing national and EU-derived regulations. A listing of the options is useful, but the challenge is to consider what is sensible and practicable and in what time frame.

9

Immigration and the UK Labour Market in Financial Services: A Case of Conflicting Policy Challenges?

Andrew Jones

9.1 Introduction

Over the last couple of decades, the financial services sector has strengthened its position as one of the leading sectors in the UK economy in terms of both employment and output (Centre for Economic and Business Research and City of London 2007; Office for National Statistics 2008). In 2005, the sector employed 1.1 million people and produced net exports valued at 19 billion, and financial services is the single largest contributor sector to the balance of payments (UK Trade and Invest 2008). Between 1996 and 2006, the UK financial services sector was the fastest-growing sector of the economy (Office for National Statistics 2008). In output terms, it grew 74.5 per cent over the decade, compared with 43 per cent growth for the service sector as a whole for the same period (Office for National Statistics 2008). Within this growth, however, there have been distinct patterns between industries and occupations. In general, banking and related activities have led the substantial employment growth of recent years, with brokering and fund management increasing by 35,000 jobs and banking increasing by 6,500 jobs between 2000 and 2006. In contrast, employment in insurance and pensions declined by 19 per cent over the same period (Financial Services Skills Council 2006a).

Yet this growth in financial services employment has suffered a significant reversal since the global economic downturn that commenced in 2007. Employment in key financial services sectors like investment banking began to shrink rapidly during 2008, as the 'credit crunch' produced crisis in the global financial system (FT 2008). The failure of several high-profile international leading financial firms has contributed to mounting job losses in these sectors in the UK, with this decline in employment concentrated in London and the South-East. Whilst more recently there have been some signs of stabilization in the global financial sector, it remains widely predicted that job losses will continue in many financial service sectors into 2010 (FT 2009a), and that the ongoing recession will lead to declining employment beyond banking and those concentrated around the City of London.

The challenges facing the UK financial services sector at the current time are considerable. In seeking to address the primary purpose of this chapter—to understand the relationship between immigration and the financial services sector—it is therefore important to unpack the specific nature of the industries covered by the umbrella category of financial services. Even before the precipitous impacts of the recent economic downturn, the UK financial services labour market corresponded to a diverse set of significantly different occupations requiring different levels of education and expertise from the workforce. Furthermore, the implications of recent trends in this diverse sector for public policy on immigration are complicated, and to some extent, I will argue, potentially contradictory. This chapter therefore develops its analysis in a series of steps. The first step is to unpack the diversity of industries covered in the financial services sector, and to identify specific sub-sectors. Section 9.2 outlines some of the characteristics of the financial services labour market as a whole, and points to regional variations and current trends. The third section considers the nature of employer demand in financial services, followed by an analysis in Section 9.4 of labour supply, and the recruitment practices employed by firms in various sub-sectors. The fifth section considers what options employers have in responding to staff shortages in financial services. I then assess the wider public policy implications of the discussion before drawing together some concluding arguments.

9.2 The UK Financial Services Sector and its Labour Markets

The term 'financial services sector' covers a large number of different industries and activities in the UK economy, and the concept has no clear or consistent definition amongst different users. For the purpose of this chapter, to assess the demand for migrant labour and immigration in relation to financial services, it is important to establish a definition and to clarify what industries and occupations will be examined.

Three major definitional and measurement issues and challenges arise. First, financial services can be broadly divided into a number of industry 'sub-sectors' which themselves are composed of different specific financial service industries. Six sub-sectors have been proposed by the Financial Services Skills Council (Financial Services Skills Council 2006a):

- Credit and Finance
- Insurance and Risk
- Financial Advice
- Banks and Building Societies
- Business to Business Services
- Business Support

This six-fold typology of sub-sectors in financial services is not universally used in the academic literature. For example, academics often treat financial services and business services as separate categories (Wood 2002; Grosse 2004). When the six sub-sectors are considered together, the term more usually referred to within the academic literature is 'Financial and Business Services' (FBS) (Bryson et al. 2004).

For the purposes of the subsequent discussion, the focus will be on industries in the following four sub-sectors (and outlined above): Credit and Finance, Insurance and Risk, Financial Advice, and Banks and Building Societies. Concerning the latter two categories, I adopt, however, a narrower focus and consider only industries and activities that are considered 'purer' financial services. To illustrate, the analysis is concerned with assessment of the labour market in accountancy and tax consultancy, but not management or strategy consultancy. It should also be noted that while many of the factors that influence demand for migrant labour in financial services are applicable to the business services sector as a whole, the discussion will not address 'business services' in their entirety.

Secondly, a key distinction exists across many of these sub-sectors between 'producer' (business-related) and 'consumer' (retail) financial services. Producer financial services correspond to services provided by firms to other firms in the UK economy and abroad (Lewis 1999; Sassen 2001). These services are only offered to other firms, not to individuals. Included in this category are investment banking, equity trading, fund management, and corporate audit. In contrast, consumer financial services are those offered to individuals or small groups of consumers and include services such as retail (high street) banking, financial advice, credit cards, personal loans, and all forms of personal insurance.

Although there is a distinction between producer and consumer financial services, a degree of overlap exists in classification of the two at both the industry and occupational level. For example, insurance and accountancy services are provided to both firms and individuals. In general, however, the distinction is important in assessing the wealth generation and labour market characteristics of different sector activities.

Finally, in relation to the overall objectives of the chapter, the issue of data sources needs to be addressed. In contrast to many other economic sectors, academic research has paid little attention to the issue of migrant labour in financial services. Part of the reason for this is that the term 'migrant' is not generally imagined to apply to people who work in financial services, especially for the most highly skilled workers. The analysis and findings in this chapter are therefore drawn from the limited data that exist, which are mostly qualitative and not quantitative. Existing research and datasets do not allow quantitative measurement of the demand for migrants within financial service sub-sectors and, at present, relevant data are not collected for many of these labour markets. For the limitations outlined above, general rather than specific conclusions may be drawn about the demand for migrant labour in financial services occupations. Consequently, the more specific arguments made about different segments of the financial services sector labour market must be treated as cautious propositions rather than as definitive findings. It is also important to note that the recent data concerned with shifts in the financial services labour market since the economic downturn of 2007 are very limited, and in many cases based on estimates rather than accurate measurement.

9.2.1 *The Financial Services Sector Labour Market*

With regard to the key features of the labour market in financial services, four major characteristics of the workforce are important. First, as with other service sector activities, occupations in financial services involve social contact and interaction with customers and clients (Thrift 1994, 1997). The labour process is principally concerned with social interaction in a variety of forms, and labour represents a very high proportion of total costs for financial service firms (Faulconbridge et al. 2008). Business activity is intrinsically a social process, and this sector has very limited scope for substituting labour with new forms of technology or automation.

Secondly, the financial services sector is skewed towards skilled and highly skilled workers (Financial Services Skills Council 2006b). The majority of occupations in financial services require a first degree, and a high proportion of very skilled jobs require postgraduate qualifications (Financial Services Skills Council 2006b). In terms of labour market segmentation, the key distinction is, as explored above, between 'producer' and 'consumer' financial services. Higher skilled and better paid occupations dominate producer or business financial services with the greater proportion of mid- or lower skill and wage occupations associated with consumer financial services (for example, retail finance, call-centres, and data processing).

Thirdly, in comparison to other sectors in the UK economy, wage levels are high overall (Financial Services Skills Council 2006a). There exists a tier of lower wage semi-skilled employment linked primarily to data processing and routinized customer services (for example, call-centres); however, the average wage level is higher than the national average, reflecting the predominantly skilled and highly-skilled composition of the workforce (Lewis 1999; Grosse 2004).

A fourth and related point is that there are a number of distinct segments to the labour market. While the gender balance in these sectors varies between occupations and industries, in the lowest skill segment, the routinized jobs in data processing and call-centres in the UK are characterized by a feminized labour market, with predominantly a younger workforce (under 35 years old) (Belt et al. 2002; Higgs 2004). There has been little research undertaken on the use of migrant labour in these industries, but it is worth noting that the interactive nature of call-centre work favours UK nationals in terms of the ability of workers to relate to customers in linguistic and cultural terms (Knights and McCabe 2003).

The 'middle segment' of the labour market, characterized by retail banking and credit services, is also characterized by feminization and, since the 1990s, has become increasingly dominated by a younger workforce (under 35 years old) (Halford et al. 1997; Leyshon and Pollard 2000). Academic research has not engaged specifically with the question of migrant labour in these industries, but indicates that the characteristics of the labour process in retail banking and similar activities have not, to date, led to significant recruitment of migrant workers (Alexander and Pollard 2000).

The top segment of highest skill and highest paid occupations in the financial services sector labour market is also dominated by a younger workforce (under 40) (Jones 2003), and is almost exclusively composed of graduates. A high proportion of those employed have a postgraduate degree or other postgraduate professional qualifications (Sassen 2001; Financial

Services Skills Council 2006a). Existing academic research suggests this segment of the financial service workforce is male-dominated, although the degree has diminished to some extent over the last 20 years (McDowell 1997; Jones 1998). There are few temporary or part-time workers in this sector, and a very low degree of unionization. There is also evidence to suggest under-representation of Black and Minority Ethnic (BME) workers (Jones 2003).

A further characteristic of this 'top segment' is the considerable use of highly skilled migrant workers. UK banking and finance, for example, operate in a global labour market for a large number of highly skilled occupations (Beaverstock and Smith 1996; Beaverstock 2002), recruiting workers from the European Union (EU), United States, Asia, and the Far East. There is also some evidence to suggest that over the last decade a growing proportion of highly skilled workers in banking and finance are migrants, and an increasingly global labour market operates among many occupations in the top segment of the financial services labour market (Beaverstock and Smith 1996; Beaverstock 2002).

9.2.2 Regional Variations and Recent Developments in the Economic Downturn

A large body of data and research identifies a distinct geography to the financial services labour market in the UK. Three issues are worth highlighting in this respect. The first is that the highly skilled and highest paid occupations in financial services are heavily concentrated in London and the South-East, with secondary concentration in leading regional cities (for example, Manchester, Leeds, Edinburgh, and Bristol) (Bryson and Daniels 2000). A significant number of the highest skill and wage occupations are only found in central London and are associated with highly specialized financial services being provided to a global market (Sassen 2001; Castells 2002).

Secondly, and conversely, the lowest skilled and paid financial services jobs are located in peripheral regions and cities in the UK. For example, call-centre and data-processing employment is concentrated in 'core cities' and regional cities (for example, Nottingham, Newcastle, Belfast, and Liverpool), and the decentralized 'outer South-East' (Reading, Basingstoke, and Harlow, for example) (Wood 2006). Finally, while relatively fewer financial services sector jobs exist in rural or peripheral regions of the UK, the size of the sector as a whole means that even small urban centres have a significant and growing number of jobs in this sector. Here the jobs are not the highest in terms of skills or wages, but they are still characterized by predominantly graduate-level employment. For example, small market towns have experienced a substantial growth in financial services sector employment in the last decade (Countryside Agency 2004). The occupational composition of this growth is complex, with a mixture of lower- and middle-tier jobs.

These regional variations have previously persisted through different stages of the economic cycle, and it seems likely that they will do so through the present economic downturn. However, whilst it is still early to provide an accurate measure of job losses since what now appears to have been a 2006/7 peak in employment, a number of preliminary pieces of research have sought to estimate the reduction. Notably, the research firm Experian suggested that up to 40,000 jobs will be lost in financial services in the 2008–11 period (Experian 2009). More recently, a Confederation of British Industry/PricewaterhouseCoopers report estimated that 15,000 jobs will be lost from UK financial services in the second quarter of 2009 (CBI/PwC 2009), and confirmed that the pace of employment decline in the first quarter of 2009 was at a 15-year high. It is clear that many of these job losses are currently concentrated in London and the South-East region, and there is evidence that different sub-sectors are faring differently. For example, the CBI/PwC research suggests that insurance and risk has suffered the least employment decline (ibid.).

9.2.3 Occupations in Financial Services

Following the earlier discussion of the different labour market segments, it is useful to distinguish between 'high-', 'mid-', and 'low-' order occupations in the sector. The criteria by which these three occupational orders can be distinguished are based around the three dimensions of the work: which sub-sector, the corporate function, and skills and knowledge required. These are overlapping because occupations in each of the three 'orders' share similar attributes in each of these dimensions. The concept of an 'order' aims to provide some measure of the value placed on employees by employers. Occupational order is therefore, to a large extent, reflected in salary levels and educational or experience prerequisites for employment in a given occupation. However, these orders neither map directly onto any one sub-sector nor fit the Standard Occupation Codes (SOCs), which conflate quite diverse occupations ranging from high, mid- to low.

'High-order' financial services occupations correspond to the most highly skilled and highly paid occupations. They are concentrated in high value-added sub-sector industries which serve a global rather than a national market. Key sub-sectors include investment banking, accountancy, private equity, insurance, and corporate finance. A significant proportion of these occupations are dominated by those with 'elite' educational backgrounds and postgraduate qualifications (for example, Master's degrees, MBAs, and doctorates) and they fulfil 'high value-adding' functions within firms. Major high-order occupations in financial services include, for example, investment banker, financial or fund manager, analyst, and finance officer.

'Mid-order' occupations in financial services include a variety of skilled occupations in a range of sub-sector industries within financial services. However, on average, these occupations are less highly skilled and create less value than 'high-order' occupations. They are more prevalent in industries serving a national, regional, or local market in the UK economy and do not command as high salaries as the highest order occupations. Major mid-order occupations in financial services include:

- Bank Manager
- Mortgage Broker
- Financial Advisor
- Chartered and Certified Accountant (2421)
- Insurance Underwriter/Broker (3533)
- Taxation Expert (3535)
- Credit Controller (4121)
- IT Professional (2131/3131)

In line with the distinctions identified above, the majority of those employed in mid-order financial services occupations are employed in consumer (retail or related) rather than producer (business service) financial services.

Finally, in the financial services sector, the main 'lower order' occupations include:

- Bank Clerk (4123)
- Account/Filing Clerk (4131)
- Pension and Insurance Clerk (4132)
- Finance and Accounting Technician (3537)
- Call-Centre Agent (7211)
- Customer Care (7212)
- Database Assistant/Clerk (4136)
- Computer Engineer (5245)
- Elementary Office Occupations (9219)

These occupations often involve more routinized work (Leidner 1993), and add less value through the work process than do mid- or high-order occupations. However, such occupations exist across all sub-sectors within the financial services sector.

Also related and worth noting, the financial services sector employs a large number of staff in related support services. It is difficult to demarcate the boundary of the sector in this sense because in some firms and sub-sectors, related support service employment may be sub-contracted out to specialist non-financial service firms. For example, in retail banking, some firms may provide software and information technology (IT) support from an 'in-house' division within the firm, while others may instead sub-contract this to a specialist firm.

9.2.4 *Key Policy Issues for the UK Financial Services Labour Market*

The existing academic and policy literature suggests at least four major public policy issues in relation to the future development of the financial services sector labour market. First, there is the UK economy's need for highly skilled migratory labour in 'high-order' financial services. A large body of social science research has established the continuing development of a global labour market for highly skilled migrant workers in higher order financial services (Sassen 2001; Sklair 2001; Jones 2003). This demand for migratory labour in the UK is concentrated in London (Salt and Millar 2006), although there is evidence of demand in key regional cities like Leeds, Manchester, Edinburgh, and Bristol, where some higher order financial service activity occurs (Salt and Millar 2006). The development of this global labour market for highly skilled workers is complex, and current research does not provide a full explanation of the differential demand for such labour in high-order financial services activities. However, it is clear that the 'top end' UK-based firms compete for highly skilled workers in a competitive international labour market that operates at a global level. The consequence of this in the current economic downturn is not straightforward, since there is evidence that when highly skilled workers lose their jobs, they can easily leave the UK, provoking concerns of a 'flight of talent' (FT 2009b).

A second issue is the vulnerability of the lower skilled, lower paid occupations to the economic transformations associated with globalization. In particular, considerable attention has been paid to the process of 'offshoring', where back-office, call-centre and data-processing jobs in financial services are being lost in the UK as firms relocate activities to cheaper wage locations in South Asia, notably India. Such a process is relevant to the concerns of this chapter in so far as research is yet to establish whether this process is likely to create a surplus pool of lower skilled labour in financial services in the UK (James and Vira, forthcoming).

Thirdly, there is a considerable literature assessing the issues that surround the uneven geography of high- and low-order financial services sector employment. This has several dimensions to it. Foremost are the policy implications for economic development and planning around the concentration of financial services employment in London and the South-East. Research suggests that few of the highest skilled and highest paid financial services sector jobs are outside this region, which represents a significant structural weakness in the economies of the other UK regions (Wood 2006). A policy debate thus continues as to whether other city-regions in the UK can compete with London and the South-East for the top segment of the labour market, and whether it is feasible to achieve a more even balance in the geography of financial services sector employment (Sokol 2007).

Finally, a more recent policy discussion has emerged concerning the future of the financial services labour market in relation to the downturn, the potential for over-dependence of the UK labour market on financial services sector (and related) employment, and the need to mitigate the impact of, or prevent off-shoring among, lower skilled financial services occupations.

9.2.5 The Demand for Migrant Labour

Assessing the demand for migrant labour across the financial services sector as a whole is a difficult task which has received relatively little direct attention. There is a substantial amount of literature that examines the nature of working practices (McDowell 1997; Leyshon and Pollard 2000), the globalization of the sector (Lewis 1999; Jones 2003), the sector's central role in UK economic development (Wood 2002, 2006) and, to a lesser extent, the development of a global labour market for highly skilled financial services sector occupations (Beaverstock 2002; Taylor et al. 2003). However, there appears to be no work that has sought to accurately quantify the demand for migrant labour in financial services. Most of the research that is relevant to understanding the demand for migrant labour in this sector does so by inference rather than by explicitly engaging with the issue.

However, two sources of quantitative data on the demand for migrant labour in financial services were identified. The first is the Labour Force Survey, which, as discussed in Chapter 3, can be analysed to provide an overview of the migrant labour share both for the sector as a whole, and for groups of some of the occupations by SIC code. Table 9.1 shows analysis from the LFS in 2008, showing the percentage of foreign-born workers in occupations within the sector. This indicates that for most occupations, around 10–15 per cent of financial services sector workers are migrants, a figure slighter higher than the median 7 per cent for skilled occupations (MAC 2008). This appears to support the significant presence of a minority of skilled migrant workers in financial services, further reinforced by the lower percentages found in lower skilled occupations such as insurance and pension clerks. However, a second source of data comes from work permit data (cf. Salt and Millar 2006). In the 1995–2005 period, the number of work permits granted for financial service firms increased from 3,194 to over 6,500. Whilst financial services accounted for a smaller proportion of all work permits granted (down from 13.2% to 7.4% in 2005), this does provide an insight into the growth in absolute demand for migrant labour over this period.

Beyond these general indicators, existing research suggests that demand for migrants in financial services is divided among different labour market segments, and this broadly corresponds to the three 'orders' that characterize such occupations. This labour market approach is more useful than either a firm- or sub-sector-based analysis because the various 'orders' of occupations in all three segments of the labour market transcend firm and sub-sector boundaries, while in terms of the qualifications and skills required of workers, occupations within different labour market segments are often comparable. It therefore makes sense to adopt this skills-based typology of the labour market in any analysis of the demand for migrants.

Table 9.1 Percentage foreign-born of UK labour force, 2008 (financial services occupations)

	% employees born non-EEA	% employees born EEA, excl. UK
Financial managers & chartered secretaries	12	3
Financial institution managers	12	3
Chartered & certified accountants	13	3
Management accountants	16	4
Brokers	13	5
Insurance underwriters	1	3
Finance & investment analysts/advisors	12	5
Taxation experts	7	2
Finance & accounting technicians	10	6
Accounts & wage clerks, book-keepers, other financial clerks	9	3
Pensions & insurance clerks	5	2

Source: MAC (2008).

With respect to high-order occupations, the evidence clearly indicates that highly skilled migrants play a crucial and increasingly significant part in the UK workforce (Taylor et al. 2003; Organisation for Economic Cooperation and Development 2007). The high-order occupations identified above require an elite education background (McDowell 1997; Hall 2006) and a range of skills that are in short supply in the UK and other national labour markets (Hall 2009). A substantial body of research confirms that employers compete in a global labour market for workers in these occupations, and that a growing proportion of workers in these occupations in the UK, as in other advanced industrial economies, are migrants (Jones 2003).

The evidence for mid-order financial services occupations is less clear-cut. There is no identifiable research that has investigated the demand for migrants in consumer financial services industries in the UK. There is no evidence to suggest that migratory labour plays a significant role in the occupations identified. Whilst there is some quantitative evidence of a small fraction of migrant employment in these occupations, this appears to be equivalent to other similar skilled occupations. A key reason for this is likely to be the 'socially interactive' dimension to many mid- and lower-tier financial services occupations. Many occupations in retail financial services involve dealing with customers, either face-to-face or over the telephone (Leyshon and Pollard 2000), and this may present a number of barriers to migrant workers. For example, issues around language and cultural understanding have been emphasized as crucial in the way in which retail banking and other retail financial services have developed their customer experiences. Migrant workers who are not highly fluent in English, or are unfamiliar with UK culture and values, are less likely to fit the characteristics desired by employers. A number of middle-segment financial services occupations also have a qualification-based barrier that is a barrier to migrants (for example, UK accountancy qualifications).

Finally, evidence on low-order financial services occupations is also limited. No research that directly engages with the issue has been identified, although the lower skill level required by employers does mean that some of the barriers to entry that migrant workers experience in the mid-order occupations are possibly less significant. However, research into customer-oriented occupations such as call-centre agents and office clerks suggests very limited migrant participation, which might be associated with the 'soft skills' and linguistic and cultural background issues identified above. Research into UK-based call-centres, for example, has highlighted the desirability of regional accents and UK cultural familiarity among firms recruiting call-centre agents (James and Vira, forthcoming). Such attributes suggest significant barriers to entry for many migrant workers in these occupations.

The remainder of this chapter explores this overall assessment of the role of migrant workers in financial services in greater depth. The next issue to be examined is an assessment of the characteristics and dimensions of labour demand in each segment of the sector's labour market.

9.3 Demand in the UK Financial Services Labour Market

In order to understand the characteristics of demand for labour in financial services as a whole, it is necessary to discuss each of the different 'orders' of financial service activity in the UK separately. The nature of high-order financial service occupations and their associated labour markets are very different to that of the mid- and low-order occupations.

9.3.1 *High-Order Financial Service Occupations*

Across several social science disciplines, there exists research that examines the characteristics and dimensions of high-order occupations in financial services. These 'elite' occupations can be broadly grouped around the highly skilled jobs that are heavily concentrated in the UK in the City of London (Taylor et al. 2003). At least three major features are of significance in understanding employer demand.

First, the skills and attributes required by employers for high-order financial services sector occupations relate to specialist expertise gained through elite postgraduate and vocational qualifications and previous work experience. Such characteristics include specialist knowledge of financial markets; experience in key foreign financial centres; elite postgraduate qualifications; and managerial experience in a different financial jurisdiction. Typically, high-order occupations require a good first degree as an absolute minimum. In the UK, many firms recruit graduates exclusively through a 'milk round' at top universities (for example, in Oxford, Cambridge, Bristol, Durham, Edinburgh, and London) (Jones 1998; Financial Services Skills Council 2006b).

Secondly, elite formal qualifications are a prerequisite but are not in themselves sufficient for gaining a position. For high-order financial services occupations, employers also place great importance on 'soft skills' and personal characteristics. These are generally acquired from a mixture of (elite) educational background and career experience (Thrift 2000).

Employers in these occupations generally seek high educational achievers who are competent in a range of crucial soft and 'performative' skills (Thrift 2000). Research with recruiters in these occupations has identified a number of skills criteria: team work; interpersonal and communication skills; organizational and time management skills; and leadership ability.

The social science literature on 'work' has pointed to the gendered nature of many of these 'soft' skills criteria, arguing that the continued dominance of men in many of the highest paid and most senior financial services jobs reflects 'masculine' criteria around which desirable skills are defined and 'performed' in the workplace (McDowell 1997; Jones 1998). There is also a high degree of employee turnover between firms and across sub-sectors in this segment of the financial services labour market (Lewis 1999)[1] and, as a consequence, firms must invest considerable resources in recruiting staff at all levels and career stages. This high turnover reflects the competitive nature of the labour market in 'boom' periods, and the strong emphasis on personal performance and established career progression pathways for many highly skilled occupations, where experience in different firms, roles, and countries is an advantage for individuals (Lewis 1999; Jones 2003).

Thirdly, for these high-order financial services occupations, 'training' builds on the elite educational background and includes a range of socializing and acculturating experiences in workplace culture (Jones 2003). Graduate requirements aside, the 'skills' required by employers largely centre on less tangible 'soft skills', and personal characteristics (for example, skills in socializing) (Thrift 2000). The 'quality' of work in these high-order occupations is thus heavily determined by interpersonal skills and personal characteristics because of the 'social' nature of the work process. These are the primary factors influencing employer preferences in recruitment at all career stages, and they provide an explanation for the extensive use of specialist recruitment agencies to find employees who 'fit' a wide-ranging set of educational and personal criteria (Beaverstock et al. 2006).

9.3.2 Mid-Order Financial Services Occupations

The academic literature on employer demand in mid-order financial services occupations largely focuses on consumer or retail financial services jobs because they feature heavily in this segment of the sector's labour

---

[1] Employee turnover in highly skilled 'City' occupations such as investment banking can reach 30–40% per year in 'boom' periods where labour market conditions are tight (Jones 2003).

market. In terms of skills and the nature of employer demand, three major factors emerge.

First, most of the mid-order occupations in financial services are skilled or highly skilled, with a majority of occupations requiring a first degree and many occupations requiring a postgraduate professional or vocational qualification.

Secondly, in contrast to the business-oriented nature of many high-order financial services occupations, the mid-order occupations require skills more aligned to interacting with retail finance customers. Whilst they are certainly 'skilled', these occupations are less highly skilled than business-oriented financial services occupations. Employers in mid-order occupations have less rigorous and tightly defined requirements for recruitment in terms of educational background and previous experience.

Thirdly, as a consequence of the focus on the customer, interpersonal skills are extremely important in many mid-order occupations (Beaverstock 1996; Pollard 1999). The quality of work provided by mortgage advisors or retail bank managers is heavily influenced by customer experience, so interpersonal and communication skills are important (O'Loughlin and Szmigin 2006). Existing research suggests that migrants, especially those with poor English-language skills and lack of socialization into UK culture and values, are at a significant disadvantage with respect to these customer-oriented skills (Alexander and Pollard 2000). They are also excluded because they are likely to lack UK-based or recognized professional qualifications.

9.3.3 *Low-Order Financial Services Occupations*

With respect to the low-order financial services occupations identified, research indicates greater diversity in the nature of the skills associated with different jobs in this group. It also suggests that skill requirements are very different from those associated with the high-order occupations. Three major features of employer demand are identifiable.

First, many low-order financial services occupations involve routinized work that does not require a degree-level qualification (Leidner 1993). The National Vocational Qualifications (NVQ) levels used to formally describe skill requirements for occupations may therefore more accurately capture the skills employers are looking for. Low-order financial services occupations in retail banks, accounts, and as pension or insurance clerks, are characterized as semi-skilled jobs because a good secondary school education is required, but entry-level recruitment employers also seek basic but good skills in language, numeracy, communication, and organization. There are no specific vocational qualifications for many of these occupations.

However, a small number of occupations identified (for example, as data-base assistants or computer technicians) require a higher level of formal qualifications, necessitating further education or higher education levels.

Secondly, a significant sub-group of the identified low-order occupations require 'soft skills', which is consistent with the customer-oriented nature of consumer financial services. Occupations such as call-centre agents or customer care assistants require interpersonal, communication, and other 'soft skills' similar to those needed in the mid-order occupations in consumer financial services. Whilst the work practices of call-centre agents are more routinized and regulated, employers still require workers who have good communication skills in English and an ability to relate to 'UK cultural values' (James and Vira, forthcoming). There is a growing body of research examining the specific nature of call-centre work which highlights the need for agents to relate to and interact with customers in ways that provide good service. Research has also examined how call-centre employers are investing significantly in training in order to develop these kinds of skills in their employees (Belt et al. 2002).

9.4 Labour Supply and Recruitment in Financial Services

We now turn to consider research into the nature of the labour supply available to employers. Due to the relative distinctiveness between occupations in each occupational order, they will be examined separately.

With regard to high-order occupations, the key factor that emerges is that the pool of British workers within the UK is very limited. This is not surprising given the generally high degree of skill specialism that is required, and that this category is composed of a large number of specific specialized occupations that each employ relatively few individuals (Beaverstock and Smith 1996; Sassen 2002; Jones 2003; Liaw 2006). Due to the degree of specialism, the UK has a small pool of suitable labour that could potentially fill vacancies and there exists a global pool of labour which is concentrated in a limited number of key financial centres in Europe, North America, and Asia. In effect, many of these occupations thus recruit from an increasingly global labour market with little difference between national labour markets in terms of their characteristics. Research suggests that UK employers expend considerable time and effort recruiting for these occupations and there is generally no 'reserve' pool of labour that they are not currently seeking to recruit from (Beaverstock 2002; Jones 2003). In the context of the recent economic downturn, it is significant that there is limited evidence that despite substantial job losses in sectors such as banking in London, the highest skill occupations do not appear to generate a significant reserve pool of labour in the UK. Large numbers of nominally unemployed but highly skilled workers from Lehman Brothers and Merrill Lynch, for example, have been immediately recruited by competitors Nomura and J. P. Morgan, respectively (cf. FT 2009b), reinforcing the high value placed on human capital in the industries. The evidence thus suggests that the supply of workers for high-order occupations remains tight even in the downswing phase of the business cycle.

Regarding mid-order financial services occupations, there is less research into the nature of the labour supply in the UK. There is also likely to be more variation in the nature of potential labour pools between the different occupations identified. Research does, however, indicate a number of general characteristics of the labour supply. First, for many customer-oriented mid-order occupations, there is a good supply of graduate labour in the UK. Employers can recruit accountants or retail bank managers from a substantial pool of graduates from the UK higher education sector, which, at the international comparative level, provides the UK labour market with a high proportion of graduates with degrees suitable for entry into these occupations. Research suggests that UK accountancy firms, for example, recruit primarily from UK Higher Education (HE) institutions, and that over the last two decades there has been a sufficient supply of UK graduates, the majority of whom are British nationals (Beaverstock and Smith 1996; Walker 2004). For many mid-order occupations, there is a potential pool of non-British workers in the EEA who could be recruited if shortages in the labour supply emerged, but they are likely to be less attractive to employers because of the need for English-language fluency in these occupations. There is only limited evidence that employers seek to recruit outside the UK (Hanlon 1999). In the context of the economic downturn, it is likely that the supply pool has been considerably increased, with job losses occurring across retail financial services. The Lloyds-TSB merger and Royal Bank of Scotland 'rescue' have already led to widespread retail bank branch rationalization and concomitant job losses in these occupations (FT 2009a).

Turning to the labour supply in low-order financial services jobs, there has been limited research on a limited number of occupations. Given the relatively lower skill requirements, there exists a substantial pool of potential workers for occupations such as banking, accountancy, or filing clerks amongst British workers. While there was evidence of tight labour market conditions in London and the South-East, where many of the jobs were concentrated during the 2000s 'boom' (Office for National Statistics 2008),

275

an available pool exists in the economy as a whole which could theoretically have filled vacancies at the national level. The economic downturn since 2007 has eased supply constraints, and whilst there is some scope for employers to draw on labour from the EEA, again, language limitations and lack of other 'soft skills' make this pool less attractive to employers for many low-order occupations.

Finally, rather than being concerned with the domestic labour supply for these occupations, research has been more concerned with the policies of employers to 'off-shore' several of these job categories. Several major financial services employers have off-shored call-centre and back-office data-processing operations out of the UK to lower wage locations elsewhere in Europe and in Asia. This reinforces evidence from regional policy and industrial location literatures that, in these activities, there is no evidence of labour shortages in the UK. Furthermore, the literature identifies the strong representation of British workers in call-centres, reflecting the linguistic and 'soft' skill dimensions to the jobs (Belt et al. 2002; James and Vira, forthcoming). One implication of this is that the potential barriers to entry to call-centre work for unemployed UK workers appear to be low (apart from an uneven regional geography of call-centre locations). Many financial firms in this sector offer on-the-job training and flexible working arrangements that make part-time and non-traditional working patterns possible (Belt et al. 2002; James and Vira, forthcoming). However, in the recessionary economic climate since 2008, there is evidence of job losses for these kinds of occupations both in the UK *and* in the off-shoring locations (*Financial Express* 2009).

9.5 Responses to Labour Shortages in Financial Services

The specific nature of demand for migrant labour in financial services, and of how migration relates to the various alternatives available to employers to meet labour shortages, varies considerably between the three different orders of occupation identified. Accordingly, each segment of the labour market will be considered separately.

9.5.1 *Migration*

For the high-order occupations, a substantial body of research points to the ongoing significance of highly skilled migrant workers in financial services. Whilst there is a clear cyclical dimension to this demand, the research indicates that in several sub-sectors the percentage of highly skilled migrants in high-order occupations has increased over the last decade. Cyclical variations notwithstanding, there appears to be a long-term trend for greater use of highly skilled migrants. This demand is concentrated around London and the South-East region for three reasons.

The first reason is the status of London as a leading global city and one of three top financial centres in the global economy (Hyde and Dilnot 2000; Sassen 2001). Secondly, UK demand for highly skilled migrants in financial services reflects the structural developments of the sub-sectors with high-order occupations (Jones 2003). In particular, there is greater diversity and specialism in occupational terms as finance services fracture into an ever-increasing number of specialized activities (Liaw 2006). This is producing a global labour market for high-order occupations as the pool of suitably skilled persons in any single national economy is very small. Firms seeking to fill these occupations make extensive use of (international) recruitment agencies to identify suitable workers for a specific role (Beaverstock et al. 2006). Research suggests that this has led to an increasing internationalization or 'cosmopolitanization' of the labour force in London and the South-East. Compared to 20 years ago, the number of highly skilled migrants working in the financial services sectors in London has grown significantly (Hamnett 2003). Whereas in the early 1980s, migrant employment in these occupations was probably less than 5 per cent (Thrift and Leyshon 1992; Sassen 2001), firm-level research in banking and related financial services suggests that this figure is now likely to be over 10 per cent and may be in the 15-20 per cent range for high-order occupations (Sassen 2001; Jones 2003).

Thirdly, industry globalization in many financial services sub-sectors is leading to a transformation of working practices that is increasing the demand for migrants (Morgan 2001). As a leading global city, research suggests that London is increasingly playing a key role as a 'hub' for highly skilled migrants in global financial services sector labour markets (Koser and Salt 1997), and workers in this sector (both UK nationals and migrants) are increasingly mobile, both in the short and long term. Working practices in many high-order financial services occupations require a high degree of short-term business travel, and for many occupations secondment periods overseas as expatriate workers are becoming the norm in terms of individual worker career paths (Beaverstock 2004; Jones 2008). Perhaps most importantly, there is evidence that international mobility is an explicitly desirable characteristic of employee experience. Firms need senior and professional employees who have worked overseas, who are familiar with different cultures and ways of working, and who have a detailed understanding of

277

different regulatory jurisdictions (Jones 2003; Faulconbridge 2004; Hall 2006).

This leads to a complicated set of implications for the role of immigration. Overall, the factors identified suggest that a 'global labour market' operates for high-order financial services occupations, which means employers around the world recruit internationally. Therefore, whilst the numbers of migrants have increased through the '2000s boom', this remains a characteristic even in a recession. However, within these occupations, an important distinction needs to be made between types of migrant, and in particular between intra-firm transfers and new recruitment. Regarding the former, research suggests that many London-based financial services firms employ a growing portion of their workers in the UK on 'secondments' from overseas (Taylor et al. 2003). Such 'internal transfers' in transnational firms range between six months and four years, and involve employees who are established in their respective occupations.[2] In most cases, employees anticipate leaving the UK at the end of their secondment (Jones 2003; Beaverstock 2004). However, in a context where firms are competing for highly specialized skills in a global labour market, some of these intra-firm transfers remain in the UK for longer.

Turning to recruitment practices in high-order occupations, the primary modes of recruitment are either through interpersonal contact networks of UK-based employees, or through the use of international recruitment firms (Beaverstock 2004; Faulconbridge et al. 2008). Career mobility produces circumstances where senior managers in the UK can recruit migrants whom they or colleagues have encountered through professional networks. There is also limited evidence to indicate that UK-based recruitment at the graduate level is leading to some non-UK workers on student visas being recruited from elite educational institutions (McDowell 1997), but many UK firms (for example, banks and accountancy firms) recruit directly at this level from elite institutions across Europe (Jones 1998). At more advanced career levels, however, the primary method of hiring is through recruitment agencies that maintain an international network of offices and contacts to fill specialized occupations (Faulconbridge et al. 2008). Given the recent growth of China and other Asian economies, there is anecdotal evidence of a growing demand, and an increase in recruitment efforts from financial services employers, for highly skilled nationals from that region.

---

[2] No quantitative data on financial services firm internal transfers were identified. Existing research is based on some partial quantitative data from specific firms, but relies more on qualitative commentary from key business managers (Jones 2003; Faulconbridge 2004).

With regard to the demand for migrant workers in mid-order occupations, the picture is a rather different one from that for high-order financial services. Although there is little direct research, the evidence suggests that most mid-order occupations have limited proportions of migrant workers (probably less than 5%), and there is little or no specific demand from employers for them (Hanlon 1999; Leyshon and Pollard 2000). There appears to be an adequate supply within the UK for most occupations, and there is only very limited evidence of employers seeking to recruit outside the UK (Hanlon 1999; Leyshon and Pollard 2000). It is likely that job losses during the recent recession mean there is no real impetus for employers to recruit outside national labour markets.

In the low-order financial services occupations, research and evidence in relation to the demand for migrant labour is sparse. This is perhaps indicative of the relative insignificance of migrants in the occupations identified. While it is likely that some migrant labour is employed in occupations such as data processing and in clerical roles, there is no evidence to suggest any specific use of, or demand for, migrant labour. Employers appear to recruit in regional labour markets, with the possible exception of London, where tight labour market conditions periodically lead to recruitment in national markets (Leyshon and Pollard 2000). As discussed above, in the customer-centred occupations in this group, there is some evidence of barriers for migrant labour in linguistic, cultural, and 'soft skills' terms. For sub-sectors involved in call-centre activity, existing research points to 'off-shoring' as the dominant labour market strategy rather than the use of migrant labour. In general, given the decentralization of many low-order financial services activities out of the high cost South-East region (Coe and Townsend 1998), there is no indication of recruitment difficulties for employers. Again, the recent recession is only likely to further reinforce this situation.

9.5.2 *Alternatives to Immigration for Responding to Perceived Labour Shortages*

Potential responses to labour shortages in the different segments of the financial services sector labour market need to be considered for each of the three labour market 'order' segments.

Regarding high-order occupations, a significant body of research supports the view that there is no real alternative to immigration (Salt 1997; Beaverstock and Boardwell 2000; Sassen 2001; Beaverstock 2002; Jones 2003). This is due to a variety of factors, including: the very limited pool of workers in the labour market with appropriate skill sets (Sklair 2001); the fact that wages in these occupations are already high and benchmarked with regard to salaries in global labour markets (Financial Services Skills Council 2006a); the specialist skills and knowledge required by employers; the lack of scope to alter the work process; the reliance on the personal characteristics of employees (Beaverstock et al. 2006).

With regard to the last point made above, the socially interactive dimensions of undertaking high-order financial services work cannot easily be substituted with new forms of technology, and the centrality of co-presence means that off-shoring highly skilled work is not possible (Jones 2005). Given the substantial salary costs involved in locating these workers to the highest-cost region of the UK economy, it is likely that firms would have invested in new technologies and/or adopted off-shoring strategies already if this were feasible. Research thus suggests that the likely consequence of reducing access to non-EEA workers in the top segment of the financial services labour market would be highly detrimental to UK economic competitiveness and the attractiveness of the UK as a location for producer-oriented financial services (Sassen 2001; Sklair 2001; Wood 2006; Beaverstock et al. 2006). Such a conclusion holds even in a period of recession. The literature also suggests that current immigration policy has little or no impact on the training opportunities for British workers in these occupations, and that given the limited size of the potential pool of workers, up-skilling is not a feasible alternative to recruiting highly skilled migrants. Overall, there are no real alternatives to immigration in this top segment and there are no reserve pools of labour within the UK that could provide an alternative supply of workers.

With regard to the mid-order occupations, research has not explored alternatives to immigration (primarily because of the low levels of migrants in these occupations). For the reasons stated earlier, in the event of labour shortages in many of these occupations, research suggests immigration is a less attractive means of tackling the problem (Hanlon 1999; Leyshon and Pollard 2000). Immigrant workers are likely to require more training and to be less able to fulfil 'soft skill' requirements. There is scope for up-skilling among UK workers to fill labour shortages that arise, and policy measures might link to improved higher education training courses that equip and re-skill British workers to fill these roles. As with the high-order financial services occupations, off-shoring is not viable because of the face-to-face customer-oriented nature of the work. Some research suggests that new forms of technology do provide opportunities to reduce the labour processes in some of these financial services occupations (Financial Services Skills Council 2006a; Durkin et al. 2007). For example, in retail banking over the last decade, a number of leading employers have reduced customer-facing staff for routinized services in high street banks and replaced them with automated transaction-processing machines (Farquhar and Panther 2007). In light of the significant job losses in many of these occupations since 2008, there appears to be little need or incentive for employers to turn to immigrant workers to fill vacancies.

In the low-order occupations, there is little migrant labour employed, and an adequate labour supply within the UK economy even during the upswing phase of an economic cycle. In terms of addressing any regional shortages of workers, this is most likely relevant for London and the South-East; employers are likely to favour up-skilling or raising wages to attract internal UK migration because of the importance of language, communication, and 'soft' skills.

The impact of reducing access to non-EEA workers in financial services would appear to be largely confined to high-order occupations. This would be highly detrimental to a key set of activities and drivers of growth in the UK economy in the long term even if the recent recession has eased some potential shortages. Beyond these high-order occupations, there is no evidence to suggest that reducing employer access to non-EEA workers would be significant. To a large extent, for many mid- and low-order financial services occupations, immigration is a less desirable response to labour shortages than seeking to fill shortages from the wider UK labour market by increasing training, raising wages, or encouraging inter-regional migration to increase the labour supply.

9.6 The Implications for Public Policy

In light of the discussion of the nature of the labour market in financial services, and its use of migrant labour, I want to highlight four key issues in relation to how public policy (including immigration policy) conditions and shapes the labour market in this sector.

First, the clear conclusion which can be drawn from research is that the labour market for highly skilled financial services workers is highly competitive and globalized (Taylor et al. 2003), and there is a very limited supply of the workers in the labour market within the UK (as there is in any national economy) (Salt 2002). The force driving this is the globalization of financial services sector activities based in the UK (and concentrated in London), along with the absolute growth of the sector in employment and, in terms of Gross Domestic Product, the UK economy. The growth in non-British workers is also a response to the highly specific and non-codified skills that employers are seeking. Thus, even in a recession that has heavily impacted key sub-sectors in financial services, the evidence suggests that any public policy measures that restrict the ability of firms to recruit highly skilled migrants could be very detrimental to the UK economy. The use of migrants is an integral and important aspect of firm and industry competitiveness (Sassen 2001; Jones 2003) which must be understood in the wider context of globalization processes in many financial services sub-sectors (Lewis 1999; Bryson and Daniels 2000) and the fracturing and specialization of high-order financial services occupations. To date, UK immigration policy has recognized this and it is strongly desirable in terms of the competitiveness of the UK as a location for these financial services activities that immigration policy allows firms to recruit non-EEA workers as they see fit.

Secondly, and related, there is no evidence that current UK immigration policies act as a significant constraint on the ability of firms to fill high-order financial services sector jobs with highly skilled migrants (McLaughlan and Salt 2002; Clarke and Salt 2003). There is no evidence of any significant constraint that damages UK-based firm competitiveness. However, future UK immigration policy might consider further streamlining and facilitating the process by which high-order occupations in financial services can be filled by non-EEA migrants. Furthermore, it would be sensible for public policy to become more sensitive to the global workforce circulation practices of transnational financial services firms and make it easier for firms to operate the secondment schemes that are an increasingly prevalent feature of this sector in the global economy. Similarly, many highly skilled migrant workers spend a period in the UK as part of an international career path. Public policy should recognize the transnational nature of such career paths, and not create unnecessary barriers in relation to areas such as access to healthcare or children's education.

Thirdly, in the mid-order financial services sector occupations, there is no research to indicate significant employment of migrant workers (either EEA or non-EEA). Many of these occupations are in 'consumer' financial services, which require high degrees of customer interaction associated with interpersonal 'soft' skills not suited to migrant workers coming from outside the UK context. In that sense, immigration policy has a very limited impact on the nature of the labour market in many of these occupations. Thus, the barriers to entry for migrant workers in terms of 'soft skills' mean that policy is unlikely to have much impact on labour market conditions for these occupations. With respect to the current economic downturn, the more pertinent public policy issue may be the provision of educational opportunities for workers formerly employed in these occupations to re-skill after a period of considerable rationalization in sub-sectors like retail banking.

The fourth point is in relation to the low-order financial services occupations. Whilst there is no evidence to suggest significant employment of non-EEA migrant workers at present, several occupations do represent jobs that could relatively easily be filled by migrant workers. At the UK national level, there is no current basis for staff shortages in these lower skill occupations, and in peripheral regions of the UK, some jobs in these sectors are being lost as firms 'off-shore' activities to cheaper wage locations in Asia. Again, therefore, in terms of immigration policy, research suggests that their relatively lower skill requirement means that staff shortages can be effectively tackled in the UK by re-skilling, inter-regional migration, raised wage levels, and the utilization of new technologies. The major public policy challenge in relation to these occupations is therefore addressing the re-skilling or up-skilling of workers in these occupations who have lost their jobs due to off-shoring or the impact of the recent economic downturn.

9.7 Conclusion: Conflicting Policy Challenges after the Global Economic Downturn?

For certain industries within the UK financial services sector, migrant labour has been an essential and integral part of growth and success over the last 20 years. London's now established place at the forefront of global financial services would not have been possible without significant flows of migrant workers moving in and out of key occupations in the City of London and (to a lesser extent) the greater South-East. To some degree, such a point also holds true for other key city-regions in the UK as they have also emerged as hubs of financial service specialism in developing global city networks. Yet taking the UK financial services sector as a whole leads to a more uneven picture of the role for migration. The evidence presented suggests that for many sub-sectors in financial services, migrant labour has had only a very limited role to play. For many 'mid-order' occupations, such as those in retail banking, the soft skills sought have meant that migrant labour has been little in demand. This has also influenced the lack of migrant labour demand within the numerically significant 'lower-order' financial services occupations, such as call-centre work. In fact, the major issues facing the future of these lower-order financial services labour markets have more to do with the potential for such jobs to be 'off-shored' rather than with new pools of migrant labour.

However, the late 2000s also represents a period of significant change and challenge for UK financial services. It is no exaggeration to suggest that the global economic downturn has brought crisis to some key financial services sectors, along with significant job losses, and that this suggests future developments in UK financial services are likely to look somewhat different from the past couple of decades. How different this landscape will be remains to be seen, but in drawing this chapter's analysis to a conclusion, I want to identify some major issues that form the basis for public policy in relation to migrant workers and the financial services sector labour market.

The first issue is how the changed landscape of UK financial services interacts with the demand for migrant labour in high-order financial services occupations. At the time of writing, it has become clear that this downturn has impacted hard on the UK economy and in particular on the financial services sector. The full implications of this have yet to play out, but by mid-2009, City financial services employment rates were estimated to have already declined 16 per cent from their 2007 peak. It appears likely that employment in UK financial services is unlikely to begin to recover until well into 2010 at the earliest. For public policy-makers, the temptation in such adverse labour market conditions is to use immigration policy to restrict the supply of migrants, particularly given the unprecedented nature of recent jobs losses in high-order financial services occupations like banking and broking. However, the evidence suggests that this represents a potentially dangerous short-term path for UK policy which would stand in contradiction to the continued complex and globalized nature of the financial services labour markets, particularly in high-order, high value-adding occupations. Any measures to restrict migrant recruitment are likely to restrict the flexibility and competitive capacity of high value-adding specialist financial services sub-sectors concentrated in the City of London.

A second issue is the recent (and relatively dramatic) changing nature of several financial services sub-sectors. Whilst detailed academic analyses of the origins and causes of the so-called 'credit crunch' have yet to be developed, it is clear that this downturn was triggered by an array of unacceptable and misguided practices within banking and other financial services sub-sectors that led to major losses and the failure of several leading players. Looking forward from 2009, it seems that the sub-sectoral landscape of both investment and retail banking in the UK has shifted significantly. Probably more important than the collapse and part or total nationalization of several banks are the implications of the crisis for the nature of future financial services activity. The development of growth in certain strands of banking, broker, insurance, and hedge funds over the last decade has been dramatically checked, and the future will be one where a different and more restrictive regulatory landscape means any upturn is unlikely to see a return to the previous pattern of sectoral development. Future employer demand for specialist migrant labour may well be quite different from that of the last decade, and may include different or new financial services occupations.

Thirdly, and arguably in fact most important, initial indications suggest that job losses in financial services in the recent downturn have by no means been confined to high-order occupations or to London and the South-East. High-order financial services sector job losses in the City make news headlines, but more numerically important in terms of total employment are sub-sectors prevalent in the more peripheral regions of the UK. Whilst the limited evidence here suggests many mid- and low-order financial services occupations experience little participation by migrant workers, sectoral restructuring, combined with the continued attraction of off-shoring to employers, may mean many of the jobs lost in the current downturn do not re-appear in a future economic recovery. The key issue for immigration policy is that this contributes to substantially increasing the available pool of labour to a range of other sectors beyond financial services, since financial services sector workers generally have a wide range of transferable soft skills applicable in sub-sectors that include, for example, business services, hospitality, and leisure. Any long-term decline in the demand for workers in financial services may mean that a substantial pool of labour is available that could act as a substitute for migrant labour in other sectors of the UK economy.

References

Alexander, A. F., and Pollard, J. S. (2000), 'Banks, Grocery Retailers and the Changing Retailing of Financial Services', *Journal of Retailing and Consumer Services*, 7(3): 137–47.

Beaverstock, J. (1996), 'Sub-contracting the Accountant! Professional Labour Markets, Migration, and Organizational Networks in the Global Accountancy Industry', *Environment and Planning A*, 28(2): 303–26.

——(2002), 'Transnational Elites in Global Cities: British Expatriates in Singapore's Financial District', *Geoforum*, 33: 525–38.

——(2004), 'Managing across Borders: Knowledge Management and Expatriation in Professional Legal Service Firms', *Journal of Economic Geography*, 4: 1–25.

Beaverstock, J. and Boardwell, J. (2000), 'Negotiating Globalization, Transnational Corporations and Global City Financial Centres in Transient Migration Studies', *Applied Geography*, 20(3): 277–304.

——Hall, S., and Faulconbridge, J. (2006), 'The Internationalization of Europe's Contemporary Transnational Executive Search Industry', in J. W. Harrington (ed.), *Knowledge-Based Services: Internationalisation and Regional Development* (Aldershot: Ashgate), 125–52.

——and Smith, J. (1996), 'Lending Jobs to Global Cities: Skilled International Labour Migration, Investment Banking and the City of London', *Urban Studies*, 33(8): 1377–94.

Belt, V., Richardson, R., and Webster, J. (2002), 'Women, Social Skill and Interactive Service Work in Telephone Call Centres', *New Technology, Work and Employment*, 17(1): 20–34.

Bryson, J., and Daniels, P. (2000), *Service Industries in the Global Economy* (Cheltenham: Edward Elgar).

—— —— and Warf, B. (2004), *Service Worlds: People, Organizations, Technologies* (London: Routledge).

Castells, M. (2002), *The Rise of the Network Society* (Oxford: Blackwell).

CBI/PwC (2009), Report cited in 'Forecast of 15,000 Job Losses in Financial Services Sector', *The Herald*, 1 May 2009.

Centre for Economic and Business Research and City of London (2007), *The Importance of Wholesale Financial Services to the EU Economy* (London: Centre for Economic and Business Research and City of London).

Clarke, J., and Salt, J. (2003), 'Work Permits and Foreign Labour in the UK: A Statistical Review', *Labour Market Trends*, 111(11): 563–74.

Coe, N., and Townsend, A. (1998), 'Debunking the Myth of Localized Agglomerations: The Development of a Regionalized Service Economy in South-East England', *Transactions of the Institute of British Geographers*, 23(3): 385–404.

Countryside Agency (2004), *A Toolkit for Market Towns: Growth Prospects* (Chichester: Countryside Agency).

Durkin, M., O'Donnell, A., Mullholland, G., and Crowe, J. (2007), 'On e-banking Adoption: From Banker Perception to Customer Reality', *Journal of Strategic Marketing*, 15(2–3): 237–52.

Experian (2009), Report cited in 'Banking Job Losses could Hit 40,000', *The Times*, 10 May.

Farquhar, J., and Panther, T. (2007), 'The More, the Merrier? An Exploratory Study into Managing Channels in UK Financial Services', *The International Review of Retail, Distribution and Consumer Research*, 17(1): 43–62.

Faulconbridge, J. R. (2004), 'London and Frankfurt in Europe's Evolving Financial Centre Network', *Area*, 36(3): 235–44.

——Engelen, E. V., Hoyler, M., and Beaverstock, J. V. (2007), 'Analysing the Changing Landscape of European Financial Centres: The Role of Financial Products and the Case of Amsterdam', *Growth and Change*, 38(2): 279–303.

——Hall, S. J. E., and Beaverstock, J. V. (2008), 'New Insights into the Internationalization of Producer Services: Organizational Strategies and Spatial Economies for Global Headhunting Firms', *Environment and Planning A*, 40(1): 210–34.

Financial Express (2009), 'Job Losses in India May Rise in the Coming Months', *Financial Express*, 2 Feb.

Financial Services Skills Council (2006a), *UK Financial Services: Five Years Forward* (London: Financial Services Skills Council/Corporation of London).

——(2006b), *Graduate Skills and Recruitment in the City* (London: Financial Services Skills Council/Corporation of London).

Financial Times (FT) (2008), 'Financial Services Job Losses "Could Hit 40,000" in Britain', *Financial Times*, 10 May.

——(2009a), 'More Job Losses at Money Managers', *Financial Times*, 22 Mar.

——(2009b), 'Merry-Go-Round as Banks Lure Talent', *Financial Times*, 7 Apr.

Grosse, R. (2004), *The Future of Global Financial Services* (Chichester: Wiley).

Halford, S., Savage, M., and Witz, A. (1997), *Gender, Careers And Organizations: Current Developments in Banking, Nursing and Local Government* (Basingstoke: Macmillan).

Hall, S. (2006), 'What Counts? Exploring the Production of Quantitative Financial Narratives in London's Corporate Finance Industry', *Journal of Economic Geography*, 6(5): 661–78.

——(2009), 'Ecologies of Business Education and the Geographies of Knowledge', *Progress in Human Geography*, 33(5): 599–618.

Hamnett, C. (2003), *Unequal City: London in the Global Arena* (London: Routledge).

Hanlon, G. (1999), 'International Professional Labour Markets and the Narratives of Accountants', *Critical Perspectives on Accounting*, 10(2): 199–221.

Higgs, M. (2004), 'A Study of the Relationship between Emotional Intelligence and Performance in UK Call Centres', *Journal of Managerial Psychology*, 19(4): 442–54.

Hyde, W., and Dilnot, S. (2000), 'The Financial Services Sector in London and New York', in *The London–New York Study* (London: Corporation of London).

James, A., and Vira, B. (forthcoming), '"Unionising" the New Spaces of the New Economy? Alternative Labour Organising in India's ITES-BPO Industry', *Geoforum*.

Jones, A. (1998), '(Re)producing Gender Cultures: Theorizing Gender in Investment Banking Recruitment', *Geoforum*, 29(4): 451–74.

——(2003), *Management Consultancy and Banking in an Era of Globalization* (Basingstoke: Palgrave Macmillan).

——(2005), 'Truly Global Corporations? Organizational Globalization in Advanced Business Services', *Journal of Economic Geography*, 5: 177–200.

——(2008), 'The Rise of Global Work', *Transactions of the Institute of British Geographers*, 33: 12–26.

Knights, D., and McCabe, D. (2003), 'Governing through Teamwork: Reconstituting Subjectivity in a Call Centre', *Journal of Management Studies*, 40(7): 1587–619.

Koser, K., and Salt, J. (1997), 'The Geography of Highly Skilled International Migration', *International Journal of Population Geography*, 3(4): 285–303.

Leidner, R. (1993), *Fast Food, Fast Talk: Service Work and the Routinization of Everyday Life* (Berkeley, Calif.: University of California Press).

Lewis, M. (ed.) (1999), *The Globalization of Financial Services* (Cheltenham: Edward Elgar).

Leyshon, A., and Pollard, J. S. (2000), 'Geographies of Industrial Convergence: The Case of Retail Banking', *Transactions of the Institute of British Geographers*, 25(2): 203–20.

Liaw, R. (2006), *The Business of Investment Banking* (Chichester: Wiley).

McDowell, L. (1997), *Capital Culture: Gender at Work in the City of London* (Oxford: Blackwell).

McLaughlan, G., and Salt, J. (2002), *Migration Policies towards Highly Skilled Foreign Workers* (London: The Home Office).

Migration Advisory Committee (MAC) (2008), *Skilled, Shortage, Sensible* (London: Migration Advisory Committee), available at <http://www.ukba.homeoffice. gov.uk/sitecontent/documents/aboutus/workingwithus/mac/first-lists/0908/ shortageoccupationlistreport?view=Binary>.

Morgan, G. (2001), 'The Multinational Firm: Organizing across Institutional and National Divides', in G. Morgan, P. Kristensen, and R. Whitley (eds.), *The Multinational Firm* (Oxford: Oxford University Press), 1–26.

Office for National Statistics (2008), 'Financial Services: Top Growth Sector 1996 to 2006' (London: Office for National Statistics).

O'Loughlin, D., and Szmigin, L. (2006), 'Customer Relationship Typologies and the Nature of Loyalty in Irish Retail Financial Services', *Journal of Marketing Management*, 22(3): 267–93.

Organisation for Co-operation and Economic Development (OECD) (2007), *OECD Economic Surveys: United Kingdom 17* (Paris: OECD).

Pollard, J. S. (1999), 'Globalisation, Regulation and the Changing Organisation of Retail Banking in the United States and Britain', in R. L. Martin (ed.), *Money and the Space Economy* (Chichester: Wiley), 49–70.

Salt, J. (1997), *International Movements of the Highly Skilled* (Paris: OECD, Directorate for Education, Employment, Labour and Social Affairs, International Migration Unit).

——(2002), 'Global Competition for Skills: An Evaluation of Policies', in *Migration: Benefiting Australia* (Canberra: Department of Immigration and Multicultural and Indigenous Affairs), 201–43.

——and Millar, J. (2006), *Foreign Labour in the United Kingdom: Labour Market Trends* (London: Office for National Statistics), 335–55.

Sassen, S. (2001), *The Global City* (Princeton: Princeton University Press).

——(2002), *Global Networks, Linked Cities* (London: Routledge).

Sklair, L. (2001), *The Transnational Capitalist Class* (Cambridge: Polity).

Sokol, M. (2007), 'Space of Flows, Uneven Regional Development and the Geography of Financial Services in Ireland', *Growth and Change*, 38(2): 224–59.

Taylor, P., Beaverstock, J., Cook, G., Pundit, N., Pain, K., and Greenwood, H. (2003), *Financial Services Clustering and its Significance for London* (London: Corporation of London).

Thrift, N. (1994), 'On the Social and Cultural Determinants of International Financial Centres: The Case of the City of London', in S. Corbridge, R. Martin, and N. Thrift (eds.), *Money, Power and Space* (Oxford: Blackwell), chapter 14.

——(1997), 'The Rise of Soft Capitalism', *Cultural Values*, 1: 29–57.

——(2000), 'Performing Cultures in the New Economy', *Annals of the Association of American Geographers*, 90(4): 674–92.

——and Leyshon, A. (1992), 'In the Wake of Money: The City of London and the Accumulation of Value', in L. Budd, and S. Whimster (eds.), *Global Finance and Urban Living* (London: Routledge).

UK Trade and Invest (2008), *Financial Services UK: A Promotional Strategy for the City of London and UK Financial and Business Related Services* (London: UK Trade and Invest).

Walker, S. (2004), 'The Genesis of Professional Organisation in English Accountancy', *Accounting, Organizations and Society*, 29(2): 127–56.

Wood, P. (2002), 'Services and the New Economy: An Elaboration', *Journal of Economic Geography*, 2: 109–14.

——(2006), 'Urban Revival and Knowledge Intensive Services: the Case of the English 'Core Cities', in P. Daniels, and J. Harrington (eds.), *Knowledge-Based Services', Internationalization and Regional Development* (Aldershot: Ashgate), chapter 12.

Immigration and the UK Labour Market in Financial Services: A Commentary

Jonathan V. Beaverstock

From the end of the nineteenth century, the UK's financial services industry has welcomed foreign capital and workers into cities like London, Manchester, and Edinburgh. Today, the sector represents one of the country's most globalized industries and is dominated by foreign firms, both transnational corporations and 'boutiques'. Successive UK governments have recognized that for London's financial services industry to remain globally competitive, it requires the world's best-qualified labour, irrespective of nationality, to ensure the continual growth of, and contribution to, 'UK plc'. Accordingly, Jones's chapter on 'Immigration and the UK Labour Market in Financial Services' provides a benchmark to understand: first, the explanations which account for immigration in this sector of economy; and, secondly, the almost *laissez-faire* approach of the state to the entry of qualified non-EEA immigrants.

Jones is correct when discussing the demand and supply determinants which reproduce the conditions for 'high-order' immigration into the UK financial services labour market. The overriding factor which stimulates the demand for immigration is the unique characteristics of this particular *labour* market. These workers are highly skilled, knowledge-rich experts who have significant fee-earning capacities, which often can be quantified in millions of US dollars, British pounds, or Euros. Firms recruit 'high-' and selected 'mid-order' immigrants to bring particular knowledge, skills, judgement, and decision-making and leadership capabilities to the organization, which cannot be obtained from the national labour market. In the financial services industry, it is often the employee alone who makes money for the firm. As Seifert et al. (2000: 8) note, '[it is] . . . the skill and commitment of individuals that ... makes the difference between success and failure, between trading profits and losses, and between clients returning or taking their business elsewhere'. This is why in many financial services the performance of 'high-order' segments of the labour market is much more critical to the firm in terms of fee-income or gains from financial markets than the number of offices (Beaverstock 2007a; Economist Intelligence Unit 1999; Greenwood et al. 1999). Also, as many financial services firms have their full or European HQs in London, they employ a large and highly specialized pool of talented labour who are multinational in citizenship to service the firm and clients on a global scale. Thus, London's labour market for financial services is truly cosmopolitan and characterized by a constant through-flow of immigrants (Cook et al. 2007). I suggest that 'high-order' immigrants in the UK's financial services labour market have several 'salient' characteristics:

- They fill highly specialized vacancies driven by skill shortages, new business opportunities, leadership requirements, global management development programmes, and client requests to employ particular individuals or teams of people.
- They originate from EEA and non-EEA countries, and there are specific flows to London from other financial centres.
- The temporality of their stay may be short- to medium-term (from one to three years) within inter-company transfers (ICTs), but might become permanent in particular circumstances for both ICTs and EEA 'free-movers'.
- They are drawn from a globally functioning labour market for highly skilled financial labour, where a 'war of talent' exists for their skills between global financial centres.

The desire to win the 'war for talent' between global financial centres is fostered by many UK stakeholders as a rationale for the continual entry of immigrant financial talent in order to maintain London's competitiveness in banking, financial, and professional services (see Hall et al. 2009). Wigley's (2008: 6) recent study of the global competitiveness of London's financial centre recognizes that its 'deep talent pool and welcoming culture' is an important driver of its leadership in the global market place for banking, finance, and business services.

Jones (Chapter 9, this volume) is right to observe that quantifying immigration is a difficult task beyond official sources like the Labour Force Survey. The Office for National Statistics (ONS), Total International Migration Trends MN Series does provide data on professional and managerial immigration into the UK, but not in fine enough detail to distinguish financial services-related jobs in this occupational category (Dobson et al. 2001). However, other immigration data on financial services are available from other official sources.

One key official data source that records the number of foreign workers entering the UK to work in the financial services is the Home Office's Work Permits data. For example, of the 86,191 work permits granted to non-EEA workers in 2005, 6,526 were in financial services (7.6%), and if law-related activities were to be included, the number of work permits would have totalled 7,513 (8.7% of the total number of work permits for 2005). Interestingly, whilst the number of work permits granted for financial services has increased by just over 100 per cent between 1995 and 2005 (from 3,194 to 6,526), the total share of work permits granted has declined from 13.2 to 7.6 per cent as other occupational groups have seen dramatic rises in successful applications, for example in health and medical services (Salt and Millar 2006).

Another official data source which quantifies the characteristics of foreign-born labour in the UK's financial services labour market is the Annual Population Survey (APS), published by the ONS. A recent report published by the Corporation of London (2007) used the APS for 2005–6 to report that of the 190,000 foreign-born workers who have been in the UK for under three years, 15,000 were employed in financial services and 36,000 in business services, the combined figure of 51,000 representing a 13 per cent share of all London foreign-born employment.

In order to unpack the detailed specifics of immigration in UK financial services, much knowledge and understanding can be derived from 'unofficial' case-study research, which focuses on analysing immigration through the corporate mechanism of ICTs. My own recent research has investigated immigration of both EAA and non-EEA citizens into the UK's financial services labour market, in sectors like accounting (Beaverstock 2007b), investment banking (Beaverstock 2007a), and legal services (Beaverstock 2004). Two common denominators characterize these analyses of 'high-order' immigration. First, such immigration is relatively short in duration, nominally from one to three years, and gone are the days of long postings. Secondly, many of these immigrants are 'high net worth' individuals who normally enter the UK via an ICT with a generous relocation and remuneration package. To illustrate the significance of 'unofficial' studies of immigration in financial services, research into the magnitude of ICTs within eight leading 'bulge-bracket' investment banks showed that 650 foreign bankers came to work in London from European (Amsterdam, Frankfurt,

Paris), North American (New York), and Asian (Hong Kong, Tokyo, Singapore) financial centres for more than one year. They were posted to London to fill specific occupational vacancies that could not be filled by UK citizens, to work for named clients, to provide leadership and managerial roles (at Chief Executive level), and for training purposes (Beaverstock 2007a).

'Managing' immigration in the UK financial services labour market is driven by the prevalent global market conditions of the banking and financial services industry rather than any state apparatus. The current economic downturn has been characterized by dramatic job losses in 'upper' and 'mid-order' employment (as defined by Jones, Chapter 9 in this volume), which will inevitably be accompanied by retrenchment in ICTs and a reduced demand for foreign labour as firms curtail their hiring and ICT programmes. From a corporate perspective, in times of efficiency savings and lean business models, an important substitute for immigration is the use of business travel for short and extended periods (Falconbridge et al. 2009). On the supply side, think-tanks like Z/Yen (2009) predict that the UK's future high levels of personal taxation, with the proposed 'Non-Dom' regime and the 50 per cent rate for those earning over 150,000 per annum, will discourage talented immigrant labour from entering the UK. It is highly likely, however, that London's financial district will remain one of the pre-eminent international financial centres and a place where talented labour of all nationalities will continue to seek enhanced career opportunities, financial reward, and the opportunity to live in one of the world's most cosmopolitan cities.

References

Beaverstock, J. V. (2004), 'Managing across Borders: Transnational Knowledge Management and Expatriation in Legal Firms', *Journal of Economic Geography*, 4(2): 157–79.

——(2007a), 'World City Networks from Below: International Mobility and Inter-City Relations in the Global Investment Banking Industry', in P. J. Taylor, B. Derudder, P. Saey, and F. Witlox (eds.), *Cities in Globalization: Practices, Policies, Theories* (London: Routledge), 52–71.

——(2007b), 'Transnational Work: Global Professional Labour Markets in Professional Service Accounting Firms', in J. Bryson and P. Daniels (eds.), *The Handbook of Service Industries* (Cheltenham: Edward Elgar), 409–31.

Cook, G., Pandit, G., Beaverstock, J., Taylor, P., and Pain, K. (2007), 'The Role of Location in Knowledge Creation and Diffusion: Evidence of Centripetal and Centrifugal Forces in the City of London Financial Services Agglomeration', *Environment and Planning A*, 39(6): 1325–45.

Corporation of London (2003), *Financial Services Clustering and its Significance for London* (London: Guildhall).

——(2007), *The Impact of Recent Immigration on the London Economy* (London: Guildhall).

Dobson, J., Koser, K., McLaughlan, G., and Salt, J. (2001), 'International Migration and the United Kingdom: Recent Patterns and Trends', Home Office RDS Occasional Paper No. 75 (London).

Economist Intelligence Unit (1999), *Global Investment Banking Strategy* (London: EIU).

Faulconbridge, J., Beaverstock, J. V., Derudder, B., and Witlox, F. (2009), 'Corporate Ecologies of Business Travel: Working Towards a Research Agenda', *European Urban and Regional Studies*, 16(3): 295–308.

Greenwood, R., Rose, T., Brown, J., Cooper, D., and Hinings, B. (1999), 'The Global Management of Professional Services: The Example of Accounting', in S. R. Clegg, E. Ibarra-Colado, and L. Bueno-Rodriquez (eds.), *Global Management* (London: Sage), 265–9.

Hall, S., Beaverstock, J. V., Faulconbridge, J., and Hewitson, A. (2009), 'Exploring Cultural Economies of Internationalization: The Role of "Iconic" Individuals and "Brand" Leaders in the Globalization of Headhunting', *Global Networks*, 9(3): 399–419.

Salt, J., and Millar, J. (2006), 'Foreign Labour in the United Kingdom', *Labour Market Trends* (London: Office for National Statistics), 335–55.

Seifert, W. G., Achleitner, A., Mattern, F., Streit, C. C., and Voth, H. (2000), *European Capital Markets* (London: Macmillan).

Wigley, R. (2008), *London: Winning in a Changing World. Review of the Competitiveness of London as a Financial Centre* (London: Merrill Lynch).

Z/Yen (2009), *The Global Financial Centres Index 5* (London: Z/Yen).

10

A Need for Migrant Labour? UK–US Comparisons

Philip Martin

10.1 Introduction

Foreign-born workers constitute 5 to 15 per cent of the labour force in most high-income countries (OECD 2008). In the United Kingdom, 13 per cent of the working age population was born abroad in 2008, up from 7 per cent in the mid-1990s (Migration Advisory Committee 2009). In the US, the share of foreign-born workers in the labour force increased from 11 per cent in 1995 to 15 per cent in 2008 (Passel and Cohn 2009).

In almost all high-income countries, including the UK and the US, the number of migrant workers, that is, those admitted as temporary workers and whose employment can be restricted to specific occupations and/or sectors that are considered to suffer from labour shortages, is increasing faster than the number of immigrants who may settle permanently and freely choose jobs.[1] The rapid growth in temporary migrant workers raises questions about whether and where migrants are 'needed' and about their effects on local workers (including on immigrants or settled foreigners), employers, and the wider host economy in the short and long term.

Britain, the most populous high-income country to significantly increase legal admissions of migrant workers, recently established a Migration Advisory Committee (MAC) to provide advice on which skilled occupations

---

[1] In line with US terminology, this chapter will use the term 'migrant' to refer to foreign-born workers with temporary permission to work (some of whom may eventually gain permanent residence status) and the term 'immigrant' to denote foreign-born workers who have a permanent right to stay. This distinction in terminology is less prevalent in the UK where 'migrant' and 'immigrant' are often used interchangeably.

suffer from labour shortages that can sensibly be met by immigration from outside the European Economic Area (EEA[2]). The MAC's advice is based on analysis of three questions (the '3 S's'): Is the occupation skilled? Is there a shortage of local (i.e. British, settled immigrant, and EEA) labour? Is it sensible to use non-EEA workers to help fill the vacancies? Made up of five academic economists and a small secretariat, the independent MAC provides advice to the government on these '3 S' questions, creating a potential model for other countries that are considering how to respond to employer requests for more temporary migrant workers to help fill alleged 'labour and skills shortages'.

This chapter discusses research and policy approaches to assessing labour shortages and the implications for immigration policy in the UK and the US, with a particular focus on the potential lessons of the MAC for current debates about immigration reform in the US. The analysis reviews research on labour shortage complaints and the demand for migrant labour in the specific economic sectors discussed in the other chapters of this book.

There is rarely an open debate over the trade-offs between the conflicting goals inherent in temporary migration programmes. For example, which should get higher priority, providing care to the maximum number of elderly and disabled residents in their homes with limited funds or ensuring high wages and benefits for care workers? The MAC's approach to assessing labour shortages and the review of particular British labour markets employing or requesting migrants highlights the importance of obtaining and reviewing both top-down and bottom-up data on labour supply and demand, and of considering the alternatives to foreign workers in response to perceived labour shortages in specific sectors and occupations. These are the two key insights of the current British model for US debates about labour shortages and immigration reform.

To set the scene, the chapter begins with brief reviews of long-term labour market changes, and the role of immigration policy and employer recruitment of migrants in high-income countries, with a focus on the UK and US. This is followed by a discussion of the key features and consequences of past and existing temporary migration programmes that aim to admit migrant workers to fill shortages in specific sectors and/or occupations. The next two sections comparatively discuss UK and US research and debates on shortages and immigration in specific sectors, and the

---

[2] The EEA includes the 27 member states of the European Union (EU) plus Iceland, Liechtenstein, and Norway.

implications of the UK's experience with the MAC for current debates about immigration reform in the US.

10.2 Labour Market Changes and Immigration Policy

Labour markets in high-income countries have changed in the past half-century in several major ways. The locus of employment has shifted from agriculture and industry to services, fewer workers have lifetime jobs with a single employer, and a higher share of jobs are part-time or non-traditional in other ways, as with the rising number of workers who are employed by a temp firm rather than the owner of the workplace. One result is an increased variance in wages, benefits, and job security between workers doing similar jobs (OECD 2007).

The supply of labour in high-income countries has changed to include more employed married women with children, later labour force entry for youth due to less child labour and more post-secondary education, and earlier retirement associated with better pensions. For example, between 1960 and 2000, the US labour force doubled from 66 million to 133 million people, but the female labour force almost tripled from 22 million to 64 million (Council of Economic Advisers (CEA) 2009: 328). The share of males of 16 years and older who were employed or looking for work fell from 83 per cent to 75 per cent between 1960 and 2000, while the female labour force participation rate rose from 38 per cent to 60 per cent (CEA 2009: 331).

The most recent projections of US labour supply growth, made before the 2008–9 recession, projected relatively rapid growth in the older US labour force (Franklin 2007: 5). However, foreign-born workers are expected to account for at least half of net labour force growth (Congressional Research Service 2005: 11).

The operation of the labour market has changed as well. The share of private sector workers represented by unions has decreased significantly, more workers are brought to workplaces by intermediaries such as temp agencies, there has been a rise in self-employment, and profits have risen in most industrial countries at the expense of wages as a share of economic output. During the 1950s, for example, over a third of US private sector workers were union members; today, fewer than 10 per cent of US private sector workers are union members. In the UK, the rate of union membership among employees fell from over half in the late 1970s to just over a quarter in 2009. However, this masks a significant difference between the private and the public sector. Though public sector union membership is declining more rapidly in the UK, it is nevertheless notably higher. In 2008, union density in the private sector was 15.5 per cent, whereas in the public sector it was 57.1 per cent (BERR 2009).

These structural changes in labour demand, supply, and labour market operation are expected to persist, albeit with variation across countries. However, the economic changes associated with globalization are likely to accelerate the shift toward workers having more employers in the course of their working lives, women becoming half or more of wage workers, and to maintain unfolding processes that often yield labour markets with several entities or layers between workers and the beneficiaries of their work.

While these trends seem clear, there are also significant uncertainties about the evolution of labour demand, supply, and labour market operation, including future fertility rates, the usual age of retirement, and the share of new workers who were born in other countries. Will most workers continue to retire in their early 60s and rely on public and private resources for another 20 to 25 years, or will more people elect to work longer so that retirement remains close to the current average of 15 to 20 years despite increased longevity?[3] Finally, will newcomers from abroad continue to expand their role in high-income country labour markets?

Factors ranging from new technologies, changing trade patterns, government policies, and shifting individual preferences shape labour markets, as do migration policies. Migrants tend to be concentrated in particular occupations and industries, so migration policy has a major influence on labour demand, supply, and labour market operation in particular sectors of industrial economies. In a world of demographic and economic inequalities that give some employers incentives to hire workers from poorer countries, and individuals incentives to cross borders for higher wages, migration policy may become one of the most important factors shaping the structure and functioning of certain very specific labour markets in industrial countries (Martin et al. 2006).

In 2005, there were about 3 billion workers in the global labour force, including 20 per cent, or 600 million in what the International Labour Organization calls more-developed countries.[4] The labour force of the more-developed countries is expected to remain stable over the next

---

[3] In the US, the average age at retirement dropped from 70 in 1940 to 65 in 1970 and 62 in 2000. The average number of years in retirement was 10 in 1940, 13 in 1970, and 18 in 2000 (Aaron 1999).

[4] ILO, <http://laborsta.ilo.org/>, accessed 25 June 2009.

decade, while the labour force in less-developed countries is projected to expand by 600 million between 2005 and 2020. In other words, the projected growth in the size of the less-developed countries' labour force equals the current size of the more-developed countries' labour force. Employers in the UK and the US, as in other high-income countries, already recruit workers in a wide range of low, middle, and high-income countries.

Employer requests for more migrant workers because of alleged 'labour and skills shortages' have become common in high-income countries. Evaluating these claims is a core aspect of labour immigration policy. The major labour immigration policy questions facing governments include how many workers to admit, from where, and in what status to admit them. Most governments grappling with these questions are responding by permitting employers to hire more workers from abroad, raising questions that range from the criteria employers must satisfy before they receive permission to employ migrants, to the importance of examining labour shortage complaints in a comprehensive way rather than focusing only on jobs and workers at a point in time.

As a traditional country of immigration, the US has a long history of labour immigration and labour immigration policy, including longstanding debates about how best to respond to employer requests for foreign workers. The US government has at least 15 visas that allow foreigners to be wage earners in the US, ranging from F-1 visas for foreign students allowed to work part-time while studying, to TN visas for Canadians and Mexicans with university degrees.

The major visas for temporary foreign workers in the US are three types of H-visas, H-1B, H-2A, and H-2B. The number of H-visas issued by the US Department of State, some valid for more than a year, more than quadrupled from 98,000 in fiscal year 1994 to 424,400 in fiscal year 2007 (Wasem 2009: 10).

H-1B visas are available to foreign workers with at least a first university degree who are requested by US employers to fill US jobs that require such degrees. The H-1B programme was created in 1990 by revising then extant programmes. A compromise that gave employers easy access to foreign university graduates in exchange for an annual cap of 65,000 visas a year. This was almost three times the annual admissions in the early 1990s. A combination of the information technology (IT) boom in the 1990s, and the development of an infrastructure to move Indian and other foreign university graduates into US jobs, soon led to the annual number of employer requests far exceeding 65,000. Employers pressed Congress to raise the H-1B cap, Congress obliged temporarily, and the current limit is 65,000 plus 20,000 H-1B visas a year for foreigners with advanced degrees from US universities and an unlimited number for those employed in non-profit institutions (such as universities).

After two decades, the H-1B programme is mired in controversy. Microsoft's Bill Gates asserted that:

The terrible shortfall in the visa supply for highly skilled scientists and engineers stems from visa policies that have not been updated in more than 15 years. We live in a different economy now, and it makes no sense to tell well-trained, highly skilled individuals—many of whom are educated at our top universities—that they are not welcome here.[5] (*Daily Labor Report* 2007)

Critics disagree, arguing that there is no 'shortage' of science and engineering (S&E) workers in the United States, only a dearth of career opportunities in S&E occupations that offer lifetime earnings comparable to those available to high-ability individuals in non-S&E fields such as law or business (Matloff 2003).

There are similar stories of growth and controversy in the H-2A and H-2B programmes that admit low-skilled workers. The H-2A programme admits temporary foreign workers to fill temporary farm jobs, while the H-2B programme admits temporary foreign workers to fill temporary non-farm jobs. There is no cap on the number of H-2A visas, but the programme is criticized by employers for being 'cumbersome' despite government approval of 95 per cent of employer requests within 15 days. Worker advocates are also critical, arguing that protections that should prevent adverse effects on US workers are insufficient. The H-2B programme, which can issue up to 66,000 visas a year, is criticized by employers for not providing enough visas and by worker advocates for not protecting US and foreign workers (Martin 2009). Thus, each of the three major US temporary worker programmes is subject to conflicting claims about the need for and effects of foreign workers.

There appeared to be less controversy in the UK when the Labour government aggressively opened doors to migrant workers. Immigration was not a significant issue in the 1997 election campaign that brought the Labour Party to power; the major migration issue under the outgoing

[5] The H-1B programme was created by the Immigration Act of 1990, which more than doubled the number of immigrant visas available for foreigners and their families desired by US employers and imposed a cap on immigration. The intent was to raise the share of immigrants selected for economic reasons from about 10 to 20%. This did not happen because the immigration cap was pierceable, and family immigration rose sharply. Immigrants and their families selected for employment reasons are about 15% of annual immigration.

Conservative government was the perception that many applicants for asylum were economic migrants (Spencer 2007: 341–2). Home Office officials began to speak of immigration as economically beneficial for the UK after 2001, softening its traditional control mentality (Spencer 2007: 348–50).

Beginning in the late 1990s, the British government significantly increased the number of work permits issued to skilled and highly skilled non-EU migrants. The consequent increase in labour immigration was further accelerated by the British government's decision in May 2004 to allow so-called A8 nationals, citizens of the eight Central European countries that joined the EU on 1 May 2004, to enter and work without any restrictions. Ireland and Sweden were the only other EU-15 countries that adopted similar policies, and most Eastern Europeans headed for the UK.[6] More than a million A8 migrants have taken up employment in the UK since May 2004, about half of whom are thought to have left the UK (Migration Advisory Committee 2009).

Introduced in 2008, the UK's new points-based system for managing immigration admits highly skilled migrant workers without a job offer (Tier 1) and skilled workers with a job offer in the UK (Tier 2) (see Migration Advisory Committee 2009).

10.3 Labour Markets and Employer Recruitment of Migrants

Although contexts differ across countries, employers generally make three key employment-related decisions that shape labour markets. The first is recruitment, the process of attracting desired workers to fill jobs. Second is remuneration, broadly understood as workers exchanging their effort for the reward of wages. Third is retention, keeping desired workers and improving their productivity over time. The availability of migrant workers can affect each of these '3 R' labour market parameters.

Recruitment can be a costly process because employers lack complete information about workers who apply to fill vacancies, and workers lack information about the job offers they are likely to receive. This lack of information is one reason why all high-income countries, including the

---

[6] Relatively few migrants moved to Sweden, in part because collective bargaining agreements required that migrants be paid the same wages as Swedish workers. With even traditional migrant sectors largely unionized, Swedish employers found fewer cost advantages in hiring migrants than British and Irish employers did (Ruhs and Martin 2008).

US and the UK, maintain no-fee exchanges where employers can register their job vacancies and workers can search for jobs. Employment exchanges play relatively larger roles in matching workers and jobs at the bottom rather than the top of the labour market, in part because both employers and workers are usually willing to invest less in job matching for low-skill jobs.

Policies that make migrants readily available may change employers' recruitment strategies. In the US and UK, public employment exchanges serve primarily employers and workers who are in the area in which the job is located. Most governments require employers seeking permission to hire foreign workers to post vacant jobs at these employment exchanges and to interview any 'local'[7] workers who respond before granting the employer permission to recruit workers from abroad. However, most US employers identify the migrant workers they prefer before posting their job vacancies, suggesting many do not want to hire local workers who may apply (US Department of Labor, Office of the Inspector General 1998). For this reason, policies that aim to 'protect' local workers by requiring employers to try to recruit local workers are rarely successful (Martin 2007).

Work is the exchange of effort for reward, and the level of remuneration is used to attract the desired type of workers and encourage them to perform their jobs well. Most workers are paid on a per-hour, week, or month basis, and a variety of mechanisms have evolved to monitor and assess their performance. However, since monitoring and firing workers can be costly, employers have an incentive to invest sufficient resources in recruitment to find workers who will perform satisfactorily for the required time.

This poses a complication with respect to migrants, who are outside the country and may not speak the language of the employer. Some employers rely on bilingual intermediaries to recruit and supervise workers. These intermediaries, often settled migrants from the same country, know both the job and the qualities of their compatriots.

A second response is a piece-rate or pay-for-performance system that keeps employer costs constant regardless of variation in employee productivity. In agriculture, for example, the cost of picking ten bins of apples at $20 a bin is $200 whether one fast worker or two slower workers pick them, but worker pay varies. Piece-rates are most often used in agriculture, but

---

[7] 'Local' is defined differently in different countries, for example, in the UK 'local workers' generally refer to all EEA nationals and settled migrants (not only UK citizens). In the US, local workers include US citizens and legal immigrants. It is important to remember, however, that in debates, popular understandings and usage of 'local' may differ from these official terminologies.

employers in many service jobs that offer hourly wages may establish minimum productivity standards, such as the number of hotel rooms to be cleaned per hour or shift, that make their costs of getting work done predictable.

Migrants tend to be more productive than local workers who fill jobs in the bottom rungs of the labour market (Congressional Research Service 1980). The reason is simple: many local workers applying for low-skill farm, construction, and care jobs often have personal characteristics that prevent them from holding higher wage jobs, including lack of education and skills, mental and drug or alcohol problems, and motivation issues (Waldinger and Lichter 2003). Newcomers from abroad, whose frame of reference is a lower wage rate at home, are sometimes described as the 'professionals' of low-wage labour markets abroad (Piore 1980).

For example, US sugar-cane growers offered jobs to cane cutters guaranteeing an hourly wage that was above the minimum, but ended up with over 99 per cent foreign workers who 'trained' for the opportunity to be selected for six months of US work. By contrast, many of the US workers who responded to required job advertisements did so in order to preserve their access to jobless benefits (Martin 2009).

The third 'R' is retention. Workers typically learn skills on the job, increasing their value to the employer. Most employers devise strategies to identify and keep their most productive workers by, for example, increasing wages and benefits with seniority. The increased productivity of workers who learn job-specific skills often offsets some of these higher labour costs.

In some low-wage jobs, productivity may not rise significantly with experience, and could in some cases fall, as with fruit-picking jobs in which younger workers tend to be more productive than older workers. For such jobs, employers have an incentive to find replacements for workers who move on to better jobs and whose productivity falls over time. Young migrants are often ideal in the eyes of employers, especially if they can achieve the required productivity standard quickly.

In most US and UK labour markets, the three Rs of recruitment, remuneration, and retention have evolved in ways that favour more employer investment in screening workers who will be paid higher wages as they perform their jobs better over time. However, for some jobs on the bottom rungs of the job ladder, employers may favour the recruitment of migrants via intermediaries and networks, use piece-rate or other pay systems that make labour costs predictable, and replace workers who leave with fresh recruits from abroad. These employers are most often found in particular sectors, including agriculture and related food processing, residential construction, and in services including back-room hotel and restaurant jobs and care-giving.

10.4 Key Features of Temporary Migration Programmes

There is a long history of temporary migration programmes (TMPs) that aim to add temporary workers to the labour force, but not necessarily settled residents to the population. TMPs can seem to be the ideal solution for governments caught between competing interests, including employers requesting migrants, migrants eager for higher wages, and public opinion that wants migration reduced.

Unlike permanent migration programmes that generally involve the right to freely chose and change jobs, TMPs enable receiving countries to restrict the employment of migrants to specific sectors and/or occupations and employers. To understand whether and how temporary labour immigration may be a desirable response to perceived shortages, it is necessary to understand the key features and challenges of TMPs which, based on past international experience, can easily lead to unintended consequences (for more comprehensive analyses of TMPs, see e.g. Martin 2007; Ruhs 2006).

10.4.1 *Certification and Monitoring Migrant Employment*

There are three key administrative elements of TMPs in migrant-receiving countries: what criteria must employers satisfy to receive permission to recruit and employ migrants; how is migrant employment monitored; and how do governments ensure that migrant workers depart as scheduled or transfer to permanent residence? These issues may obscure an even more important one—how are employer preferences, local workers' attitudes, and the operation of labour markets affected by the presence of migrants over time?

The US government relies on a certification process to determine whether employers can recruit migrant workers to fill low-skill jobs, which means that a US employer must try and fail to find local workers despite active recruitment with wages and working conditions approved by the Department of Labor. Employers post jobs at local employment exchanges, interview workers who respond, and record the reasons why local workers were not hired. In the US, employers requesting certification to hire 100 migrants have their request for migrants reduced on a one-for-one basis for each local worker they hire.

The alternative to certification, government checking of employer recruitment efforts, is attestation, a trust-the-employer approach. Attestation allows the employers to attest that they have satisfied recruitment regulations, leading to almost automatic approval to recruit and employ foreign workers. Under an attestation system, there are no checks or enforcement before the migrant worker is admitted. In the US, for example, internet-based attestation under the H-1B TMP usually occurs in seconds, and enforcement responds to complaints after admission. As with the H1-B programme in the US, admission of non-EEA workers under Tier 2 of the UK's points-based system requires employers to attest that they have first made efforts to recruit British and/or other EEA workers. There are, however, no checks or any enforcement measures before the migrant is admitted (Migration Advisory Committee 2009). Naturally, most employers prefer attestation to certification.

Certification becomes contentious when workers who are supposed to have priority access to jobs respond to employer recruitment efforts but are not hired. If these rejected local workers complain that the employer preferred migrants, government agencies are often not well equipped to review employer decisions on who is best qualified to fill a particular job. Some employers reveal their preferences for migrants quite explicitly. For example, Mordechai Orian, the president of recruiter Global Horizons, testified during a July 2007 trial that Thai migrants were preferable to local workers because 'they work really hard' and were less likely to 'abscond' or leave their employers.

Temporary foreign workers are normally entitled to the same wages and benefits as local workers, although they cannot usually change employers. As with the enforcement of all labour laws, the best assurance that migrants are treated equally is market incentives. If employers who offer substandard wages and benefits cannot recruit workers, local or migrant, they are likely to have to improve their offer. Secondly, most labour law enforcement depends on complaints, and few migrants complain because they fear the loss of their jobs and removal from the country. In some cases, unions and NGOs aware of migrant rights can sometimes help enforcement authorities to ensure that violating employers are detected and punished without migrants losing their jobs.

Deregulated labour markets and minimal labour law enforcement in both the UK and the US mean that many employers can 'get away' with paying migrant workers substandard wages with minimal risk of enforcement

(Bernhardt et al. 2009).[8] Migrants assigned to a particular employer must weigh the risk of losing their jobs and being removed from the country against the additional wages and benefits they may receive by filing a complaint. In practice, there are remarkably few complaints filed by migrant workers about employer violations of labour laws.

The third administrative issue with TMPs is ensuring that migrants depart as required. Returns may occur 'naturally' if migrants hold seasonal jobs and are parents whose families remain at home. However, migrants holding year-round or permanent jobs, but having time-limited work visas, may need economic incentives to depart, especially if both they and their employers want to prolong employment. The clash between rules that require departure and incentives for a longer employment relationship can contribute to path dependence.

10.4.2 *Path Dependence*

Employers hire migrants because they cannot find workers with the requisite skills willing to fill jobs for the wages and benefits they offer. Economic distortion or path dependence can increase the reliance of employers on migrant workers over time as they make investments based on the assumption that doors to migrants will remain open. The lower labour costs made possible by the availability of migrants are sometimes capitalized into asset values, giving asset owners an incentive to keep hiring migrants.

For example, farm wages lowered by the availability of migrant workers raise land prices, giving landowners (including those who paid high prices to buy land) an incentive to maintain access to migrant workers to preserve the value of their land. If migrants were not available to pick fruits and vegetables that were planted in remote areas at wage levels that make the investment profitable, the value of the land would drop. In effect, access to migrants acts as a subsidy that raises land prices in the same way that water or crop subsidies raise land prices, giving landowners incentives to maintain open doors for migrants (Kilkenny 1993).

---

[8] Bernhardt et al. surveyed 4,400 workers in low-wage industries in 2008 in Los Angeles, Chicago, and New York and found that workers received on average 15% less than they should have because employers did not pay them appropriate overtime or required off-the-clock work. About 40% of the interviewed workers were unauthorized, 30% were legal immigrants, and 30% US-born. The report emphasized that violations of basic labour laws were widespread, with the failure to pay premium wages for overtime work most common (a quarter of those surveyed worked more than 40 hours the previous week).

There can be similar path dependence among migrants, as families, regions, and countries become dependent on earnings and remittances from a foreign labour market. If the money remitted by migrants is not invested to create jobs and generate stay-at-home development, there may be continuing incentives to migrate for employment. In both the US and Europe, decades of guest worker recruitment were followed, with lags, by unauthorized migration from Mexico and by asylum seeking from Turkey (Martin 2009, Chapter 2; Martin 2004).

Path dependence helps to explain why temporary migration programmes often get larger and last longer than expected. Many migrant worker programmes began in wartime or at other 'extraordinary' times, allowing employers to persuade governments to admit migrant workers to cope with 'emergency' labour shortages. This anticipation that TMPs are short-lived efforts to deal with emergencies minimizes serious discussion of alternatives to migrants and the trade-offs between migrant numbers and migrant rights (Ruhs and Martin 2008).[9] The fact that the British government created the MAC, and gave it sufficient resources to examine labour markets in the sectors in which employers requested migrants, opens a rare window on demand, supply, and labour market operation in economic sectors that hire large numbers of migrants.

10.5 Labour Shortages, Demand For Migrant Labour, and Sectoral Analysis

Research and policy debates about shortages and immigration policy in the UK and the US grapple with similar questions, including how to define and identify a labour shortage; whether, why, and when employers develop a preference for migrant workers; and how the demand for and role of migrants varies across sectors and occupations.

10.5.1 *Labour Shortages and Policy Responses*

What is a 'labour shortage?' Employers who want border gates opened wider for migrant workers typically assert that they face a 'shortage' of

---

[9] Migrant rights can cost employers money. With a negatively sloped demand for labour, ensuring full or equal rights can reduce the number of temporary foreign workers employed (Ruhs and Martin 2008).

workers, even when labour market indicators such as the unemployment rate suggest that there are more jobless workers than job vacancies.

There is no standard definition or measure of labour shortage. Market economies embody self-clearing mechanisms, the changes in wages and prices that bring supply and demand into balance. If the demand for labour exceeds the supply, which is what the term 'shortage' suggests, wages should rise, setting in motion forces that reduce the demand for labour via automation, job restructuring, or other adjustments, and increase the supply of workers.

In market economies, labour demand should not exceed supply for sustained periods because of rising wages, which suggests that governments should not pay much attention to employer labour shortage complaints. Indeed, decades of economic studies of labour shortage complaints generally discount them. Blank and Stigler (1957), for example, found that the earnings of engineers did not rise faster than average in the 1950s despite US employer complaints of a shortage of engineers. Cohen (1995) studied top-down labour market indicators for several years in an effort to predict labour shortages at the state or regional level, largely without success.[10] More recently, Veneri (1999) used faster than average employment and wage growth, and lower than average unemployment rates, as indicators to find that only seven of 68 'labour shortage' occupations satisfied all three criteria.[11]

Governments nonetheless pay attention to labour shortage complaints for reasons including the political clout of employers, practical budgetary considerations, and the distinction between fixed and variable costs. First is the nature of the sectors that make labour shortage complaints, such as agriculture. Agriculture is the oldest industry in almost all countries, and farmers are well organized to get the attention of governments—no other

---

[10] Cohen (1995) used six top-down indicators for 193 occupational groups: the occupational unemployment rate and the change in occupational employment; the change in weekly wages of full-time workers in the occupation; the expected long-run employment growth for the occupation; the total replacement demand for the occupation; the number of certifications to employ foreign workers issued for the occupation; and the specific vocational preparation required. This methodology led to projections of shortages of several types of college-educated workers, including physical and medical scientists, veterinarians, physical therapists, physicians, registered nurses, speech therapists, chemists, biological and life scientists, computer programmers, and airline pilots.

[11] Veneri (1999: 18–19) used three criteria to examine 68 occupations for labour shortages in the 1990s: employment growth was at least 50% higher than the average for all occupations; growth in median weekly earnings was at least 30% greater than the average for all occupations; and the occupational unemployment rate was at least 30% lower than the average for all occupations. These 50, 30, 30 indicators did not find shortages of computer workers, RNs, and construction workers, three occupations in which employers claimed there were labour shortages.

sector accounting for less than 5 per cent of GDP, for example, has a cabinet ministry in most countries. Agriculture is riddled with paradoxes, including policies that transfer tax monies to richer-than-average farmers to keep the sector larger than it would be in the absence of subsidies. One legacy of 'agricultural exceptionalism' is that it is relatively easy for farmers in most industrial countries to win governmental approval to employ migrant workers. The question is whether such exceptionalism will spread to other sectors in which employers are requesting easy access to foreign workers, including healthcare, IT, and services that range from janitors to catering.

Second are the practical budgetary difficulties of allowing wages to rise in order to bring labour demand and supply into balance. Governments strongly influence both the demand for and supply of labour in some sectors, especially healthcare. If government policies increase the demand for healthcare by expanding eligibility and keeping direct costs to consumers low, but restrict the supply of healthcare workers by limiting the number of slots in institutions that train them or by holding down their wages, there will be 'shortages' of healthcare workers. In such cases, governments may find it politically easier to open border gates to foreign healthcare workers than to raise expenditures in ways that reduce healthcare demand or increase domestic labour supply.

Third is the distinction between fixed and variable costs. Labour is considered a variable cost in most production processes, meaning that employers can lay off workers and have minimal future responsibilities for them. Labour-saving machinery, on the other hand, is a fixed cost, meaning that the employer must pay for the machine whether it is used or not. In seasonal industries such as agriculture and food processing, where machinery will not be used year-round, and in sectors in which the demand for the product or service is uncertain, employers often prefer to maximize their variable costs, which gives them an incentive to hire migrants rather than invest in labour-saving machinery.

The final factor that encourages a migrant worker response to labour shortage complaints is increased globalization and mobility. Both employers and workers today know far more about wages and worker characteristics in other countries than in the past, and a variety of bilateral, regional, and global agreements allow or encourage migration over national borders (OECD 2004). With more workers in low-wage countries aware of better opportunities abroad, and a proliferation of bilateral and regional agreements easing the flow of goods and some types of workers over national borders, more international labour mobility seems to be a 'natural' part of globalization.

10.5.2 *A Specific Demand for Migrant Labour?*

The researchers whose contributions are included in this book examined economic sectors along four major dimensions: what do employers seek in the workers they recruit; what do workers seeking jobs want; why do employers recruit migrants; and what are the alternatives to migrant workers in a particular sector. Research on these questions shows that employers can, for a variety of reasons, develop a preference for recruiting specific types of migrant rather than local workers. Whether and to what extent this happens is highly specific to sector and/or occupation and, as discussed in this book, results from a combination of factors related to labour demand, supply, and recruitment methods.

A key finding of employer surveys in both the UK and the US is that many value so-called 'soft skills', including a good attitude, loyalty to the employer and job, and willingness to work as instructed. Many US employers report that they prefer Spanish-speaking Mexican-born migrants with less education to English-speaking US-born Blacks with more schooling because the migrants are perceived to be 'more suited' to filling low-level jobs than the Blacks (Waldinger and Lichter 2003). Similarly, UK research has found many employers praising migrants' superior 'attitudes' and 'work ethic' (e.g. Anderson et al. 2006).

Secondly, local workers who might fill low-skill jobs temporarily typically want 'better' jobs that offer higher wages, more status, and more opportunities for advancement. Some will fill low-wage migrant jobs until they can find better jobs, but many employers do not consider such local workers 'loyal', meaning that the employer fears they will quit as soon as better jobs become available. The children of newcomers tend to shun their parents' jobs, putting employers in some industries and occupations on an immigration treadmill, seeking to replace workers who move up in the labour market with additional newcomers from abroad.

Thirdly, employer recruitment systems are intimately linked to the types of workers recruited. Most employers of migrants rely on network hiring, which means that current workers are asked to refer their friends and relatives when additional workers are needed, or a bilingual intermediary taps his or her network for additional workers (Commission on Agricultural Workers 1992). In the US, cell phones sometimes make it possible for potential workers in remote Mexican villages to learn of US job openings sooner than jobless US workers near the work site.

Finally, there is rarely serious policy discussion of alternatives to migrant workers. Opening border gates to migrant workers is often perceived as a short-term response to an emergency or to slow labour market adjustments, suggesting that migrants will not be needed when 'normal' economic circumstances return, or after employers and local workers have more time to adjust. It is very hard to chart the adjustment trajectory of a particular labour market, since one adjustment can beget others that are hard to anticipate, even when migrants are not involved. For example, the switch to self-service gasoline stations or self-service airport ticket counters, jobs that did not involve migrants, was not widely anticipated.

10.5.3 *Sectoral Analyses: UK–US Comparisons*

HEALTH AND CARE GIVING

Providing healthcare and other care to the elderly and disabled in their homes or in group facilities are sectors that are heavily reliant on migrant workers in the UK and the US. The National Health Service, the world's largest publicly funded healthcare system, employs most of the healthcare professionals in the UK, and the Department of Health, of which the NHS is part, is responsible for most of the training and certification of healthcare professionals.

As discussed by Bach's chapter in this book (Chapter 4), over the past decade, the British government moved aggressively to reduce waiting times and increase the quality of care provided by expanding the number of healthcare professionals employed by the NHS. In order to expand the number of healthcare workers quickly, both doctors and nurses were recruited from abroad. By September 2008, 32 per cent of UK doctors and 19 per cent of nurses were born outside the European Economic Area.

International recruitment was a 'quick fix' to find healthcare workers and reduce public dissatisfaction with lengthy waits at the NHS. The underlying reasons for the healthcare worker shortage included relatively low wages and limited government-financed training slots. Migration was an 'easy' solution because there was a supply of English-speaking healthcare professionals trained to British standards abroad who were eager to migrate for higher wages or perhaps to move from the UK to other countries, as with Filipino nurses in Saudi Arabia who migrate first to the UK and later to the US.

As a former colonial power that established healthcare training systems abroad, the UK is in a unique position to recruit foreign healthcare professionals. The social-care sector is slightly different. The government provides the funds to hire 2 million workers to provide care to children, the elderly, and the disabled in their homes, but local government councils often contract with private agencies to employ care workers.

Women constitute 80 per cent of the UK's social-care labour force, and the share of foreign-born care workers doubled in the decade to 2008 to about 16 per cent (Moriarty, Chapter 5, this volume). Surveys suggest that, unlike the international recruitment of healthcare professionals, most of the migrant care workers entered the UK via non-work channels such as as students, and then found jobs as care workers. Turnover among both UK-born and migrant care workers is very high, reflecting both low wages and the low status of the work.

The alternatives to migrant care workers include raising their wages and status.[12] Both are costly, and raising required levels of training to raise pay and status could wind up increasing the 'shortage', since fewer UK workers will have the required credentials. Care working may evolve into a multi-tiered sector, with those cared for in regulated group settings served by credentialized and higher-wage workers, while less or non-credentialized workers, including migrants, provide care services in private homes.

The US has a less generous health and care sector. Nonetheless, health-care facilities in remote areas tend to recruit foreign doctors and nurses, and care workers in private homes include a large number of migrants.

CONSTRUCTION

The British construction industry is unusual in having about one self-employed worker for every two wage-workers—almost a third of the 1.9 million workers in the sector are self-employed (Chan et al., Chapter 8, this volume). It is also where several 'British jobs for British workers' disputes arose in 2009, especially at the Lindsey Oil Refinery after some work was subcontracted to Italian company IREM, which planned to use Italian workers.

The major story of the British (and American) construction industry is the rise in subcontracting and erosion of the apprenticeship training system. Average skill levels declined along with wages, especially in residential and remodelling work, and the migrant share of the construction labour force rose, especially as older workers, who were trained when the apprenticeship system was more robust, began to retire. Construction has long been a network industry, meaning that sons followed fathers into building trades, and such network hiring, plus the high share of self-employed workers, allowed so-called 'Polish plumbers' from the Central European countries that joined the EU on 1 May 2004, to expand their presence in the UK construction labour market (Chan et al., Chapter 8, this volume).

---

[12] Senior care givers earning at least £7.80 an hour were on the Tier 2 shortage list in May 2009.

The US has three distinct construction labour markets: construction of building, which is subdivided into residential homes and other buildings; heavy and civil engineering, which involves building roads, bridges, and other infrastructure; and specialty trade contractors, including plumbers, electricians, and carpenters and masons. These specialty trades, which account for two-thirds of total construction employment, include workers with skills such as carpenter or electrician and unskilled workers who are employed by firms that act as subcontractors to the general contractor in charge of building or infrastructure projects (<http://www.bls.gov/oco/cg/cgs003.htm>).

Construction is a geographically dispersed industry that employs workers whose skills are also used in other industries, so that workers are often more mobile than employers. Historically, worker mobility was an advantage for unionized workers, who could call a strike in one town and go to work in another, putting many of the costs of the strike on relatively small employers. US construction workers traditionally identify with their craft or occupation, not with any particular employer, and US unions often operate hiring halls to deploy carpenters, electricians, and other craft workers to employers according to union rules.

The workers employed in the construction industry have occupations ranging from executive to helper, but two-thirds are in 'construction occupations' such as carpenter, labourer, or electrician. Foreign-born workers in the US construction labour force are concentrated in six of the 14 construction occupations, including carpet installers, cement masons, labourers and helpers, drywall installers, and roofers.

In Britain, a combination of relatively low entry-level wages in a sometimes-seasonal industry with low status means that many youths shun construction jobs. Migrants from countries that have more formal construction training systems can provide the UK with some of the missing skills that arise from its inadequate training system. The major recommendation to deal with employer complaints of labour shortages is a revamped skills training system that helps Britain to grow more of its own construction workers (Chan et al., Chapter 8, this volume).

HOSPITALITY

The British hospitality industry includes 14 industries, ranging from hotels and restaurants to tourist services. Some 1.9 million people are employed in 180,000 mostly small establishments, with less than ten employees, and few establishments are unionized (Lucas and Mansfield, Chapter 6, this volume).

The US divides the hotel and restaurant industry into two segments, accommodations and food services, and drinking places. The accommodations industry, which employed 1.8 million workers in the Economic Census of 2002, was very diverse. About 75 per cent of the establishments were hotels and motels, and they had 1.4 million employees in the pay period that included 12 March 2002. The 500,000 food services and drinking place establishments in 2002 included 230,000 limited-service eating places such as McDonald's, 195,000 full service restaurants, and 50,000 drinking places—foreign-born workers tend to be concentrated in full-service restaurants.

In both the UK and the US, hospitality involves employers, employees, and customers, so that the employee becomes the 'face' of the employer or business when providing the service. Since the employee may become part of the service that the business is providing, many employers seek 'personality' and other soft skills, such as enthusiasm and a good attitude. Most employers offer the minimum wage, and many say they cannot raise wages without reducing consumer demand.

The hospitality sector wants different types of workers at different service points. In the UK, 'white and middle-class' employees are preferred as hotel receptionists; many employers say that minorities are more acceptable in food preparation and cleaning. Migrants are more likely to accept the (low) wages than British workers, and those housed on-site or nearby are far more willing to work overtime and weekends as required.

Since the service is usually provided to the consumer on site, the major alternative to migrants is self-service in restaurants and hotels, which can change the 'product', or mechanization, such as computers, that make staff more efficient, and hotel rooms designed to save labour. Temp agencies supply many of the lower-skill employees, such as hotel cleaning staff, to hospitality employers in both the UK and the US, shifting the cost of recruitment, training, and retention to another business. As in construction, the availability of migrants has allowed systems that in the past recruited and trained local workers to erode at a time when migrant networks expanded, increasing the migrant share of the hospitality labour force over time.

AGRICULTURE AND FOOD PROCESSING

Agriculture has long been reliant on migrant workers, especially to fill seasonal jobs. However, a combination of 'better' non-farm jobs, an expanded social safety net, and mechanization induced by rising wages, reduced the employment of hired farm workers. In the UK as elsewhere, the best way to help seasonal farm workers to improve their incomes has been to help them find non-farm jobs. In contrast to declining employment on farms, employment in the non-farm food-processing industry has increased, as busy households buy more products that are fully or partially prepared in food-processing establishments.

Migrant workers play important roles in both agriculture and food processing. A majority of those employed seasonally on British crop farms were born outside the UK, as were 40 per cent of those employed in food processing industries. About a third of the workers hired in UK agriculture and food processing are supplied by temp agencies, including gangmasters or labour contractors. The Gangmasters Licensing Authority, established in 2005, a year after 23 Chinese cockle pickers drowned in Morecambe Bay, reported that 1,200 labour contractors were licensed in September 2009 to provide workers to farmers and food processors.

The UK has for decades had a Seasonal Agricultural Workers Scheme (SAWS) under which 'operators' could recruit non-EU workers to fill seasonal jobs on crop farms. The UK government gradually tightened employer access to SAWS workers, reducing the maximum number who could be admitted and restricting the countries in which migrants can be recruited. A maximum 16,250 nationals of Bulgaria and Romania could enter the UK under the SAWS programme in 2008, and the SAWS programme is to be phased out by 2010 and replaced by Tier 3.

There is a strong 'ethical trading' movement in the UK that pressures the four dominant supermarket chains to improve conditions in their supply chains at home and abroad. Many critics of the migrant labour system in British agriculture and food processing blame the supermarkets for putting downward pressure on farm wages by demanding that their suppliers reduce prices (Geddes and Scott, Chapter 7, this volume). Some call farmers and food processors 'captives' of the supermarkets, and migrant and local workers 'captives' of farmers and food processors.

The US has a longer tradition of employing migrants, especially in seasonal farm jobs in the southwestern states. The major change over the past 25 years has been the spread of foreign-born workers from seasonal crop farms in the southwest to crop and livestock farms throughout the US, as well as to food processing and meat-packing. Animal slaughtering and processing employed a third of the 1.5 million workers employed in food manufacturing in 2002.

In the US, food manufacturing pays less than the average wage in the private sector, and meat-packing pays less than the average wage in food manufacturing. Meat-packing is one of the most dangerous manufacturing jobs in the US, with common injuries including muscular trauma, repetitive motion disease, cuts, and strains.[13]

A high rate of injuries is a long-standing feature of US meat-packing, but not lower-than-average earnings. Union strength peaked in meat-packing in the 1960s, when over 90 per cent of production workers belonged to unions and the average meat-packing wage of $3.45 an hour in 1968 was 15 per cent above the average manufacturing wage of $3 an hour; by 1990, the $8.73 wage was 24 per cent below the $10.85 average manufacturing wage (Craypo 1994: 71).

Anthropologists have examined employer preferences for Hispanic migrants and hiring additional workers as needed via migrant networks (Griffith 1988), but it should be emphasized that Hispanics comprise only about half of the production workers in meat-packing.

10.6 MAC and its Implications for the US

The UK had a near doubling of the foreign-born share of the labour force to 13 per cent in the decade to 2008. For a US audience, the surprise is that this opening to migrants occurred under a 'New Labour' government that was at least nominally close to unions, and that the government maintained relatively open doors for migrants despite an anti-migrant tabloid press. The Labour Party government supported a number of studies that concluded migrants generated significant economic benefits to the UK economy (Glover et al. 2001).[14]

Migration policy changed in 2008 with the introduction of a five-tier system to select immigrants and migrants. A major aim of the new system was to increase the skills of migrants employed in the UK, and the major mechanism to achieve up-skilling was a points system that gives priority to foreigners with more education and knowledge of English. Extra points are awarded to applicants who will be used to fill jobs on a UK labour shortage list.

The Migration Advisory Committee (MAC) plays a critical role in determining whether the foreign workers requested by employers are needed by establishing occupational shortage lists for Tier 2 admissions. Its charge is

---

[13] Meat-packing is near the top in the annual survey of workplace injuries and reports by industry—with over 10% of workers having a reportable incident each year (<http://www.bls.gov/iif/oshwc/osh/os/ossm0014.pdf>).

[14] Glover et al. (2001, p. viii) found 'little evidence that native workers are harmed by migration . . . [and] considerable support for the view that migrants create new businesses and jobs and fill labour market gaps, improving productivity and reducing inflationary pressures'.

embodied in the three S's: skilled,[15] shortage, and sensible—that is, for occupations requiring skills—is there evidence of labour shortages that can sensibly be filled by migrant workers?

The major work of the MAC involves considering 12 top-down indicators of labour shortage and the bottom-up evidence submitted by employers, unions, and other interested parties. In order for the MAC to determine that an occupation has a labour shortage, at least six of the 12 top-down indicators must suggest one, for example, that wages and employment in an occupation are rising faster than average (median plus 50%). If the MAC determines that there is a shortage of workers in a particular occupation, it must also determine that migrants are a sensible solution.

The tier-selection system and the MAC represent a change for the UK, which began to admit a large number of migrant workers in the late 1990s at the request of employers. Entry channels for foreign workers proliferated, so that by 2007 there were over 80 ways in which foreigners could enter the UK to work. In 2008, the tier system reduced the number of entry channels to five, and the MAC was created to advise the government.

There are three major reasons why the MAC may be more applicable to other countries than the five-tier system. First, the MAC is an independent body, not a government agency, which may help to insulate its deliberations from political pressure. Secondly, the MAC considers both top-down and bottom-up labour market indicators, filling a lacuna evident in US efforts to use top-down indicators that generally do not suggest widespread labour shortages (Cohen 1995; Veneri 1999). US employers often complain that top-down national and regional indicators cannot deal with their particular situations, a gap that the systematic submission and consideration of bottom-up evidence can help to fill.

Thirdly, the MAC can explore alternatives to labour immigration and weigh the sensibleness of filling any labour shortages it finds with migrant workers. In the case of the British social-care sector, for example, it can highlight the discrepancy between the expectation that care workers should be highly skilled and the limited government budgets that result in low wages. By helping to de-politicize decisions on whether to admit migrant workers, the MAC can serve a very useful advice-giving role.

However, allowing an independent MAC to weigh bottom-up evidence is not a panacea for often difficult discussions about whether migrant workers are a sensible solution to identified labour shortages. In the US, proposals

---

[15] By MAC criteria, 192 of the 353 occupations are skilled.

for an independent MAC-like commission to provide advice or determine how many economic immigrants and migrant workers should be admitted have been resisted by employers, who are not certain that a commission would reach the 'right' answers.

The US has been debating what to do about the growing number of unauthorized foreigners, an estimated 12 million in 2008, for a decade (Passel and Cohn 2009). The spectrum of policy options is framed by two extremes: enforcement and attrition, and comprehensive immigration reform. Enforcement and attrition means making life in the US increasingly difficult for unauthorized foreigners, so that many leave on their own, and then dealing with the few who remain. Comprehensive immigration reform, endorsed by the now President Obama and his then Republican rival Senator John McCain before the November 2008 elections, involves legalizing most of the unauthorized foreigners and developing a secure ID system that discourages additional illegal foreigners from entering the US to seek jobs.

The new twist in the US immigration reform debate, euphemistically called 'future flows', is determining how many guest workers to admit. Less than a sixth of the million immigrants a year admitted come because US employers prove to the Department of Labour that the foreigner is uniquely qualified to fill a particular job, and over half of these 150,000 foreigners who receive immigrant visas for economic reasons are members of the principal worker's family. The US has an alphabet soup of visas for non-immigrants or guest workers, and at least twice as many arrive each year as immigrants.[16]

Immigration reform failed in 2006 and 2007 in part because of union opposition to employer proposals for new 'market-based' guest worker programmes that would automatically add work visas if employers demanded all those available before the end of the year. In an effort to bridge the gap between employers, who have demonstrated their ability to persuade Congress to include new guest worker programmes in any comprehensive immigration reform bill, and sceptical unions, there have been proposals for a MAC-like commission to examine the impacts of migrants on the US labour market and recommend an appropriate number of guest workers (Marshall 2009).

---

[16] There are about 70,000 immigrant visas issued each year to 'principals', foreigners whose US employers must normally demonstrate that US workers are not available to fill a particular job. Almost four times more temporary workers are admitted, and the stock of unauthorized foreign workers rose by an average 350,000 a year between 2003 and 2007.

Employers have resisted a MAC-like commission, preferring to enact into law new guest worker programmes and the criteria employers must satisfy to obtain migrants. President Obama met with 30 Congressional leaders on 25 June 2009 to begin 'an honest discussion about the issues' involved in comprehensive immigration reform. Obama singled out McCain for special praise, noting that he went against many in the Republican Party by supporting comprehensive immigration reform. However, McCain expressed strong opposition to a MAC-like commission, saying: 'We don't need a commission. I can't support any proposal that doesn't have a temporary worker program'.[17]

The MAC is likely to play an important role in generating knowledge of how labour markets in sectors employing large numbers of migrants function. By combining top-down and bottom-up labour market indicators to examine shortage complaints and determine whether admitting migrant workers is a sensible solution, the MAC can pioneer a more rigorous approach to dealing with employer complaints of too few workers and some unions' responses that there is no shortage of workers, only a shortage of decent wages.

References

Aaron, H. (1999), *Behavioral Dimensions of Retirement Economics* (Washington: Brookings Institution).

Anderson, B., Ruhs, M., Rogaly, B., and Spencer, S. (2006), *Fair Enough? Central and East European Migrants in Low Wage Employment in the UK* (London: Joseph Rowntree Foundation (JRF)).

Bernhardt, A., Milkman, R., Theodore, N., Heckathorn, D., Auer, M., DeFilippis, J., González, A., Narro, V., Perelshteyn, J., Polson, D., and Spiller, M. (2009), 'Broken Laws, Unprotected Workers: Violations of Employment and Labour Laws in America's Cities', National Employment Law Project, available at <http://www.nelp.org>.

BERR (Department for Business, Enterprise and Regulatory Reform) (2009), *Trade Union Membership 2008*.

Blank, D., and Stigler, G. (1957), *The Demand and Supply of Scientific Personnel* (Washington: National Bureau of Economic Research).

Cohen, M. (1995), *Labour Shortages as America Approaches the Twenty-First Century* (Ann Arbor: University of Michigan Press).

---

[17] See 'Obama: Immigration Reform?' *Migration News*, 16(3), July 2009, available at <http://migration.ucdavis.edu/mn/more.php?id=3522_0_2_0>.

Commission on Agricultural Workers (1992), 'Report of the Commission on Agricultural Workers', Nov.

Congressional Research Service (1980), 'Temporary Worker Programs: Background and Issues', prepared for US Senate Committee on the Judiciary, Feb.

——(2005), 'The Role of Immigrants in the US Labour Market', prepared for US Senate Finance Committee, Nov.

Council of Economic Advisors (2009), 'Economic Report of the President', available at <http://www.whitehouse.gov/cea/pubs.html>.

Craypo, C. (1994), 'Meat-Packing: Industry Restructuring and Union Decline', in Paula Voos (ed.), *Contemporary Collective Bargaining in the Private Sector* (Madison: Industrial Relation Research Association), 63–96.

Daily Labor Report (2007), 'Gates Urges Change in H-1B Visa Program', *Daily Labor Report*, 8 Mar., p. A-8.

Franklin, J. (2007), 'An Overview of BLS Projections to 2016', *Monthly Labour Review*, 3–12 Nov.

Glover, S., Gott, C., Loizillon, A., Portes, J., Price, R., Spencer, S., Srinivasan, V., and Willis, C. (2001), *Migration: An Economic and Social Analysis* (London: Home Office, Research, Development and Statistics Directorate Occasional Paper No. 67).

Griffith, D. (1988), 'The Impact of the 1986 IRCA on the US Poultry Industry: A Comparative Analysis', Mimeo, Sept.

Kilkenny, M. (1993), 'Rural/Urban Effects of Terminating Farm Subsidies', *American Journal of Agricultural Economics*, 75(4), Nov.: 968–80.

Marshall, R. (2009), *Immigration for Shared Prosperity—A Framework for Comprehensive Reform*, Economic Policy Institute, May, available at <http://www.epi.org/publications/entry/book_isp/>.

Martin, P. (2004), 'Germany: Managing Migration in the 21st Century', in W. A. Cornelius, T. Tsuda, P. L. Martin, and J. F. Hollifield (eds.), *Controlling Immigration: A Global Perspective* (Stanford, Calif.: Stanford University Press), 221–52.

——(2007), 'Guest Workers: New Solution or New Problem', *University of Chicago Legal Forum*, 289–318.

——(2009), *Importing Poverty? Immigration and the Changing Face of Rural America* (New Haven: Yale University Press).

——Abella, M., and Kuptsch, C. (2006), *Managing Labour Migration in the Twenty-First Century* (New Haven: Yale University Press).

Matloff, N. (2003), 'On the Need for Reform of the H-1B Non-Immigrant Work Visa in Computer Related Occupations', *University of Michigan Journal of Law Reform*, 36(4), Fall: 815–914.

Migration Advisory Committee (2009), *Analysis of the Points-Based System: Tier 2 and Dependents* (London), available at <http://www.ukba.homeoffice.gov.uk/aboutus/workingwithus/indbodies/mac/reports-publications/>.

Moriarty, J. (2010), 'Competing with Myths: Migrant Labour in Social Care', in B. Anderson, and M. Ruhs (eds.) *Who Needs Migrant Workers? Labour Shortages, Immigration, and Public Policy*, (Oxford: Oxford University Press).

OECD (2004), *Migration for Employment: Bilateral Agreements at a Crossroads* (Paris: OECD), available at <http://www.oecd.org/document/60/0,3343,en_2649_33931_34019452_1_1_1_1,00.html>.

——(2007), *Benefits and Wages 2007* (Paris: OECD).

——(2008), *International Migration Outlook*, SOPEMI 2008 (Paris: OECD).

Passel, J., and Cohn, D. (2009), 'A Portrait of Unauthorized Immigrants in the United States', Pew Hispanic Center, available at <http://pewhispanic.org/reports/report.php?ReportID=107>, accessed, Apr. 2009.

Piore, M. (1980), *Birds of Passage: Migrant Labour and Industrial Societies* (Cambridge: Cambridge University Press).

Ruhs, M. (2006), 'The Potential of Temporary Migration Programmes in Future International Migration Policy', *International Labour Review*, 146(1–2): 7–36.

——and Martin, P. (2008), 'Numbers vs. Rights: Trade Offs and Guest Worker Programs', *International Migration Review*, 42(1): 249–65.

Spencer, S. (2007), 'Immigration', in Anthony Seldon (ed.), *Blair's Britain, 1997–2007* (Cambridge: Cambridge University Press), 341–60.

US Department of Labor, Office of the Inspector General (1998), 'Consolidation of Labor's Enforcement Responsibilities for the H-2A Program Could Better Protect U.S. Agricultural Workers', 04-98-004-03-321, 31 Mar.

Veneri, C. M. (1999), 'Can Occupational Labour Shortages be Identified Using Available Data?' *Monthly Labour Review*, 122, Mar.: 15–21.

Waldinger, R., and Lichter, M. (2003), *How the Other Half Works: Immigration and the Social Organization of Labour* (Berkeley, Calif.: University of California Press).

Wasem, R. (2009), 'Immigration of Foreign Workers: Labour Market Tests and Protections' (Congressional Research Service, RL33977), available at <http://opencrs.com/document/RL33977/>, accessed 20 Mar. 2009.

World Bank (2005), *Global Economic Prospects: The Economic Implications of Remittances and Migration*, available at <http://www.worldbank.org/prospects/gep2006>.

Index